SUPREME COURT CONFIRMATION HEARINGS AND CONSTITUTIONAL CHANGE

Before Supreme Court nominees are allowed to take their place on the high Court, they must face a moment of democratic reckoning by appearing before the Senate Judiciary Committee. Despite the potential this holds for public input into the direction of legal change, the hearings are routinely derided as nothing but empty rituals and political grandstanding. In this book, Paul M. Collins, Jr., and Lori A. Ringhand present a different view. Using both empirical data and stories culled from more than seventy years of transcripts, they demonstrate the hearings are a vibrant and democratic forum for the discussion and ratification of constitutional change. As such, they are one of the ways in which "We the People" take ownership of the Constitution by examining the core constitutional values of those permitted to interpret it on our behalf.

Paul M. Collins, Jr., is Associate Professor of Political Science at the University of North Texas. His research focuses on judicial politics, with a particular interest in the democratic nature of the courts. The recipient of numerous research awards, he has published articles in the *Journal of Empirical Legal Studies*, the *Journal of Politics*, *Law & Social Inquiry*, *Law & Society Review*, the *Notre Dame Law Review*, *Political Research Quarterly*, and other journals. Collins is also the author of *Friends of the Supreme Court: Interest Groups and Judicial Decision Making*, which received the 2009 C. Herman Pritchett Award from the Law and Courts Section of the American Political Science Association.

Lori A. Ringhand is J. Alton Hosch Professor of Law at the University of Georgia School of Law. Her research focuses on the Supreme Court confirmation process and has been published in journals such as *Constitutional Commentary*, the *American University Law Review*, the *William & Mary Bill of Rights Journal*, and the *University of Pennsylvania Journal of Constitutional Law*. Ringhand is also the recipient of the 2010 Ronald Ellington Award for Excellence in Teaching.

For Rose and Maggie

and

In loving memory of Michael, Jillian, Makayla, and Bryce Casey

– PMC

For Mom and Dad

– LAR

Supreme Court Confirmation Hearings and Constitutional Change

PAUL M. COLLINS, JR.

University of North Texas

LORI A. RINGHAND

University of Georgia

CAMBRIDGE
UNIVERSITY PRESS

CAMBRIDGE
UNIVERSITY PRESS

32 Avenue of the Americas, New York NY 10013-2473, USA

Cambridge University Press is part of the University of Cambridge.

It furthers the University's mission by disseminating knowledge in the pursuit of
education, learning and research at the highest international levels of excellence.

www.cambridge.org
Information on this title: www.cambridge.org/9781107502659

© Paul M. Collins, Jr., and Lori A. Ringhand 2013

First published 2013
First paperback edition 2015

A catalogue record for this publication is available from the British Library

Library of Congress Cataloguing in Publication data

Collins, Paul M.
Supreme Court confirmation hearings and constitutional change / Paul M. Collins, University
of North Texas, Lori A. Ringhand, University of Georgia.
    pages cm
Includes bibliographical references and index.
ISBN 978-1-107-03970-4 (hardback)
1. United States. Supreme Court.   2. Judges – Selection and appointment – United States.
3. Constitutional law – United States.   I. Ringhand, Lori A.   II. Title.
KF8742.C625   2013
347.73′2634–dc23   2013000441

ISBN 978-1-107-03970-4 Hardback
ISBN 978-1-107-50265-9 Paperback

Contents

List of Illustrations

List of Tables

Preface

The idea for this book began when Kirk Randazzo, a political scientist at the University of South Carolina, convened a workshop to bring together an interdisciplinary group of scholars interested in law and politics. It was the fall of 2009, and the country had just witnessed yet another contentious confirmation hearing. The highlight roll of this particular hearing, that of Sonia Sotomayor, featured clips about "wise Latinas" and the evils of judicial empathy. It also included the usual litany of complaints about senatorial posturing and nominee reticence, and revived the decades-old debate about the 1987 Robert Bork hearing.

As often happens at such workshops, the conversations of the day carried over into dinner, and we found ourselves huddled together at a sushi bar talking about our mutual frustration with the lack of comprehensive information about what actually happens at the confirmation hearings of Supreme Court nominees. Do Senators really just latch onto whatever is politically useful when preparing their questions for a given hearing, or do the hearings follow a more deliberative path? Have nominees actually become more reluctant to answer questions, or is that perception just a self-perpetuating post-Bork myth? Most importantly, are the hearings truly pointless exercises in political grandstanding, or is there a more positive story to be told about the role they play in our governing system?

We both believed there was, and the result is this book. The book uses empirical data, as well as historical vignettes culled from our review of hearing transcripts, to tell the story of the role the confirmation hearings play in ratifying constitutional change. In doing so, we have strived to make the book both accessible and appealing to a wide array of audiences. Political scientists are provided with an abundance of data to mull over, gathered from an original data collection effort, documenting the relationship among confirmation dialogue, public opinion, and the Court's precedents. Legal scholars will value our discussions of cases and doctrines, as well as our choice to present our data within a larger normative framework, thus providing a new way of thinking about how the hearings intersect with constitutional change. Non-academics will appreciate our efforts to translate both the data and the legal doctrines into readily accessible and thought-provoking themes of self-governance and the role of courts in a constitutional system.

We also hope that all of our readers will enjoy the stories we tell in the "Sidebars" sprinkled throughout the book. These stories use scenes from more than seventy years of confirmation hearings to show the striking, moving, and occasionally even humorous side of the hearings. They complement our empirical and normative work by providing an overarching view of the hearings that is too often lost in the heat of a given confirmation fight. The hearings discussed in this book span two world wars, the growth of America as a superpower, the civil rights movement, the cracking of the glass ceiling, and the fall of the Iron Curtain. Each and every one of these changes was discussed, debated, and fought over in front of the Senate Judiciary Committee. The hearing transcripts let us explore these changes through the words of those who lived through them, and show us how senators and nominees alike struggled to be true to our deepest constitutional commitments in a rapidly transforming world.

The story told by the changing faces of the nominees who have come before the Committee over the years is equally inspiring. As time passes, more and more of us become *present* on these pages. The New England aristocracy of Oliver Wendell Holmes shifts and makes room for Felix Frankfurter, a Jewish immigrant who came to this country at age twelve unable to speak English. Thurgood Marshall, the great civil rights lawyer, takes his seat after dismantling, step by painful step, the legalized apartheid system that tarnished our nation for so long. Sandra Day O'Connor sets aside her doubts and answers her President's call to become the first woman to sit on the Court. Antonin Scalia, Clarence Thomas, Ruth Bader Ginsburg, Sonya Sotomayor – more and more, these transcripts ring with the varied voices of America herself. We consider ourselves lucky to have spent the past few years immersed in this rich history, and we hope the Sidebars will give our readers a taste of the story these transcripts tell.

None of this would have been possible, however, without a great deal of help. Special thanks are due to Kirk, the University of South Carolina, and the National Science Foundation, who hosted and supported the conference that led to this book. Funding was also provided by the Dirksen Congressional Center and the Southern Political Science Association (through its recognition of a portion of this work as the recipient of the Neal Tate Award). Our own institutions, the University of North Texas and the University of Georgia School of Law, have given us their unwavering support, as have our colleagues at those institutions. An early article based on some of the data used in this book appeared as "May It Please the Senate: An Empirical Analysis of the Senate Judiciary Committee Hearings of Supreme Court Nominees, 1939–2009" in the *American University Law Review* (Volume 60, pp. 589–641). We also are indebted to a host of graduate and law students who have provided able research assistance, including Anna Batta, Bryan Calvin, and Tom Miles, as well as Patrick Baldwin, Douglas Gladden, Nathan Goodrich, Nick Jones, Alexander King, Jonathan Milby, Kristin Rigdon, and Alex Sklut.

Numerous friends and colleagues provided valuable feedback at different stages of the project, including Henry Abraham, Sara Benesh, Ryan Black, Bethany Blackstone, Eileen Braman, Jonathan Cardi, Pam Corley, Jolly Emery, Matt Eshbaugh-Soha, David Fontana, Barry Friedman, Amanda Frost, Ben Gross, Paul Heald, Lisa Holmes, Stefanie Lindquist, Wendy Martinek, Joe Miller, Chris Nemacheck, Elizabeth Oldmixon, Ryan Owens, Rich Pacelle, Eve Ringsmuth, Neil Siegel, Amy Steigerwalt, Geoffrey Stone, Christian Turner, Rich Vining, Art Ward, Justin Wedeking, Elizabeth Weeks-Leonard, Sonja West, and Margie Williams. Special thanks are also owed to Frank Baumgartner and Bryan Jones for making their Policy Agendas Project data publicly available, and to Stacy Harvey, who played an essential role in keeping us organized and on track. We are additionally grateful for the comments we received on earlier versions of this work presented at the meetings of the Midwest Political Science Association, Southeastern Association of Law Schools, and Southern Political Science Association, as well as the American University Washington College of Law.

We also wish to extend our deepest thanks to John Berger, Rishi Gupta, and the team at Cambridge University Press, and to the anonymous reviewers whose insightful comments significantly improved the quality of this book.

Paul M. Collins, Jr., expresses his sincere gratitude to his family and friends for their continuing encouragement, good humor, and inspiration. He is especially indebted to his wife, Lisa, whose love, patience, and kindness make life a pleasure to live. Paul dedicates this book to his amazing daughters, Rose and Maggie, and to the loving memory of Michael, Jillian, Makayla, and Bryce Casey, who were with us for far too short a time.

Lori A. Ringhand thanks her family and friends for their ongoing support. She is especially grateful to her husband, Dan Lorentz, and her parents, to whom she dedicates this book. Without their love and support, this work would not have been possible.

Finally, as this book was going to print we learned of the death of Senator Arlen Specter. Senator Specter served on the Senate Judiciary Committee for decades, and always fought to protect the role of the Senate in the confirmation process. For this he deserves our gratitude and thanks.

1

A Confirmation Process Worth Celebrating

Since 1939, almost every candidate nominated to serve on the Supreme Court has appeared to testify before the Senate Judiciary Committee. Each time one of these hearings occurs, Americans reengage in a debate about the meaning of the Constitution. Not only do the nominees respond to question after question from the senators, but these questions (and the nominees' answers) also frequently spark intense and colorful debate within the larger public. Nominees are grilled on everything from iconic and sublime cases such as *Brown v. Board of Education*[1] to deceptively mundane issues like spending Christmas Day at a Chinese restaurant – which sometimes turn out to have important cultural and political resonances.

To understand the confirmation hearings through this swirl of contemporary public debate is to get a rich education about what the Constitution means to us at a given moment in time. One might think, therefore, that these hearings would be viewed as important constitutional moments – essential discussions about constitutional meanings that would be welcomed, even celebrated, in a democratic system of governance such as ours. But the confirmation hearings are rarely thought of in this way. Instead, they are much maligned. The hearings are routinely criticized as empty rituals (at best) or deceptive debacles (at worst).[2] Some legal scholars have even called for abolishing them entirely.[3] (See footnote 3 on next page)

---

[1] Brown v. Board of Education, 347 U.S. 483 (1954).

[2] See, e.g., Richard Brust, "No More Kabuki Confirmations," 95 *American Bar Association Journal* 39 (2009); Stephen L. Carter, *The Confirmation Mess: Cleaning Up the Federal Appointments Process* (New York: Basic Books, 1994); Richard Davis, *Electing Justice: Fixing the Supreme Court Nomination Process* (New York: Oxford University Press, 2005); Ronald Dworkin, "Justice Sotomayor: The Unjust Hearings," *The New York Review of Books*, September 24, 2009; Christopher L. Eisgruber, *The Next Justice: Repairing the Supreme Court Appointments Process* (Princeton, NJ: Princeton University Press, 2007); Brian Fitzpatrick,

This book defends the celebratory view. Far from being empty rituals that degrade all involved, the confirmation hearings play an important but underappreciated role in our constitutional system: they provide a democratic forum for the discussion and ratification of constitutional change.[4] They do so by creating moments of democratic accountability during which senators debate what should be considered part of our constitutional consensus, and aspiring justices are expected – in public and under oath – to accept that consensus before being allowed to assume a seat on the high Court. Over time, the process of debating and repeatedly affirming (or, in some cases, rejecting) once deeply contested constitutional choices ratifies a new constitutional canon, one that reflects the broad and deep support of those who agree to live under it. In doing so, the confirmation process provides a key mechanism through which each generation of Americans defines and shapes our changing constitutional consensus.

Recognizing that public opinion shapes constitutional meaning is not novel. After all, the framers set up a Constitution that provides for indirect public input into the selection of federal judges through the public's representatives in the Senate and the White House, thereby ensuring that the Court's decisions would rarely stray too far from the public's preferences.[5] Moreover, numerous scholars have demonstrated that the Court is politically constrained and rarely deviates from deeply held majoritarian preferences.[6] Others have examined

"Confirmation 'Kabuki' Does No Justice," *Politico*, July 20, 2009. Retrieved from: http://www.politico.com/news/stories/0709/25131.html (Accessed July 24, 2012); Elena Kagan, "Confirmation Messes, Old and New," 62 *University of Chicago Law Review* 919 (1995); Scott Lemieux, "Can Kagan Win Over Liberals?" *American Prospect*, May 12, 2010. Retrieved from: http://prospect.org/article/can-kagan-win-over-liberals-0 (Accessed July 24, 2012,); John P. MacKenzie, "The Trouble with Hearings," *New York Times*, September 24, 1991; Stuart Taylor, Jr., "The Lessons of Bork," *National Journal*, July 22, 2009. Retrieved from: http://ninthjustice.nationaljournal.com/2009/07/the-lessons-of-bork.php (Accessed July 25, 2012); David A. Yalof, "Confirmation Obfuscation: Supreme Court Confirmation Politics in a Conservative Era," 44 *Studies in Law, Politics and Society* 143 (2008).

3 See Stephen Choi and Mitu Gulati, "A Tournament of Judges?" 92 *California Law Review* 299 (2004); Glenn Harlan Reynolds, "Taking Advice Seriously: An Immodest Proposal for Reforming the Confirmation Process," 65 *Southern California Law Review* 1572 (1992).

4 Our focus throughout this book is on constitutional, not statutory, law. As we demonstrate in Chapter 4, there is very little discussion of statutory law at the confirmation hearings: from 1939 to 2010, only 1% of all hearing dialogue involved matters of statutory interpretation.

5 Robert A. Dahl, "Decision-Making in a Democracy: The Supreme Court as a National Policy-Maker," 6 *Journal of Public Law* 279 (1957).

6 See, e.g., Alexander M. Bickel, *The Least Dangerous Branch: The Supreme Court at the Bar of Politics* (Indianapolis: Bobbs-Merrill, 1961); Tom S. Clark, "The Separation of Powers, Court-curbing and Judicial Legitimacy," 53 *American Journal of Political Science* 971 (2009); Barry Friedman, *The Will of the People: How Public Opinion Has Influenced the Supreme Court and Shaped the Meaning of the Constitution* (New York: Farrar, Straus & Giroux, 2010); Mark A.

various ways in which public opinion acts as a constraint on judicial decision making,[7] investigated how constitutional changes can obtain democratic validity,[8] and theorized why democratic input into constitutional meaning is normatively desirable.[9]

What our work adds to this rich literature is evidence that the confirmation hearings are one of the important ways in which the public contributes to constitutional change. When constitutional choices made by the Court gain acceptance by the public at large, nominees are expected to pledge their adherence to those choices at their confirmation hearings. Over time, subsequent nominees from across the political spectrum voice their support for those changes, allowing the hearings to function as a formal mechanism through which the Court's constitutional choices are ratified as a part of our constitutional consensus – the long-term constitutional commitments embraced by the public.[10] In doing so, the constitutional choices made by an otherwise largely insulated judiciary are affirmed through a formal, public, and law-focused process.

The hearings are uniquely positioned to play this role, in that they are conducted in the language of constitutional law and feature nominees testifying under oath and in the glare of substantial media attention, often for days on end. This separates the hearings from myriad other ways in which public

Graber, "The Nonmajoritarian Difficulty: Legislature Deference to the Judiciary," 7 *Studies in American Political Development* 35 (1993); Thomas R. Marshall, *Public Opinion and the Rehnquist Court* (Albany: State University of New York Press, 2008); Kevin T. McGuire and James A. Stimson, "The Least Dangerous Branch Revisited: New Evidence on Supreme Court Responsiveness to Public Preferences," 66 *Journal of Politics* 1018 (2004).

[7] See, e.g., Lee Epstein and Andrew D. Martin, "Does Public Opinion Influence the Supreme Court? Possibly Yes (But We're Not Sure Why)," 13 *University of Pennsylvania Journal of Constitutional Law* 263 (2010); Barry Friedman, "Dialogue and Judicial Review," 91 *Michigan Law Review* 577 (1993); Michael W. Giles, Bethany Blackstone, and Richard L. Vining, Jr., "The Supreme Court in American Democracy: Unraveling the Linkages between Public Opinion and Judicial Decision Making," 70 *Journal of Politics* 293 (2008); Terri Jennings Peretti, *In Defense of a Political Court* (Princeton, NJ: Princeton University Press, 2001).

[8] See, e.g., Jack M. Balkin and Sanford Levinson, "Understanding the Constitutional Revolution," 87 *Virginia Law Review* 1045 (2001); David A. Strauss, "The Irrelevance of Constitutional Amendments," 114 *Harvard Law Review* 1457 (2001); Cass R. Sunstein, "If People Would Be Outraged By Their Rulings, Should Judges Care?" 60 *Stanford Law Review* 155 (2007).

[9] See, e.g., Bruce Ackerman, *We the People*, Vol. 1: *Foundations* (Cambridge, MA: Harvard University Press, 1991); Larry D. Kramer, *The People Themselves: Popular Constitutionalism and Judicial Review* (New York: Oxford University Press, 2004); Peretti, *In Defense of a Political Court*, supra, n. 7.

[10] "Ratification" means to approve and give formal sanction to, which is the sense in which we are using the term here. See Joseph P. Pickett, ed., *The American Heritage Dictionary of the English Language* (Boston: Houghton Mifflin, 2000).

opinion influences constitutional change.[11] These differences are important, in that their very formality provides a measure of democratic accountability that looser mechanisms lack. Simply put, the Senate's ability to refuse to confirm a nominee who fails to accept or reject a particular constitutional doctrine provides a tangible moment at which elected officials, acting on our behalf, can choose one legally viable constitutional meaning and reject another.

Focusing on the role the confirmation hearings play in ratifying the current constitutional consensus, rather than on the ways in which they fail to impose a democratic check over the Court's handling of currently contested issues, has implications for the way we think about constitutional meaning and the role of the Court in our governing system. Although academic discourse has largely moved past this, much of the public mythology about constitutional lawmaking rests on the idea that smart justices acting in good faith can use the tools of constitutional interpretation to ascertain a single, "correct" meaning of the Constitution and apply that meaning in a determinative way to specific cases.[12] Though this view might be appealing, it is not the system we have. Legal and political science scholars have shown beyond reasonable dispute that our most careful methods of constitutional interpretation simply cannot eliminate judicial discretion in hard cases.[13] That is, to put it simply, what makes them hard. In such cases, the tools of legal reasoning may constrain judicial discretion, but they cannot eliminate it. Supreme Court justices therefore necessarily make choices among the constitutionally acceptable answers the tools of legal reasoning leave open to them. These choices are within those the Constitution allows, but they are not exclusively mandated by the Constitution. They are judicial *choices* – constructions built to operationalize

---

[11] Contrast, for example, the formal nature of the confirmation hearings with Ackerman's effort to legitimate constitutional change by identifying somewhat nebulously defined moments of "higher law making." See Bruce Ackerman, "The Living Constitution," 120 *Harvard Law Review* 1737 (2007).

[12] See, e.g., Erwin Chemerinsky, "Seeing the Emperor's Clothes: Recognizing the Reality of Constitutional Decision Making," 86 *Boston Law Review* 1069 (2006) (discussing how the myth of discretion-free decision making in constitutional law hinders the ability of the confirmation process to function as a democratic check on an unelected judiciary).

[13] See, e.g., Mitchell Berman, "Originalism Is Bunk," 84 *New York University Law Review* 1 (2009); Paul M. Collins, Jr., *Friends of the Supreme Court: Interest Groups and Judicial Decision Making* (New York: Oxford University Press, 2008); Daniel Farber and Suzanna Sherry, *Desperately Seeking Certainty: The Misguided Quest for Constitutional Foundations* (Chicago: University of Chicago Press, 2002); Friedman, *The Will of the People*, supra, n. 6; Brian Z. Tamanaha, *Beyond the Formalist-Realist Divide: The Role of Politics in Judging* (Princeton, NJ: Princeton University Press, 2009); Keith E. Whittington, *Political Foundations of Judicial Supremacy: The Presidency, the Supreme Court, and Constitutional Leadership in U.S. History* (Princeton, NJ: Princeton University Press, 2007).

the words of the Constitution in ways that make sense to the people living under it.

But our public rhetoric, dominated by debates about "umpires" and "activists,"[14] has little patience for a Constitution that offers multiple legally viable answers to hard constitutional questions. Acknowledging such a thing would, after all, require facing up to the fact that we live in a system in which we give unelected justices the power to choose among the legally acceptable outcomes the Constitution leaves open to them. Giving such power to judges seems intolerable.[15]

As other scholars have noted, this picture changes if we instead see those judicial choices as constrained over time by constitutional commitments made by the people and their elected officials, rather than just by the judiciary.[16] But Supreme Court confirmation hearings are rarely seen as contributing to this process, in part because they have proven unable to draw from nominees their opinions on our most hotly contested constitutional issues.[17] Focusing our lens instead on the role the hearings play in formally recognizing previously contested cases as part our constitutional consensus allows us to see how the confirmation hearings can in fact contribute to this process. Major constitutional changes, from this perspective, are not "mistakes" that must be grudgingly tolerated because people have come to rely on them,[18] but rather are constitutional choices, made by the people and ratified through the confirmation process. Constitutional meaning, in the process we describe here, is

---

[14] See, e.g., Kim McLane Wardlaw, "Umpires, Empathy, and Activism: Lessons from Judge Cardozo," 85 *Notre Dame Law Review* 1629 (2010); Aaron S.J. Zelinsky, "The Justice as Commissioner: Benching the Judge-Umpire Analogy," 119 *Yale Law Journal Online* 113 (2010).

[15] See, e.g., Raoul Burger, *Government by Judiciary: The Transformation of the Fourteenth Amendment* (Indianapolis: Liberty Fund, 1997). See also Richard A. Posner, "The Rise and Fall of Judicial Self-Restraint," 100 *California Law Review* 519 (2012) at 536 (discussing how the rise of constitutional theory, and its focus on finding "correct" constitutional answers, generates a belief that judging unrestrained by the "correct" method of interpretation necessarily results in "lawless" decisions).

[16] See, e.g., Kramer, *The People Themselves*, supra, n. 9; Mark Tushnet, *Taking the Constitution Away from the Courts* (Princeton, NJ: Princeton University Press, 2000).

[17] See, e.g., Eisgruber, *The Next Justice*, supra, n. 2 at 4 (arguing that the hearings have become little more than a forum for "platitudes, anecdotes, and scandals" and that the senators, unable to extract anything of constitutional substance from the nominees, have instead "fished for evidence of wrongdoing"). See also Vikram David Amar, "How Senate Confirmation Hearings Should Better Educate Senators and the American Public: The Instructional Necessity of Case Specific Questioning," 61 *Hastings Law Journal* 1407 (2010) (arguing that democratic discourse requires that nominees answer questions about specific issues and cases).

[18] For a discussion of the problem constitutional change poses for certain theories of constitutional interpretation, see Jack M. Balkin, "Nine Perspectives on Living Originalism," 2012 *University of Illinois Law Review* 815 (2012) at 821.

not pulled from the parchment by nine legal seers, but rather is created in fits and starts as the Court issues decisions that are accepted, rejected, ignored, and passionately argued about by us.

As our empirical analyses show, this understanding of the value of the confirmation hearings has the important advantage of resting on a descriptively accurate picture of how the Supreme Court and the Constitution actually work. In providing both the data and the theory to support our view, we hope this book will thus work to lessen the grip of the incomplete story so many of us feel compelled to tell about the Constitution and the Court. We have found, however, that people of all political persuasions bring strong preconceptions to discussions of the confirmation hearings, the Supreme Court, and the Constitution, and that those perceptions sometimes lead readers to leap ahead and reach conclusions we reject in this book. We therefore find it helpful at the onset to lay out with some specificity what we are *not* saying.

We do not believe that it is the job of the Supreme Court to track short-term public opinion (although it frequently will do so), nor do we believe Supreme Court justices have an obligation to vote the way their political allies or "constituencies" want them to. We do not think nominees should be required to answer every question put to them by senators (although we do think that senators could get better answers if they asked better questions) and we certainly do not think justices should be impeached for failing to always vote in accordance with the answers they gave at their hearings (although we think they should feel a special obligation to explain such deviations in their written opinions). Nor do we believe that every decision issued by the Supreme Court is equally valid. The tools of legal reasoning constrain judicial discretion even if they cannot eliminate it, and there will always be better and worse legal arguments. Likewise, although the Constitution in almost all hard cases allows for more than one legally correct answer, it is not infinitely flexible. To say there is unlikely to be a single correct answer is not to say there are no *wrong* answers. Finally, we do not assert that the hearings are the only important means by which Supreme Court decisions gain democratic acceptance.[19] There are many ways this occurs,

---

[19]   It is important to note that we are concerned with the ratification of the Court's decisions, not the legitimacy of the Court as an institution. For excellent treatments of the factors shaping the legitimacy of the Supreme Court, see, e.g., Gregory A. Caldeira and James L. Gibson, "The Etiology of Public Support for the Supreme Court," 36 *American Journal of Political Science* 635 (1992); James L. Gibson and Gregory A. Caldeira, *Citizens, Courts, and Confirmations: Positively Theory and the Judgments of the American People* (Princeton, NJ: Princeton University Press, 2009); Timothy R. Johnson and Andrew D. Martin, "The Public's Conditional Response to Supreme Court Decisions," 92 *American Political Science Review* 299 (1998).

including through long-term constitutional conversations,[20] the construction and re-construction of constitutional meaning,[21] and the acceptance of new constitutional understandings advanced by various social movements.[22]

What we *are* saying is this. The Constitution rarely gives determinative legal answers to complex constitutional questions. Supreme Court justices therefore necessarily make choices among the constitutionally acceptable answers the tools of legal reasoning leave open to them. These choices are within those the Constitution allows, but are rarely uniquely mandated by the Constitution itself. They are judicial choices. Accordingly, they draw their legitimacy not from any constitutional decree, but rather by acceptance, over time, by broad and deep swaths of the public. The confirmation hearings contribute to this process by providing a forum in which those choices are ratified in a democratically legitimated way. *Brown v. Board of Education* is accepted, *Plessy v. Ferguson*[23] is rejected, and what was once controversial is recognized as part of our constitutional understanding.

This celebratory view of the confirmation hearings – as a forum through which constitutional choices are, over time, embraced through a formal, public, and legalized process – builds on existing literature about constitutional construction, public opinion, and social movements. Scholars working in this tradition have argued that constitutional lawmaking is a constructive process in which the Court legitimates and rationalizes constitutional meanings developed through social movements and ordinary politics.[24] In doing so, they have shown how constitutional understandings can be changed through sustained and broad-based public action.[25] We add to this work by demonstrating how the confirmation process acts as one of the mechanisms used to validate those changes. We show that nominees testifying at the hearings do in fact repeatedly affirm their allegiance to (or rejection of) what were once disputed constitutional meanings.[26] Over time, these repeated avowals help to turn those

---

[20] See, e.g., Bruce A. Ackerman, "The Storrs Lectures: Discovering the Constitution," 93 *Yale Law Journal* 1013 (1984); Friedman, "Dialogue and Judicial Review," supra, n. 7.

[21] See, e.g., Kramer, *The People Themselves*, supra, n. 9.

[22] See, e.g., Reva Siegel, "Dead or Alive: Originalism as Popular Constitutionalism in *Heller*," 122 *Harvard Law Review* 191 (2008).

[23] Plessy v. Ferguson, 163 U.S. 537 (1896).

[24] See, e.g., Jack M. Balkin, *Living Originalism* (Cambridge, MA: Harvard University Press, 2011); Sanford Levinson, *Constitutional Faith* (Princeton, NJ: Princeton University Press, 1989).

[25] See, e.g., Ackerman, *We the People*, supra, n. 9; Akhil Reed Amar, *America's Unwritten Constitution: The Precedents and Principles We Live By* (New York: Basic Books, 2012).

[26] Balkin has referred to these "must" affirm or reject issues as the "constitutional catechism." Jack M. Balkin, "The Constitutional Catechism." January 11, 2006. Retrieved from: http://balkin.blogspot.com/2006/01/constitutional-catechism.html (Accessed September 5, 2012).

once-disputed meanings – the constitutional choices made by the judiciary – into part of our constitutional fabric. They become constitutional meanings that "We the People" accept, acting not as a metaphysical abstraction, but as we actually think, live, and vote today.

This view of the importance of the hearings stands in stark contrast to the claim that the hearings lack value because senators are unable to pull from nominees their opinions on currently contested constitutional issues.[27] Focusing on the nominees' refusal to answer questions about unsettled areas of law, although meaningful in some contexts, overlooks the valuable role of the hearings in solidifying our common understandings of what areas *are* settled.[28] Thus, although nominees are unlikely to tell us much about their opinions of currently contested issues, such as abortion, affirmative action, and gay rights, the repeated affirmation of seminal cases, such as *Brown*, plays an important role in both validating the Court's choices in previously contested areas and defining the constitutional issues that are and are not actively in play.

PLAN OF THE BOOK

Although there is no shortage of critiques of the confirmation process, there has been very little empirical research examining exactly what happens when nominees appear before the Senate Judiciary Committee.[29] As a result, many of the calls for changes to the process are based primarily on anecdotes or the analysis of a few nominees,[30] as opposed to a large-scale investigation of

---

[27] See, e.g., Amar, "How Senate Confirmation Hearings Should Better Educate Senators and the American Public," supra, n. 17; Eisgruber, *The Next Justice*, supra, n. 2.

[28] In this light, senatorial discussions of "super precedents," addressed in Chapter 8, are best understood as efforts to define what is and is not part of the consensus that makes up our constitutional canon. John Roberts' confirmation hearing, for example, involved a great deal of debate about the role of such precedents in judicial law making. See, e.g., Michael J. Gerhardt, "Super Precedent," 90 *Minnesota Law Review* 1204 (2006).

[29] For exceptions to this, see, e.g., Dion Farganis and Justin Wedeking, "'No Hints, No Forecasts, No Previews': An Empirical Analysis of Supreme Court Nominee Candor from Harlan to Kagan," 45 *Law & Society Review* 525 (2011); Frank Guliuzza III, Daniel J. Reagan, and David M. Barrett, "The Senate Judiciary Committee and Supreme Court Nominees: Measuring the Dynamics of Confirmation Criteria," 56 *Journal of Politics* 773 (1994); Ayo Ogundele and Linda Camp Keith, "Reexamining the Impact of the Bork Nomination to the Supreme Court," 52 *Political Research Quarterly* 403 (1999); Margaret Williams and Lawrence Baum, "Questioning Judges about Their Decisions: Supreme Court Nominees before the Senate Judiciary Committee," 90 *Judicature* 73 (2006).

[30] See, e.g., Bruce A. Ackerman, "Transformative Appointments," 101 *Harvard Law Review* 1164 (1988); Amar, "How Senate Confirmation Hearings Should Better Educate Senators and the American Public," supra, n. 17; Carter, *The Confirmation Mess*, supra, n. 2; Davis, *Electing Justice*, supra, n. 2; Eisgruber, *The Next Justice*, supra, n. 2; Bruce Fein, "A Circumscribed

every nominee who has testified before the Judiciary Committee. Bucking this trend, we ground our normative picture of the confirmation hearings in an empirically rigorous examination of what actually happens at the hearings. Our conclusions, however, are far from the mundane cataloging of confirmation questions and answers. Rather, our close inspection of the hearings allows us to draw not just on dry data, but also on stories and illustrations, plucked from hearing transcripts going back to before World War II, to show the various ways in which the hearings do in fact play a role in democratically ratifying the Court's constitutional choices.

In so doing, we are attentive to the fact that the research question should drive one's choice of methods, rather than the reverse. Consequently, we employ both quantitative and qualitative methods throughout this book. For example, we use quantitative methods to determine the extent to which public opinion and Supreme Court precedent influence confirmation hearing dialogue, a question we believe is best answered through the tools of statistical analysis. Conversely, we rely on qualitative methods to assess the extent to which various nominees affirmed or rejected core constitutional principles at their hearings, as this question calls out for the in-depth analysis of hearing dialogue. Thus, some chapters feature primarily statistical methods, others primarily qualitative methods, and still others utilize both methodological orientations. We are confident that employing this mixed-methods approach will result in a deeper understanding of the nuanced relationship between confirmation hearings and constitutional change.

The data we use throughout this book are based on the transcripts of the Senate Judiciary Committee hearings of Supreme Court nominees. Our quantitative analyses make use of an original database we have created. The database codes every question asked and every answer given at every open public hearing of a Supreme Court nominee since Felix Frankfurter testified in 1939. This data set includes nominees who appeared to testify and were confirmed, as well as nominees who testified but were not confirmed, either because they withdrew from the process or because their confirmation failed in the Senate. This database, the first of its kind, provides a rich source of information on hearing dialogue.[31] Our qualitative analyses likewise make use of hearing transcripts. In particular, we rely primarily on hearing transcripts to develop a compelling narrative exploring how hearing discourse evolves over time, thus providing

---

Senate Confirmation Role," 102 *Harvard Law Review* 672 (1989); David A. Strauss and Cass R. Sunstein, "The Senate, the Constitution, and the Confirmation Process," 101 *Yale Law Journal* 1491 (1992).

[31] A full treatment of our database is provided in the Appendix.

a vivid illustration of just how the senators' questions and nominees' answers contribute to the ratification of our evolving constitutional understandings.

We begin our story in Chapter 2 by presenting an overview of the Supreme Court nomination and confirmation process. The chapter offers an in-depth treatment of all stages of the process of filling a vacancy on the nation's highest Court. We start by discussing how vacancies arise on the Court. We then cover the means by which the president selects a nominee and the various influences on the president's decision as to whom to nominate. Next, we provide an exposition of the significant role the Senate Judiciary Committee plays in the process, as well as that of the full Senate. Following this, we discuss what happens after a nominee is confirmed and prepares to take his or her seat on the Supreme Court. As a way of highlighting this process in action, the chapter closes with a case study of the nomination and confirmation of the Court's newest Justice (as of the time of this writing), Elena Kagan.

While Chapter 2 provides necessary background for understanding the confirmation process, the remainder of the book is dedicated to advancing our thesis: Supreme Court confirmation hearings are a democratic forum for the discussion and ratification of constitutional change. Supporting this claim requires we do three things. First, we need to show that the hearings are democratic, in the sense that they feature the discussion of issues that are important to the American public. In this way, the hearings gain a large part of their democratic legitimacy insofar as the senators fulfill their representational duties by relaying the concerns of the citizenry to nominees.[32] Second, we need to illustrate that the hearings feature the discussion of constitutional issues of contemporary relevance to the public. Rather than merely follow an idiosyncratic path determined by the traits or personal histories of the nominees,[33] our thesis necessitates that we show that hearing dialogue centers around

---

[32] One might argue that the hearings are implicitly democratic because, at least since the passage of the Seventeenth Amendment (which predates the hearings), senators are directly elected. We believe the dialogical nature of the thesis we are advancing requires more than just reliance on the direct election of senators: it involves demonstrating that senators relay the concerns of the citizenry to nominees. For more general discussions of the democratic nature of the Senate relating to the effects of the Seventeenth Amendment, see, e.g., Vikram David Amar, "Indirect Effects of Direct Election: A Structural Examination of the Seventeenth Amendment," 49 *Vanderbilt Law Review* 1347 (1996); Jay S. Bybee, "Ulysses at the Mast: Democracy, Federalism, and the Sirens' Song of the Seventeenth Amendment," 91 *Northwestern University Law Review* 500 (1997).

[33] The discussion of Sonia Sotomayor's "wise Latina" comment at her confirmation hearing is the most high-profile, recent example of nominee-specific factors driving hearing discourse. In that statement, Sotomayor appeared to suggest that minority judges would reach "better" conclusions than white male judges because of their life experiences. That such idiosyncratic conversations do not dominate the hearings is demonstrated in Chapters 3 and 4. See Sonia

constitutional issues, most notably the constitutional reasoning embodied in the Court's prior decisions.[34] Finally, we need to demonstrate that the hearings help ratify constitutional change by showing that they are in fact a mechanism through which the senators strive to define, and nominees are expected to embrace, previously controversial judicial choices that have been absorbed into our constitutional agreement. Chapters 3, 4, and 5 accomplish the first two tasks, while Chapters 6, 7, and 8 carry out the latter.

Chapter 3 provides the first empirical test of our theory of confirmation hearings by examining the extent to which both public opinion and Supreme Court precedent influence hearing dialogue. Although nominees (as well as Supreme Court justices) have multiple ways to obtain information about public opinion,[35] establishing that the hearings are one such mechanism is significant. The confirmation process, we argue, is an important procedural "check point" at which democratically accountable actors directly engage changes in our governing consensus as explicitly constitutional changes. For the hearings to assume this role, hearing discourse must reflect the salient legal and political issues of the day, including the very issues with which the Supreme Court grapples. Indeed, it is almost impossible to imagine a situation in which the hearings provide the occasion for public input into the direction of constitutional change *absent* a link between public opinion and hearing dialogue. Likewise, the hearings cannot ratify constitutional change unless nominees and senators directly engage the Court's prior constitutional choices. To test this, we use original data on hearing dialogue, coupled with information regarding public opinion and Supreme Court precedents. Although the statistical methods employed in this chapter are somewhat sophisticated, readers should take heart that we have translated our results in a straightforward manner by relying on numerous graphs to provide a more accessible understanding of our findings.

Sotomayor, "A Latina Judge's Voice." Retrieved from: http://www.law.berkeley.edu/4982.htm (Accessed May 6, 2011).

[34] This is because, simply put, there can be no ratification of constitutional change absent a discussion of constitutional issues, particularly those involving the Court's precedents. The chapters devoted to demonstrating this point illustrate not just that the hearings involve the discussion of constitutional issues, but also that this discourse is driven by deep and long-lasting concerns over constitutional meaning, as opposed to political opportunism on the part of the Senators. For a discussion of senatorial roles at the hearings, see George Watson and John Stookey, "Supreme Court Confirmation Hearings: A View From the Senate," 71 *Judicature* 186 (1988).

[35] See, e.g., Epstein and Martin, "Does Public Opinion Influence the Supreme Court?" supra, n. 7; Giles, Blackstone, and Vining, "The Supreme Court in American Democracy," supra, n. 7.

In Chapters 4 and 5, we build on our key findings in Chapter 3 by further demonstrating the links among public opinion, Supreme Court precedent, and hearing dialogue. Chapter 4 delves more deeply into the issues discussed at the hearings by illustrating how those issues change over time as their importance rises and falls in American society. For example, we illustrate how racial discrimination, once a focal point of hearing colloquy, has waned, almost certainly reflecting our current consensus that the Constitution proscribes intentional discrimination against racial minorities. As comments regarding racial discrimination declined, statements about discrimination based on gender and sexual orientation arrived to fill the gap – a shift in focus that corresponded to the increased public debate surrounding first gender and then sexual orientation discrimination. Chapter 5 further develops our theoretical story by illustrating how both nominees and senators use Supreme Court precedents to construct a broadly accepted set of constitutional commitments that change over time as new legal debates develop in the American polity.

Chapters 6, 7, and 8 address how the hearings ratify constitutional change. In Chapter 6, we take a closer look at the use of particular precedents to demonstrate how the Court's seminal decisions are affirmed or rejected by senators and nominees. In doing so, we illustrate how those precedents function as "confirmation conditions" – the judicial choices nominees are expected to accept or rebuff before being allowed to join the high Court. To establish this central role of the hearings in ratifying constitutional change, we follow the trajectory of three cases and one issue that represented a significant change in our constitutional understandings: *Brown v. Board of Education, Griswold v. Connecticut,*[36] *District of Columbia v. Heller,*[37] and the issue of gender discrimination.

In Chapter 7, we focus on two specific nominations – the failed nomination of Robert Bork and the subsequent successful nomination of Anthony Kennedy – to illustrate this point further. In contrast to many claims about the failure of the Bork nomination, we argue that Bork failed to garner Senate confirmation not because he answered too many questions, but because he gave the wrong answers.[38] Kennedy, as we show, was every bit as forthcoming as Bork on the issues that proved problematic for Bork. Unlike Bork's, however, Kennedy's responses in regard to those issues were consistent with what

---

[36]   Griswold v. Connecticut, 381 U.S. 479 (1965).

[37]   District of Columbia v. Heller, 171 L. Ed. 2d 637 (2008).

[38]   See, e.g., Nancy Benac, "Tough Confirmation Hearings Relatively New," *Telegraph Herald*, August 29, 2005; Linda Greenhouse, "Judge Ginsburg: A Nominee with a Short 'Paper Trail,'" *New York Times*, November 1, 1987; Henry J. Reske, "Did Bork Say Too Much?" *ABA Journal*, December 1, 1987; Guy Taylor, "Politics and Justice for All," *Washington Times*, July 24, 2005.

the Bork hearing itself had helped to reveal as the then-existing constitutional consensus. Importantly, that consensus held through more than a decade of subsequent nominations: the nominees immediately following Kennedy, a group that included individuals put forth by both Democratic and Republican presidents, embraced the positions articulated by Kennedy and rejected those espoused by Bork. Far from being a travesty, the failed Bork confirmation is thus reframed as an important moment in which a new constitutional consensus was recognized and subsequently embraced over a series of nominations made by a variety of presidents and voted on by differently composed Senates.

Chapter 8 further addresses the ratification of constitutional change by tackling the vexing problem of the role played in the confirmation hearings by questions involving issues on which there is no constitutional consensus – questions, in other words, about currently contested constitutional meanings. As we show, this "problem," which commands so much attention,[39] may be less about a general lack of responsiveness than it is about *Roe v. Wade*[40] and abortion rights. Nonetheless, although we believe that nominees could answer more questions about currently contested issues than they do, we argue that confirmation dialogue about such issues is constructive even in the face of nominee reticence. Such questions give nominees and senators a focused opportunity in which to present their best case for bringing currently contested constitutional choices into the constitutional canon. In this capacity, they illustrate the scope of our existing constitutional agreement, while also providing a platform from which to advocate changes to that agreement.[41] We show this process in action by examining how the notion of "super precedents" is used at the hearings. We also explore certain ways in which nominees' confirmation statements compare with the positions they take once on the high Court. In doing so, we address the extent to which apparent "mismatches"

---

[39] See, e.g., Michael Comiskey, "Can the Senate Examine the Constitutional Philosophies of Supreme Court Nominees?," 26 PS: *Political Science and Politics* 495 (1993); William G. Ross, "The Questioning of Supreme Court Nominees at Senate Confirmation Hearings: Proposals for Accommodating the Needs of the Senate and Ameliorating the Fears of the Nominees," 62 *Tulane Law Review* 109 (1987); Denis Steven Rutkus, "CRS Report for Congress, Questioning Supreme Court Nominees about Their Views on Legal or Constitutional Issues: A Recurring Issue" (2005). Retrieved from: http://www.fas.org/sgp/crs/misc/R41300.pdf (Accessed December 13, 2011); Denis Steven Rutkus, "CRS Report for Congress, Proper Scope of Questioning of Supreme Court Nominees: The Current Debate" (2005). Retrieved from: http://assets.opencrs.com/rpts/RL33059_20050901.pdf (Accessed December 13, 2011).

[40] Roe v. Wade, 410 U.S. 113 (1973).

[41] In other words, they are a way of talking about what issues are on and off the constitutional wall. See Balkin, *Living Originalism*, supra, n. 24.

between the positions nominees take at the hearings and those they take on the Court are and are not problematic for our theory.

Although the primary purpose of this book is to demonstrate that the confirmation hearings are valuable because they act as a democratic forum for the discussion and ratification of constitutional change, our work also contributes to our understanding of the Court and the confirmation process in other ways. For example, our discussion of the connection between public opinion and confirmation dialogue in Chapters 3 and 4 enhances our understanding of the Supreme Court by providing a novel window into the means by which public opinion is transmitted to the justices. By illustrating how the hearings provide an effective opportunity for the American people, acting through their representatives on the Judiciary Committee, to shape the meaning of the Constitution, we add fresh nuance to this debate. In so doing, we provide empirical evidence for previously developed theories arguing that constitutional law is formed by a dialogue among the public, elected officials, and future justices themselves.[42]

Chapters 3 and 5, in addition to establishing that the hearings are a forum for constitutional discourse, also show how the confirmation process enables the Supreme Court to communicate *its* constitutional understandings to the public. Just as scholars have long concerned themselves with the democratic nature of the Court, so too have they been concerned with how the Court in turn affects American law, politics, and society.[43] We add to this important discussion by demonstrating that the Court's decisions, through the spirited debates they generate at the confirmation hearings, help the judiciary both initiate and shape a national dialogue about the Constitution. Far from being the passive institution that some have suggested,[44] the Court actively shapes

---

[42] See, e.g., Ackerman, "The Storrs Lectures," supra, n. 20; Christine Bateup, "The Dialogical Promise: Assessing the Normative Potential of Theories of Constitutional Dialogue," 71 *Brooklyn Law Review* 1109 (2005); Neal Devins and Louis Fisher, *The Democratic Constitution* (New York: Oxford University Press, 2004); Richard H. Fallon, Jr., *Implementing the Constitution* (Cambridge, MA: Harvard University Press, 2001); Friedman, "Dialogue and Judicial Review," supra, n. 7; Robert C. Post and Reva B. Siegel, "Popular Constitutionalism, Departmentalism, and Judicial Supremacy, 92 *California Law Review* 1027 (2004).

[43] See, e.g., Bradley C. Canon and Charles A. Johnson, Jr., *Judicial Policies: Implementation and Impact* (Washington, DC: CQ Press, 1999); Michael J. Klarman, "How *Brown* Changed Race Relations: The Backlash Thesis," 81 *Journal of American History* 81 (1994); Gerald N. Rosenberg, *The Hollow Hope: Can Courts Bring about Social Change?* (Chicago: University of Chicago Press, 1991); Francine Sanders, "*Brown v. Board of Education*: An Empirical Reexamination of Its Effects on Federal District Courts," 29 *Law and Society Review* 731 (1995).

[44] See, e.g., Donald L. Horowitz, *The Courts and Social Policy* (Washington, DC: Brookings Institution, 1977); Rosenberg, *The Hollow Hope*, supra, n. 43; Stuart A. Scheingold, *The*

American constitutional debate by generating precedents that are vigorously and publicly debated at the confirmation hearings. That debate, in turn, plays a major role in how we evaluate future members of our high Court. Confirmation dialogue, in other words, is a two-way street. Senatorial questioning acts as one of the ways in which nominees receive information about contemporary public opinion, while the nominees' answers help share with the public the complexity of constitutional decision making by explaining the Court's prior choices in the language and reasoning of constitutional law rather than ordinary politics.

More generally, this book informs our understanding of proposals to reform the confirmation process. Whether the confirmation process is or is not working properly, and how it should be fixed if it is not, has been the subject of endless legal, political, and popular debate.[45] A belief that the process has changed – and changed for the worse – has led to a chorus of calls for reform. But these reform proposals suffer from the lack of a firm empirical understanding of what actually happens at the hearings. This book provides that essential foundation by presenting quantitative data documenting confirmation discourse. This alone is a significant contribution to the existing literature, in that it allows theorists working in various areas finally to have an empirical foundation on which to rest their arguments.

The picture of the Supreme Court confirmation hearings that emerges from this work steps back from the cynicism about the process that has dominated public discourse in recent decades. Instead of focusing on what the hearings cannot do, we explore what they can do. And we find much to celebrate. The confirmation hearings as we present them are an essential part of our system of self-governance and an auspicious opportunity for nominees, elected officials, and the public to engage in the complex project of constitutional lawmaking. Moreover, the analyses presented here show that this understanding of the hearings is not just normatively appealing but also empirically substantiated. Accordingly, this book brings us one step closer to accepting – and celebrating – the Court and the Constitution we actually have, rather than the mythical one we seem to think we need.

Politics of Rights: Lawyers, Public Policy, and Political Change (New Haven: Yale University Press, 1974).

45   See, e.g., Brust, "No More Kabuki Confirmations," supra, n. 2; Carter, *The Confirmation Mess*, supra, n. 2; Dworkin, "Justice Sotomayor," supra, n. 2; Eisgruber, *The Next Justice*, supra, n. 2; Kagan, "Confirmation Messes, Old and New," supra, n. 2; Yalof, "Confirmation Obfuscation," supra, n. 2.

2

How It Works

The Nuts and Bolts of the Confirmation Process

The United States Constitution says very little about the Supreme Court nomination and confirmation process. Article II, Section 2 grants the president the "Power, by and with the Advice and Consent of the Senate, to . . . appoint . . . judges of the Supreme Court."[1] Article III, Section 1 holds that "The judges, both of the supreme and inferior Courts, shall hold their Offices during good Behaviour."[2] With these few words, the Constitution set up a system in which the president is charged with nominating Supreme Court justices and the Senate is tasked with confirming the president's nominees. Once confirmed, Supreme Court justices effectively enjoy life tenure, thus limiting their political accountability. In fact, the only way to constitutionally remove a Supreme Court justice is through the cumbersome and rarely used impeachment process. The Constitution also is silent as to requirements for sitting on the Supreme Court. That is, although the Constitution dictates age and residency requirements for members of Congress and the president, there are no formal requirements for service on the Supreme Court. Indeed, one need not even be an attorney, although every nominee to the Court to date has practiced law.[3]

Throughout the nation's history, there have been 160 nominations to the Supreme Court.[4] Of these, 123 nominations received Senate confirmation, and 26 nominations were rejected by the Senate. The remaining nominations

---

[1] U.S. Constitution, Article II, Section 2.

[2] U.S. Constitution, Article III, Section 1.

[3] Lee Epstein, Thomas G. Walker, Nancy Staudt, Scott Hendrickson, and Jason Roberts, "The U.S. Supreme Court Justices Database." Retrieved from: http://epstein.law.northwestern .edu/research/justicesdata.html (Accessed January 26, 2011).

[4] This figure, and those reported throughout this chapter, excludes the thirteen recess appointments made by presidents. We provide a separate discussion of recess appointments later in this chapter in a sidebar.

were either withdrawn by the president or never considered by the Senate.[5] Thus, statistically speaking, presidents are quite successful in obtaining Senate support for their nominees: more than 75% of presidential nominations gained Senate approval.

This success rate, however, is notably lower than in other presidential nominations. For example, from 1945 to 2004, the Senate confirmed more than 80% of appointments to the U.S. Courts of Appeals and the U.S. District Courts.[6] Moreover, from 1965 to 2008, the Senate confirmed 93% of appointments to the cabinet and the Executive Office of the President and 88% of appointments to independent agencies and executive corporations.[7] Thus, it is clear that Supreme Court nominations are among the most contentious appointments made by presidents.

The purpose of this chapter is to shed light on the nomination and confirmation process. We demonstrate that the process has been marked by both continuity and change. For example, although the constitutional procedures for the nomination and confirmation of Supreme Court justices have never been formally amended, the manner in which they have been implemented has changed. We begin by discussing how vacancies occur on the Supreme Court, followed by an analysis of the president's role in the process, including the factors influencing the president's decision of whom to nominate. Next, we discuss the considerable role played by the Senate Judiciary Committee, as well as that of the full Senate. To illustrate the process in action, we conclude the chapter with a case study of President Obama's nomination of Elena Kagan.

SUPREME COURT VACANCIES

The nomination of a Supreme Court justice is a major milestone in a president's career, particularly in the modern era. Because the Court is a policymaking institution, nominations provide presidents with the opportunity

---

[5] Epstein, Walker, Staudt, Hendrickson, and Roberts, "The U.S. Supreme Court Justices Database," supra, n. 3; Denis Steven Rutkus, "CRS Report for Congress, Supreme Court Appointment Process: Roles of the President, Judiciary Committee, and Senate" (2010). Retrieved from: http://www.fas.org/sgp/crs/misc/RL31989.pdf (Accessed December 13, 2011).

[6] Lee Epstein and Jeffrey A. Segal, *Advice and Consent: The Politics of Judicial Appointments* (New York: Oxford University Press, 2005) at 99; Wendy L. Martinek, Mark Kemper, and Steven R. Van Winkle, "To Advise and Consent: The Senate and Lower Federal Court Nominations, 1977–1998," 64 *Journal of Politics* 337 (2002).

[7] Jon R. Bond, Richard Fleisher, and Glen S. Krutz, "Malign Neglect: Evidence That Delay Has Become the Primary Method of Defeating Presidential Appointments," 36 *Congress & the Presidency* 226 (2009).

to shape public policy long after they leave office: although presidents now can serve a maximum of eight years, the average tenure of a Supreme Court justice has been fifteen years. Since 1970, justices have served for an average of twenty-four years.[8] Of course, before the president can nominate an individual to the Court, a vacancy must occur. There are four means by which vacancies can open on the Supreme Court: the creation of new seats, impeachment, death, and voluntary departures through either retirement or resignation.

The first of these options – the creation of new seats – is rare, but it is not unprecedented. Although the Supreme Court has remained a nine-member institution since 1869, this stability is neither constitutionally required nor historically sacred. The Constitution does not specify the size of the Court, and Congress has changed the Court's makeup many times. The Judiciary Act of 1789 set the size of the Court at six justices: one chief justice and five associate justices. In 1807, Congress expanded the Court to seven justices; in 1837, two additional seats were allocated to the Court; and in 1863, the Court increased to a ten-member panel. In 1866, Congress reduced the size of the Court to seven justices and also prohibited the president from appointing new justices until the Court had seven members. (This statute was passed as an attempt to prevent President Andrew Johnson, unpopular with the Republican-controlled Congress for his resistance to its reconstruction plans, from appointing new justices.[9]) This act was revised in 1869, when the Supreme Court's size was set at nine justices, which corresponded to the number of federal judicial circuits at the time.[10]

A second means by which a vacancy can occur on the Supreme Court involves the impeachment of a sitting justice for "treason, bribery, or other high crimes and misdemeanors."[11] As with all impeachable federal offices, such as those of the president, vice president, and cabinet officials, judicial impeachment follows a two-step procedure. The impeachment stage takes place in the House of Representatives, which brings and votes on articles of

---

[8] Epstein, Walker, Staudt, Hendrickson, and Roberts, "The U.S. Supreme Court Justices Database," supra, n. 3.

[9] Henry J. Abraham, *Justices, Presidents, and Senators: A History of U.S. Supreme Court Appointments from Washington to Bush II* (Lanham, MD: Rowman & Littlefield, 2008) at 99.

[10] Charles L. Zeldon, ed., *The Judicial Branch of Federal Government: People, Process, and Politics* (Santa Barbara, CA: ABC-CLIO, 2007) at xi.

[11] U.S. Constitution, Article II, Section 4. However, there is some debate as to whether the Constitution's provision that federal judges serve for "good Behaviour" indicates that they may be impeached for activities that fall below the standard articulated in Article II, Section 4. See, e.g., John D. Feerick, "Impeaching Federal Judges: A Study of the Constitutional Provisions," 39 *Fordham Law Review* 1 (1970); Michael J. Gerhardt, *The Federal Impeachment Process: A Constitutional and Historical Analysis* (Chicago: University of Chicago Press, 2000) at 83–6.

impeachment. Impeachment in the House requires only a simple majority vote. The trial and removal phase of the impeachment process takes place in the Senate and requires a two-thirds majority to remove the accused from office. Although no justice on the Supreme Court has ever been removed from the Court through impeachment, the Republican-controlled House did vote to impeach Justice Samuel Chase, a strong supporter of Federalist policies, in 1804. Though the House vote was down party lines, Republicans in the Senate failed to garner the necessary two-thirds majority necessary for conviction. This failed impeachment effort is widely regarded as establishing a precedent that justices would not be impeached for solely political reasons.[12]

A third way for a seat to open on the Supreme Court involves the death of a sitting justice. Since the Court's inception in 1789, forty-nine justices have died while serving on the Court.[13] Most recently, Chief Justice William Rehnquist died on September 3, 2005, after a year-long battle with thyroid cancer. Rehnquist's death provided President George W. Bush with the opportunity to appoint John Roberts as the leader of the high Court.

The final means by which a vacancy can arise on the Court involves a justice voluntary departing from the bench, either through retirement or resignation. During the Court's history, fifty-four justices have left the Court voluntarily,[14] usually after reaching pension eligibility. Since 1984, this occurs when a justice satisfies the "Rule of Eighty:" when the combined age and number of years of service equals at least eighty for a justice who has reached the age of sixty-five.[15] For example, if a justice is seventy years of age and has served at least ten years on the Court, he or she is eligible to receive for life his or her full salary at the time of retirement. In 2010, this amounted to $223,500 for the chief justice and $213,900 for associate justices.[16] A retired justice is also entitled to maintain chambers at the Court, employ at least one law clerk and other administrative

---

[12] Richard B. Lillich, "The Chase Impeachment," 4 *American Journal of Legal History* 49 (1960); Rutkus, "Supreme Court Appointment Process," supra, n. 5 at 2; Keith E. Whittington, "Reconstructing the Federal Judiciary: The Chase Impeachment and the Constitution," 9 *Studies in American Political Development* 55 (1995).

[13] Epstein, Walker, Staudt, Hendrickson, and Roberts, "The U.S. Supreme Court Justices Database," supra, n. 3; Christopher J. W. Zorn and Steven R. Van Winkle, "A Competing Risks Model of Supreme Court Vacancies, 1789–1992," 22 *Political Behavior* 145 (2000).

[14] Epstein, Walker, Staudt, Hendrickson, and Roberts, "The U.S. Supreme Court Justices Database," supra, n. 3; Zorn and Van Winkle, "A Competing Risks Model of Supreme Court Vacancies," supra, n. 13.

[15] Artemus Ward, *Deciding to Leave: The Politics of Retirement From the United States Supreme Court* (Albany: State University of New York Press, 2003) at 195.

[16] Robert Barnes, "Supreme Court Chief Justice Roberts Opts Not to Ask Congress to Raise Judicial Salaries," *Washington Post*, January 1, 2010.

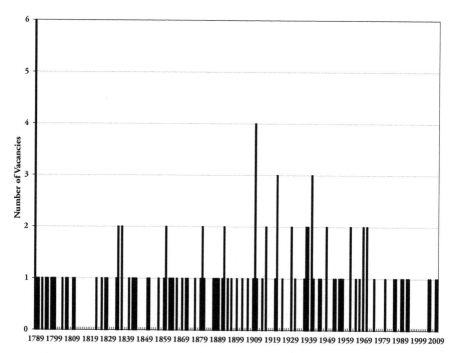

FIGURE 2.1. Number of Supreme Court vacancies, 1789–2010.

personnel, and hear cases in the lower federal courts as a visiting judge.[17] Conversely, a justice who resigns from the Court without satisfying the Rule of Eighty is not eligible for these pension benefits and retirement perks.

Figure 2.1 reports the number of vacancies on the Court from 1789 to 2010.[18] Years are aligned along the *x*-axis, and the *y*-axis reports the number of open seats. As this figure makes clear, vacancies on the Supreme Court occur at irregular rates. Although, on average, a vacancy on the Court opens up about every two years, there have been several periods in history in which the number of years between vacancies was far longer. For example, from 1812 to 1822, there were no vacancies on the Court. Similarly, no vacancies occurred during the entire presidency of Jimmy Carter. More recently, there was no membership change on the Court from Justice Breyer's appointment in 1994 until the appointment of Chief Justice Roberts in 2005, a strikingly long eleven-year period.

---

[17] Ward, *Deciding to Leave*, supra, n. 15 at 191.
[18] This information was collected from Epstein, Walker, Staudt, Hendrickson, and Roberts, "The U.S. Supreme Court Justices Database," supra, n. 3, and Zeldon, ed., *The Judicial Branch of Federal Government*, supra, n. 10, updated to reflect the retirement of Justice Stevens.

There is no single reason why justices voluntarily leave the Court, which may be why vacancies occur so irregularly. Rather, a variety of occasionally interrelated factors appear to influence a justice's decision to depart from the bench. First, a justice's age is important: older justices are more likely to retire.[19] In part, this is because the Rule of Eighty works to deprive younger retirees of full pension benefits. In addition, because infirmity is likely to play a larger role for older justices, departures related to medical issues often correspond with a justice's advancing age.[20]

Of course, health concerns can strike at any age, and numerous justices have left the Court because of illness, particularly before the advent of modern medicine.[21] For example, Justice Gabriel Duvall, who served from 1811 to 1835, went deaf while on the bench, rendering oral argument proceedings, the primary means by which cases were argued at the time, effectively useless.[22] Charles Whittaker, who suffered from mental anxiety and depression before joining the Court, retired after enduring a mental breakdown in 1962, which his son attributed in part to Felix Frankfurter's relentless efforts to secure Whittaker's vote.[23] More recently, Justice Thurgood Marshall retired after serving on the Court for more than two decades (1967–1991). His retirement, however, came only after he suffered a heart attack, glaucoma, recurrent pneumonia, and viral bronchitis.[24]

A third factor that influences – or at least used to influence – the decision to leave the bench is ambition.[25] Although justices on the contemporary Supreme Court enjoy the prestige of serving at the zenith of the American legal system, a position on the Court was not always seen as so desirable. For example, until 1911, the justices were required to engage in circuit-riding duties, traveling throughout the country, often on horse and carriage, to preside over cases in the circuit courts.[26] For justices presiding over the Southern Circuit, this amounted to 1,800 miles of travel over rough terrain.[27]

[19] Kjersten R. Nelson and Eve M. Ringsmuth, "Departures from the Court: The Political Landscape and Institutional Constraints," 37 *American Politics Research* 486 (2009); Zorn and Van Winkle, "A Competing Risks Model of Supreme Court Vacancies," supra, n. 13.

[20] David N. Atkinson, *Leaving the Bench: Supreme Court Justices at the End* (Lawrence: University Press of Kansas, 1999); Richard L. Vining, Christopher Zorn, and Susan Navarro Smelcer, "Judicial Tenure on the U.S. Supreme Court, 1790–1868: Frustration, Resignation, and Expiration on the Bench," 20 *Studies in American Political Development* 198 (2006).

[21] Vining, Zorn, and Smelcer, "Judicial Tenure on the U.S. Supreme Court," supra, n. 20.

[22] Atkinson, *Leaving the Bench*, supra, n. 20 at 28.

[23] Ward, *Deciding to Leave*, supra, n. 15 at 164–5.

[24] Atkinson, *Leaving the Bench*, supra, n. 20 at 156.

[25] See, e.g., Atkinson, *Leaving the Bench*, supra, n. 20; Ward, *Deciding to Leave*, supra, n. 15.

[26] Vining, Zorn, and Smelcer, "Judicial Tenure on the U.S. Supreme Court," supra, n. 20.

[27] Ward, *Deciding to Leave*, supra, n. 15 at 30.

Moreover, the Court itself moved ten times from 1789 until 1935, further adding to the hardship endured by the justices. Finally, formal retirement provisions, including pension benefits, were not available until 1869.[28]

Consequently, many justices in the eighteenth and nineteenth centuries left the bench to pursue other, more prestigious opportunities. For example, Chief Justice John Jay, President Washington's first nominee to the Court, left after only six years to become Governor of New York.[29] Justice David Davis, who served from 1862 to 1877, departed from the Court on his election to the U.S. Senate. Davis later served as president pro tempore of the Senate and president of the Illinois Bar Association.[30] As the Court developed into the powerful institution it is today, fewer and fewer justices left the bench to follow other opportunities, although the occasional departure to pursue another position still has occurred. For example, Chief Justice Warren Burger, who served from 1969 to 1986, retired to oversee the nation's bicentennial celebration of the signing of the Constitution at the request of President Reagan.[31]

Although it is ultimately a justice's choice to depart voluntarily from the bench, external pressures can shape a justice's decision to resign or retire. For example, after allegations of Justice Abe Fortas' role in some unscrupulous financial transactions surfaced in *Life* magazine, the threat of impeachment and the failure of the Senate to confirm him as chief justice likely influenced his decision to leave the Court in 1969 after only five years on the bench.[32] Family pressures can also play a role in a justice's decision to depart. Indeed, despite being in good health and only sixty-five years of age, Justice Potter Stewart retired in 1981 to spend more time with his family.[33] More recently, Justice Sandra Day O'Connor retired in 2006 to look after her husband, who was suffering from Alzheimer's disease.[34]

A fifth factor that influences a justice's decision to leave the Court involves job satisfaction. That is, justices who are satisfied with their positions on

---

[28] In part, the Retirement Act of 1869 was enacted by the Republican-controlled Congress as a means of inducing Democratic Justices Robert Grier and Samuel Nelson to step down. This was apparently successful in that Grier retired in 1870, while Nelson retired in 1872. See Ward, *Deciding to Leave*, supra, n. 20 at 4, 9.

[29] Atkinson, *Leaving the Bench*, supra, n. 20 at 13.

[30] Ibid. at 55–7.

[31] Ibid. at 150.

[32] Ibid. at 140.

[33] Ibid. at 149.

[34] Patricia Sullivan, "Sandra Day O'Connor's Husband Dies," *Washington Post*, November 11, 2009. Retrieved from: http://voices.washingtonpost.com/postmortem/2009/11/sandra-day-oconnors-husband-di.html (Accessed December 13, 2011).

the Court are more likely to remain on the bench.[35] Lower levels of job satisfaction were particularly acute prior to 1925, when the Supreme Court had a virtually mandatory docket (meaning that the justices were compelled to hear almost every case brought before the Court). This resulted in heavy workloads, taxing the justices' time and energy, which was further exacerbated by their circuit-riding duties.[36] Consequently, it should come as no surprise that several justices in that era left the Court as a result of job dissatisfaction. For example, Justice Thomas Johnson resigned in 1793 after serving only fourteen months because of his frustration with riding the Southern Circuit.[37] More recently, Justice Owen Roberts retired in 1945 after serving for fifteen years as a result of his unhappiness with his position, as reflected in the fact that his relationships with other members of the Court, especially Justice Hugo Black, were less then friendly.[38] Justice James Byrnes retired in 1942, after serving only two terms, apparently as a result of his boredom with the Court's caseload and because he believed he was better suited to a more overtly political life directing President Franklin D. Roosevelt's Office of Economic Stabilization.[39] Justice Souter's recent departure at the relatively young age of sixty-nine also may be attributable to a lack of satisfaction with the job, as his distaste for living in the nation's capital was well known.[40]

Finally, political considerations can influence a justice's decision to leave the Court. In particular, there is conflicting evidence that the partisan makeup of the legislative and executive branches plays a role in a justice's decision to depart voluntarily.[41] A justice who is in relatively good health may choose to

---

[35] See, e.g., Atkinson, *Leaving the Bench*, supra, n. 20; Zorn and Van Winkle, "A Competing Risks Model of Supreme Court Vacancies," supra, n. 13.

[36] Zorn and Van Winkle, "A Competing Risks Model of Supreme Court Vacancies," supra, n. 13.

[37] Atkinson, *Leaving the Bench*, supra, n. 20 at 15.

[38] Ibid. at 115.

[39] Ibid. at 118.

[40] Nina Totenberg, "Supreme Court Justice Souter to Retire," *NPR*, April 30, 2009. Retrieved from: http://www.npr.org/templates/story/story.php?storyId=103694193 (Accessed December 13, 2011).

[41] The literature on this topic is rife with contradictory findings. Studies supporting strategic retirement theory include Timothy M. Hagle, "Strategic Retirements: A Political Model of Turnover on the United States Supreme Court," 15 *Political Behavior* 25 (1993); Nelson and Ringsmuth, "Departures From the Court," supra, n. 19; Ross M. Stolzenberg and James Lindgren, "Retirement and Death in Office of U.S. Supreme Court Justices," 47 *Demography* 269 (2010); and Ward, *Deciding to Leave*, supra, n. 15. Studies providing limited or no evidence for strategic retirement theory include Saul Brenner, "The Myth That Justices Strategically Retire," 36 *Social Science Journal* 431 (1999); Peverill Squire, "Politics and Personal Factors in Retirement from the United States Supreme Court," 10 *Political Behavior* 180 (1988); Vining,

retire when he or she believes the president will appoint, and the Senate will confirm, a nominee who shares the justice's ideological orientation. Correspondingly, a justice whose ideology differs from that of the president may put off retiring until a more ideologically compatible president is elected. For example, Chief Justice Burger, a Republican, retired in 1986 at a time when the Republican Party controlled both the White House and the Senate. On the day after the election of President Clinton, Justice Harry Blackmun scribed the following note during oral argument: "What do I do now? Retire at once; Retire at 6/30/93; Retire at 6/30/94."[42] When television news incorrectly called the 2000 presidential election in favor of Al Gore, Justice O'Connor is said to have responded "This is terrible" at a dinner party upon hearing the news.[43] The comment was reported as being in reference to her plans to retire in the near future, which would have resulted in Gore naming her successor.[44] O'Connor instead chose to remain on the bench until 2006, thereby allowing President George W. Bush to appoint Samuel Alito to fill her seat.

Of course, justices' attempts to retire strategically are not always successful. For example, Chief Justice Earl Warren announced his retirement in 1968, conditional on his successor's confirmation in the Senate. Warren did this in hopes that President Johnson, in his last year in office, would appoint the next chief justice. This strategy ultimately backfired after Associate Justice Abe Fortas' elevation to chief justice was filibustered in the Senate.[45] Johnson subsequently withdrew the nomination, and President Nixon, Johnson's successor, appointed Warren Burger to fill the chief justice position in 1969. In addition, Justice Thurgood Marshall, who suffered poor health for years, was unable to hold out until a Democratic president was elected and retired during the administration of President George H.W. Bush, resulting in President Bush's appointment of Clarence Thomas.[46]

As the preceding discussion illustrates, vacancies at the Supreme Court occur at irregular rates and for various reasons. In recent years, seats have opened on the Court as a result of deaths, retirements, and resignations. When

Zorn, and Smelcer, "Judicial Tenure on the U.S. Supreme Court," supra, n. 20; and Zorn and Van Winkle, "A Competing Risks Model of Supreme Court Vacancies," supra, n. 13.

[42] Nelson and Ringsmuth, "Departures from the Court," supra, n. 19 at 486.

[43] Michael Isikoff and Evan Thomas, "The Truth behind the Pillars," *Newsweek*, December 24, 2000. Retrieved from: http://www.newsweek.com/2000/12/24/the-truth-behind-the-pillars.html (Accessed December 13, 2011).

[44] Richard K. Neumann, "Conflicts of Interest in *Bush v. Gore*: Did Some Justices Vote Illegally?" 16 *Georgetown Journal of Legal Ethics* 375 (2003).

[45] Atkinson, *Leaving the Bench*, supra, n. 20 at 138.

[46] Ward, *Deciding to Leave*, supra, n. 15.

justices choose to depart the Court voluntarily, a variety of often interrelated factors come into play, including age, health, ambition, external pressures, job satisfaction, and political considerations. Regardless of how a vacancy arises, however, the next step in the process is the same: the president gets the opportunity to nominate a new justice.

PRESIDENTIAL APPOINTMENTS TO THE SUPREME COURT

The first step in the appointment process involves the president putting together a list of names to fill a Supreme Court vacancy. Though presidents typically begin compiling a list of potential nominees only after a vacancy opens on the Court, a president may enter the Oval Office with specific individuals in mind. For example, immediately after George W. Bush was sworn in as president, his staff began putting together a list of potential nominees to the bench, anticipating Chief Justice Rehnquist's retirement.[47]

There are many actors involved in the process of creating this list of potential nominees. Within the administration, the president relies closely on numerous advisors, including the attorney general, White House legal counsel, and other high-ranking executive branch officials.[48] In addition, the president may consult with members of the Senate, paying particular attention to the input of party leaders and members of the Senate Judiciary Committee.[49] Such consultations provide an opportunity for the President to obtain senators' views of a potential nominee's strengths and weaknesses, thus giving the president a sense of how a nominee might fare in the Senate. Presidents also may rely on the advice of individuals outside of government, including attorneys, representatives from interest groups, and members of the media.[50] Moreover, sitting Supreme Court justices can provide the president with their insights into potential nominees. For example, Chief Justice Earl Warren was influential in convincing President Kennedy to nominate Arthur Goldberg to the Court to replace Justice Felix Frankfurter, who himself also consulted with the president on his replacement.[51]

---

[47] Jan Crawford Greenburg, *Supreme Conflict: The Inside Story of the Struggle for Control of the United States Supreme Court* (New York: Penguin Press, 2007) at 241.

[48] David Alistair Yalof, *Pursuit of Justices: Presidential Politics and the Selection of Supreme Court Nominees* (Chicago: University of Chicago Press, 1999).

[49] Rutkus, "Supreme Court Appointment Process," supra, n. 5 at 7.

[50] Abraham, *Justices, Presidents, and Senators*, supra, n. 9; Rutkus, "Supreme Court Appointment Process," supra, n. 5.

[51] Abraham, *Justices, Presidents, and Senators*, supra, n. 9 at 25. Of course, the extent to which individual presidents rely more or less on each of these advisors varies by administration.

As the president puts together a list of potential nominees, two types of background checks occur.[52] The Federal Bureau of Investigation conducts a private investigation, including an analysis of each candidate's financial affairs. An investigation of a candidate's public record and professional abilities is conducted by Department of Justice officials; White House aides; and, on occasion, private attorneys. In addition to scrutinizing each nominee's record, including reading the nominee's judicial opinions if he or she is being elevated from another court, nominees may be interviewed by members of the president's administration or by the president. Further, the president may request that nominees fill out questionnaires regarding their jurisprudential philosophies.[53] The purpose of these background checks is to obtain as much information as is possible about potential nominees to ensure that no surprises arise later in the process. These screening mechanisms also enhance the president's ability to appoint like-minded nominees to the Court, a particularly important consideration in that the appointment of Supreme Court justices provides the president with the opportunity to shape the course of American law long after he or she leaves the Oval Office.

A variety of dynamics influence the president's decision of whom to appoint. Certainly, a nominee's formal qualifications for office play a major role.[54] Although it is somewhat difficult to pin down exactly the characteristics that make a nominee "qualified" to serve on the Court, several factors come into play. Prior experience as a judge, either on the lower federal bench or on state courts, frequently is viewed as relevant, both because such experience is seen as beneficial and because it allows the president and the Senate to evaluate the type of justice the nominee is likely to be. Indeed, some 65% of Supreme Court nominees had previous judicial experience,[55] and this percentage has increased in recent years as presidents have favored nominees with prior judicial experience as compared to those with prior political experience.[56] Of course, service in the judiciary in and of itself is not sufficient. For example,

---

[52] Rutkus, "Supreme Court Appointment Process," supra, n. 5.

[53] Epstein and Segal, *Advice and Consent*, supra, n. 6 at 64.

[54] See, e.g., Abraham, *Justices, Presidents, and Senators*, supra, n. 9; Epstein and Segal, *Advice and Consent*, supra, n. 6; Neil D. McFeeley, *Appointment of Judges: The Johnson Presidency* (Austin: University of Texas Press, 1987); Jeffrey A. Segal and Harold J. Spaeth, *The Supreme Court and the Attitudinal Model Revisited* (New York: Cambridge University Press, 2002).

[55] Epstein, Walker, Staudt, Hendrickson, and Roberts, "The U.S. Supreme Court Justices Database," supra, n. 3.

[56] See, e.g., Lee Epstein, Jack Knight, and Andrew D. Martin, "The Norm of Prior Judicial Experience and Its Consequences for Career Diversity on the U.S. Supreme Court," 91 *California Law Review* 903 (2003).

President Nixon nominated G. Harrold Carswell, who served as a district court judge for the Northern District of Florida and as a judge on the U.S. Court of Appeals for the Fifth Circuit, to the Supreme Court in 1970. Despite having served on the federal bench for twelve years, Carswell was thought to be unqualified for the Supreme Court, in part because he was the most reversed judge in the Fifth Circuit.[57]

For individuals who do not have prior judicial experience, presidents often look to those with governmental service, frequently in the executive branch of the federal government. For example, numerous nominees have served in the Office of Solicitor General, the group of attorneys who represent the executive branch in the Supreme Court. Justice Elena Kagan, former justice Thurgood Marshall, and nominee Robert Bork all served as solicitor general, while Chief Justice John Roberts and Justice Samuel Alito served as principal deputy solicitor general and assistant to the solicitor general, respectively. In addition, several nominees have come from the Office of Attorney General, including Justices Warren Burger, Stanley Reed, William Rehnquist, Antonin Scalia, and John Paul Stevens.[58] Outside of the federal government, numerous nominees brought with them experience in state and local politics, including Frank Murphy (mayor, Detroit, Michigan), Sandra Day O'Connor (senator, Arizona), David Souter (attorney general, New Hampshire), and Earl Warren (governor, California).[59]

It is also apparent that presidents seek nominees from the highest echelons of law schools. Although there are hundreds of law schools throughout the country, only thirty-three have been represented on the Supreme Court.[60] Of these, Ivy League law schools are exceptionally well represented, with twenty-two nominees from Harvard and ten each from Yale and Columbia. In fact, every member of the current Court has studied at either Harvard or Yale during the course of his or her law school career. In addition, several nominees enjoyed prestigious positions in law schools prior to their appointment to the

---

[57] Epstein and Segal, *Advice and Consent*, supra, n. 6 at 66. In responding to allegations of Carswell's lack of qualifications, Senator Hruska (R-NE) famously proclaimed, "Even if he were mediocre, there are a lot of mediocre judges and people and lawyers. They are entitled to a little representation, aren't they, and a little chance? We can't have all Brandeises, Frankfurters and Cardozos." William H. Honan, "Roman L. Hruska Dies at 94; Leading Senate Conservative," *New York Times*, April 27, 1999.

[58] Epstein, Walker, Staudt, Hendrickson, and Roberts, "The U.S. Supreme Court Justices Database," supra, n. 3.

[59] Ibid.

[60] Two of the law schools represented on the Supreme Court are from outside of the United States: Middle Temple (England) and the University of Paris (France). Ibid.

Court, including Justice Elena Kagan (dean, Harvard Law School), Justice Antonin Scalia (professor, University of Chicago), and Robert Bork (professor, Yale Law School).

Although a nominee's formal qualifications play a major role in shaping the president's decision of whom to nominate, politics also enters into the picture. Most obviously, presidents seek to appoint nominees who share their ideological orientation.[61] For example, conservative presidents look to nominate justices who will support the government over the criminal defendant, business over labor, states' rights over federal powers, and those who will be generally unfavorable toward civil rights plaintiffs, while liberal presidents pursue the opposite strategy.[62] During the course of the nation's history, presidents have appointed individuals who share their political party affiliation more than 85% of the time.[63]

Although presidents generally are successful at appointing like-minded justices to the Court,[64] they are not unconstrained and must select their nominees with an eye on senatorial preferences and intraparty disputes. These dynamics certainly entered into George H. W. Bush's nomination of David Souter in 1990. Although Souter had more than a decade of experience as a judge in New Hampshire and sat on the U.S. Court of Appeals for the First Circuit at the time of his nomination, his appointment was viewed by some as a "stealth nomination" in that his record lacked any major controversial rulings.[65] This was useful for an administration trying to navigate controversial social issues within the Republican Party itself, but perhaps less so for a president trying to make an imprint on the evolution of constitutional law: upon his confirmation to the Court, Justice Souter proved himself to be a reasonably reliable liberal justice, often voting with Justices Breyer and Ginsburg, both Clinton appointees.[66]

---

[61] See, e.g., Abraham, *Justices, Presidents, and Senators*, supra, n. 9; Epstein and Segal, *Advice and Consent*, supra, n. 6; Segal and Spaeth, *The Supreme Court and the Attitudinal Model Revisited*, supra, n. 54.

[62] Epstein and Segal, *Advice and Consent*, supra, n. 6;. Segal and Spaeth, *The Supreme Court and the Attitudinal Model Revisited*, supra, n. 54.

[63] Abraham, *Justices, Presidents, and Senators*, supra, n. 9 at 52; Segal and Spaeth, *The Supreme Court and the Attitudinal Model Revisited*, supra, n. 54.

[64] See, e.g., Epstein and Segal, *Advice and Consent*, supra, n. 6; Jeffrey A. Segal, Richard J. Timpone, and Robert M. Howard, "Buyer Beware? Presidential Success through Supreme Court Appointments," 53 *Political Research Quarterly* 557 (2000).

[65] Jeffrey Rosen, "The Stealth Justice," *New York Times*, May 1, 2009.

[66] Epstein and Segal, *Advice and Consent*, supra, n. 6 at 62. Souter's relative liberalism should not have come as a surprise to those who paid attention to the answers he provided at his confirmation hearing.

In addition to ideological compatibility, politics enters into the president's decision in a number of other ways. Presidents frequently use Supreme Court appointments as a means of building political support by appeasing various constituencies.[67] During the Court's earliest years, geography (which heavily influenced politics in early American history) played a major role. This corresponded to the fact that the Judiciary Act of 1802 required justices to reside within the circuit on which they supervised. Although the need for geographical representation on the Court faded with the demise of the justices' circuit-riding duties, geography would periodically continue to factor into the president's selection process. For example, President Nixon sought to gain the support of voters from the southern United States, who traditionally aligned themselves with the Democratic Party, in part by appointing a southerner to replace Justice Black in 1971.[68]

Today, it seems that geography is a lesser consideration, evidenced by the fact that four members of the current Supreme Court hail from New York City: Justices Ginsburg, Kagan, Scalia, and Sotomayor. Presidents now are more likely to use Supreme Court appointments to appeal to nongeographic constituencies. Although the Court has been overwhelmingly dominated by white men of European descent, the appointment of minority and female nominees has provided presidents with an opportunity to reach out to new constituencies, including interest groups representing racial, ethnic, and gender minorities.[69] For example, President Reagan's nomination of Justice Sandra Day O'Connor fulfilled a campaign promise to appoint the first woman to the Court – a promise made in part to bridge the Republican Party's chronic gender gap in voter support.[70] Likewise, on the retirement of Thurgood Marshall, the first black justice, President George H. W. Bush nominated Clarence Thomas, also an African American, to fill Marshall's seat.[71] Justices themselves have acknowledged the importance of racial and gender diversity on the Court. After President George W. Bush announced that he was appoint-

[67] Kevin J. McMahon, "Presidents, Political Regimes, and Contentious Supreme Court Nominations: A Historical Institutional Model," 32 *Law and Social Inquiry* 919 (2007); Segal and Spaeth, *The Supreme Court and the Attitudinal Model Revisited*, supra, n. 54.

[68] Segal and Spaeth, *The Supreme Court and the Attitudinal Model Revisited*, supra, n. 54 at 183.

[69] See, e.g., Lauren Cohen Bell, *Warring Factions: Interest Groups, Money, and the New Politics of Senate Confirmation* (Columbus: Ohio State University Press, 2002).

[70] Abraham, *Justices, Presidents, and Senators*, supra, n. 9 at 265.

[71] Ibid. at 51.

ing John Roberts to replace Justice Sandra Day O'Connor, the first female justice in the nation's history, O'Connor responded rather clearly: "He's good in every way, except he's not a woman."[72] More recently, President Obama's appointment of Justice Sonya Sotomayor was met with great enthusiasm by the increasingly important Hispanic voting population.

The president may also use a Supreme Court appointment as a means of rewarding personal friends and political allies. Indeed, about 60% of Supreme Court appointments have involved individuals with personal ties to the president.[73] For example, Chief Justice Fred Vinson was an old friend of President Truman who served as Truman's secretary of commerce.[74] President Johnson unsuccessfully nominated his long-time comrade, Abe Fortas, to the position of chief justice.[75] President Kennedy was friends with Justice Byron White, who assisted in Kennedy's election by chairing Citizens for Kennedy–Johnson.[76] President George W. Bush unsuccessfully nominated his long-time associate and former personal attorney, Harriet Miers, in 2005.[77]

Finally, presidents also are constrained by both public opinion and the composition of the Senate.[78] Whereas presidents who enjoy the support of the American public and face a friendly Senate have a large amount of leeway in determining whom to nominate to the Court, unpopular presidents facing a hostile Senate have more limited choices. For example, although President Ford would have surely preferred in 1975 to appoint a more conservative nominee than John Paul Stevens, the political environment constrained his ability to do so. In particular, Ford had low approval ratings, in part due to his pardon of former President Nixon. Ford also faced a filibuster-proof Democratic majority in the Senate. Seeking to avoid a clash in the Senate, Ford chose the moderate Stevens, who went on to become one of the leading justices on the Court's left-wing block.[79]

---

[72] Dan Balz and Darryl Fears, "Some Disappointed Nominee Won't Add Diversity to Court," *Washington Post*, July 21, 2005.

[73] Robert Scigliano, *The Supreme Court and the Presidency* (New York: The Free Press, 1971) at 95; Segal and Spaeth, *The Supreme Court and the Attitudinal Model Revisited*, supra, n. 54 at 184.

[74] Scigliano, *The Supreme Court and the Presidency*, supra, n. 73 at 94.

[75] Segal and Spaeth, *The Supreme Court and the Attitudinal Model Revisited*, supra, n. 54 at 184.

[76] Scigliano, *The Supreme Court and the Presidency*, supra, n. 73 at 94.

[77] Abraham, *Justices, Presidents, and Senators*, supra, n. 9 at 319.

[78] See, e.g., Epstein and Segal, *Advice and Consent*, supra, n. 6; Segal and Spaeth, *The Supreme Court and the Attitudinal Model Revisited*, supra, n. 54.

[79] Segal and Spaeth, *The Supreme Court and the Attitudinal Model Revisited*, supra, n. 54.

Sidebar: Recess Appointments

Recess Appointments to the U.S. Supreme Court, 1789–2010

Appointee	Year	President	Outcome
Thomas Johnson	1791	Washington	Confirmed to lifetime appointment
John Rutledge	1795	Washington	Rejected for lifetime appointment
Bushrod Washington	1798	Adams, J.	Confirmed to lifetime appointment
Henry Brockholst Livingston	1806	Jefferson	Confirmed to lifetime appointment
Smith Thompson	1823	Monroe	Confirmed to lifetime appointment
John McKinley	1837	Van Buren	Confirmed to lifetime appointment
Levi Woodbury	1845	Polk	Confirmed to lifetime appointment
Benjamin Curtis	1851	Fillmore	Confirmed to lifetime appointment
David Davis	1862	Lincoln	Confirmed to lifetime appointment
Oliver Wendell Holmes	1902	Roosevelt, T.	Confirmed to lifetime appointment
Earl Warren	1953	Eisenhower	Confirmed to lifetime appointment
William Brennan	1956	Eisenhower	Confirmed to lifetime appointment
Potter Stewart	1958	Eisenhower	Confirmed to lifetime appointment

Article II, Section 2, Clause 3 of the Constitution grants the president the ability to appoint Supreme Court justices, lower court judges, and other officials requiring confirmation when the Senate is in recess. These appointments expire at the end at the next congressional session and do not require senatorial approval, typically lasting for about two years. The original purpose of recess appointments was to authorize the president to fill critical vacancies when the Senate was not in session, which was a common occurrence in the early history of the country.[80] As the Senate began to meet for longer periods of time, with shorter recesses, the need for recess appointments diminished and today they are occasionally used to appoint controversial nominees to lower federal courts who may not survive the Senate confirmation process.[81]

Although recess appointments to the judiciary most commonly involve lower court judges, thirteen Supreme Court justices reached the Court by way of recess appointments, the most recent in 1958.[82] Every one of these justices, save one, was

---

[80] See, e.g., T. J. Halstead, "CRS Report for Congress, Judicial Recess Appointments: A Legal Overview" (2005). Retrieved from: http://fpc.state.gov/documents/organization/50801.pdf (Accessed December 12, 2011); Rutkus, "Supreme Court Appointment Process," supra, n. 5.

[81] Scott E. Graves and Robert M. Howard, *Justice Takes a Recess: Judicial Appointments from George Washington to George W. Bush* (Lanham, MD: Lexington Books, 2009); Halstead, "Judicial Recess Appointments," supra, n. 80.

[82] Epstein, Walker, Staudt, Hendrickson, and Roberts, "The U.S. Supreme Court Justices Database," supra, n. 3.

later confirmed through the traditional Senate confirmation process. Only John Rutledge failed to garner Senate support when President Washington reappointed him to the Court. Interestingly, Rutledge was appointed to the Court on three separate occasions. In 1789, he was appointed and confirmed by the Senate to an associate justiceship, although he never actually served on the Court, opting instead to resign before it convened in order to accept the position of chief justice of the South Carolina Court of Common Pleas and Sessions. In 1795, President Washington used a recess appointment to appoint him to chief justice of the United States of America. Washington then formally nominated him to chief justice, but because of a hostile Senate environment and allegations of mental instability, the Senate rejected his appointment by a 14–10 vote.[83]

In the modern era, once the president has picked a nominee, the president announces the individual's nomination in a press conference. Typically, this involves the president speaking to the nominee's background, experience, integrity, and fitness for office, followed by remarks from the nominee. For example, on May 26, 2009, President Obama, joined by Vice President Biden, announced his nomination of Second Circuit Court of Appeals Judge Sonia Sotomayor to fill the seat vacated by Justice Souter. During his announcement, Obama discussed Sotomayor's experience as a private practice attorney, a prosecutor, a federal trial judge, and a federal appellate judge. Obama, a baseball fan, used the occasion to praise Sotomayor for her district court opinion that helped end the Major League Baseball strike of 1994–5. He also described her moving personal story as the embodiment of the American Dream, in that she is a first-generation American whose parents emigrated from Puerto Rico during World War II.[84] Sotomayor spoke next, accepting the nomination, discussing her career path to the bench, and thanking many of her friends and family for their assistance on her journey to the Court.

Prior to, or in tandem with, the referral of the nomination to the Senate, the appointee's name is sent to the American Bar Association (ABA),[85] which has rated nominees according to their qualifications for office since 1956.[86] Currently, the ABA uses a three-tier ranking system: "well

---

[83] Abraham, *Justices, Presidents, and Senators,* supra, n. 9.

[84] John T. Woolley and Gerhard Peters, "The American Presidency Project." Retrieved from: http://www.presidency.ucsb.edu/ws/?pid=86204 (Accessed December 13, 2011).

[85] The ABA first began rating federal court nominees below the Supreme Court in 1946. Its role in rating Supreme Court nominees did not begin until 1956. Abraham, *Justices, Presidents, and Senators,* supra, n. 9 at 27.

[86] Abraham, *Justices, Presidents, and Senators,* supra, n. 9; Rutkus, "Supreme Court Appointment Process," supra, n. 5; Susan Navarro Smelcer, Amy Steigerwalt, and Richard L. Vining, Jr.,

qualified," "qualified," and "not qualified." The ABA's assessment of a nominee is based on professional competence, integrity, and judicial temperament, using information culled from a review of a nominee's legal experience, writing samples, and interviews with the nominee and members of the legal community.[87] The purpose of the ABA's role is to provide an unbiased view of a nominee's qualifications for office, irrespective of a nominee's ideological orientation.[88]

Although the ABA has rated Supreme Court nominees since 1956, its role has changed over time. Three presidents, Eisenhower in 1957, Nixon in 1971, and Ford in 1975, authorized the ABA to vet candidates prior to their nomination, thus giving the ABA substantial input into the selection of a nominee.[89] In other nominations, the ABA has rated candidates only after the president nominated an individual to the Court.[90] In 2001, President George W. Bush stopped sending nominees' names to the ABA, arguing that the organization was biased against conservative nominees and should not be given such a prominent role in the selection process.[91] Nonetheless, the Senate Judiciary Committee continued to rely on the ABA's ratings for Bush nominees, forwarding nominee names to the ABA itself.[92] Soon after his election, President Obama reinstated the ABA's traditional role in the process.[93]

As stated previously, appointments to the Supreme Court provide presidents with the opportunity to influence public policy long after they leave office. In the process of selecting nominees to the Court, the president relies on the input of numerous advisors from the executive, legislative, and judicial branches, as well as from actors outside of government. Ultimately, however, the decision of whom to nominate is the president's alone. A number of factors

---

"Bias and the Bar: Evaluating the ABA Ratings of Federal Judicial Nominees," 65 *Political Research Quarterly* 827 (2012).

[87] American Bar Association, "Standing Committee on the Federal Judiciary: What It Is and How It Works." Retrieved from: http://www.abanet.org/scfedjud/federal_judiciary09.pdf (Accessed December 12, 2010).

[88] Abraham, *Justices, Presidents, and Senators*, supra, n. 9; Smelcer, Steigerwalt, and Vining, "Bias and the Bar," supra, n. 82.

[89] Rutkus, "Supreme Court Appointment Process," supra, n. 5 at 12. Compare Abraham, *Justices, Presidents, and Senators*, supra, n. 9 at 27.

[90] Rutkus, "Supreme Court Appointment Process," supra, n. 5.

[91] Smelcer, Steigerwalt, and Vining, "Bias and the Bar," supra, n. 82. President George W. Bush's nominees, John Roberts and Samuel Alito, both received unanimous "well qualified" ratings from the ABA. Because the nomination of Harriet Miers was withdrawn before it reached the Senate Judiciary Committee, she did not receive a rating. Epstein, Walker, Staudt, Hendrickson, and Roberts, "The U.S. Supreme Court Justices Database," supra, n. 3.

[92] Rutkus, "Supreme Court Appointment Process," supra, n. 5.

[93] Smelcer, Steigerwalt, and Vining, "Bias and the Bar," supra, n. 82.

shape the president's decision, including a nominee's qualifications, ideology, election concerns, and the political environment. Once the president makes his choice, responsibility for the nomination moves to the next key actor in the confirmation process: the Senate Judiciary Committee.

THE SENATE JUDICIARY COMMITTEE

Once the president makes an appointment to the Court, that nomination is forwarded to the Senate for its consideration. To assist in its role of providing the president advice and consent, the Senate in 1816 established the Committee on the Judiciary as a standing committee. Prior to the creation of the Judiciary Committee, nominations were handled by the full Senate without consideration by committee. From 1816 to 1867, two-thirds of nominations were referred to the Judiciary Committee. Since 1868, almost all nominations have been automatically referred to the Senate Judiciary Committee.[94]

Like that of other congressional committees, the makeup of the Senate Judiciary Committee is based on partisan control of the Senate. For example, in July of 2009, the Senate was made up of fifty-eight Democrats, forty Republicans, and two independents who caucused with the Democratic Party. Thus, when Sonia Sotomayor was nominated by President Obama, the Judiciary Committee was composed of twelve Democrats and seven Republicans. The chair, who schedules the Committee's agenda, calendar, and hearings, is elected by the full Senate. This allows the party that controls the majority of the Senate to ensure one of its members is chair of the Committee. It is important, however, to note that seniority also plays a large role in the selection of the chair, although the prominence of seniority has changed from time to time.[95] Minority party leadership is represented by the ranking member of the

---

94 See Denis Steven Rutkus and Maureen Bearden, "CRS Report for Congress, Supreme Court Nominations, 1789–2009: Actions by the Senate, the Judiciary Committee, and the President" (2009). Retrieved from: http://fpc.state.gov/documents/organization/124658.pdf (Accessed December 13, 2011). There have been seven exceptions to this, all involving individuals who served in some federal government capacity prior to, or at the time of, their appointment, including a president, an attorney general, senators, a secretary of war, and a sitting Supreme Court justice. All of these nominees were subsequently confirmed, the last of which in 1941 (Senator James F. Byrnes). This reflected the Senate's one-time deference to former federal officials, who usually received quick confirmation without Judiciary Committee hearings. See Rutkus, "Supreme Court Appointment Process," supra, n. 5 at 18.

95 See, e.g., Lawrence A. Becker and Vincent G. Moscardelli, "Congressional Leadership on the Front Lines: Committee Chairs, Electoral Security, and Ideology," 41 *PS: Political Science & Politics* 77 (2008); Christopher J. Deering and Steven S. Smith, *Committees in Congress* (Washington, DC: CQ Press, 1997); George Goodwin, Jr., "The Seniority System in Congress," 53 *American Political Science Review* 412 (1959).

Committee, who typically becomes chair when the minority party regains control of the Senate. In addition to handling judicial appointments, the Committee's jurisdiction includes constitutional amendments, the judiciary, immigration, antitrust laws, and civil liberties.[96]

In the contemporary era, once a nomination is referred to the Judiciary Committee, the chair schedules hearings.[97] The current practice of holding public hearings featuring question-and-answer sessions with the nominees, however, is relatively new. The first confirmation hearing held in an open session involved Louis Brandeis' appointment in 1916, although Brandeis did not testify. Instead, testimony at the hearing was limited to outside witnesses.[98] In 1925, Harlan Stone, at the request of President Calvin Coolidge, took the unprecedented step of agreeing to appear before the Committee. Stone's appearance was limited, however, to defending himself against charges related to the Teapot Dome scandal during his tenure as attorney general.[99]

In 1939, Felix Frankfurter became the first nominee to take unrestricted questions in an open, transcribed, public hearing. At the beginning of his hearings, numerous witnesses accused Frankfurter, a founder of the American Civil Liberties Union, with being a radical with ties to the Communist Party. Although Frankfurter did not plan on testifying, his advisors, reacting to the advice of members of the Committee, persuaded him to appear in person and refute these claims.[100] Frankfurter's hearings became somewhat of a media circus, centered on allegations of his alleged sympathy to communist and socialist causes. When Frankfurter unequivocally and dramatically renounced any allegiance to communism or the Communist Party, the crowd reacted enthusiastically, reportedly standing on chairs, cheering, and rushing forward to shake his hand.[101]

---

[96] David R. Tarr and Ann O'Connor, eds., *Congress: A to Z* (Washington, DC: CQ Press, 1999) at 243.

[97] Although the Chair of the Judiciary Committee routinely schedules hearings for Supreme Court nominees, provided their nominations are not withdrawn, this practice does not necessarily translate to appointments to the lower federal courts. Should a nominee fail to receive a hearing, the nomination dies in Committee and is not referred to the full Senate for an up or down vote. Epstein and Segal, *Advice and Consent,* supra, n. 6 at 89.

[98] Rutkus and Bearden, "Supreme Court Nominations, 1789–2009," supra, n. 90 at 6.

[99] United States Senate Committee on the Judiciary, "History of the Senate Committee on the Judiciary." Retrieved from: http://judiciary.senate.gov/about/history/index.cfm (Accessed December 13, 2011).

[100] John Anthony Maltese, *The Selling of Supreme Court Nominees* (Baltimore: Johns Hopkins University Press, 1995) at 105.

[101] Ibid. at 107.

Sidebar: Hugo Black and the Ku Klux Klan

Many things contributed to the Senate Judiciary Committee's decision in the 1930s to conduct its examination of Supreme Court nominations in open public hearings, rather than in closed sessions. The Seventeenth Amendment, effective in 1913, gave voters direct control over the election of senators, thus increasing the accountability senators felt toward their constituents. A growing and diverse electorate also played a role: the Nineteenth Amendment, ratified in 1920, gave the franchise to women, while the emerging civil rights movement was expanding and changing the voices, interests, and concerns the senators needed to be responsive to. No single event, however, did as much to open the hearings to public scrutiny as did the disastrous attempt of the Judiciary Committee to prevent public discussion of nominee Hugo Black's involvement with the Ku Klux Klan (KKK).

Black was nominated to the Supreme Court by President Franklin Delano Roosevelt in 1937. Black represented Alabama in the U.S. Senate for more than a decade and was a strong supporter of the president's New Deal agenda. Senatorial courtesy ensured Black a speedy confirmation. Concerns about his past, however, were raised within the Senate, and the nomination was referred to the Senate Judiciary Committee for further consideration. The Judiciary Committee, aware of rumors about Black's association with the KKK, debated the nomination in closed session, voted to approve it, and then hurried it to the full Senate for a quick vote.

It was only through the work of a pioneering reporter, Ray Sprigle of the *Pittsburgh Post-Gazette*, that the public learned a week later that the nomination had been rushed through in order to avoid public discussion of Black's KKK ties.[102] In a series of reports that would win him a Pulitzer Prize, Sprigle revealed that Black joined the Klan prior to running for elected office. This itself was (unfortunately) not particularly shocking – Black after all was a white politician in Alabama during the height of the Klan's popularity. Sprigle went on to report, however, that Black had not, as he claimed, resigned his Klan membership ten years before taking his seat in the U.S. Senate. Instead, Sprigle reported, Black accepted and never relinquished a lifetime membership in the organization. If true, that meant that the Senate just approved the appointment of a Klan member to the nation's highest Court.

The revelation shook the country. The press questioned the Judiciary Committee's decision to consider the nomination in private and the Senate's apparent rush to approve it. The sense of a cover-up intensified when it was revealed that President Roosevelt deviated from tradition by having Black sworn in as an associate justice in a private ceremony held at the White House just days after the Senate vote, rather than having Black wait, as was customary, to take the constitutionally required oath on the opening day of the Court's October term.

Northern Democrats David Walsh of Massachusetts and Prentiss Brown of Michigan vocally criticized both the process and the president. They demanded that Black

---

[102] See, e.g., William E. Leuchtenburg, "A Klansman Joins the Court: The Appointment of Hugo L. Black," 41 *University of Chicago Law Review* 1 (1973).

publicly respond to the accusations. Senator Walsh, an anti-New Deal Democrat and long-time opponent of the KKK, told *The New York Times* that Black had been confirmed by the Senate under "misunderstanding and misapprehension" and that the president should demand Black's resignation.[103] Brown, usually an ally of the president, said he would not have voted for Black had he known of the Klan affiliation.[104] The sitting imperial wizard of the Klan did not help matters by publicly speaking out about the nomination, declaring that opposition to Black based on his KKK membership was "un-American."[105] Newspapers across the country protested the lack of public scrutiny the nomination received and echoed calls for Black's resignation.[106]

Black, who had remained silent on the issue during much of the fervor, eventually was forced to give a radio address denouncing the Klan and explaining his association with the organization. He acknowledged that he joined the Klan as a young man, but reiterated that he resigned his membership before first being seated in the Senate. He did admit that he received an "unsolicited" KKK lifetime membership card, but insisted that he had not considered himself a member of the organization since his initial resignation a decade earlier.[107]

Black silently took his seat on the Court just three days after his radio talk. He did so in front of a courtroom packed with protestors. There was no ceremony, and Black did not reiterate the oath of office he had taken earlier at the White House. Instead, the chief justice simply announced the presence of the Court's newest member and then began the business of the day.

Black would go on to become a highly regarded justice and a frequent supporter of expanding civil liberties, including those of African Americans. The Senate, however, learned an important lesson about the changing nature of its own public accountability. When Felix Frankfurter's nomination was announced two years later, the Senate Judiciary Committee immediately agreed to hold open public hearings on the nomination. "In view of criticism of the Senate's speedy confirmation" of Justice Black, *The New York Times* reported, the Judiciary Committee Chair declared that the Frankfurter nomination would be "scrutinized thoroughly" before being approved by the Committee.[108]

Between Frankfurter's hearing in 1939 and John Harlan's testimony in 1955, nominees appeared only intermittently. Some notable jurists nominated in this time frame, such as Earl Warren, did not appear. Since 1955, however, every Supreme Court nominee, other than those whose names were withdrawn before hearings began (e.g., Douglas Ginsburg and Harriet Miers), has

---

[103] "Black Ouster Now Is Held Impossible," *New York Times*, September 13, 1937.
[104] Ibid.
[105] "Walsh Says Black Won by Deception," *New York Times*, September 22, 1937.
[106] "Nation's Press Almost United in Denouncing Black Speech," *New York Times*, October 3, 1937.
[107] "Radio Talk Is Brief," *New York Times*, October 2, 1937.
[108] "Hearings Are Set on Frankfurter," *New York Times*, January 8, 1939.

appeared and testified before the Committee.[109] Beginning with the O'Connor hearing in 1981, the hearings have been televised.[110]

Before the Judiciary Committee hearings commence, both the Judiciary Committee and the nominee do several things. Once the Committee receives the president's nomination, it begins its own investigation of the nominee's background, conducted by Committee staff. The primary source of information during this investigation is the nominee's response to a Committee questionnaire. This is an extensive document, covering a host of topics, including detailed biographical information, financial disclosure statements, copies of published writing and statements, a list of any potential conflicts of interest relevant to serving on the Court, and a description of services to the disadvantaged.[111] To get a sense of the thoroughness of this document, consider that Elena Kagan's questionnaire totaled 202 pages, and Sonia Sotomayor's questionnaire was 173 pages long.[112]

Individual members of the Committee also may request that the nominee provide written responses to their own questions, the answers of which are made available to all Committee members and become part of the nominee's public record. For example, Elena Kagan's answers to individual senators' questions totaled seventy-seven pages. A series of thirteen questions from Senators Sessions (R-AL), Hatch (R-UT), Grassley (R-IA), Kyl (R-AZ), Graham (R-SC), Cornyn (R-TX), and Coburn (R-OK) queried Kagan as to her role in the development of, and legal challenges to, the Patient Protection and Affordable Care Act, the healthcare reform bill passed early in President Obama's first term. Additional questions, touching on everything from cases in which she may have to recuse herself, to her views on the death penalty, to her role as solicitor general, were asked individually by the aforementioned senators.[113] In addition, members of the Committee may direct their staff to compile supplemental information about the nominee from previous employers, professional

---

[109] Rutkus, "Supreme Court Appointment Process," supra, n. 5; Rutkus and Bearden, "Supreme Court Nominations, 1789–2009," supra, n. 90.

[110] Michael Comiskey, "Not Guilty: The News Media in the Supreme Court Confirmation Process," 15 *Journal of Law and Politics* 1 (1999).

[111] Rutkus, "Supreme Court Appointment Process," supra, n. 5 at 22.

[112] United States Senate Committee on the Judiciary, "Associate Justice of the U.S. Supreme Court – Elena Kagan." http://judiciary.senate.gov/nominations/SupremeCourt/KaganIndex .cfm (Accessed December 13, 2011); United States Senate Committee on the Judiciary, "Associate Justice of the U.S. Supreme Court – Sonia Sotomayor." Retrieved from: http:// judiciary.senate.gov/nominations/SupremeCourt/SotomayorIndex.cfm (Accessed December 13, 2011).

[113] United States Senate Committee on the Judiciary, "Associate Justice of the U.S. Supreme Court – Elena Kagan," supra, n. 101.

associations, and interviews with relevant individuals who can shed light on a nominee's background.

The Committee also obtains information regarding a nominee's background from the dozens of letters that make their way into the record from individuals, interest groups, former employers, and other actors who feel that their input into the Committee's consideration of the nominee might prove useful. For example, 149 letters were submitted to the Committee during the Sotomayor hearing. These letters, both supporting and opposing her confirmation, came from a diverse assortment of individuals and institutions, including law professors; former law clerks; members of Congress; the American Federation of State, County and Municipal Employees; the National Rifle Association; the Sierra Club; and the U.S. Chamber of Commerce.[114]

In addition to submitting letters to the Senate Judiciary Committee, interest groups also publicly line up for or against a nominee, frequently mobilizing their members to contact senators to express their support or opposition to a nominee.[115] Groups follow a variety of tactics in this role, including using direct mail, the Internet, television, radio, and newspaper space. In this capacity, groups opposing the nominee frequently try to paint the appointee as unqualified and out of the mainstream, whereas groups supporting the nominee highlight the potential justice's experience, judicial temperament, and even-handedness. For example, during the confirmation of Samuel Alito, advocacy organizations on both ends of the ideological spectrum spent more than $2 million in their attempts to shape public opinion about the nominee. Conservative groups successfully portrayed Alito as an everyday American who would bring years of experience to the high Court, whereas liberal organizations were unable to convince the public that Alito was an extremist who sought to overturn *Roe v. Wade*[116] and give the president unlimited power.[117]

While the Committee conducts its background investigation, the nominee pays a series of visits to senators, including members of the Judiciary Committee. These visits, part of a longstanding tradition, allow senators to obtain a sense of a nominee's views of the issues most important to the senators. In addition, this is often the only opportunity for senators who are not members of the Judiciary Committee to personally engage nominees. Although the exact number of courtesy calls varies by nominee, most appointees make an effort

---

[114] United States Senate Committee on the Judiciary, "Associate Justice of the U.S. Supreme Court – Sonia Sotomayor," supra, n. 101.

[115] See, e.g., Bell, *Warring Factions*, supra, n. 69.

[116] Roe v. Wade, 410 U.S. 113 (1973).

[117] Lois Romano and Juliet Eilperin, "Republicans Were Masters in the Race to Paint Alito; Democrats' Portrayal Failed to Sway the Public," *Washington Post*, February 2, 2006.

to meet with a goodly number of senators. For example, John Roberts visited with more than half of the hundred-member Senate, and Sonia Sotomayor paid visits to eighty-nine senators.[118]

Prior to the commencement of the hearings, both Senate Judiciary Committee members and nominees undergo substantial preparation. Members of the Committee begin preparing their opening remarks and formulating the questions they will ask nominees. The nominees prepare for the hearings by appearing in front of "murder boards:" mock hearing sessions in which various individuals, often members of the legal community and White House staff, play the role of senators by pressing the nominee on the questions each member of the Committee is likely to ask.[119] These preparation sessions are typically quite intense and may carry on for weeks at a time. For example, Samuel Alito appeared before a "murder board" for four hours a day for three weeks,[120] while John Roberts was grilled in ten mock hearings, lasting two to three hours each.[121]

Since John Harlan initiated the norm of nominees appearing in an open session of the Senate Judiciary Committee in 1955, the hearing procedure has remained relatively consistent. The hearings commence with the opening statements of members of the Judiciary Committee or with the presentation of the nominee by his or her presenters, who are usually the nominee's home state senators, representatives, and/or other political leaders with a connection to the nominee.[122] For example, Granite State native David Souter's hearing began with the presentation of the nomination by New Hampshire Senators Gordon Humphrey and Warren Rudman. A statement of then-Senate Judiciary Chairman Joseph Biden followed, in which Biden outlined how the hearings would proceed. Members of the Judiciary Committee then each make an opening statement. The nominee's opening statement follows, and usually focuses on the nominee's background and commitment to sound judicial temperament.

The heart and soul of the confirmation hearings, the questioning by senators, comes next. While the exact format of the question-and-answer session varies with the preferences of the chairs, the process is typically as follows. Each member of the Judiciary Committee is granted a set amount of time to question nominees, traditionally thirty minutes. The colloquy begins with questioning from the Committee chair, followed by the ranking minority member of the

[118] Rutkus, "Supreme Court Appointment Process," supra, n. 5 at 24.

[119] Ibid. at 28.

[120] Romano and Eilperin, "Republicans Were Masters in the Race to Paint Alito," supra, n. 106.

[121] Elisabeth Bumiller, "Lengthy Practices Prepare Court Nominee for His Senate Hearings," *New York Times*, September 1, 2005.

[122] Rutkus, "Supreme Court Appointment Process," supra, n. 5 at 29.

Committee. The remaining members of Committee, in descending order of seniority and alternating between majority and minority party members, question the nominee. Once the first round of questions is completed, at the discretion of the chair, the Committee may begin a second or third round of questioning.[123] Each successive round usually involves a shorter time allocation for each senator.

To provide a sense of the extent of the dialogue that takes place at the hearings, Figure 2.2 reports the number of comments made by nominees and senators at Senate Judiciary Committee confirmation hearings from 1939 to 2010.[124] The nominees are aligned along the y-axis, and the x-axis reports the total number of comments made by nominees (the white bars) and senators (the black bars). This figure reveals two significant things. First, there is a strong association between the number of comments made by nominees and senators. Using the hearing as the unit of analysis, the correlation between the number of comments made by nominees and senators is 0.99 ($P < 0.001$). Despite the appearance at times that senators are using the hearings primarily to give speeches, it is evident from our data that confirmation hearings take place in a question-and-answer format, with senators traditionally moving first by asking questions, followed by the nominees responding in turn.

Second, the number of comments made by both nominees and senators has increased rather dramatically over time. For example, from 1939 to 1981, the average number of comments made by nominees was 210, while the average number of comments made by senators was 294. Since Rehnquist's chief justice hearing in 1986, however, the average number of comments made by nominees was 770 and the average number of comments made by senators was 1,009.[125]

Following the question-and-answer session, the Judiciary Committee hears testimony by individuals, interest groups, or other actors supporting or

---

[123] Ibid.

[124] This figure excludes comments made during the three days of testimony at the hearing of Clarence Thomas that focused on allegations of sexual harassment brought by Anita Hill.

[125] Although the Bork hearing represents the greatest number of comments, with 1,587 statements made by Bork and 1,931 remarks made by senators, it is notable that the increase in the number of statements made at the hearings began not with Bork, but with Rehnquist's nomination for chief justice in 1986. During that hearing, Rehnquist made 727 statements and senators contributed 1,135 questions and comments. Thus, although the Bork hearing certainly stands as an outlier in terms of the number of statements made, Bork's nomination does not represent the point at which the number of comments made at confirmation hearings saw its most radical transformation. We verified this employing a regression model that used the total numbers of comments as the dependent variable and Rehnquist and Bork dummy variables as predictors. The results corroborate that the increase in hearing dialogue is attributable primarily to Rehnquist's chief justice hearing in 1986.

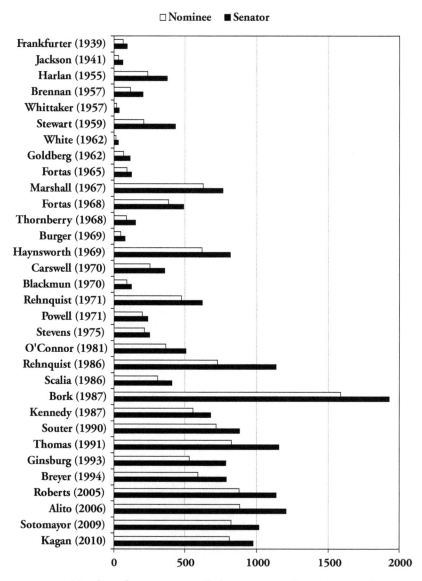

FIGURE 2.2. Number of comments made by senators and nominees at Supreme Court confirmation hearings, 1939–2010.

opposing the nominee.[126] These witnesses are authorized to testify at the discretion of the Committee chair and typically take questions regarding their

[126] See, e.g., Bell, *Warring Factions*, supra, n. 69; Gregory A. Caldeira and John R. Wright, "Lobbying for Justice: Organized Interests, Supreme Court Nominations, and the United

testimony from members of the Committee.[127] For example, at the confirmation hearing of Anthony Kennedy in 1987, a variety of groups and individuals testified, including attorneys, law professors, and representatives from the International Association of Chiefs of Police, the National Association of Criminal Defense Lawyers, and the National Organization for Women. The ABA plays a special role at this stage, with its representatives appearing among the first witnesses to testify for the purpose of explaining its ranking of the nominee's qualifications.[128]

Perhaps the most significant change in the hearing procedure was instituted in 1992, when the Judiciary Committee began meeting in a closed session with each nominee.[129] The purpose of this closed-door session is to question the nominee regarding any sensitive issues that arose from the confidential investigations conducted by the Federal Bureau of Investigation and the Committee staff. These hearings take place as a matter of procedure, irrespective of whether any issues have been brought to the Committee's attention, so as to not give the impression that they are held only if the Committee receives negative information about the nominee. The closed-door sessions may be held at any point in the hearing process. For example, the closed-door hearings for Alito and Roberts took place after the nominees were questioned by the senators but before the Committee took outside witness testimony, whereas the closed-door session for Sotomayor was held between the Committee's first and second round of questions.

Once the Senate Judiciary Committee concludes its hearings, it meets in an open session to determine how to report the nomination to the full Senate, a practice instituted in 1870.[130] The Committee has four options: report the nomination favorably; report the nomination negatively; provide no recommendation; or do not report the nomination.[131] A favorable Committee report indicates that at least a majority of Committee members support the nominee's confirmation. The Committee has favorably reported seventy-four nominations, sixty-eight of which were confirmed by the full Senate. A negative Committee report indicates that a majority of members recommend that the Senate reject the nomination. Seven nominations have been unfavorably

States Senate," 42 *American Journal of Political Science* 499 (1998); Maltese, *The Selling of Supreme Court Nominees*, supra, n. 96.

[127] Bell, *Warring Factions*, supra, n. 69 at 113.

[128] Rutkus, "Supreme Court Appointment Process," supra, n. 5 at 31.

[129] Ibid. at 31–2.

[130] Prior to this, the Committee typically reported nominations to the full Senate without a recommendation (although two nominations, those of John Crittenden and Ebenezer Hoard, were accompanied by negative recommendations). Rutkus and Bearden, "Supreme Court Nominations, 1789–2009," supra, n. 90 at 8–9.

[131] Rutkus, "Supreme Court Appointment Process," supra, n. 5 at 32.

reported to the Senate, only two of which were confirmed.[132] When the Committee reports a nomination without a recommendation as to whether the appointment should be confirmed or rejected, it signals to the Senate that a good number of Judiciary Committee members have reservations about the nomination. Four nominations have been reported without recommendation, three of which were confirmed.[133] Finally, if a majority of Committee members oppose the nominee's confirmation, the Committee can decide not to report the nomination to the full Senate. However, it has been the Committee's practice to report all Supreme Court nominees to the full Senate for an up-or-down vote.[134]

Since the Committee's creation in 1816, only eight nominations have not been reported out of Committee. Five of these nominees were never confirmed, and three were confirmed only after being renominated by the president. Notably, the failure of each of these nominations to be reported out of Committee was due to the actions taken by those *other* than the Committee. Such actions include the president withdrawing a nomination (e.g., Harriet Miers) or Congress eliminating the vacant seat (Henry Stanbery).[135]

When the Judiciary Committee reports a nomination to the full Senate, it typically does so by providing the Senate with a written Committee report.[136] This report provides the Senate with a single document containing the views of Committee members, both positive and negative, along with the perspectives of other actors, such as interest groups, on the nomination. Although it has become commonplace for the Committee to provide the Senate with a report, not all nominations are sent to the Senate with a printed Committee report. For example, the nominations of John Roberts, Samuel Alito, and Sonia Sotomayor were all sent to the Senate without a Committee report, apparently in an effort to expedite the full Senate's consideration of the nominations.[137]

The Senate Judiciary Committee plays a vital intermediary role in the process of confirming Supreme Court justices. In addition to conducting background investigations of nominees, the Committee provides the first

---

[132] The Committee unfavorably reported the nominations of John Crittenden (1829), Ebenezer Hoard (1869), Stanley Matthews (1881), Lucius Lamar (1888), William Hornblower (1894), John Parker (1930), and Robert Bork (1987). Only Matthews and Lamar were confirmed. See Rutkus and Bearden, "Supreme Court Nominations, 1789–2009," supra, n. 90 at 9.

[133] The Committee reported the nominations of Melville Fuller (1888), George Shiras (1892), Wheeler Peckham (1894), and Clarence Thomas (1991) without a recommendation. Only Peckham was rejected by the Senate. Ibid. at 9.

[134] Rutkus, "Supreme Court Appointment Process," supra, n. 5 at 32.

[135] Rutkus and Bearden, "Supreme Court Nominations, 1789–2009," supra, n. 90 at 10.

[136] Rutkus, "Supreme Court Appointment Process," supra, n. 5 at 33.

[137] Ibid. at 33–4.

opportunity for nominees to face democratic accountability in the question-and-answer sessions that are the heart and soul of the confirmation process. Once the hearings conclude, the Committee recommends nominations to the full Senate, which typically agrees with the Committee's recommendations. Indeed, only two nominees who were reported out of the Committee with an unfavorable recommendation were eventually confirmed, and the full Senate has agreed with the Committee's recommendations more than 90% of the time, thus indicating the deference the full Senate grants to the Committee's judgments.[138] We now turn to a discussion of the full Senate's role in the confirmation process.

SENATE TREATMENT OF SUPREME COURT NOMINEES

Once a nomination is reported to the Senate, the executive clerk of the Senate places the nomination on the executive calendar.[139] The calendar contains a variety of information about the nominee, including his or her name, the name of the justice whom the nominee is replacing, and the Senate Judiciary Committee's recommendation on the nomination.[140] The Senate majority leader, in consultation with the minority leader, sets aside time for the consideration of the nomination on the Senate's executive calendar. Before a nomination is considered by the Senate, the Senate proceeds into executive session,[141] normally through a unanimous consent agreement. An alternative to considering a nomination by unanimous consent is making a debatable motion calling for the Senate to take up the nomination.[142]

The unanimous consent agreement typically includes setting a time limit for the amount of debate on a nomination and the time and date the nomination vote will occur. Senate debate over a nomination usually is divided evenly between members of the majority and minority parties. During Senate debate, senators are given the opportunity to speak in favor of, or against, a nominee. Frequently, senators discuss the nominee's qualifications for office, judicial philosophy and temperament, as well as any other factors that may influence

[138] See, e.g., Epstein and Segal, *Advice and Consent*, supra, n. 6 at 97.

[139] The executive calendar constitutes the list of pending nominations and treaties awaiting consideration by the Senate. See Rutkus, "Supreme Court Appointment Process," supra, n. 5 at 35.

[140] Elizabeth Rybicki, "CRS Report for Congress, Senate Consideration of Presidential Nominations: Committee and Floor Procedure" (2009). Retrieved from: http://www.policyarchive .org/handle/10207/bitstreams/1768.pdf (Accessed December 13, 2011).

[141] An executive session is used when the Senate considers nominations and treaties, whereas regular legislative business is conducted during a legislative session. Ibid.

[142] Rutkus, "Supreme Court Appointment Process," supra, n. 5 at 36–7.

the senators' evaluations of the nominee. Unanimous consent on a time limit for debate prevents a single senator from filibustering a nomination. If a time limit is not set, a filibuster is possible.[143] If the nomination is considered by the Senate through a motion, as opposed to a unanimous consent agreement, there are two additional opportunities for filibusters to enter the process. First, a senator can filibuster the nomination when the motion to consider the nomination is being debated. Second, a senator can filibuster the nomination when the nomination itself is being debated.[144]

A filibuster allows a single senator to block or delay consideration of a nomination by indefinitely extending debate.[145] To end a filibuster, a supermajority of sixty or more senators must vote to invoke cloture. Only four votes to invoke cloture have taken place since 1949, when the option of bringing a cloture motion regarding unlimited debate on a nominee was first initiated. In 1968, the Senate failed to invoke cloture over Abe Fortas' nomination to chief justice by a 45–43 vote. Fortas' nomination was subsequently withdrawn by President Lyndon Johnson. In 1971, a cloture motion failed to garner the necessary three-fifths support to end debate over the nomination of William Rehnquist by a 52–42 vote, although he was confirmed later that day by a 68–26 vote after the Senate rejected a motion to postpone his confirmation vote by more than a month. When Rehnquist was nominated to the chief justice position in 1986, the Senate voted 68–31 to invoke cloture. Most recently, in 2006, the Senate supported a motion to invoke cloture on Samuel Alito's nomination by a 72–25 vote.[146]

Between the time in which the nomination has been reported to the Senate and debate on the Senate floor concludes, two additional steps may be taken by the Senate. First, the Senate may recommit a nomination to the Senate Judiciary Committee. There have been eight attempts to recommit, only two of which have succeeded. This tactic is typically used either to gather additional information about the nominee in Committee or as an attempt to kill the nomination in Committee. The nomination of George H. Williams was recommitted in 1873 when allegations surfaced after his nomination was

---

[143] Ibid. at 36.

[144] However, if the motion to consider the nomination is made while the Senate is in a legislative session, the motion to consider the nomination is not debatable, thus protected from the possibility of a filibuster. Ibid. at 37.

[145] As a result of changes to Senate rules in the 1970s, it is no longer necessary for a senator to hold the floor during a filibuster. See Sarah A. Binder and Steven S. Smith, *Politics or Principle? Filibustering in the United States Senate* (Washington, DC: The Brookings Institution Press, 1997).

[146] Rutkus, "Supreme Court Appointment Process," supra, n. 5 at 43–4.

reported out of Committee that he used his position as attorney general for personal gains. This was apparently a successful effort to kill the nomination by returning it to the Committee, in that the Committee refused to re-report the nomination to the Senate and the nomination was subsequently withdrawn by President Grant. In 1925, the nomination of Harlan Stone was recommitted to the Judiciary Committee to investigate his role in the Teapot Dome scandal. After holding hearings, at which Stone took the then-unprecedented step of appearing before the Committee, the nomination was favorably reported to the full Senate, which confirmed Stone's appointment by a 71–6 vote.[147]

A second option is for the Senate to delay the confirmation vote for additional hearings absent a formal recommittal. This has occurred only once.[148] In 1991, after the Senate received the nomination of Clarence Thomas, allegations of sexual misconduct were made by law professor Anita Hill. The Senate delayed its vote on the nomination in order to allow the Committee to conduct additional hearings centering on these allegations. After holding three days of hearings, at which both Hill and Thomas testified, the Committee re-reported the nomination without recommendation to the full Senate, which confirmed Thomas' nomination by a 52–48 vote.[149]

Many of the aforementioned factors that shape the president's evaluation of potential nominees also influence the senators' perceptions of those nominees.[150] It is clear that a nominee's qualifications matter, with better credentialed nominees enjoying smoother paths to confirmation. The ABA's ratings of a nominee's fitness for office thus play an important role in a nominee's fate in the Senate. In addition, the nominee's partisanship and ideology factor into senators' evaluations. Senators are more likely to support nominees who share their partisan affiliation and ideological orientation, the latter of which can be gleaned from the nominee's prior work and judicial records, as well as statements at the confirmation hearings. Moreover, nominees who will alter the Court's existing ideological balance tend to garner less senatorial support than those who replace justices who share their ideological orientations.[151]

Senators also are likely to pay attention to their constituents' views of a nominee, as well as the perspectives of interest groups who might influence the

---

[147] Ibid. at 52–3.
[148] Ibid. at 53.
[149] Ibid. at 53.
[150] See, e.g., Caldeira and Wright, "Lobbying for Justice," supra, n. 115; Epstein and Segal, *Advice and Consent*, supra, n. 6; Segal and Spaeth, *The Supreme Court and the Attitudinal Model Revisited*, supra, n. 54.
[151] See, e.g., L. J. Zigerell, "Senator Opposition to Supreme Court Nominees: Reference Dependence on the Departing Justice," 35 *Legislative Studies Quarterly* 393 (2010).

senators' reelection prospects. If supporting or opposing a nominee provides the senator with the opportunity to appease his or her constituents, the senator will likely do so.[152] For example, Senator Ben Nelson (D-NE) opposed the nomination of Elena Kagan, noting "concerns raised by Nebraskans."[153] The strength of the president also is an important factor that senators consider. If the president enjoys widespread electoral support, senators are likely to support the president's nominee. If, however, the president is in a weak position, for example, in his or her last year in office, the Senate will likely be less supportive of the nominee.[154]

Individual senators also may take cues from their Senate colleagues. A senator may defer to a close colleague who championed the nominee through the confirmation process.[155] Similarly, senators look to the recommendation of the Senate Judiciary Committee and its members.[156] The extent to which the president consulted with the Senate regarding the selection of the nominee also may come into play. Generally speaking, the president can expect more senatorial support if he or she consulted with a wide array of senators regarding the appointment.[157]

Finally, the nominees' performance before the Judiciary Committee also affects their likelihood of confirmation. Nominees hoping to secure confirmation are expected to affirm their agreement with the constitutional consensus of their era, a topic we explore throughout the remainder of this book.

Once floor debate on a nomination comes to a conclusion, the presiding officer of the Senate calls for a confirmation vote. The question before the Senate is traditionally framed as follows: "The question is, Will the Senate advise and consent to the nomination of [nominee's name] of [state of residence] to be an Associate Justice [or Chief Justice] on the Supreme Court?"[158] Prior to 1967, most (but certainly not all) confirmation votes were conducted by voice votes or unanimous consent. Since 1967, all confirmation votes have been conducted by roll call. Before a policy change in 1991, senators were free to come and go during the roll call vote. However, since the nomination of Clarence Thomas in 1991, the majority leader has requested that senators

---

[152] See, e.g., Caldeira and Wright, "Lobbying for Justice," supra, n. 115.

[153] Don Walton, "Ben Nelson Will Not Vote for Elena Kagan," *Lincoln Journal Star*, July 30, 2010.

[154] See, e.g., Segal and Spaeth, *The Supreme Court and the Attitudinal Model Revisited*, supra, n. 54.

[155] See, e.g., Rutkus, "Supreme Court Appointment Process," supra, n. 5.

[156] See, e.g., Epstein and Segal, *Advice and Consent*, supra, n. 6.

[157] See, e.g., Rutkus, "Supreme Court Appointment Process," supra, n. 5.

[158] Ibid. at 46.

remain seated at their desks during the roll call vote, rising to vote only when their names are called.[159]

Figure 2.3 provides an overview of the outcome of Supreme Court appointments, by president, from 1789 to 2010.[160] The nominating presidents appear on the vertical y-axis, and the outcomes of their appointments are indicated by the horizontal bars. As this figure makes evident, most appointments are confirmed by the Senate. Indeed, of the 160 appointments made to the Court, 123 have been confirmed by the Senate (76.9%), although eight of these nominees never actually served on the Court. The last nominee to win Senate confirmation, but who did not serve on the Court, was Roscoe Conkling, who was nominated by President Chester Arthur in 1882. Five days after being confirmed by a 39–12 margin, Conkling declined his commission.[161]

Twenty-six nominees were rejected by the Senate, the last of which was Robert Bork in 1987. Bork's nomination was reported out of the Senate Judiciary Committee unfavorably by a 9–5 vote, making his chances of being confirmed by a Democratically controlled Senate very unlikely. However, rather than withdraw his name from consideration, Bork pressed for a full Senate vote on his nomination. In a statement delivered at the White House, Bork had rather strong words for his opponents, including the hundreds of interest groups who lined up against him. He spoke to the importance of holding a confirmation vote for the purpose of sending a message to those who politicized the appointment process. In part, Bork argued:

> There should be a full debate and a final Senate decision. In deciding on this course, I harbor no illusions.

> But a crucial principle is at stake. That principle is the way we select the men and women who guard the liberties of all the American people. That should not be done through public campaigns of distortion. If I withdraw now, that campaign would be seen as a success, and it would be mounted against future nominees.

> For the sake of the Federal judiciary and the American people, that must not happen. The deliberative process must be restored. In the days remaining, I ask only that voices be lowered, the facts respected and the deliberations

---

[159] Although it is technically possible for a Senator who voted with the majority on the confirmation vote to move to reconsider the confirmation vote, this has never occurred. Ibid. at 46–8.

[160] This information was collected from Epstein, Walker, Staudt, Hendrickson, and Roberts, "The U.S. Supreme Court Justices Database," supra, n. 3, updated to reflect the confirmation of Elena Kagan.

[161] Abraham, *Justices, Presidents, and Senators*, supra, n. 9 at 111.

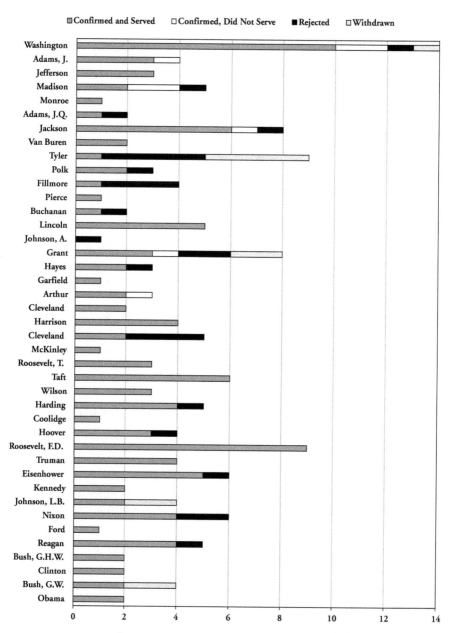

FIGURE 2.3. Supreme Court appointments by president, 1789–2010.

conducted in a manner that will be fair to me and to the infinitely larger and more important cause of justice in America.[162]

Whether or not Bork was defeated because of "distortions" of his record, something we discuss in Chapter 7, the Senate ultimately rejected his nomination by a 42–58 vote.

Figure 2.3 also reveals that eleven nominations were withdrawn by presidents prior to their confirmation votes in the Senate. In 2005, President George W. Bush withdrew two nominations. After Justice O'Connor announced her retirement, Bush nominated John Roberts to her associate justice position. This nomination was withdrawn after Chief Justice Rehnquist died and Bush reappointed Roberts to fill the seat vacated by Rehnquist, a position Roberts currently holds. The second of Bush's withdrawals involved Harriet Miers, who Bush appointed to replace O'Connor after nominating Roberts for chief justice. Miers' appointment did not sit well on either side of the aisle. Both Democrats and Republicans believed she lacked the necessary qualifications and constitutional vision to be a justice. In addition, many conservatives questioned her conservative credentials and were especially troubled by her positions on abortion and other social issues. Ultimately, Miers requested that Bush accept her letter of withdrawal, which he did before her confirmation hearing began.[163]

To provide a sense of Senate support for the president's nominees, Figure 2.4 plots the vote percentage for each nominee who received a roll call vote from 1795 to 2010.[164] The percentage of votes supporting the nomination is denoted by the solid black line, and the dashed line represents the linear fitted trend. The average vote percentage for Supreme Court nominees in the Senate is 70.9%, thereby corroborating the fact that the Senate confirms most nominations. The mean vote percentage for successful nominees is 80.8%, whereas the average vote percentage for unsuccessful nominations is 43.4%. Thus, of those appointees who fail to win Senate support, the vote is typically quite close. In fact, it ranges from 27.3% (Alexander Wolcott) to 49.0% (George Badger and Jeremiah Black).

[162] Associated Press, "Bork Gives Reasons for Continuing Fight," *New York Times*, October 10, 1987.

[163] Abraham, *Justices, Presidents, and Senators*, supra, n. 9 at 320.

[164] These data were collected from Epstein, Walker, Staudt, Hendrickson, and Roberts, "The U.S. Supreme Court Justices Database," supra, n. 3, updated to reflect the confirmation vote of Elena Kagan. This figure excludes the cloture vote that failed to break the filibuster of Abe Fortas in 1968. Because our intent is to illustrate that there has been little systematic alteration in Senate support for nominees over time, we refrain from putting each nominee's name on the x-axis. This decision also enables us to provide a cleaner (i.e., less cluttered) presentation of the data.

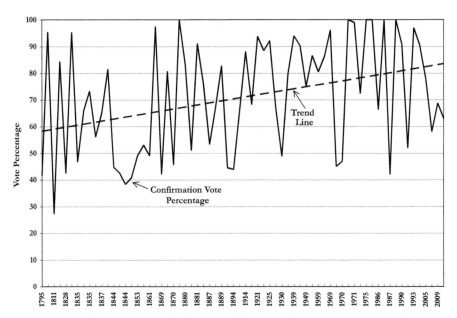

FIGURE 2.4. Senate support for Supreme Court nominees who received roll call votes, 1795–2010.

When considering Senate support for recent members of the Court, one might be tempted to conclude that the confirmation process has become increasingly politicized over time, with smaller vote percentages for more recent nominees. For example, Justice Scalia, one of the Court's most conservative members, enjoyed a 98–0 vote in 1986, whereas Justice Sotomayor, a moderately liberal justice, garnered a 68–31 vote in 2009. However, Figure 2.4 reveals that there is, in fact, a slight increase in Senate support for more recent nominees, as illustrated by the trend line in Figure 2.4.[165] Thus, it is clear that the process has always been politicized, with controversial nominees

[165] A regression model, using the vote percentage as the dependent variable and the year of nomination as the independent variable, indicates a small, but statistically significant, increase in Senate support for more recent nominees. Note that, when we include voice votes in the data and assume that voice votes constitute unanimous support for a nominee, the same regression model returns a small, and statistically insignificant ($P = 0.496$), negative coefficient on the year of nomination variable. Thus, even when we make the questionable assumption of treating voice votes as unanimous support for a nominee (despite the fact that their use does not necessarily signal a lack of controversy about a nominee), it is clear that the hearings have always been political in nature. For a discussion of the use of voice votes throughout American history, see Michael S. Lynch and Anthony J. Madonna, "Viva Voce: Implications from the Disappearing Voice Vote, 1865–1996," *Social Science Quarterly* forthcoming (2013).

generating smaller vote percentages, regardless of the era in which they were nominated.[166]

The Senate vote is the final barrier an individual must pass as he or she makes the transformation from nominee to justice. During this phase, senators debate the merits of a nominee's candidacy for the Court and individual senators may even attempt to filibuster a nomination, preventing the full Senate from conducting an up-or-down vote. Considered in tandem with the role played by the Senate Judiciary Committee, it is clear that the Senate takes its role to provide the president with advice and consent regarding Court nominees very seriously. Although most nominees make it through the process and find their way to the bench, if a majority of senators view a nominee as unfit for office, they can prevent that nominee from taking a seat on the high Court, thereby influencing the direction of our constitutional development.

AFTER CONFIRMATION

If a nominee receives a positive Senate vote, the secretary of the Senate transmits a resolution of confirmation to the White House. Once signed by the president, this resolution acts as the nominee's commission to the Court. The commission is then sent to the Justice Department, which engraves on it the date of appointment and the Justice Department's seal, along with the signature of the attorney general. The commission is then delivered to the new justice.[167]

The new justice takes two oaths of office. First, the nominee takes a judicial oath, which is required by the Judiciary Act of 1789.[168] Second, the nominee takes a constitutional oath, which is required by Article VI of the Constitution.[169] The judicial oath is traditionally taken in private, typically

---

[166] See also Epstein and Segal, *Advice and Consent*, supra, n. 6; Of course, characteristics of the legislative and executive branches frequently make some nominations more controversial than others, which is often reflected in certain periods of American history. Richard D. Friedman, "The Transformation in Senate Response to Supreme Court Nominations: From Reconstruction to the Taft Administration and Beyond," 5 *Cardozo Law Review* 1 (1984).

[167] Rutkus, "Supreme Court Appointment Process," supra, n. 5 at 54.

[168] "I, [name], do solemnly swear (or affirm) that I will administer justice without respect to persons, and do equal right to the poor and to the rich, and that I will faithfully and impartially discharge and perform all the duties incumbent upon me as [Associate Justice or Chief Justice of the United States of America] under the Constitution and laws of the United States. So help me God." Office of the Curator, "Text of the Oaths of Office for Supreme Court Justices." Retrieved from: http://www.supremecourt.gov/about/oath/textoftheoathsofoffice2009.aspx (Accessed March 21, 2011).

[169] "I, [name], do solemnly swear (or affirm) that I will support and defend the Constitution of the United States against all enemies, foreign and domestic; that I will bear true faith and allegiance to the same; that I take this obligation freely, without any mental reservation or

at the Supreme Court, and the constitutional oath recently has been administered at the White House in a nationally televised ceremony. In 2009, however,
Justice Sotomayor took both oaths at the Supreme Court, with the judicial
oath broadcast on national television. Apparently, this was at the urging of
President Obama, who was responding to the concerns of some sitting justices who believed that administering the constitutional oath in the White
House suggested that nominees are unduly accountable to their appointing
president.[170]

After a nominee takes his or her oaths of office, the Court welcomes its
newest member with an investiture ceremony. This invitation-only event,
attended by all of the sitting justices as well as the new justice's family, friends,
and associates (typically including the president and attorney general), usually
takes place right before the new justice takes his or her seat on the high Court
bench for the first time.[171] During this ceremony, the justice is sworn in for a
third time, providing an excellent photo opportunity.

Having outlined the process, from the time when vacancies on the Court
open up through the investiture ceremony, we now turn to a case study of the
nomination and confirmation of the Court's newest member, Elena Kagan,
to illustrate this process in action.

THE NOMINATION AND CONFIRMATION OF ELENA KAGAN

On April 9, 2010, Justice John Paul Stevens informed President Obama of his
intention to retire from the Court, effective on the day after the Court began
its summer recess.[172] Stevens enjoyed a storied career on the Court, serving
for thirty-five years, the third longest tenure in the Court's history. Though
Stevens was appointed by Republican Gerald Ford, he often found himself
anchoring the liberal wing of the Court. For example, during his tenure on
the Court, Stevens cast liberal votes in 61% of all cases heard.[173]

Like President George W. Bush before him, Obama began assembling
a list of potential nominees soon after his election.[174] This is not surprising:

purpose of evasion; and that I will well and faithfully discharge the duties of the office on
which I am about to enter. So help me God." Ibid.

[170] Rutkus, "Supreme Court Appointment Process," supra, n. 5 at 54–5.

[171] Ibid. at 55.

[172] Robert Barnes, "Justice John Paul Stevens Announces His Retirement from Supreme Court,"
Washington Post, April 10, 2010.

[173] Harold J. Spaeth, Lee Epstein, Ted Ruger, Keith Whittington, Jeffrey Segal, and Andrew
D. Martin, "The Supreme Court Database." Retrieved from: http://scdb.wustl.edu/ (Accessed
November 23, 2010).

[174] Peter Baker and Adam Nagourney, "Sotomayor Pick a Product of Lessons From Past Battles,"
New York Times, May 27, 2009.

Obama, a former law professor, surely recognized the importance of a Supreme Court appointment. As Obama began the process of putting together a list of potential nominees, he sought the input of numerous advisors, including Vice President Biden (the former chair of the Senate Judiciary Committee), David Axelrod (senior advisor to the president), Rahm Emanuel (White House chief of staff), Cynthia Hogan (counsel to the vice president), and Ronald Klain (vice president's chief of staff).[175]

On being informed of Stevens' pending retirement, Obama consulted with his team of advisors for the purpose of formulating a list of potential nominees for Stevens' seat. Because Justice Souter retired a year earlier, much of the legwork on assembling this list was already completed. Many of the names considered to replace Souter also appeared on the list of possible replacements for Stevens' seat. In assembling his short list, Obama sought the input of numerous senators, paying particular attention to the views of members of the Senate Judiciary Committee, as he did when considering a replacement for Souter.[176]

Although press reports vary as to exactly who was on Obama's short list, some names stood out. Key contenders included several sitting or former judges, such as District of Columbia Court of Appeals Judge Merrick Garland, former Georgia Supreme Court Chief Justice Leah Ward Sears, Ninth Circuit Court of Appeals Judge Sidney Thomas, and Seventh Circuit Court of Appeals Judge Diane Wood. The names of several non-judges reportedly also made their way onto the short list, including Governor Jennifer Granholm of Michigan, Homeland Security Secretary Janet Napolitano, and Solicitor General Elena Kagan.[177]

As Department of Justice officials, White House staff, and the Federal Bureau of Investigation conducted background checks on the potential nominees, President Obama personally met with four of the candidates: Garland, Kagan, Thomas, and Wood.[178] Two of these individuals, Kagan and Wood,

---

[175] Ibid.

[176] Ibid.; Patricia Zengerle, "Obama Meets Supreme Court Candidate, Republicans," *Reuters*, May 5, 2010. Retrieved from: http://www.reuters.com/article/idUSTRE6444HN20100505 (Accessed December 13, 2011).

[177] Barnes, "Justice John Paul Stevens Announces His Retirement from Supreme Court," supra, n. 161; Caren Bohan, "Judge from Montana Interviewed for Supreme Court," *Reuters*, April 29, 2010. Retrieved from: http://www.reuters.com/article/idUSTRE63T08J20100430 (Accessed December 12, 2011); Tony Mauro, "White House Said to Have Short List Ready for Justice Stevens' Slot." Retrieved from: http://www.law.com/jsp/law/LawArticleFriendly.jsp?id=1202446568098 (Accessed December 12, 2011).

[178] Peter Baker and Jeff Zeleny, "Obama Picks Kagan as Justice Nominee," *New York Times*, May 9, 2010; Tom Diemer, "Obama Interviews Diane Wood; Search for Supreme Court Nominee Narrows," *Politics Daily*, May 5, 2010. Retrieved from: http://www.politicsdaily.com/

also were interviewed by Obama when he considered possible replacements for Justice Souter in 2009, indicating they may have been at the top of the short list at that point.[179]

On May 10, 2010, President Obama nominated Solicitor General Elena Kagan to the Supreme Court. At the press conference announcing her nomination, Obama began by praising Justice Stevens' service to the Court. He then discussed Kagan's background. The granddaughter of immigrants, she excelled in the elite universities of the nation, eventually becoming the dean of Harvard Law School. He applauded her service in public sphere and as solicitor general, the lead attorney for the executive branch in the Supreme Court, noting that she stood up for the rights of what he described as ordinary citizens against powerful corporate interests in *Citizens United v. Federal Election Commission*.[180] Obama also remarked on her judicial temperament, predicting that she would be fair minded, open to a diverse array of viewpoints, and a consensus builder on the Court.[181] Kagan gave a brief address following Obama's remarks, thanking the president for her nomination and her friends and family for their support and loyalty on her path to the Court.

As noted earlier, many factors shape the president's selection of a Supreme Court nominee and Kagan's appointment was no different. In terms of qualifications, Kagan came to the bench with an impeccable educational record, having received a bachelor's degree in history from Princeton University, a master's degree in philosophy from Oxford University, and a juris doctorate from Harvard Law School, where she served as articles editor for the *Harvard Law Review*.[182]

Though Kagan had a plethora of legal experience in both the public and private sectors, she never served as a judge, an issue that her opponents would seize onto. In terms of governmental service, however, Kagan is the only justice on the current Court with experience in all three branches of government. After law school, Kagan clerked for Judge Abner Mikva of the U.S. Court of Appeals for the District of Columbia Circuit and for Justice Thurgood Marshall on the U.S. Supreme Court. In the legislative branch, she worked as special counsel to the chair of the Senate Judiciary Committee, Joseph Biden, where

2010/05/05/obama-interviews-diane-wood-search-for-supreme-court-nominee-na/   (Accessed December 12, 2011).

[179] Baker and Nagourney, "Sotomayor Pick a Product of Lessons from Past Battles," supra, n. 163.

[180] Citizens United v. Federal Election Commission, 175 L.Ed.2d 753 (2010).

[181] John T. Woolley and Gerhard Peters, "The American Presidency Project." Retrieved from: http://www.presidency.ucsb.edu/ws/index.php?pid=87859&st=kagan&st1 (Accessed December 13, 2011).

[182] Sheryl Gay Stolberg, Katharine Q. Seelye, and Lisa W. Foderaro, "A Pragmatic New Yorker on a Careful Path to Washington," *New York Times*, May 10, 2010.

she helped usher Ruth Bader Ginsburg through the confirmation process. In the executive branch, she served as associate counsel to the president, deputy assistant for domestic policy, and deputy director of the domestic policy council in the Clinton administration, and as the solicitor general of the United States in the Obama administration.[183]

In the private sector, Kagan was a litigator at Williams and Connolly in Washington, DC, from 1989 to 1991. After this, she was a faculty member at the University of Chicago Law School, where she obtained tenure in 1995. After leaving the Clinton administration, she returned to academia, first as a visiting professor at Harvard Law School (1999–2001) and then as a professor (2001–10). In 2003, she became the dean of Harvard Law School. During her tenure as dean, Kagan was well respected by her colleagues across the ideological spectrum, overseeing major changes to the curriculum and hiring twenty-two new faculty members.[184]

In terms of ideology, it is fair to say that Obama could count on Kagan to be a relatively liberal justice, akin to her predecessor, Justice Stevens, and Obama's first nominee, Justice Sotomayor. Like virtually all other Supreme Court nominees, Kagan had long been active in partisan politics. In college, she was involved with the Senate campaign of Democrat Elizabeth Holtzman (NY). It is reported that, after Holtzman lost the election to Alfonse D'Amato and Ronald Reagan was elected president, she drowned her sorrows in vodka tonics.[185] As a clerk, she worked for two Democratic appointees, Mikva and Marshall, in addition to serving under Democrat Joseph Biden in the Senate and in the administrations of Democrats Bill Clinton and Barack Obama.

Kagan's appointment also likely worked to build political support for President Obama within the Democratic Party. There is little doubt that Obama was particularly interested in diversifying the Court in terms of its gender composition, as reflected in the fact that his shortlists for openings on the Supreme Court were dominated by women.[186] Kagan's appointment marked the first opportunity in American history for three female justices to sit together on the high Court. In addition, owing to her strong connections to the Democratic Party, Obama may have seen Kagan as able to appeal to his core base, without alienating moderate voters. Indeed, Kagan earned the votes of seven Republicans during her confirmation as solicitor general, suggesting that she

[183] Federal Judicial Center, "Kagan, Elena." Retrieved from: http://www.fjc.gov/servlet/nGet Info?jid=3289&cid=999&ctype=na&instate=na (Accessed December 12, 2011).
[184] Stolberg, Seelye, and Foderaro, "A Pragmatic New Yorker on a Careful Path to Washington," supra, n. 171.
[185] Ibid.
[186] Baker and Nagourney, "Sotomayor Pick a Product of Lessons from Past Battles," supra, n. 163; Baker and Zeleny, "Obama Picks Kagan as Justice Nominee," supra, n. 167.

could attract the support of individuals across party lines. Kagan's appointment also allowed Obama to diversify the Court in terms of the backgrounds of the justices, in that she was the first non-judge confirmed to the Court since the appointment of William Rehnquist in 1971.

Like most Supreme Court appointees, Kagan has strong personal ties to the president. Kagan was a faculty member at the University of Chicago Law School alongside Obama, who was a lecturer there. In the Obama administration, she served as solicitor general, spearheading the federal government's litigation in the Supreme Court. She also, as mentioned earlier, worked with Vice President Joseph Biden in 1993 when he was chair of the Senate Judiciary Committee.[187]

With regard to the political environment, Obama's nominee would face a relatively smooth path to confirmation. During April of 2010, 47–50% of Americans had a favorable impression of the president, slightly lower than the overall average for all presidents (54%).[188] More importantly, Obama's nominee would face a friendly Senate environment, with fifty-eight members of the Senate caucusing with the Democratic Party and Democrats in firm control of the Senate Judiciary Committee. Thus, the makeup of the Senate provided the president substantial leeway in his choice of a nominee.

Prior to her hearings before the Senate Judiciary Committee, both Kagan and the Committee members engaged in substantial preparation. Kagan's questionnaire from the Committee totaled 202 pages, covering everything from her educational and employment records, to her academic publications, to her activities as solicitor general. In addition, members of the Committee requested that she answer a host of questions that were not part of the Committee questionnaire; her responses were seventy-seven pages long. Sixty-eight letters were submitted to the Committee, totaling 229 pages. These letters, both supporting and opposing her confirmation, came from a wide array of individuals and institutions, including the AFL-CIO, the American Conservative Union, Harvard Law School alumni, the Hip Hop Entertainment Law Project, the Liberty Counsel, members of the House of Representatives, the National Association for the Advancement of Colored People, the National Rifle Association, People for the American Way, as well as former solicitors general.[189] All of this information provided a foundation for the members of

---

[187] Stolberg, Seelye, and Foderaro, "A Pragmatic New Yorker on a Careful Path to Washington," supra, n. 171.

[188] Gallup, "Presidential Approval Ratings – Barack Obama." Retrieved from: http://www.gallup.com/poll/116479/barack-obama-presidential-job-approval.aspx (Accessed December 12, 2011).

[189] United States Senate Committee on the Judiciary, "Associate Justice of the U.S. Supreme Court – Elena Kagan," supra, n. 101.

the Committee to work from as they prepared their opening statements and questions for the confirmation hearings.

Kagan worked closely with her White House advisors in preparing for the hearings. She participated in numerous mock hearings in which approximately twenty different individuals grilled her for hours on the issues they believed the senators would bring up at the hearings. The mock hearings were orchestrated by White House Counsel Bob Bauer, and the "actors," playing the roles of members of the Judiciary Committee, included academics and lawyers from private practice, the White House, and the Department of Justice. Outside of these "murder boards," Kagan spent hours reading up on key cases and legal writings, ensuring that she was up to date on the material likely to come up at her hearing.[190]

During this time, Kagan began meeting with senators on Capitol Hill, a process that lasted five weeks and included visits with more than sixty senators.[191] During these meetings, Kagan received insight into the questions and concerns that would make their way into her confirmation hearings. A variety of issues were addressed at these informal meetings, including her stance on the military's "Don't Ask, Don't Tell" policy, her decision to briefly bar military recruiters from Harvard Law School facilities when she was dean, and her position on the Second Amendment. Although most of these meetings took a rather serious tone, some of her Democratic supporters seized on the opportunity to engage her lighter side. For example, Senator Durbin (D-IL) discussed Chicago-style pizza and Cubs baseball with the former Second City resident.[192]

As preparation for her confirmation hearing continued, interest groups came out for and against her nomination. Groups took out advertisements on radio, television, the Internet, and in newspapers to mobilize their constituents to contact senators in support of, or in opposition to, her confirmation. A variety of groups supported her nomination, including the Alliance for Justice, the National Association for the Advancement of Colored People, and People for the American Way. A group of liberal organizations, operating as the Coalition for Constitutional Values, ran a national television ad focusing on her modest background and strong experience in the public and educational sectors, advocating for her confirmation.[193] Groups opposing her confirmation included Americans United for Life, the American Conservative

---

[190] Associated Press, "Kagan Practices Answers, Poise in Mock Hearings," *US News and World Report*, June 23, 2010.

[191] Ibid.

[192] Sheryl Gay Stolberg, "On Capitol Hill, Kagan Gets to Know Her Voters," *New York Times*, May 12, 2010.

[193] Ibid.

Union, and the National Rifle Association.[194] The conservative Judicial Crisis Network targeted moderate Democrats in traditionally conservative states, such as Mary Landrieu (D-LA) and Ben Nelson (D-NE), in hopes of convincing them to oppose Kagan's confirmation by painting her as a left-wing extremist.[195]

Kagan's confirmation hearings took place from June 28 to July 1, 2010.[196] Committee chair Patrick Leahy (D-VT) opened the hearings by discussing hearing procedure and providing a brief background of Kagan.[197] Ranking Member Senator Jeff Sessions (R-AL) spoke next, followed by the remaining members of the Committee. Kagan, who spent much of her career in Massachusetts during her tenure at Harvard Law School, was then presented by Massachusetts Senators John Kerry (D-MA) and Scott Brown (R-MA). She was then sworn in by Leahy and was given the opportunity to make an opening statement. She did so, highlighting her background and experience in the legal and political worlds, as well as the importance of bringing an open mind to the bench.

The second day of the Kagan hearings marked the first of two days of question-and-answer sessions. As is typical, Chairman Leahy opened the colloquy, followed by Ranking Member Sessions. The remaining members of the Committee, in descending order of seniority and alternating between majority and minority party status, then questioned Kagan. Each of the nineteen members of the Committee was granted thirty minutes to engage the nominee. Following questions from Senator Franken (D-MN), the most junior member of the Committee, each member of the Committee was granted up to twenty minutes to interrogate the nominee a second time around. Leahy then authorized several senators, who asked for more time during the second round, to ask additional questions, including Sessions, Grassley (R-IA), and Coburn (R-OK). The hearings closed with remarks from Ranking Member Sessions and Chairman Leahy.

Following the question-and-answer session, the Committee went into a closed session to discuss with Kagan the results of the private background

---

[194] United States Senate Committee on the Judiciary, "Associate Justice of the U.S. Supreme Court – Elena Kagan," supra, n. 101.

[195] Associated Press, "Interest Groups See Opportunity in Kagan Fight," *CBS News*, June 9, 2010. Retrieved from: http://www.cbsnews.com/stories/2010/06/09/politics/main6565289.shtml (Accessed December 12, 2011).

[196] Because we will cover the issues discussed at the Kagan hearing, along with the topics addressed at the hearings of other nominees, throughout the remainder of the book, we limit our discussion of the Kagan hearing to providing a treatment of hearing procedure.

[197] Senator Leahy also devoted some time to discussing the legacy of the recently departed Senator Robert Byrd (D-WV).

investigations.[198] Next, it heard the testimony of a variety of individuals and interest groups both supporting and opposing her confirmation. Representatives from the American Bar Association's Standing Committee on the Judiciary were first to testify, during which they provided the Committee with a description of the ABA's "well qualified" ranking of Kagan. Witnesses appearing at the request of Committee Democrats (the party in control of the Committee) testified next and included law professors, a former solicitor general, and representatives from the National Association of Women Judges, the National Women's Law Center, and the Harvard Law Armed Forces Association. The plaintiff in a recently decided gender discrimination suit, Lilly Ledbetter, also testified on Kagan's behalf. Witnesses testifying in opposition came next. These witnesses included numerous members of the armed services, law professors, and representatives from the Heritage Foundation, the Independence Institute, the Family Research Council, and Americans United for Life.[199]

The Senate Judiciary Committee voted to report the nomination of Elena Kagan favorably to the full Senate on July 20, 2010, by a 13–6 vote. All twelve of the Committee's Democrats supported her confirmation, and only one Republican Senator, Lindsey Graham (R-SC), voted in support of the favorable Committee report. The other six Republicans on the Committee voted against recommending her confirmation. In explaining his vote in favor of Kagan, Graham noted that "elections have consequences" and that, in his view, the Constitution did not give him the right "to replace my judgment for [the President's]."[200]

On August 5, 2010, the Senate voted to confirm Elena Kagan to the Court by a 63–37 vote. One Democrat, Ben Nelson, opposed her, while she won the support of five Republicans. During two days of Senate debate, Democratic senators praised her experience and judicial temperament, while Republican senators accused her of working to advance a liberal agenda and lacking the necessary qualifications to sit on the Court.[201] The following Saturday, Kagan was sworn in at the Court by Chief Justice Roberts. Following newly

[198] Mike Memoli and Michael Muskal, "Questioning of Kagan Done, Senators Head to Closed Session," *Los Angeles Times*, June 30, 2010.

[199] Garance Franke-Ruta, "Kagan Hearings Witness List Released." *Washington Post*, June 25, 2010. Retrieved from: http://voices.washingtonpost.com/44/2010/06/kagan-hearings-witness-list-re.html (Accessed December 12, 2011).

[200] Patricia Murphy, "Elena Kagan Approved by Senate Judiciary Committee; Lindsey Graham Votes Yes," *Politics Daily*, July 20, 2010. Retrieved from: http://www.politicsdaily.com/2010/07/20/elena-kagan-approved-by-senate-judiciary-committee-lindsey-grah/ (Accessed December 12, 2011).

[201] Paul Kane and Robert Barnes, "Senate Confirms Elena Kagan's Nomination to Supreme Court," *Washington Post*, August 6, 2010.

established protocol, she was first administered the constitutional oath in a private ceremony, followed by a public recitation of the judicial oath in the Court's West Conference Room.[202] Kagan was joined by her family and friends in the public ceremony. Her investiture ceremony at the Court took place on October 1 in a special sitting of the Court before it opened its term three days later. A number of high-ranking officials attended the ceremony, including President Obama; Senators Al Franken and Arlen Specter (D-PA); retired Justices O'Connor, Stevens, and Souter; Attorney General Eric Holder; Acting Solicitor General Neal Katyal; and a host of acquaintances.[203]

On the first Monday in October 2010, Elena Kagan ascended the bench as the 112th associate justice of the United States Supreme Court.

CONCLUSIONS

The United States Constitution says very little about the Supreme Court confirmation process beyond charging the president with appointing justices and the Senate with confirming them. The purpose of this chapter was to provide an overview of the confirmation process, from the means by which a seat opens up on the Court to a justice's investiture ceremony. This process, as we have seen, has been marked by both continuity and change. Although the constitutional duties of the president and Senate have remained constant, the manner in which they perform their roles has varied over time. Perhaps the most notable change to this process involves the vital intermediary role played by the Senate Judiciary Committee. Since 1955, every nominee has testified before the Committee, creating the moment of democratic reckoning we explore in this book. Today, a nominee can expect a roller coaster ride to the Court, complete with numerous background investigations, appearances before "murder boards," visits to Capitol Hill, grilling before the Senate Judiciary Committee, public criticism from interest groups, further condemnation during Senate floor debate, and, ultimately, if the nominee weathers the process, Senate confirmation. This examination of the process shows plainly that both presidents and senators take their roles very seriously. This is no doubt recognition of the fact that Supreme Court justices are among the most powerful actors in government. It is to that power, and the role the confirmation process plays in shaping how they exercise it, that we now turn.

---

[202] Peter Baker, "Kagan Is Sworn in as the Fourth Women, and 112th Justice, on the Supreme Court," *New York Times*, August 7, 2010.

[203] Tony Mauro, "Obama Looks on As Kagan Takes Her Place on the Bench." Retrieved from: http://legaltimes.typepad.com/blt/2010/10/obama-looks-on-as-kagan-takes-her-place-on-the-bench.html (Accessed December 12, 2011).

3

Public Opinion and Precedent at Confirmation Hearings

The year 2008 was a watershed year for the Second Amendment.[1] On June 26, the Supreme Court addressed the meaning of the Second Amendment for the first time in almost seventy years.[2] In *District of Columbia v. Heller*,[3] a 5–4 majority held that the Second Amendment is broad enough to encompass an individual's right to possess a firearm, regardless of whether that individual is connected to a government-recognized militia. In so doing, the Court struck down a District of Columbia law that outlawed the possession of a handgun within District limits. Moreover, the Court's decision presaged the incorporation of the Second Amendment against states, which would take place two years later in *McDonald v. Chicago* (2010).[4]

The Court, of course, was not the lone actor in the Second Amendment debate during 2008. A Gallup Poll conducted in February indicated that 73% of Americans believed the Second Amendment guarantees the rights of individuals to own guns.[5] That October, another Gallup Poll revealed that only 44% of Americans felt that firearm sales should be subject to stricter regulation,

---

[1] "A well regulated Militia, being necessary to the security of a free State, the right of the people to keep and bear Arms, shall not be infringed." U.S. Constitution, Amendment II.

[2] In United States v. Miller, 307 U.S. 174 (1939), the Court determined that a national law, prohibiting the possession of sawed-off shotguns and similar firearms, did not run afoul of the Second Amendment on the grounds that possessing such weapons did not have a reasonable relationship to the efficacy of a militia.

[3] District of Columbia v. Heller, 171 L. Ed. 2d 637 (2008).

[4] McDonald v. Chicago, 177 L. Ed. 2d 894 (2010). Incorporation is the process by which provisions in the Bill of Rights are made binding on state governments. Because the District of Columbia is a federal enclave, as opposed to a state, the *Heller* decision did not focus on this point.

[5] Jeffrey M. Jones, "Americans in Agreement with Supreme Court on Gun Rights." Retrieved from: http://www.gallup.com/poll/108394/americans-agreement-supreme-court-gun-rights .aspx (Accessed November 3, 2010).

down 34% from the first time this question was asked in 1990.[6] Members of Congress responded to these sentiments by introducing numerous bills regarding the right to keep and bear arms. These bills included the Second Amendment Enforcement Act, the National Crime Gun Identification Act, and the End Gun Trafficking Act of 2008. Discussions of gun rights also permeated the media. *The New York Times*, for example, ran more than a dozen stories involving the Second Amendment. In addition to covering *Heller*, the *Times* reported on a variety of topics related to guns, including the decision of New Orleans officials to return handguns confiscated in the aftermath of Hurricane Katrina to their owners[7] and a detailed analysis of the relationship between guns and crime.[8]

Given the hearty debate Americans were having about the Second Amendment, one might expect that the right to keep and bear arms would become a focal point of the confirmation hearing of President Obama's first pick to join the Court. But discussion of the Second Amendment had been relatively rare at Supreme Court confirmation hearings. From 1939 to 2006, dialogue involving the Second Amendment constituted less than 0.1% of all discourse at the hearings. It did not make an appearance at all until O'Connor's hearing in 1981. Even at that hearing, the right to keep and bear arms comprised only 0.5% of discussions. Thus, from a historical standpoint, the Second Amendment has been largely missing from the hearings. But, as noted earlier, 2008 was a big year for the Second Amendment. Would members of the Senate Judiciary Committee follow tradition by largely ignoring the Second Amendment during the hearing of Obama's first nominee to the Court? Or would they reflect public opinion and Supreme Court precedent and focus a substantial amount of attention on the meaning of the right to keep and bear arms?

On May 1, 2009, Supreme Court Justice David Souter formally advised Obama of his intent to retire from the Court, effective at the beginning of the Court's summer recess. Within a month, Obama nominated Second Circuit Court of Appeals Judge Sonia Sotomayor to fill Souter's position. During her confirmation hearing, Sotomayor faced a host of questions familiar to previous nominees. For example, more than a fifth of the dialogue at the Sotomayor confirmation hearing involved matters of judicial philosophy, while about

---

[6] Jeffrey M. Jones, "In U.S., Record-Low Support for Stricter Gun Laws." Retrieved from: http://www.gallup.com/poll/123596/in-u.s.-record-low-support-stricter-gun-laws.aspx (Accessed November 3, 2010).

[7] Associated Press, "Louisiana: City Will Give Back Guns," *New York Times*, October 8, 2008.

[8] Adam Liptak, "Gun Laws and Crime: A Complex Relationship," *New York Times*, June 29, 2008.

30% of her hearing focused on civil rights, broadly defined. Breaking historic trends, though, a full 11% of Sotomayor's hearing involved discussions of the Second Amendment.

The issue was first raised by the Committee chair, Senator Leahy (D-VT):

Chairman LEAHY: Let me talk to you about another decision, *District of Columbia v. Heller*. In that case, the Supreme Court held that the Second Amendment guarantees to Americans the right to keep and bear arms and that it is an individual right. I have owned firearms since my early teen years. I suspect a large number of Vermonters do. I enjoy target shooting on a very regular basis at our home in Vermont, so I watched that decision rather carefully and found it interesting.

Is it safe to say that you accept the Supreme Court's decision as establishing that the Second Amendment right is an individual right? Is that correct?

Judge SOTOMAYOR: Yes, sir.[9]

Leahy continued to press Sotomayor on her views of the Second Amendment in light of the *Heller* decision, asking her four more questions on the topic and appearing generally satisfied by her stated commitment to upholding the spirit of *Heller*. Follow-up questions regarding the Second Amendment were posed by Senators Coburn (R-OK), Cornyn (R-TX), Feingold (D-WI), Graham (R-SC), Hatch (R-UT), Klobuchar (D-MN), Kyl (R-AZ), Sessions (R-AL), and Specter (D-PA).

Hatch, who appeared much more doubtful than Leahy about Sotomayor's commitment to *Heller*, engaged the nominee in a particularly pointed discussion of the case, devoting almost 30% of his questions to the Second Amendment. Hatch's skepticism is evident in the dialogue stemming from his second comment at the hearings:

Senator HATCH: Now, I want to begin here today by looking at your cases in an area that is very important to many of us, and that is the Second Amendment, the right to keep and bear arms, and your conclusion that the right is not fundamental.

Now, in the 2004 case entitled *United States v. Sanchez-Villar*,[10] you handled the Second Amendment issue in a short footnote. You cited the

---

9 Sotomayor transcript, questioning by Senator Leahy (D-VT) at 2.7.
10 United States v. Sanchez-Villar, 99 Fed. Appx. 256 (2nd Cir. 2004), involved the appeal of an individual convicted of cocaine possession with the intent to distribute and the possession of a firearm by an illegal alien. The Second Circuit panel upheld the conviction.

Second Circuit's decision in *United States v. Toner*[11] for the proposition of the right to possess a gun is not a fundamental right.

Toner in turn relied on the Supreme Court's decision in *United States v. Miller.* Last year, in the *District of Columbia v. Heller*, the Supreme Court examined *Miller* and concluded that, "The case did not even purport to be a thorough examination of the Second Amendment," and that *Miller* provided "no explanation of the content of the right." You are familiar with that.

Judge SOTOMAYOR: I am, sir.

Senator HATCH: Okay. So let me ask you, doesn't the Supreme Court's treatment of *Miller* at least cast doubts on whether relying on *Miller*, as the Second Circuit has done for this proposition, is proper?

Judge SOTOMAYOR: The issue before –

Senator HATCH: Remember, I'm saying at least cast doubts.

Judge SOTOMAYOR [continuing]: Well, that is what I believe Justice Scalia implied in his footnote 23, but he acknowledged that the issue of whether the right, as understood in Supreme Court jurisprudence, was fundamental. It's not that I considered it unfundamental, but that the Supreme Court didn't consider it fundamental so as to be incorporated against the states.[12]

Regardless of one's position on the Second Amendment or the wisdom of the *Heller* decision, it is evident that the members of the Senate Judiciary Committee viewed gun rights as a pressing issue of the day. Thus, rather than following historical trends and generally ignoring the topic, the senators' questions reflected both public opinion and Supreme Court precedent.

Was Sotomayor's hearing anomalous in this regard, driven by unique attributes of the nominee (such as the fact that she had joined an opinion declining to extend *Heller* to the states without clear guidance from the Supreme Court[13]), or is this connection among confirmation dialogue, public opinion, and Supreme Court precedent a regular part of the hearing process? This question is important. If the hearings are, as we argue, a democratic forum for ratifying constitutional change, then hearing dialogue must reflect issues

---

[11]   United States v. Toner, 728 F.2d 115 (2nd Cir. 1984), implicated the appeal of two individuals who were convicted of a variety of criminal offenses for violating firearms statutes stemming from the defendants' attempt to purchase 20 M-16 machine guns from FBI agents for the purpose of shipping the weapons to Northern Ireland. The Second Circuit panel affirmed the convictions.

[12]   Sotomayor transcript, questioning by Senator Hatch (R-UT) at 2.26.

[13]   Maloney v. Cuomo, 554 F.3d 56 (2nd Cir. 2009).

important to the citizenry. Accordingly, this chapter systematically investigates the democratic nature of the hearings by examining the extent to which public opinion influences the issues debated at the confirmation hearings. We also explore how Supreme Court precedent itself shapes hearing dialogue, showing hearing discourse is motivated not only by the issues the public deems important but also by the issues relevant to the role of the Court in the American political system – the very issues future justices are likely to grapple with. In so doing, we further our knowledge of both the influence of public opinion on the judiciary and the impact of Supreme Court precedent on American society.

Such knowledge of the confirmation hearings is sorely lacking in the existing literature. Although a voluminous body of scholarship examines how public opinion influences the Supreme Court, it is overwhelmingly focused on how public mood is translated to justices once they are on the Court.[14] Understanding the mechanisms by which public opinion is communicated to sitting justices is important, but we believe that it also is imperative to comprehend how public opinion is conveyed at the confirmation stage. After all, it is during the confirmation hearings that the American people, through their representatives on the Senate Judiciary Committee, most directly influence constitutional change. Throughout the question-and-answer sessions featured at the hearings, senators relay their constituents' concerns about constitutional meaning, pressing nominees to answer questions regarding the salient legal and political topics of the day.[15]

This chapter also contributes to our understanding of the impact of Court decisions themselves. Scholars have amassed an impressive understanding of

---

[14] See, e.g., Robert A. Dahl, "Decision-Making in a Democracy: The Supreme Court as a National Policy-Maker," 6 *Journal of Public Law* 279 (1957); Barry Friedman, *The Will of the People: How Public Opinion Has Influenced the Supreme Court and Shaped the Meaning of the Constitution* (New York: Farrar, Straus and Giroux, 2009); Micheal W. Giles, Bethany Blackstone, and Richard L. Vining, Jr., "The Supreme Court in American Democracy: Unraveling the Linkages between Public Opinion and Judicial Decision Making," 70 *Journal of Politics* 293 (2008); Thomas R. Marshall, *Public Opinion and the Rehnquist Court* (Albany: State University of New York Press, 2008); Kevin T. McGuire and James A. Stimson, "The Least Dangerous Branch Revisited: New Evidence on Supreme Court Responsiveness to Public Preferences," 66 *Journal of Politics* 1018 (2004).

[15] Other mechanisms for communicating constituent preferences to the Court include filing amicus curiae briefs, chastising the Court's decisions in the media, and debating altering or overriding the Court's decisions in chamber. See, e.g., Judithanne Scourfield McLauchlan, *Congressional Participation as* Amicus Curiae *Before the U.S. Supreme Court* (New York: LFB Scholarly Publishing, 2005); Walter F. Murphy, *Congress and the Court: A Case Study in the American Political Process* (Chicago: University of Chicago Press, 1962); Rorie L. Spill Solberg and Eric S. Heberlig, "Communicating to the Courts and Beyond: Why Members of Congress Participate as Amici Curiae," 29 *Legislative Studies Quarterly* 591 (2005); Harry P. Stumpf, "The Political Efficacy of Judicial Symbolism," 19 *Western Political Quarterly* 293 (1966).

how Supreme Court precedents affect American society. This research, however, focuses primarily on how precedents are interpreted by lower courts,[16] how they influence societal change,[17] and how they shape congressional policy.[18] We know practically nothing about the Court's role in shaping the dialogue that takes place at confirmation hearings. We remedy this by presenting the Court as an active participant in setting the confirmation agenda. It is through its precedents, we argue, that the Court contributes to the national dialogue about the proper interpretation of the Constitution, igniting debate regarding its constitutional choices among the American public and in Congress. The confirmation hearings provide members of the Senate Judiciary Committee the occasion to query nominees about those choices by asking the nominees about their understanding and willingness to accept the Court's existing precedents. The hearings also offer senators the opportunity to present future members of the Court with their own preferred interpretations of recently decided cases. Accordingly, confirmation hearings provide insight into how Supreme Court precedents can transform constitutional discourse.

Although a casual consideration of confirmation hearings might lead one to believe that hearing dialogue is motivated primarily by idiosyncratic events specific to each nominee (such as Sotomayor's lower court decision declining to incorporate the Second Amendment), our evidence indicates that this is not the case. As we demonstrate, the issues discussed at the hearings are not random or driven by particular facts about the person who happens to be in the hot seat. Although some discussion is certainly nominee-specific, much more of it, as we show here, closely tracks both public opinion and Supreme Court precedent. Consequently, it is clear that the confirmation hearings do in fact provide a key forum for a constitutional dialogue that is shaped by both the issues most important to the citizenry and the Court's recently decided cases.

---

[16] See, e.g., Bradley C. Canon and Charles A. Johnson, Jr., *Judicial Policies: Implementation and Impact* (Washington, DC: CQ Press, 1999); David E. Klein, *Making Law in the United States Courts of Appeals* (Cambridge: Cambridge University Press, 2002); Francine Sanders, "*Brown v. Board of Education*: An Empirical Reexamination of Its Effects on Federal District Courts," 29 *Law & Society Review* 731 (1995).

[17] See, e.g., Michael J. Klarman, "How *Brown* Changed Race Relations: The Backlash Thesis," 81 *Journal of American History* 81 (1994); Gerald N. Rosenberg, *The Hollow Hope: Can Courts Bring About Social Change?* (Chicago: University of Chicago Press, 1991).

[18] See, e.g., William N. Eskridge, Jr., "Overriding Supreme Court Statutory Interpretation Decisions," 101 *Yale Law Journal* 331 (1991); Lori Hausegger and Lawrence Baum, "Inviting Congressional Action: A Study of Supreme Court Motivations in Statutory Interpretation," 43 *American Journal of Political Science* 162 (1999).

To shed light on the factors that influence the issues discussed at the confirmation hearings, we begin by presenting our theoretical account of how
public opinion shapes hearing dialogue, as well as our expectations for the
role precedent plays at the hearings. Next, we present our research design
and methodology, followed by the empirical results. We close with a discussion of our findings and their implications for understanding the role of the
confirmation process in shaping and validating constitutional change.

PUBLIC OPINION AND CONFIRMATION HEARINGS

One of the most significant normative and empirical debates regarding the
Supreme Court is the extent to which it operates as a countermajoritarian
institution.[19] On the one hand, it is clear that Supreme Court justices have
ample opportunity to subvert the public will, replacing it with their preferred
policy preferences. Indeed, this is in some ways facilitated by the very means
in which the Court is staffed. Rather than undergo democratic election, the
justices are appointed by the president, with the advice and consent of the
Senate. Because they can be removed from office only through the exceptionally rare and cumbersome impeachment process, they also effectively enjoy
life tenure, buffering them even further from direct democratic control.[20]

On the other hand, the Court is not entirely free to substitute its will for that
of the American public or its duly elected counterparts in the legislative and
executive branches. Possessing neither the purse nor the sword, justices must
rely on the executive branch to enforce their decisions, and the goodwill of the
American people to follow those decisions.[21] Should the Court step too far out
of line with public opinion, the president might react by implementing the
Court's decisions indifferently. The citizenry also may rebel against unpopular decisions by rejecting the justices' dictates, thus reducing the Court's
institutional legitimacy and undermining its authority. Congress also has

---

[19] See, e.g., Dahl, "Decision-Making in a Democracy," supra, n. 14; Friedman, *The Will of the People*, supra, n. 14; Giles, Blackstone, and Vining, "The Supreme Court in American Democracy," supra, n. 14; Larry D. Kramer, *The People Themselves: Popular Constitutionalism and Judicial Review* (New York: Oxford University Press, 2004); Marshall, *Public Opinion and the Rehnquist Court*, supra, n. 14; McGuire and Stimson, "The Least Dangerous Branch Revisited," supra, n. 14.

[20] See, e.g., Dahl, "Decision-Making in a Democracy," supra, n. 14 (arguing that the framers did this in part to ensure that the Court could provide a counterbalance to the tyranny of the majority).

[21] See, e.g., Paul M. Collins, Jr., "Friends of the Court: Examining the Influence of Amicus Curiae Participation in U.S. Supreme Court Litigation," 38 *Law & Society Review* 807 (2004); Lee Epstein and Jack Knight, *The Choices Justices Make* (Washington, DC: CQ Press, 1998).

several formal ways to punish a Court that strays too far away from the public mood. For example, the legislative branch can override statutory decisions,[22] propose amendments to overturn constitutional decisions,[23] strip the Court of its jurisdiction to hear particular types of cases,[24] and freeze the justices' salaries.[25]

Given this, numerous scholars have argued that the justices seek to avoid these negative repercussions by rendering decisions that generally reflect the will of the American people.[26] Although our understanding of the role played by the confirmation hearings in ratifying constitutional change does not require (or even advocate) that the justices follow short-term public opinion, it does require that the constitutional commitments of the American people be communicated to the justices: in order for the justices to ratify the constitutional commitments of the people, they must be aware of what those commitments are, as well as the ongoing public debates about them.

Scholars have proposed a variety of ways in which information about the public's constitutional preferences are communicated to the justices. For example, inasmuch as members of Congress and the president are elected by the American public, these actors' ideological orientations provide a rough gauge of public opinion that is easily comprehended by the justices.[27] The justices can also obtain information regarding public opinion as a function of their everyday life experiences: by reading newspapers, listening to the radio, watching television, and talking to their neighbors.[28] Interest groups provide yet another way by which public mood is translated to the justices. By filing amicus curiae briefs, organizations supply the justices with information regarding their constituents' positions on particular disputes facing the Court.[29]

---

[22] Eskridge, "Overriding Supreme Court Statutory Interpretation Decisions," supra, n. 18.

[23] Lee Epstein, Jack Knight, and Andrew D. Martin, "The Supreme Court as a *Strategic* National Policymaker," 50 *Emory Law Journal* 583 (2001).

[24] Dawn M. Chutkow, "Jurisdiction Stripping: Litigation, Ideology, and Congressional Control of the Courts," 70 *Journal of Politics* 1053 (2008).

[25] William H. Rehnquist, "2000 Year-End Report on the Federal Judiciary." Retrieved from: http://www.supremecourt.gov/publicinfo/year-end/2002year-endreport.aspx (Accessed August 18, 2010).

[26] See, e.g., Collins, "Friends of the Court," supra, n. 21; Dahl, "Decision-Making in a Democracy," supra, n. 14; Epstein and Knight, *The Choices Justices Make*, supra, n. 21; Friedman, *The Will of the People*, supra, n. 14; Giles, Blackstone, and Vining, "The Supreme Court in American Democracy," supra, n. 14; Marshall, *Public Opinion and the Rehnquist Court*, supra, n. 14; McGuire and Stimson, "The Least Dangerous Branch Revisited," supra, n. 14.

[27] Epstein and Knight, *The Choices Justices Make*, supra, n. 21; Giles, Blackstone, and Vining, "The Supreme Court in American Democracy," supra, n. 14.

[28] Epstein and Knight, *The Choices Justices Make*, supra, n. 21.

[29] Collins, "Friends of the Court," supra, n. 21.

Each of these methods for the transmission of public opinion to the justices has garnered substantial attention from both scholars and the popular press. This work has shown that the justices' decisions, to at least some extent, reflect popular will.[30] Yet, this scholarship has thus far been limited to mechanisms through which the public conveys its mood to the justices only after they have joined the Court. Although this work has made a valuable contribution to our understanding of the democratic responsiveness of the judiciary, it is incomplete, in that it fails to examine a key point at which the public exerts control over constitutional development – the confirmation process. We posit that a fuller understanding of the interplay between public opinion and the Supreme Court thus requires understanding how public sentiment is conveyed to justices before they are allowed to join the Court.

Of course, the American public does not have the opportunity to question Supreme Court nominees directly. Although representatives from interest groups frequently testify at the hearings, they do not engage nominees in face-to-face questioning. Instead, they typically present written and oral testimony regarding a nominee's virtues or faults.[31] Thus, the primary means by which public opinion is translated to nominees at the hearings is through the publics' elected representatives on the Senate Judiciary Committee.[32] Senators, highly aware of the importance of reelection and accountable to a wider range of voters than their counterparts in the House of Representatives, must stay in tune with their constituents' desires in order to secure reelection.[33] One way they can signal their desire to do this is by sharing with nominees their constituents' positions regarding the salient legal and political issues of the day.

Consequently, it is during confirmation hearings that future members of the Court receive many of their primary lessons on the public's ideas about the Constitution. These lessons are significant inasmuch as they provide future

[30] See, e.g., Dahl, "Decision-Making in a Democracy," supra, n. 14; Epstein and Knight, *The Choices Justices Make*, supra, n. 21; Friedman, *The Will of the People*, supra, n. 14; Giles, Blackstone, and Vining, "The Supreme Court in American Democracy," supra, n. 14; Kramer, *The People Themselves*, supra, n. 19; Marshall, *Public Opinion and the Rehnquist Court*, supra, n. 14; McGuire and Stimson, "The Least Dangerous Branch Revisited," supra, n. 14.

[31] See, e.g., Lauren Cohen Bell, *Warring Factions: Interest Groups, Money, and the New Politics of Senate Confirmation* (Columbus: Ohio State University Press, 2002).

[32] As discussed in Chapter 2, interest groups also take public positions for or against nominees on various media platforms, while executive branch officials prepare nominees for their questioning. Both of these mechanisms no doubt convey some information regarding public opinion to nominees. Thus, our point is not that the question-and-answer sessions at the hearings are the only means of transmitting public opinion to nominees, only that they are a particularly significant mechanism due to their formal and public nature.

[33] See, e.g., David R. Mayhew, *Congress: The Electoral Connection* (New Haven, CT: Yale University Press, 1974).

justices with the views of the general public and the political elites who, as discussed previously, can rein in a Court that strays too far from public opinion. In this sense, members of the Senate Judiciary Committee endeavor to educate nominees on their preferences about constitutional change, while at the same time relaying their constituents' views of current law. Consider the following senatorial comments:

> Senator BROWN: I hope also, Judge Thomas, that you and the other judges who sit on the Supreme Court will understand clearly and firmly that amending the Constitution and legislating are not the province of the Court, are not now and never should be the province of the Court, but that these are reserved under our Constitution to others and ultimately to the people that they serve.[34]

* * *

> Senator McCLELLAN: Good. I hope that will have some influence with you, as you weigh some of these cases, comparable cases that have gone to the Supreme Court, where we have had 5-to-4 decisions, where one man could change what you talk about, the Constitution. It is one man's decisions that often determines what the Constitution is. You recognize that, do you not?[35]

* * *

> Senator FEINGOLD: Ms. Kagan, if you're confirmed, I hope you'll keep this in mind. I hope you'll tread carefully and consider the reputation of the Court as a whole when evaluating whether to overturn longstanding precedent in ways that will have such a dramatic impact on our political system.[36]

* * *

> Senator METZENBAUM: All I am hoping to do in these hearings is maybe sensitize you enough, and when you get on the Supreme Court, maybe you will remember, gee, I remember those questions I had when I was appearing before the Judiciary Committee, maybe the milk of human kindness will run through you and you will not be so technical.[37]

Some senators take this dialogical task even further, anticipating that nominees will recall lessons learned from the hearings, regardless of whether they are confirmed:

> Chairman SPECTER: We don't extract promises, but when Senator Leahy very adroitly asks you about the rule of four on granting cert, four Justices say the cert is granted but it takes five to stay an execution in a capital case, how ridiculous can you be? Senator Leahy wondered if you would remember

---

[34] Thomas transcript, opening statement by Senator Brown (R-CO) at 76.
[35] Marshall transcript, questioning by Senator McClellan (D-AR) at 7.
[36] Kagan transcript, opening statement by Senator Feingold (D-WI) at 16.
[37] Breyer transcript, questioning by Senator Metzenbaum (D-OH) at 149.

that. Well, I predict you will, if confirmed, remember that. In fact, I predict you will remember it even if you are not confirmed.[38]

Through the question-and-answer sessions that are the heart of the confirmation process, the hearings thus work to communicate public opinion to future members of the Court, allowing the citizenry to help shape and debate constitutional meaning. As we demonstrate throughout this book, as various constitutional propositions gain or lose support over time, a new constitutional consensus emerges, one that the public has actively helped shape. Senate confirmation hearings play a key part in this process by presenting a forum in which these constitutional conversations can occur.

We argue that there are three primary mechanisms through which public opinion influences hearing discourse. First, we believe that senators will be responsive to the public's view of the most pressing issues of the day. As public opinion about the importance of an issue rises and falls, this should be reflected in the dialogue at confirmation hearings. Insofar as senators must be responsive to the citizenry's perceptions of the critical issues facing society to enhance their reelection prospects, they should be especially likely to address these topics in confirmation hearings. Doing so allows senators to show their constituents that they are sensitive to the public's views of the issues facing society,[39] and that they identify and connect with their constituents.[40] It also, of course, allows senators to tell their constituents that they fulfilled their representational duty to convey citizen concerns to future members of the high Court. Our first hypothesis about the relationship between confirmation dialogue and public opinion, consequently, is that as the public's perception of an issue's importance increases, so too will the dialogue involving that issue at confirmation hearings.

The second means by which we believe the connection between public opinion and hearing dialogue can be shown involves the role of the media. As media coverage of an issue increases or decreases, the amount of discussion that issue receives at the hearings also should increase or decrease. One of the primary roles of the media is to illustrate to the American people the importance of particular issues through the topics it chooses to cover (or not cover). In this way, the media help set the national agenda,[41] often by

[38] Alito transcript, questioning by Senator Specter (R-PA) at 587.
[39] See, e.g., Mayhew, *Congress*, supra, n. 33.
[40] See, e.g., Richard F. Fenno, *Home Style: House Members in Their Districts* (Boston: Little, Brown, 1978).
[41] See, e.g., Frank Baumgartner and Bryan Jones, *Agendas and Instability in American Politics* (Chicago: University of Chicago Press, 1995); Maxwell E. McCombs and Donald Shaw, "The Agenda Setting Function of the Mass Media," 36 *Public Opinion Quarterly* 176 (1972).

responding to the public's interest in an issue area.[42] For example, when the media devote substantial attention to civil rights policy, we expect not only that the American public's attention to this issue will go up, but also that civil rights will appear with greater frequency at the hearings. The media also are capable of "priming" issues for public attention.[43] Consistent media attention primes an issue by heightening the public's awareness of the issue, causing the public to evaluate political actors and policies in light of the primed issue. Turning again to civil rights as an example, priming takes place when constant media attention to civil rights issues causes American (and senators) to evaluate nominees in light of their position on civil rights questions. Given the media's important roles in both setting the national agenda and priming the way the public evaluates political actors, our second hypothesis is that as media coverage of an issue increases, so too will the dialogue involving that issue at confirmation hearings.

Third, we believe that public opinion will manifest itself at the hearings as a function of congressional attention to an issue area. As legislation related to an issue area increases, we contend that the issue will generate more attention at the hearings. Although there are many reasons why members of Congress devote attention to legislation, it is clear that public opinion constitutes one significant influence.[44] After all, members of Congress win elections by appealing to voters. Ignoring the public's desires once in office diminishes their reelection hopes.[45] What is more, legislation is often introduced by members of Congress specifically to increase their election prospects,[46] frequently for the purpose

---

[42] See, e.g., James T. Hamilton, *All the News That's Fit to Sell: How the Market Transforms Information into News* (Princeton: Princeton University Press, 2003).

[43] See, e.g., Shanto Iyengar and Donald R. Kinder, *News That Matters: Television and American Opinion* (Chicago: University of Chicago Press, 1987). The media also play a role in framing issues for the American public; that is, informing the citizenry how to think about a particular issue. Because we are interested in whether particular issues are on the radar of the American public in this chapter, and not the public's views of the desirability of particular positions attached to those issues, framing is orthogonal to this chapter's focus.

[44] See, e.g., Robert S. Erikson, Michael B. MacKuen, and James A. Stimson, *The Macro Polity* (New York: Cambridge University Press, 2002); Bryan D. Jones and Frank R. Baumgartner, "Representation and Agenda Setting," 32 *Policy Studies Journal* 1 (2004); Jeff Manza and Fay Lomax Cook, "A Democratic Polity?: Three Views of Policy Responsiveness to Public Opinion in the United States," 30 *American Politics Research* 630 (2002); Alan D. Monroe, "Public Opinion and Public Policy, 1980–1993," 62 *Public Opinion Quarterly* 6 (1998); Benjamin I. Page and Robert Y. Shapiro, "Effects of Public Opinion on Policy," 77 *American Political Science Review* 175 (1983).

[45] See, e.g., Mayhew, *Congress*, supra, n. 33.

[46] See, e.g., Gabriel Almond, *The American People and Foreign Policy* (New York: Harcourt, Brace, and Company, 1950); Fenno, *Home Style*, supra, n. 40; John Zaller, *The Nature and Origins of Mass Opinion* (New York: Cambridge University Press, 1992).

of pleasing attentive publics, such as interest groups.[47] Congressional legislation, consequently, should generally reflect public opinion, albeit at times the opinion of a more informed and organized public than the citizenry as a whole. Thus, our third hypothesis is that as congressional attention to an issue increases, so too will the dialogue involving that issue at confirmation hearings.

PRECEDENT AND CONFIRMATION HEARINGS

Information about constitutional choices does not travel just from the public to the Court, however. It also moves in the other direction. The justices write their opinions at least in part to persuade the public that the Court has made the appropriate constitutional choice. Thus, another significant debate regarding the Supreme Court involves the extent to which the Court's decisions change American society and influence the beliefs of Americans themselves. Teasing this out is tricky because the effect of Supreme Court decisions is largely indirect, given that the Supreme Court has no express means to enforce its decisions. Accordingly, the justices must depend on executive branch agents at the state and federal levels to enforce the Court's dictates.[48] Similarly, because the Court cannot review every lower court decision, it must entrust lower federal and state courts to act as faithful agents and correctly apply the Court's precedents.[49] The justices also must rely on the media to inform the citizenry of the significance of the Court's decisions.[50]

Scholarship about the impact of the Court's decisions abounds. A substantial amount of research addresses how the Court's precedents affect American society, frequently focusing on seminal decisions, such as *Brown v. Board of Education*[51] and *Roe v. Wade*.[52] Other work examines the extent to which lower

---

[47] Ken Kollman, *Outside Lobbying: Public Opinion and Interest Group Strategies* (Princeton: Princeton University Press, 1998).

[48] See, e.g., Canon and Johnson, *Judicial Policies*, supra, n. 16.

[49] See, e.g., Klein, *Making Law in the United States Courts of Appeals*, supra, n. 16; Sanders, "*Brown v. Board of Education*," supra, n. 16.

[50] See, e.g., Linda Greenhouse, "Telling the Court's Story: Justice and Journalism at the Supreme Court," 105 *Yale Law Journal* 1537 (1996); Elliot E. Slotnick and Jennifer A. Segal, *Television News and the Supreme Court: All the News That's Fit to Air?* (New York: Cambridge University Press, 1998).

[51] Brown v. Board of Education, 347 U.S. 483 (1954). See, e.g., Derrick Bell, *Silent Covenants: Brown v. Board of Education and the Unfulfilled Hopes for Racial Reform* (New York: Oxford University Press, 2005); David J. Garrow, "Hopelessly Hollow History: Revisionist Devaluing of *Brown v. Board of Education*," 80 *Virginia Law Review* 151 (1994); Klarman, "How *Brown* Changed Race Relations," supra, n. 17; Rosenberg, *The Hollow Hope*, supra, n. 17; David A. Schultz, ed., *Leveraging the Law: Using the Courts to Achieve Social Change* (New York: Peter Lang, 1998).

[52] Roe v. Wade, 410 U.S. 113 (1973). See, e.g., John J. Donohue and Steven D. Levitt, "The Impact of Legalized Abortion on Crime," 116 *Quarterly Journal of Economics* 379 (2001); Susan B.

courts comply with Supreme Court precedents,[53] how the Court's decisions influence other branches of government,[54] and the means by which the Court's decisions are implemented.[55] In addition, scholars have explored the influence of the Court's precedents on public opinion[56] and media coverage of the Court.[57]

Although this body of scholarship has helped us understand how Supreme Court precedents impact American society, virtually no attention has been paid to the role of Supreme Court precedent at confirmation hearings.[58] This is unfortunate, because it is through its precedents that the Court shapes the direction of American legal and social policy, and it is through the confirmation process that we choose the individuals who will shape those precedents. Our view is that the confirmation hearings play a significant role in illuminating how the Court's decisions impact society, in that the Court's precedents actively shape the constitutional conversation that takes place at confirmation hearings and thus our choices about who will sit on the high Court. Specifically, we posit that senators will be attentive to recent Supreme Court precedents and engage nominees in discussions of the wisdom of those

Hansen, "State Implementation of Supreme Court Decisions: Abortion Rates since *Roe v. Wade*," 42 *Journal of Politics* 372 (1980); Rosenberg, *The Hollow Hope*, supra, n. 17.

[53] See, e.g., Klein, *Making Law in the United States Courts of Appeals*, supra, n. 16; Sanders, "*Brown v. Board of Education*," supra, n. 16.

[54] See, e.g., Eskridge, "Overriding Supreme Court Statutory Interpretation Decisions," supra, n. 18; Joseph Ignagni and James Meernik, "Explaining Congressional Attempts to Reverse Supreme Court Decisions," 47 *Political Research Quarterly* 353 (1994); James F. Spriggs, II, "The Supreme Court and Federal Administrative Agencies: A Resource-Based Theory and Analysis of Judicial Impact," 40 *American Journal of Political Science* 1122 (1996).

[55] See, e.g., Lawrence Baum, "Implementation of Judicial Decisions: An Organizational Analysis," 4 *American Politics Quarterly* 86 (1976); Robert H. Birkby, "The Supreme Court and the Bible Belt: Tennessee Reaction to the 'Schempp' Decision," 10 *Midwest Journal of Political Science* 304 (1966); Canon and Johnson, *Judicial Policies*, supra, n. 16.

[56] See, e.g., Charles H. Franklin and Liane C. Kosaki, "Republican Schoolmaster: The U.S. Supreme Court, Public Opinion, and Abortion," 83 *American Political Science Review* 751 (1989); Valerie J. Hoekstra, *Public Reaction to Supreme Court Decisions* (New York: Cambridge University Press, 2003).

[57] See, e.g., Rosalee Clawson, Harry C. "Neil" Strine, IV, and Eric N. Waltenburg, "Framing Supreme Court Decisions: The Mainstream versus the Black Press," 33 *Journal of Black Studies* 784 (2003); Greenhouse, "Telling the Court's Story," supra, n. 50; Slotnick and Segal, *Television News and the Supreme Court*, supra, n. 50.

[58] A recent exception to this is Margaret Williams and Lawrence Baum, "Questioning Judges about Their Decisions: Supreme Court Nominees before the Senate Judiciary Committee," 90 *Judicature* 73 (2006), which examines the questions nominees faced regarding their previous judicial decisions. Although most of these questions involved the decisions nominees rendered in the lower federal and state courts, for nominees elevated to the position of chief justice or sitting on the Court as a result of a recess appointment, Supreme Court precedents were occasionally discussed.

decisions at the hearings. The confirmation hearings thereby present a unique forum at which the Court's precedents influence national dialogue about constitutional change, particularly among attentive publics who follow the Court's decisions.[59]

We argue that there are two primary means by which the Court's precedents influence the dialogue at confirmation hearings. First, we propose that senators will be responsive to the overall workload of the Court. Although individual decisions are important, it is through a *series* of decisions that the Court directs the development of constitutional law.[60] When the Court hands down a sequence of decisions relating to an issue area, it is these decisions as a group that shape the decision making of lower courts[61] and executive branch agencies charged with implementing the Court's decisions.[62] Moreover, when the Court adjudicates a series of decisions involving a particular issue area, those decisions contribute to the national dialogue regarding constitutional change. A vivid example of this is the criminal procedure revolution ushered in by the Warren Court during the 1950s and 60s. During those decades, the Warren Court set a variety of precedents expanding on the rights of the criminally accused. These decisions then played a prominent role in broader public discussions of criminal rights – discussions that included pointed criticisms of the Court's criminal justice cases.[63] Our fourth hypothesis, therefore, is that as the percentage of Supreme Court precedents involving an issue area increases, so too will the dialogue involving that issue at confirmation hearings.

We also believe that particularly salient decisions are likely to influence discussion at confirmation hearings. Although the run of the mill decisions might occasionally capture the attention of the American public and members of Congress, salient decisions figure most prominently into media coverage

---

[59] See, e.g., Gregory A. Caldeira and James L. Gibson, "The Etiology of Public Support for the Supreme Court," 36 *American Journal of Political Science* 635 (1992); Hoekstra, *Public Reaction to Supreme Court Decisions*, supra, n. 56.

[60] See, e.g., Jack M. Balkin and Sanford Levinson, "Understanding the Constitutional Revolution," 87 *Virginia Law Review* 1045 (2001); Friedman, *The Will of the People*, supra, n. 14; Rosenberg, *The Hollow Hope*, supra, n. 17.

[61] See, e.g., Donald R. Songer, Jeffrey A. Segal, and Charles M. Cameron, "The Hierarchy of Justice: Testing a Principal-Agent Model of Supreme Court-Circuit Court Interactions," 38 *American Journal of Political Science* 673 (1994); Donald R. Songer and Reginald S. Sheehan, "Supreme Court Impact on Compliance and Outcomes: *Miranda* and *New York Times* in the United States Courts of Appeals," 43 *Western Political Quarterly* 297 (1990).

[62] See, e.g., Spriggs, "The Supreme Court and Federal Administrative Agencies," supra, n. 54.

[63] See, e.g., Yale Kamisar, "The Warren Court and Criminal Justice: A Quarter-Century Retrospective," 31 *Tulsa Law Journal* 1 (1995).

of the Court.[64] By devoting attention to the Court's landmark precedents, the media highlights the role of the Court's decisions in the American political landscape, illustrating how the Court's decisions affect the polity. Because space is scarce in media outlets, the Court's decisions must fight with a variety of other potential newsworthy sources for coverage.[65] When the Court's precedents figure prominently into the newsworthy stories of the day, this sends a reliable signal that those decisions will have broad legal and societal impact. As a result, they are likely to ignite constitutional debate among the American public, causing the citizenry and senators to evaluate future justices in light of the Court's recent contributions to major shifts in constitutional development. Consequently, when the Court hands down landmark precedents in an issue area, we expect that issue area to receive substantial attention at the hearings. This idea informs our fifth and final hypothesis: as the percentage of salient Supreme Court precedents involving an issue increases, so too will the dialogue involving that issue at confirmation hearings.

DATA AND METHODOLOGY

To subject our hypotheses to empirical testing, we examine the dialogue at all Senate Judiciary Committee confirmation hearings from 1955 to 2006 involving the 19 issue areas identified in Table 3.1, which were adopted from the Policy Agendas Project.[66] These issue areas, discussed in detail in Chapter 4, represent the major topics in American political discourse, thus allowing us to track changes in political dialogue over time. The unit of analysis is the hearing–issue dyad, meaning that each observation in the data represents each

---

[64] Lee Epstein and Jeffrey A. Segal, "Measuring Issue Salience," 44 *American Journal of Political Science* 66 (2000).

[65] Sara C. Benesh and Harold J. Spaeth, "Salient to Whom? A Measure of Salience to the Justices" (paper presented at the Annual Meeting of the American Political Science Association, San Francisco, 2001); Saul Brenner and Theodore S. Arrington, "Measuring Salience on the Supreme Court: A Research Note," 43 *Jurimetrics* 99 (2002).

[66] Frank Baumgartner and Bryan Jones, "Policy Agendas Project." Retrieved from: http://www. policyagendas.org/ (Accessed August 20, 2010). While our database contains the universe of testimony at Supreme Court confirmation hearings from 1939 to 2010, data limitations compel us to focus on the 1955–2006 time period in this chapter. In particular, the "most important problem" question, our most direct measure of public opinion, was consistently made part of Gallup Polls in 1946. See Tom W. Smith, "America's Most Important Problem-A Trend Analysis, 1946–1976," 44 *Public Opinion Quarterly* 164 (1976) at 164. As a result, we are unable to include the hearings of Frankfurter (1939) and Jackson (1941). With respect to the two most recent nominees who are excluded from the data analyses in this chapter, Sotomayor (2009) and Kagan (2010), the Baumgartner and Jones database on public opinion, from which we derive one of our key independent variables, ends in 2007. Thus, the data employed in this chapter include twenty-eight of the thirty-two Supreme Court confirmation hearings.

TABLE 3.1. *The issues under analysis*

Issue	Examples
Macroeconomics	Inflation, unemployment, taxation
Civil Rights, Minority Issues, and Civil Liberties	Racial discrimination, free speech, voting rights
Health	Health care, regulation of drugs, medical liability
Agriculture	Agricultural trade, government subsidies, agricultural research and development
Labor, Employment, and Immigration	Worker safety, fair labor standards, immigration
Education	Higher education, secondary education, specialized education
Environment	Water safety, air pollution, species protection
Energy	Nuclear energy, natural gas, energy conservation
Transportation	Mass transportation, highway construction, airlines
Law, Crime, and Family Issues	Legal issues, judicial administration, death penalty
Social Welfare	Poverty assistance, elderly issues, social services
Community Development and Housing Issues	Urban economic development, rural housing, housing assistance
Banking, Finance, and Domestic Commerce	Banking regulation, insurance, corporate mergers
Defense	National defense, military intelligence, homeland security
Space, Science, Technology and Communications	Science technology, telecommunications regulation, computer industry
Foreign Trade	Trade negotiations, competitiveness of U.S. business, tariff restrictions
International Affairs and Foreign Aid	U.S. foreign aid, international finance and economic development, human rights
Government Operations	Intergovernmental relations, presidential impeachment, federal government branch relations
Public Lands and Water Management	National parks, Native American affairs, territorial issues

Source: Frank Baumgartner and Bryan Jones, "Policy Agendas Project." Retrieved from: http://www.policyagendas.org/ (Accessed August 20, 2010).

of the issues identified in Table 3.1 tagged to each hearing. Because there are twenty-eight nomination hearings in the data, and because each hearing is tied to each of the nineteen issue areas, the number of observations in the data set employed in this chapter is 532. A full description of the data used throughout this book, along with the results of reliability tests, appears in the Appendix.

The dependent variable represents the percentage of discussion at each hearing for each issue area, based on an original data collection effort. We coded every statement made by both nominees and senators at the hearings, using the Policy Agendas Project coding rules.[67] We then transformed the data such that the hearing–issue dyad is the unit of analysis.[68]

The most commonly discussed issue at the hearings is civil rights, minority issues, and civil liberties, which constituted an average of 52.1% of discussion at the hearings; followed by law, crime, and family (30.2%); and government operations (10.6%). Three issues appearing in Table 3.1 were not discussed at any hearing: agriculture, foreign trade, and transportation. Although these issues were never addressed at the hearings, they could have theoretically appeared at any of the hearings and they do vary within the independent variables. Hence, we include these issues in our analyses. Note that if we exclude these three issue areas from our data set, our results remain substantively unchanged.

---

[67] Baumgartner and Jones, "Policy Agendas Project," supra, n. 66. Although the issue areas in the Policy Agendas Project are capable of tracking the major policy areas in the American political system, we included four additional topics in our original data collection effort: hearing administration, which includes routine administrative announcements and discussions of nominee background and qualifications; judicial philosophy, which is based on treatments of the nominee's preferred methods of constitutional interpretation; federalism, which contains discussions of the concept of federalism; and miscellaneous substantive topics, which is composed of discussions of, for example, judicial administration and standing. Because hearing administration and judicial philosophy do not appear in the Policy Agendas Project data, which provides the basis for the coding of our independent variables, we excluded hearing administration and judicial philosophy in the creation of the dependent variable. We included discussions of federalism in the government operations category in the Baumgartner and Jones data, which contains discussions of intergovernmental relations, while the miscellaneous substantive topics category was incorporated into the law, crime, and family category, which includes issues dealing with the administration of justice. In the remaining chapters of this book, we consider the federalism and miscellaneous substantive topics categories separately from government operations (federalism) and law, crime, and family issues (miscellaneous substantive topics), in addition to providing a treatment of the hearing administration and judicial philosophy categories. Finally, because Gallup's "most important problem" question does not include the "state and local government administration" category in the Policy Agendas Project database, we excluded 0.07% of the data corresponding to statements made by nominees or senators pertaining to state and local government administration.

[68] Note that we also experimented with two other dependent variables: (1) the percentage of senatorial dialogue at each hearing for each issue area; and (2) the percentage of nominee dialogue at each hearing for each issue area. These three dependent variables correlate at greater than 0.99. This exceptionally high correlation should be expected, given that the hearings take place in a question-and-answer format, with senators setting the agenda through their questions, followed by the nominees responding in turn. When we use the two alternative dependent variables in place of the dependent variable that captures the total percentage of discussion, we obtain consistent results.

Sidebar: Statements Made by Outside Actors at the Hearings

Although nominees and members of the Senate Judiciary Committee make the vast majority of statements at confirmation hearings (more than 99.7%), on very rare occasions a statement is made by someone other than a nominee or Committee member. This first occurred during the hearing of William Brennan in 1957, when almost 20% of statements were made by Senator Joseph McCarthy (R-WI), who was not a member of the Committee.[69] The chair allowed McCarthy to question Brennan as a matter of senatorial courtesy, even though it was clear by Brennan's 1957 hearing that McCarthy's personal influence in the Senate had waned. He would die later that year, of hepatitis aggravated by alcoholism. It had been seven years since the moment when McCarthy gripped the nation by claiming to have a list of hundreds of communist infiltrators working in the State Department, and three years since his self-destructive performance before the Senate Subcommittee on Privileges and Elections that earned him a formal censure from his peers.[70]

The Judiciary Committee nonetheless saw fit to let the fading anti-communist crusader throw his parting shots at the young, liberal William Brennan. He did not disappoint: "As this committee is well aware," McCarthy began, "the Supreme Court will have a number of cases before it in the months ahead concerning the Communist conspiracy . . . Justice Brennan has demonstrated an underlying hostility to congressional attempts to expose the Communist conspiracy. I can only conclude that his decisions on the Supreme Court are likely to harm our efforts to fight communism."[71] Brennan, McCarthy went on, had referred to congressional investigations of communism as "witch hunts" and "inquisitions" – statements that proved to McCarthy that Brennan failed to understand "the Communist threat to our liberties."[72]

Despite his blustery rhetoric, McCarthy was not up to the task of convincing his fellow senators to vote against Brennan. In fact, McCarthy's performance was a sad sham. Asked to identify the documents he said showed Brennan's lack of fitness for the high Court, McCarthy fell into a long ramble that provoked not fear but laughter from his audience.[73] After McCarthy ended yet another diatribe by asking Brennan if a "Supreme Court Justice can hide behind his robes and conduct a guerrilla warfare against investigating committees," the chair called an end to the day's testimony.[74] Although invited to continue his questioning the next day, Senator McCarthy did not return.

Another example of questioning by a non-Committee member took place at the hearing of Charles Whittaker, also in 1957.[75] Whittaker was asked a series of questions about two cases he presided over as a district court judge involving suits

---

[69] Brennan transcript, questioning by Senator McCarthy (R-WI) at 17–28.
[70] Arthur Herman, *Joseph McCarthy: Reexamining the Life and Legacy of America's Most Hated Senator* (New York: The Free Press, 2000).
[71] Brennan transcript, opening statement by Senator McCarthy (R-WI) at 5.
[72] Ibid.
[73] Ibid. at 7.
[74] Brennan transcript, questioning by Senator McCarthy (R-WI) at 28.
[75] Whittaker transcript at 34.

filed by Fyke Farmer, who was best known for his defense of Julius and Ethel Rosenberg (and who testified against Whittaker at the hearings). When Whittaker described one of the cases as a suit in which Farmer attempted to personally sue President Truman for two-thirds of his back taxes on the grounds that his taxes went to finance the undeclared and illegal war in Korea, Farmer demanded to be heard. Chairman Eastland (D-MS) authorized Farmer to speak, an opportunity Farmer took to explain that the lawsuit was actually about requiring the president to produce official records relating to Korean War orders – clearly a very different interpretation of the case than Whittaker offered the Committee.

More recently, Sonia Sotomayor's hearing in 2009 was interrupted by a protester screaming "Filibuster Sotomayor! She's a baby-killer!"[76] Chairman Leahy (D-VT) immediately reacted to the disruption by instructing officers to remove the protester, who was escorted out of the hearing shouting "Defend the babies! And we're losing the pro-life vote!" Following this, the chairman reminded the audience that further outbursts would not be tolerated, regardless of whether they supported or opposed the nominee (or her positions). In addition, Leahy noted that Senator Grassley (R-IA), whose questioning was disrupted by the protester, would not lose any of his allotted time because of the commotion. Grassley thanked Leahy and responded that "People always say I have the ability to turn people on."[77]

Because our dependent variable ranges from 0 to 100, it is both left and right censored in that it cannot fall below 0 or above 100. We therefore use a Tobit model to capture the factors that influence the dialogue at the confirmation hearings.[78] To account for the nonindependence of observations, in that each hearing appears in the data nineteen times, we employ robust standard errors, clustered on each hearing.[79] It is not essential to understand the technicalities of the Tobit model in order to comprehend the empirical results, however. Rather than just reporting the independent variables' coefficients and standard errors, we also graphically plot the independent variables against the predicted value of the dependent variable. The graphs provide readers less familiar with our statistical methodology an intuitive and easy-to-understand visual depiction of our findings.

We employ five independent variables to test our hypotheses. To determine whether public opinion influences the dialogue at the confirmation hearings (hypothesis 1), we use a *Public Opinion* variable. This variable indicates the

---

[76] Sotomayor transcript at 2.47.

[77] Ibid.

[78] See, e.g., Richard Breen, *Regression Models: Censored, Sample Selected, or Truncated Data* (Thousand Oaks, CA: SAGE, 1996).

[79] We obtain substantively similar results using a random effects Tobit model (in which the panel units are hearings), as well as through the estimation of a Dirichlet multinomial distribution as described in Paulo Guimareas, "A Simple Approach to Fit the Beta-Binomial Model," 5 *Stata Journal* 385 (2005).

percentage of the American public who identified each of the nineteen issues as the most important problem facing the country in Gallup Polls during the year preceding the hearing.[80] We expect this variable will be positively signed, indicating that, as the percentage of the citizenry responding that a given issue area is the nation's most important problem increases, so too will attention to that issue at the hearings.

To test whether media coverage influences attention to an issue at the hearings (hypothesis 2), we use a *Media Coverage* variable. This variable represents the percentage of stories appearing in a random sampling of *The New York Times* index involving each of the nineteen issue areas in the Policy Agendas data set, lagged one year.[81] Accordingly, it provides a proxy of media attention to an issue area. We expect this variable will be positively signed, indicating that, as media coverage of an issue increases, so too will dialogue involving that issue at the hearings.

Our third hypothesis involves the role of congressional legislation. We posit that when Congress devotes increased attention to an issue area, that increased interest will be reflected at the hearings. To test this hypothesis, we utilize a *Legislation* variable, which captures the percentage of legislative initiatives in each of the nineteen issue areas, as reported in the *Congressional Quarterly Almanac*, during the year preceding the hearing.[82] These initiatives include bills introduced into Congress that both became law and failed to gain congressional support. We expect this variable will be positively signed, revealing that increased congressional attention to an issue area will be reflected in the amount of dialogue involving that issue area at the hearings.

Our fourth and fifth hypotheses involve the role of Supreme Court precedent. To test whether the overall amount of precedents in an issue area influences the discussion at the hearings (hypothesis 4), we use a *Supreme Court Precedent* variable. This variable is the percentage of precedents in each issue area set by the Court during the calendar year before the hearing. This

---

[80] Baumgartner and Jones, "Policy Agendas Project," supra, n. 66.

[81] Ibid. Although *The New York Times* is widely regarded as a national newspaper, because it is situated in New York State, it frequently covers stories that focus on issues pertaining to New York, such as state government. To ensure this does not bias our findings, we created an alternative specification of this variable by excluding stories involving only New York State. We obtain substantively identical results when we remove coverage of New York State from the coding of this variable.

[82] Ibid. As an alternative, we used a variable that captures the percentage of public laws passed by Congress in each issue area during the year preceding the hearing. That variable correlates with our measure at the 0.68 level and multicollinearity tests reveal that both variables should not be utilized in the same model specification. Substituting it for the variable we use here does not significantly change the results.

information was obtained from Baumgartner and Jones[83] and is based on the Spaeth[84] database. Baumgartner and Jones coded each of the cases decided by the Court to fit into the nineteen issue areas in the Policy Agenda Project codebook. We expect this variable will be positively signed, revealing that hearing dialogue is influenced by the number of Supreme Court precedents involving each issue area.

Hypothesis 5 involves the role of landmark Supreme Court precedents. Our *Salient Supreme Court Precedent* variable represents the percentage of salient precedents decided by the Court in each issue area during the calendar year preceding the hearings. To create this measure, we identified salient precedents as those appearing as the lead case on stories present on the front page of *The New York Times* on the day after the decision.[85] Such a measure is particularly useful in that it captures those cases that are most likely to attract substantial discussion among the American public, which should translate to increased attention by senators. We then merged the *New York Times* data with the aforementioned Baumgartner and Jones[86] data on the Supreme Court's precedents to create this variable. We anticipate that this variable will be positively signed, indicating that, as the percentage of salient Court precedents in an issue area increases, so too will the dialogue involving that issue area at the hearings.

Readers will note that all of our independent variables are lagged one year – that is, they capture public opinion, media coverage, legislation, and Supreme Court precedents during the calendar year immediately preceding the hearing. We have opted to lag our variables one year for both theoretical and methodological reasons. Theoretically, it makes good sense to lag the variables a year in that it gives senators some time to "catch up" to the various factors we posit will influence hearing discourse. Perhaps more importantly, if we failed to lag our independent variables, we would run the risk of using information on our independent variables collected *after* the hearing in question actually occurred.[87] Note that when we employ contemporary measures of our independent variables, our empirical results do not substantively alter. In addition, it is important to recognize that, although our independent variables should theoretically correlate, in that each is intended to measure a

[83] Ibid.
[84] Harold J. Spaeth, *The Original United States Supreme Court Database, 1953–2006 Terms* (East Lansing: Department of Political Science, Michigan State University, 2007).
[85] Epstein and Segal, "Measuring Issue Salience," supra, n. 64.
[86] Baumgartner and Jones, "Policy Agendas Project," supra, n. 66.
[87] See, e.g., Giles, Blackstone, and Vining, "The Supreme Court in American Democracy," supra, n. 14; McGuire and Stimson, "The Least Dangerous Branch Revisited," supra, n. 14.

TABLE 3.2. *The influence of public opinion and precedent on the issues discussed at Supreme Court confirmation hearings, 1955–2006*

Variable	Expected direction	Coefficient
Public Opinion	+	0.444***
		(0.134)
Media Coverage	+	−0.272
		(0.251)
Legislation	+	1.61***
		(0.429)
Supreme Court Precedent	+	1.372***
		(0.362)
Salient Supreme Court Precedent	+	1.009***
		(0.215)
Constant		−44.638***
		(8.529)
McKelvey and Zavoina R-squared		0.402
F-test		24.05***
N		532

The dependent variable is the percentage of discussion at each nominee's confirmation hearing involving each of nineteen issue areas identified in Table 3.1. Entries are Tobit coefficients. Numbers in parentheses are robust standard errors, clustered on each hearing. ***$P \leq$ .01 (two-tailed tests).

different concept that contributes to American political discourse, this does not translate to multicollinearity in our empirical models. The variance inflation factor does not exceed 2.50 for any of the variables in the model and the tolerance never drops below 0.40. Moreover, the median correlation among the variables under analysis is 0.14 (mean correlation = 0.24).[88]

EMPIRICAL RESULTS

Table 3.2 reports the factors that influence the dialogue at the confirmation hearings. Recall that the dependent variable is the percentage of discussion, per hearing, for each of the nineteen issue areas under analysis. Therefore, the independent variables offer leverage over the factors that contribute to increased (or decreased) discussion of a given issue area.[89]

---

[88] See, e.g., Paul D. Allison, *Logistic Regression Using the SAS System: Theory and Application* (Cary, NC: SAS Institute Inc., 1999) at 50.

[89] Summary statistics for the independent variables are as follows: Public Opinion (mean = 4.77, standard deviation = 9.92, minimum = 0, maximum = 56.35); Media Coverage (mean = 4.10,

Turning first to the variables that capture the role of public opinion, Table 3.2 provides support for our first hypothesis. We find that, as public attention to an issue area increases, so too does discussion of that issue area at the hearings. More specifically, when the public identifies an issue as the most important problem facing the nation, senators take note and press nominees as to their positions on that issue area. In addition, we find that congressional attention to an issue area results in increased discussion of that issue at the hearings. For example, when members of Congress introduce a relatively large number of legislative initiatives involving a particular topic, members of the Senate Judiciary Committee are increasingly likely to address that issue area at the hearings, thus supporting hypothesis 3. Note, however, that our second hypothesis fails to garner support. That is, our model reveals that there is no statistically significant relationship between media coverage of a given issue and the amount of dialogue involving that issue at the hearings. Accordingly, although it is clear that members of the Senate Judiciary Committee cue off of public mood as reflected in public opinion polls and the goings-on in Congress, the media does not appear to play a key role in setting the hearing agenda.

Table 3.2 also evinces the role of precedent at the hearings, thus supporting hypotheses 4 and 5. First, it is clear that the number of Supreme Court precedents in a given issue area influences hearing discourse. When the Court decides a relatively large number of cases in an issue area, that issue area receives increased attention at the hearings. The senators, in other words, ask more questions about issue areas in which the Court has been active.

Beyond the overall number of precedents set, however, it also is apparent that senators respond to landmark precedents. As the number of salient precedents within a given issue area increases, so too does attention to that issue area at the hearings. This illustrates that particularly salient precedents within an issue area, as well as increased judicial attention to a specific issue, influence the constitutional colloquy that is the hallmark of confirmation hearings.

As summarized in the preceding text and shown in Table 3.2, we find support for four of our five hypotheses. Our theory about why some issue areas garner more attention than others at the hearings is thus supported by the data. Table 3.2, however, does not show the substantive influence of each variable

standard deviation = 4.60, minimum = 0.148, maximum = 27.92); Legislation (mean = 5.26, standard deviation = 4.24, minimum = 0, maximum = 30.09); Supreme Court Precedent (mean = 5.26, standard deviation = 7.96, minimum = 0, maximum = 42.05), Salient Supreme Court Precedent (mean = 5.26, standard deviation = 10.56, minimum = 0, maximum = 51.43). The average values for the Public Opinion and Media Coverage variables are not equal to 5.26 owing to the need to exclude categories that do not appear in the Policy Agendas Project data set from those variables.

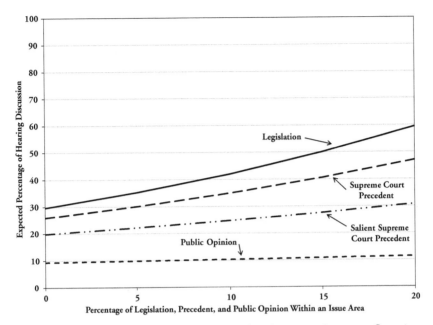

FIGURE 3.1. Influences on the issues discussed at Supreme Court confirmation hearings, 1955–2006. *Note*: The figure represents the marginal effects of the Public Opinion, Legislation, Supreme Court Precedent, and Salient Supreme Court Precedent variables on the predicted value of the dependent variable, holding all other variables at their mean values.

on the issues discussed at confirmation hearings. Figure 3.1 provides this information. This figure plots the influence of the significant variables in Table 3.2 on the predicted percentage of dialogue involving each issue at the hearings.[90] The x-axis, aligned horizontally, indicates the percentage of the public identifying an issue as the nation's most important problem (short dash line), as well as the percentage of congressional initiatives (solid line), Supreme Court precedent (long dash line), and salient Supreme Court precedent (long dash dot dot line) involving an issue area. The y-axis, aligned vertically, represents the predicted percentage of discussion of an issue area at the confirmation hearings.

This graph allows us to evaluate the relative strength of each of the independent variables on the issues discussed at confirmation hearings. For example, because all of the independent variables are on the same scale (in that they

[90] More specifically, this figure plots the marginal effects of each of the significant variables in Table 3.2 on the censored expected value of the dependent variable (i.e., the predicted value for issue areas falling within the range of the dependent variable), while holding all other variables at their mean values.

indicate the percentage of public opinion, legislation, and precedent involving an issue area), even a quick glance at this figure reveals that congressional legislation has the largest relative impact on the issues discussed at the hearings, followed by Supreme Court precedent, salient precedent, and public opinion, which has the smallest relative effect.

Figure 3.1 also allows us to provide a substantive understanding of the influence of each variable by interpreting the variable's marginal effect on hearing discourse. Our purpose here is to isolate the effect of a single variable (by holding the other variables at their average values) in order to illustrate how an increase in that variable, and that variable alone, is predicted to impact hearing dialogue involving a given issue area. For example, this figure shows that a 5% increase in congressional legislation in an issue area will, holding all else constant, generate a 6.7 percentage point increase in dialogue concerning that issue area.[91] Thus, it is clear that members of the Senate Judiciary Committee are responsive to the issues featured in congressional legislation, addressing those issues at the hearings.

Figure 3.1 also illustrates the role of Supreme Court precedent in shaping hearing discourse. A 5% increase in the percentage of the Court's precedents in an issue area leads to a 4.8 percentage point increase in attention to that issue area at the hearings. With regard to landmark precedent, we find that a 5% increase in salient precedents translates to a 2.6 percentage point increase in hearing dialogue. The combined effects of these variables are particularly interesting. For example, a 5% increase in both of these variable results in an almost 9 percentage point increase in attention to an issue area.

Finally, the figure also indicates that public opinion, as reflected in Gallup Polls, shapes the constitutional debate at the hearings, although it clearly exerts the weakest influence of all the variables in the model. For example, a 5% increase in the percentage of the American public identifying an issue as the nation's most important problem results in a 0.5 percentage point increase in hearing discussion.

A CLOSER LOOK: THE ECONOMY AND NATIONAL DEFENSE

While our empirical results indicate that public opinion influences hearing dialogue, they also show that that our most direct measure of public opinion,

---

[91] A 5% increase in the Legislation variable corresponds to approximately a one standard deviation increase in this variable, while a 5% increase in the Public Opinion, Supreme Court Precedent, and Salient Supreme Court Precedent variables corresponds roughly to a one-half standard deviation increase in those variables. For the purposes of the predicted probabilities discussed throughout this chapter, we have varied the variable of interest from 5% to 10%, while holding all other variables at their mean values (unless otherwise noted).

the percentage of Americans identifying an issue as the most important problem facing the nation, exerts the smallest substantive effect on hearing discussion among the variables we examined. This suggests that senators might take their cues on the pressing issues facing society not primarily from the general public, but instead from attentive publics that shape legislative priorities, such as interest groups (as revealed by the strong effect of the *Legislation* variable). This is potentially troubling for our theoretical perspective. It indicates that, although "the public" does shape hearing dialogue, the substantive influence of *general* public opinion, as opposed to the opinion of attentive publics (e.g., organized interests), is rather limited. That having been said, even if this inference is correct, it would mean only that the confirmations hearings over time have no less connection to public opinion than do the actions of other governmental bodies, which are subject to the same disproportionate influence by attentive publics.[92]

We believe, however, that the substantive effect of the *Public Opinion* variable is being depressed by a disconnect between two issues the public identifies as especially pressing and the limited role of the Supreme Court in shaping policy related to those issues: the economy and national defense. During the time frame under analysis (1955–2006), 25% of Americans in the Gallup Poll sample identified the economy as the nation's most important problem, and 23% viewed national defense as the most pressing issue facing the country. These two topics are thus the most frequently cited problems in the public opinion polls in our data.[93] But, cumulatively, these issues make up only 1.2% of hearing dialogue from 1955 to 2006. Thus, although the public regularly identifies both the state of the economy and national security as the country's most important problems, these issues are rarely discussed at confirmation hearings.

Rather than evidence of a theoretical flaw, therefore, we believe this disconnect between hearing dialogue and Gallup Poll results reflects instead the Court's limited role in these two specific issue areas. The Court, particularly since 1937, has had little to say about macroeconomics. Nor has the Court ever been deeply involved in issues about national defense. Senators, we believe, consequently spend less time on these issues than public concern about them would seem to warrant, choosing instead to press nominees on substantive

---

92 See, e.g., Almond, *The American People and Foreign Policy*, supra, n. 46; R. Douglas Arnold, *Congress and the Bureaucracy: A Theory of Influence* (New Haven, CT: Yale University Press, 1979); Paul S. Martin, "Voting's Rewards: Voter Turnout, Attentive Publics, and Congressional Allocation of Federal Money," 47 *American Journal of Political Science* 110 (2003).

93 That the public views these issues as the nation's most pressing problems should not be surprising. These two issues hit Americans closest to home in that they implicate their safety (defense) and economic well-being (macroeconomics).

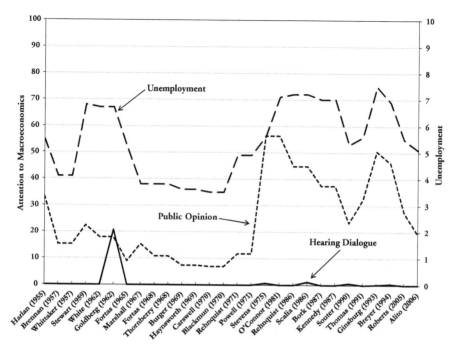

FIGURE 3.2. Public opinion, unemployment, and hearing dialogue involving macroeconomics, 1955–2006.

topics most relevant to the judiciary, including civil rights and liberties, criminal procedure, and government operations.

To put it differently, in an ideal world, we would have a perfect measure of public opinion, one that captures, for example, Americans' views of the most important problems *facing the Supreme Court*. However, to our knowledge, such a question has never been asked in public opinion polls (much less appeared regularly in polls since the 1950s). Given this data limitation, we are compelled to use an imperfect variable to capture public attention to an issue area. Our purpose in this section is to analyze further the relationship between public opinion and hearing dialogue by excluding macroeconomics and national defense issues, thereby removing some of the noise from our most direct measure of public opinion.

Figure 3.2 illustrates this with regard to macroeconomics (the issue area under which most economic concerns are coded). This figure plots the percentage of the public identifying the economy as the nation's most important problem and the percentage of hearing dialogue related to macroeconomics, alongside of the unemployment rate, as reported by the Bureau of Labor

Statistics.[94] The left vertical axis is the percentage of the public stating that the economy is the nation's most pressing problem and the percentage of hearing discussion related to the economy. The right vertical axis is the unemployment rate. Looking at this chart, two things are immediately apparent. First, it is evident that hearing dialogue does not track public opinion on the economy very closely. In fact, the correlation between these two variables is -0.05 ($P = 0.80$). The only nominee who received a good deal of questioning on economic concerns was Arthur Goldberg in 1962. During the Goldberg hearing, 20% of the discussion involved macroeconomics. This dialogue consisted entirely of a conversation with Senator Wiley (R-WI) involving Goldberg's views of the economic system in America and whether, because of his background as the secretary of labor, he was biased against business interests.[95]

Second, it is clear that public opinion on the economy very closely follows the unemployment rate: the correlation between these two variables is 0.78 ($P < 0.001$). This figure indicates that the state of the economy motivates American's economic concerns, particularly when the economy is in such rough shape that the citizens' very well-being is threatened, such as during periods of prolonged unemployment.[96] Yet, the senators do not cue of off economic conditions when grilling nominees at the hearings, presumably because the Court has a very limited role in setting the country's economic agenda.[97]

Figure 3.3 reveals that a similar picture emerges with regard to national defense. This figure plots the percentage of the public identifying national defense as the nation's most important problem and hearing debate involving

---

94 Bureau of Labor Statistics, "Employment Status of the Civilian Noninstitutional Population, 1940 to Date." Retrieved from: ftp://ftp.bls.gov/pub/special.requests/lf/aat1.txt (Accessed November 8, 2010). Consistent with our empirical models, we lag the unemployment rate one year to account for the temporal relationship between the unemployment rate and hearing discussion.

95 Goldberg transcript, questioning by Senator Wiley (R-WI) at 64.

96 See, e.g., Smith, "America's Most Important Problem," supra, n. 66; Tom W. Smith, "The Polls: America's Most Important Problems Part I: National and International," 49 *Public Opinion Quarterly* 264 (1985); Christopher Wlezien, "On the Salience of Political Issues: The Problem with 'Most Important Problem,'" 24 *Electoral Studies* 555 (2005). The correlation between the percentage of the public identifying the economy as the nation's most significant problem and the annual change in the consumer price index, capturing inflation, is 0.37 ($P = .06$).

97 Recall that Senate Judiciary Committee hearings featuring open nominee testimony began in 1939, two years after the Court's 1937 retreat from the economic realm. See, e.g., Robert G. McCloskey, "Economic Due Process and the Supreme Court: An Exhumation and Reburial," 1962 *Supreme Court Review* 34 (1962); Stuart S. Nagel, "Court-Curbing Periods in American History," 18 *Vanderbilt Law Review* 925 (1964). It was not until 1955, the time period marking the beginning of the empirical analyses in this chapter, that all nominees testified before the Committee.

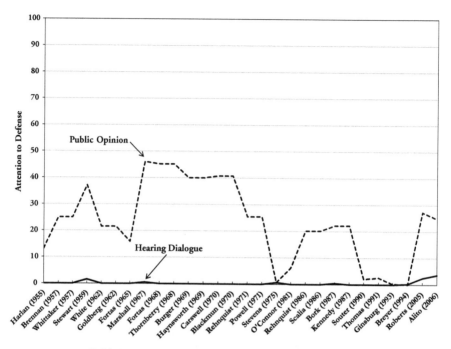

FIGURE 3.3. Public opinion and hearing dialogue involving defense, 1955–2006.

defense. As with the economy, there is a minimal correlation between public opinion and hearing dialogue relating to national defense: 0.08 ($P = 0.70$). And, as with the economy, public opinion on national defense closely tracks events that are exogenous to the Court.[98] In particular, the increase in public attention to defense in the 1950s and early 1960s corresponds to the escalation of the Cold War, while its accession during the 1965–71 era reflects the Vietnam War. The enhanced public attention to defense during the 1980s coincides with the Second Cold War, while the increase in the post–September 11th (2001) era is related to elevated threats to national security and the subsequent wars in Afghanistan and Iraq. As with the economy, because the Court does not play a major role in formulating the country's national security policies, hearing discussion does not closely track public attention to defense.[99]

---

[98] See, e.g., Smith, "America's Most Important Problem," supra, n. 66; Smith, "The Polls," supra, n. 87; Wlezien, "On the Salience of Political Issues," supra, n. 87.

[99] Hearing dialogue involving national defense did increase during the hearings of Roberts, Alito, Sotomayor, and Kagan. Whereas the overall percentage of discussion of national defense issues from 1939 to 1994 was 0.06%, from 2006 to 2010 it increased to 2.92%. The enhanced attention to national defense since the Roberts hearing is consistent with our theory in that it reflects not

Senators thus appear to filter public opinion through their understanding of the issues most relevant to the Supreme Court, such as civil rights and liberties, criminal procedure, and intergovernmental relations. This is not, of course, to say that the Court does not adjudicate disputes involving economic concerns or national security. To be sure, the Court has handed down hundreds of decisions in these issue areas.[100] But, relative to its influence in other areas, the Court's role in formulating the nation's economic and national security policies is limited.[101] With regard to economic affairs, the Court has been quite deferential to Congress's economic prerogatives ever since it retreated from the realm of economic regulation in 1937.[102] As to defense, the Supreme Court and lower federal courts have determined that some controversies involving national security are not open to judicial review, relying on the political questions and act of state doctrines.[103] Moreover, even when the Court does adjudicate disputes involving national defense, it tends to be deferential to the president's foreign policy priorities.[104] Consequently, the Court has a more

just the increased public attention to national security in the post–September 11, 2001 era, but also the Court's subsequent and unusual foray into a variety of cases involving national defense, such as those relating to appeals from individuals detained in Guantanamo Bay, Cuba.

[100] See, e.g., Baumgartner and Jones, "Policy Agendas Project," supra, n. 66. Thomas Brennan, Lee Epstein, and Nancy Staudt, "The Political Economy of Judging," 93 *Minnesota Law Review* 1503 (2009); Lee Epstein, Daniel E. Ho, Gary King, and Jeffrey A. Segal, "The Supreme Court During Crisis: How War Affects Only Non-War Cases," 80 *New York University Law Review* 1 (2005); Kimi Lynn King and James Meernik, "The Supreme Court and the Powers of the Executive: The Adjudication of Foreign Policy," 52 *Political Research Quarterly* 801 (1999); Spaeth, *The Original United States Supreme Court Database*, supra, n. 75.

[101] See, e.g., Brennan, Epstein, and Staudt, "The Political Economy of Judging," supra, n. 91; Epstein, Ho, King, and Segal, "The Supreme Court During Crisis," supra, n. 91; Michael P. Fix and Kirk A. Randazzo, "Judicial Deference and National Security: Applications of the Political Question and Act of State Doctrines," 6 *Democracy and Security* 1 (2010); Kirk A. Randazzo, "When Liberty and Security Collide: Foreign Policy Litigation and the Federal Judiciary," 94 *Kentucky Law Journal* 629 (2005); Ernest A. Young and Erin C. Blondel, "Does the Supreme Court Follow the Economic Returns? A Response to A *Macrotheory of the Court*," 58 *Duke Law Journal* 1759 (2009).

[102] See, e.g., Tony Caporale, and Harold Winter, "A Positive Political Model of Supreme Court Economic Decisions," 68 *Southern Economic Journal* 693 (2002); McCloskey, "Economic Due Process and the Supreme Court," supra, n. 88; Nagel, "Court-Curbing Periods in American History," supra, n. 88; Pablo T. Spiller and Rafael Gely, "Congressional Control or Judicial Independence: The Determinants of U.S. Supreme Court Labor-Relations Decisions, 1949–1988," 23 *RAND Journal of Economics* 463 (1992).

[103] See, e.g., Fix and Randazzo, "Judicial Deference and National Security," supra, n. 92. Briefly stated, the political questions doctrine holds that the federal courts should not decide issues that are more properly under the purview of the elected branches of government, and the act of state doctrine asserts that the federal courts should not hear cases that implicate the actions of sovereign foreign nations.

[104] See, e.g., King and Meernik, "The Supreme Court and the Powers of the Executive," supra, n. 91.

limited role in the province of economic and national defense policy than in the other issue areas contained in our data set.

Moreover, when the average American thinks about the most important problems facing the nation, it is unlikely that he or she does so primarily with an eye toward the constitutionality of government programs related to these issues. Instead, responses to the "most important problem" question track broad issues of general importance to society as a whole or to the individual survey respondent.[105] With regard to the economy and national defense, a number of questions may cross a respondent's mind. Americans who view the question in broad, national terms may ask themselves questions such as: Will the country recover from the recession? Will the dollar be devalued? Will the nation face a nuclear attack from North Korea or Iran? Will the events of September 11th happen again? Those citizens who view the question at a more personal level may ask things like: Will I be able to feed my family? Will I be able to send my children to college? Will my son return home safely from Afghanistan? Will my family be safe from terrorist attacks if I move to a major city? When Americans search for answers to such questions, it is doubtful they turn to the Supreme Court.

To evaluate more rigorously whether the influence of public opinion is being diminished by the inclusion of economic and national security issues in the empirical model, we reestimated our statistical model excluding these topics, the results of which appear in Table 3.3. This model provides strong support for our contention that the inclusion of economic and national security issues dampens the substantive impact of the *Public Opinion* variable. When we exclude these issues from the data set, the coefficient for the *Public Opinion* variable nearly triples in size. With this exception, the results in Table 3.3 are consistent with those of Table 3.2. That is, we provide evidence that hearing dialogue reflects public opinion, legislation, Supreme Court precedent, and salient Supreme Court precedent, but not media attention to an issue area.

To more clearly see the substantive effects of this model, Figure 3.4 plots the influence of the significant variables in Table 3.3 on the predicted percentage of dialogue involving each issue at the hearings, excluding macroeconomics and defense. As before, the *Legislation* variable has the strongest relative impact on hearing discussion. A 5% increase in congressional legislation in an area is predicted to generate a 10.3 percentage point increase in dialogue concerning the issue area.[106] Most significantly, however, we find that public opinion now

---

[105] See, e.g., Smith, "America's Most Important Problem," supra, n. 66; Smith, "America's Most Important Problem," supra, n. 87; Wlezien, "On the Salience of Political Issues," supra, n. 87.

[106] Once economics and national defense issues are removed from the data, summary statistics for the independent variables are as follows: Public Opinion (mean = 2.47, standard

TABLE 3.3. *The influence of public opinion and precedent on the issues discussed at Supreme Court confirmation hearings, excluding macroeconomics and defense, 1955–2006*

Variable	Expected direction	Coefficient
Public Opinion	+	1.196***
		(0.300)
Media Coverage	+	−0.276
		(0.243)
Legislation	+	1.957***
		(0.423)
Supreme Court Precedent	+	1.202***
		(0.372)
Salient Supreme Court Precedent	+	0.981***
		(0.217)
Constant		−46.494***
		(8.545)
McKelvey and Zavoina R-squared		0.442
F-test		23.16***
N		476

The dependent variable is the percentage of discussion at each nominee's confirmation hearing involving the issue areas identified in Table 3.1, excluding macroeconomics and defense. Entries are Tobit coefficients. Numbers in parentheses are robust standard errors, clustered on each hearing. ***$P \leq .01$ (two-tailed tests).

exerts the second strongest influence on hearing discussion, tied with Supreme Court precedent.[107]

Specifically, Figure 3.4 reveals that a 5% increase in the percentage of the American public identifying an issue as the nation's most important problem leads to a 4 percentage point increase in attention to that issue area at the hearings. Thus, there now is almost a 1:1 ratio in terms of how public opinion translates to hearing dialogue. That is, for every 1% increase in the percentage of the public identifying an issue as the country's most important problem, there is, after accounting for the Court's reduced role in economic and national

deviation = 5.77, minimum = 0, maximum = 43.23); Media Coverage (mean = 4.03, standard deviation = 4.69, minimum = 0.148, maximum = 27.92); Legislation (mean = 4.99, standard deviation = 4.23, minimum = 0, maximum = 30.09); Supreme Court Precedent (mean = 5.67, standard deviation = 8.29, minimum = 0, maximum = 42.05), Salient Supreme Court Precedent (mean = 5.60, standard deviation = 10.95, minimum = 0, maximum = 51.43).

[107] Although the marginal effect of the Public Opinion variable is slightly greater than that of the Supreme Court Precedent variable, a statistical test indicates that the coefficients for these variables are indistinguishable from one another ($F = 0$, $P = 0.99$). In other words, this difference is not statistically significant.

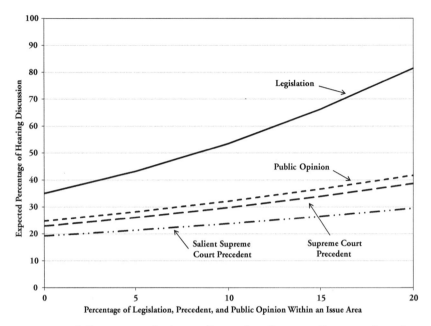

FIGURE 3.4. Influences on the issues discussed at Supreme Court confirmation hearings, excluding macroeconomics and defense, 1955–2006. *Note:* The figure represents the marginal effects of the Public Opinion, Legislation, Supreme Court Precedent, and Salient Supreme Court Precedent variables on the predicted value of the dependent variable, excluding macroeconomics and defense, holding all other variables at their mean values.

defense issues, an approximately 0.8 percentage point increase in attention to that issue area at the hearings.

As before, we continue to find that hearing dialogue tracks Supreme Court precedent. A 5% increase in the percentage of precedents in an issue area is predicted to have a 3.7 percentage point increase in hearing dialogue. With regard to landmark precedent, we find that a 5% increase in salient precedents in a given issue area results in a 2.4 percentage point increase in hearing dialogue devoted to that issue area. Taken as a whole, it is clear that the senators involved in confirmation hearings are responsive to both public opinion and Supreme Court precedent, and this is especially evident once the Court's limited role in economic and national defense policy is recognized.

CONCLUSIONS

A casual observer of Supreme Court confirmation hearings might be tempted to think that the hearings are so nominee specific that they cannot be explained through a general theoretical framework. After all, Sonia Sotomayor was asked repeatedly about her "wise Latina" remark; William Rehnquist was interrogated about a memo he wrote arguing that *Plessy v. Ferguson*[108] should not be overturned; and William Brennan was grilled about his alleged communist sympathies. Examples such as these could lead one to conclude that such situation-specific events drive the bulk of confirmation dialogue. The data, however, show otherwise. Although some of the topics discussed at the hearings are idiosyncratic to the specific nominee, we have demonstrated that the issues addressed at confirmation hearings are in fact quite predictable, and that they closely track both public opinion and Supreme Court precedent. Moreover, we suspect that even those nominee-specific issues that capture senatorial attention do so *because* they touch upon issues – affirmative action, racial integration, and antigovernment activities – that are *already* highly salient to the public. Even issues we think of as idiosyncratic, in other words, become confirmation issues only when they resonate with areas of public concern.

Because we believe that confirmation hearings are a key point at which the American people take ownership of the Constitution, we expected senators to question nominees on the salient political issues of the day, and they do: our empirical models reveal that senators' questions closely reflect contemporary legal and political debates relevant to the Court's role in the American political system. We thus have provided a novel window into how the public influences constitutional change. This finding is essential to our perspective that the hearings afford the American people a meaningful opportunity to shape constitutional development in that it demonstrates the democratic nature of the hearings. Indeed, it is difficult to imagine a situation in which the hearings provide the occasion for public input into the ratification of constitutional change absent a link between public opinion and hearing dialogue.

This link between public opinion and hearing discourse also provides a window into the operation of representative government in the United States. The extent to which government is responsive to the public's preferences has long been a focal point of normative democratic theory and for good reason. If government institutions, such as the U.S. Senate, do not respond to the concerns of the citizenry, the notion of representative government is little more than a façade. Although some have provided theories and evidence for why institutions might respond to public opinion,[109] others posit that political institutions have failed to live up to their promise as outlets for representative

---

[108] Plessy v. Ferguson, 163 U.S. 537 (1896).

[109] See, e.g., Anthony Downs, *An Economic Theory of Democracy* (New York: Harper and Row, 1957); Erikson, MacKuen, and Stimson, *The Macro Polity*, supra, n. 44; Jones and Baumgartner, "Representation and Agenda Setting," supra, n. 44; Manza and Cook, "A Democratic Polity?," supra, n. 44; Monroe, "Public Opinion and Public Policy," supra, n. 44; Page and Shapiro, "Effects of Public Opinion on Policy," supra, n. 44.

democracy, frequently pointing to the power wielded by interest groups[110] or the self-interested concerns of political actors.[111] Our empirical evidence stands in stark contrast to claims made by the latter, in that it evinces a powerful link between the preferences of the citizenry and the actions taken by members of the Senate Judiciary Committee. We thus join a host of scholars in demonstrating that political actors are influenced by public opinion.[112]

These findings are also of note in that they illustrate that senators are responsive to the public in a context other than how we traditionally think about the roles of legislators, such as sponsoring legislation and voting.[113] To the extent that confirmation hearings are especially visible forums, frequently sparking intense national debate and voluminous media coverage, this should not be surprising. That is, the high-profile nature of the hearings provides powerful incentives for members of the Judiciary Committee to probe nominees on the pressing issues of the day, allowing them to demonstrate, in a highly public manner, that they are in touch with the concerns of the American citizenry. Thus, just as senators can employ roll call votes on nominations to enhance their reelection prospects,[114] so too can they use their questions at the hearings to do so.

Also of interest is our finding that members of the Judiciary Committee attend to changes in national opinion, rather than solely responding to the preferences of their individual constituencies. This suggests that senators view their role on the Judiciary Committee as more than representing their individual states. Instead, Committee members are in tune with the concerns of citizens across the country and are willing to question nominees on behalf of the nation as a whole. This is perhaps to be expected in that senators represent the largest legislative constituencies in the nation, thus compelling them to be especially attentive to national concerns.[115] This is particularly important

---

[110] See, e.g., E. E. Schattschneider, *The Semisovereign People: A Realist's View of Democracy in America* (New York: Holt, Rinehart, and Winston, 1960).

[111] See, e.g., C. Wright Mills, *The Power Elite* (Oxford: Oxford University Press, 1956).

[112] See, e.g., Dahl, "Decision-Making in a Democracy," supra, n. 14; Erikson, MacKuen, and Stimson, *The Macro Polity*, supra, n. 44; Friedman, *The Will of the People*, supra, n. 14; Jones and Baumgartner, "Representation and Agenda Setting," supra, n. 44; Manza and Cook, "A Democratic Polity?," supra, n. 44; Monroe, "Public Opinion and Public Policy," supra, n. 44; Page and Shapiro, "Effects of Public Opinion on Policy," supra, n. 44.

[113] See, e.g., Scott R. Meinke, "Institutional Change and the Electoral Connection in the Senate: Revisiting the Effects of Direct Election," 61 *Political Research Quarterly* 445 (2008).

[114] Charles M. Cameron, Albert D. Cover and Jeffrey A. Segal, "Senate Voting on Supreme Court Nominees: A Neoinstitutional Model," 84 *American Political Science Review* 525 (1990).

[115] See, e.g., Lonna Rae Atkeson and Randall W. Partin, "Economic and Referendum Voting: A Comparison of Gubernatorial and Senatorial Elections," 89 *American Political Science Review* 99 (1995).

for members of the Judiciary Committee, who are active participants in the processes of determining who can and cannot interpret the Constitution on behalf of all of us.[116]

In addition, we have investigated the extent to which Supreme Court precedents influence confirmation dialogue. We proposed that the Court's precedents contribute to the constitutional colloquy that takes place during the hearings, thereby providing an opportunity for the American public to debate the wisdom of those decisions. As with the role of public opinion, our expectations were confirmed by the data: we found that confirmation dialogue closely reflects the Court's precedents. Thus, we have provided additional insight into the impact of the Court's decisions on the functioning of government. Although some question whether courts can contribute to social change,[117] our findings reveal that the Court's precedents play a major role in how we evaluate and judge its future members. It is therefore clear that the Court's decisions do help shape public dialogue regarding constitutional development, which is on vivid display at the confirmation hearings.

As we argue throughout this book, Supreme Court confirmation hearings provide a democratic forum for the discussion and ratification of constitutional change. For this to work, it is essential that public concerns are conveyed to future justices and that hearing dialogue is motivated by the Court's decisions. The former ensures the hearings are democratic, while the latter speaks to the ability of the hearings to act as forums for meaningful discussions about the Court's constitutional choices. The fundamental purpose of this chapter was to illustrate that the hearings serve these two roles. Having established that confirmation hearing discourse closely reflects both public opinion and Supreme Court precedents, the two chapters that follow address these issues in closer detail. In Chapter 4, we explore more thoroughly the issues discussed at confirmation hearings, while Chapter 5 sheds light on the precedents that are accepted, refuted, and debated at the hearings.

---

[116] We make these statements with the caveat that we are unable to test for the influence of state-level public opinion on hearing dialogue because of data limitations. That is, Gallup Poll data on the most important problem question do not exist at the state level for the time period under analysis in this chapter. Should such data become available, this would be a most fruitful avenue for future research.

[117] See, e.g., Donald L. Horowitz, *The Courts and Social Policy* (Washington, DC: Brookings Institution, 1977); Rosenberg, *The Hollow Hope*, supra, n. 17; Stuart A. Scheingold, *The Politics of Rights: Lawyers, Public Policy, and Political Change* (New Haven, CT: Yale University Press, 1974).

4

An Issue-by-Issue Look at the Hearings

Issues are important. We evaluate candidates for political office based on our perceptions of how well those individuals handle particular issues.[1] We think about political parties in terms of their devotion to, and competence in, policy domains.[2] We talk about media bias in terms of the media's attention to particular issues.[3] Because issues are so important, we routinely describe the work of the executive, legislative, and judicial branches with regard to the policies on their agendas.[4] We point to Franklin Delano Roosevelt's economic programs during the New Deal; congressional legislation relating to civil rights issues in the 1960s; and the Warren Court's revolution in criminal procedure in the same era. Issues, in short, are central to our understanding of public policy: when we debate matters of public policy, we do so with an eye toward the issues most meaningful to us. Issues are the currency of how we think about the legal and political systems.

Thus far, we have treated the issues discussed at Supreme Court confirmation hearings somewhat abstractly, focusing on the factors that cause increased or decreased attention to a given issue area. The purpose of this chapter is to move beyond this abstraction by showing exactly what issues are addressed at confirmation hearings, and how those issues have changed over time. In

---

[1] See, e.g., Edward G. Carmines and James A. Stimson, "The Two Faces of Issue Voting," 74 *American Political Science Review* 78 (1980).

[2] See, e.g., John R. Petrocik, "Issue Ownership in Presidential Elections, with a 1980 Case Study," 40 *American Journal of Political Science* 825 (1996).

[3] See, e.g., Dave D'Alessio and Mike Allen, "Media Bias in Presidential Elections: A Meta-Analysis," 50 *Journal of Communication* 133 (2000).

[4] See, e.g., Matthew Eshbaugh-Soha, "The Politics of Presidential Agendas," 58 *Political Research Quarterly* 257 (2005); Bryan D. Jones and Frank R. Baumgartner, "Representation and Agenda Setting," 32 *Policy Studies Journal* 1 (2004); Richard L. Pacelle, Jr., *The Transformation of the Supreme Court's Agenda: From the New Deal to the Reagan Administration* (Boulder, CO: Westview Press, 1991).

doing so, we illuminate how the confirmation hearings can function as a forum through which senators debate the appropriate meaning of our Constitution, testing constitutional alternatives while attempting to convince the nominees – and the country – to adopt their preferred positions.

Our findings paint an interesting picture, one that again evidences both continuity and change in confirmation dialogue. For example, we show how racial discrimination, once a focal point of hearing colloquy, has waned over time as our society has reached a consensus that the Constitution proscribes intentional discrimination by state actors against racial minorities. As comments regarding racial discrimination declined, statements about gender and sexual orientation discrimination arrived to fill the gap, corresponding to the hearty constitutional debate surrounding discrimination on those grounds that has appeared in more recent years. Thus, although the issues discussed frequently change, they tend to do so consistent with the attention devoted to them among the American public.

We begin the chapter with an overview showing just what it is that the senators and nominees spend their time talking about at the hearings. The chapter then examines how hearing dialogue about the most frequently addressed issues has changed over time. These issues include civil rights; hearing administration; nominee background; judicial philosophy; and law, crime, and family issues. Because civil rights is the most frequently addressed issue at the hearings, we devote particular attention to examining this issue area, providing an in-depth look at the subissues discussed within it, including racial and gender discrimination, the right to privacy (both in general and pertaining to abortion), and the freedoms of speech and religion. As a whole, this chapter sheds light on how our constitutional commitments, as well as our constitutional debates, have evolved over time.

AN OVERVIEW OF CONFIRMATION HEARING DIALOGUE

Chapter 3 demonstrated that the questions senators ask closely follow changes in public attention to the relevant issues of the day and to Supreme Court precedent. Although Chapter 3 was essential to establishing this empirical relationship, it did not address in detail the topics that are actually discussed at the hearings. In other words, we know from Chapter 3 that public opinion and Supreme Court precedent influence hearing dialogue, but we do not know what issues constitute that dialogue.

This chapter breaks new ground in the story of the confirmation process by going beyond anecdotal and impressionist accounts and reporting the actual issues addressed at the hearings by both senators and nominees. Our data extend from 1939 to 2010. Although a full discussion of the data appears in the Appendix, a few brief words are warranted here. First, the unit of analysis in the data is the change of speaker, meaning that we have coded a new observation whenever the speaker changes. For example, the following exchange between Senator Kennedy (D-MA) and John Paul Stevens constitutes two observations in the data, one for Kennedy and one for Stevens:

> **Senator KENNEDY:** I'm just trying to find out how concerned you are about the question of sex discrimination. Would you say that you have been more disturbed by discrimination against blacks rather than women? Or, are you equally disturbed about both? Is this a matter that you feel that the American people are very much interested in and concerned about? What can you tell us of your own views about the subject?

> **Judge STEVENS:** Well, I am certainly concerned, and I agree that the American people are and should be concerned. I have not thought in terms of placing priorities; two wrongs, both of which we want to eliminate completely, if we possibly can. I suppose, if I am asked to do so, I would be more concerned about the racial discrimination because I think they are a more disadvantaged group in the history of our country than the half the population that is female.[5]

We have coded each statement according its primary issue and any relevant subissues. A single observation can have only one issue, but it may have multiple subissues. For example, in the preceding conversation between Kennedy and Stevens, the main issue is "civil rights," while the subissues are "racial discrimination" and "gender/sexual orientation discrimination."[6] Finally, note that senatorial and nominee comments are coded separately and therefore need not (although usually do, as in the preceding example) involve the same issue and subissue(s). The purpose of coding statements made by nominees and senators separately is to recognize that on occasion the issues discussed in a line of questioning may change from speaker to speaker. Distinguishing comments made by nominees from those made by senators also allows us to investigate the extent to which the topics discussed by senators and nominees differ.

---

[5] Stevens transcript, questioning by Senator Kennedy (D-MA) at 16.

[6] In the interest of brevity, we have shortened the names of several of the issue and subissue categories in the tables and figures presented in the remainder of this book from their full names used in the Policy Agendas Project codebook. Frank Baumgartner and Bryan Jones, "Policy Agendas Project." Retrieved from: http://www.policyagendas.org/index.html (Accessed August 20, 2010). Specifically, we refer to "Civil Rights, Minority Issues, and Civil Liberties" as "Civil Rights;" "Labor, Employment, and Immigration" as "Labor and Employment;" "Banking, Finance, and Domestic Commerce" as "Banking and Finance;" and "Ethnic Minority and Racial Group Discrimination" as "Racial Discrimination."

TABLE 4.1. *The issues addressed at the Senate Judiciary Committee confirmation hearings of Supreme Court nominees, 1939–2010*

Issue	Senators	Nominees	Total
Civil Rights	25.7 (4,623)	32.2 (4,335)	28.5 (8,958)
Hearing Administration	27.6 (4,950)	10.2 (1,348)	20.0 (6,298)
Nominee Background	14.8 (2,663)	17.5 (2,351)	16.0 (5,014)
Judicial Philosophy	11.3 (2,026)	14.2 (1,903)	12.5 (3,929)
Law, Crime, and Family	7.1 (1,273)	8.9 (1,202)	7.9 (2,475)
Government Operations	3.4 (611)	4.2 (570)	3.8 (1,181)
Court Administration	2.9 (528)	3.7 (501)	3.3 (1,029)
Federalism	1.2 (220)	1.6 (214)	1.4 (434)
Labor and Employment	0.9 (161)	1.2 (156)	1.0 (317)
Statutory Interpretation	0.8 (147)	1.1 (150)	1.0 (297)
Banking and Finance	0.7 (130)	0.9 (127)	0.8 (257)
National Defense	0.7 (125)	0.9 (116)	0.8 (241)
Standing/Access to Courts	0.5 (96)	0.6 (89)	0.6 (185)
Best/Favorite Justices	0.3 (60)	0.5 (70)	0.4 (130)
Other Issues	2.0 (356)	2.4 (320)	2.2 (676)
Totals	99.9 (17,969)	100.1 (13,452)	100.2 (31,421)

The column entries represent the percentage of comments regarding each issue area. The percentages do not necessarily sum to 100% due to rounding. The numbers in parentheses indicate the total number of comments pertaining to each issue area. Issue areas representing less than 0.4% of the total column are combined into the "Other Issues" category.

Table 4.1 reports the issues addressed by senators and nominees who appeared before the Senate Judiciary Committee from 1939 to 2010. The issue areas appear in the first column; the percentage of statements made by senators and nominees corresponding to each issue area is reported in the second and third columns, respectively; and the fourth column provides the total percentage of comments involving each topic.

As this table illustrates, the most common issue area addressed at the hearings is civil rights. Civil rights dialogue constitutes 26% of all senatorial comments and 32% of all nominee comments contained in the data set. Taking senatorial and nominee comments together, statements about civil rights thus comprise 29% of all of our observations. Civil rights statements typically pertain to racial, gender, age, and sexual orientation discrimination; freedoms of speech and religion; the right to privacy (involving both abortion and non-abortion matters); voting rights; antigovernment activities; and the right to keep and bear arms.

The next most frequently addressed issue area involves hearing administration. Not surprisingly, this is where we see the biggest gap between the comments made by nominees and senators. Twenty-eight percent of senatorial comments involve hearing administration, whereas only 10% of nominee statements touch on hearing administration. This vast difference is largely explainable by the fact that this category contains administrative matters, such as the scheduling of breaks and other hearing logistics, which are initiated by senators, as opposed to nominees. In addition, this category includes social chit chat and nonsubstantive clarifications such as "excuse me," or "could you repeat that?"

Discussions of the nominees' backgrounds make up the third most frequently addressed category at the hearings. Fifteen percent of the senators' comments are about the nominees' backgrounds, and nominees devote 18% of their statements to similar discussions. These exchanges typically pertain to the nominees' education, prior employment (including any previous judicial posts), health, and family. They also quite often include ethical concerns senators believe (or claim to believe) are relevant to the nominee's fitness for office.

Table 4.1 also reveals that two additional substantive issues have played a large role in the hearings: judicial philosophy and law, crime, and family. Judicial philosophy, which includes comments about methods of constitutional interpretation, *stare decisis*, the role of the Court, and "judicial activism," constitutes 13% of all comments. Law, crime, and family issues round out the top four substantive areas, accounting for 8% of total comments. Although law, crime, and family is a seemingly broad category, in fact, this issue area is absolutely dominated by discussions of criminal justice, including treatments of criminal procedure, such as *Miranda* rights, double jeopardy, and due process (71%); capital punishment (17%); and executive branch agencies dealing with law and crime, such as the Department of Justice and the Federal Bureau of Investigation (6%).[7] The remaining issue areas reported in Table 4.1 are discussed relatively infrequently, with no single issue area representing more than 4% of hearing commentary.

Looking at Table 4.1, the importance of civil rights issues at the hearings is immediately apparent. This category comprised more statements at the hearings than did even administrative matters. The second thing of note is the *relatively* small role played by comments involving judicial philosophy. Although this substantive issue area is one of the top four such issue areas addressed at the hearings, Table 4.1 shows that it nonetheless constitutes less than 13% of all hearing statements. Even when the nonsubstantive hearing administration category is excluded, fewer than 16% of all comments made at

---

[7] The "family" part of this category includes discussion of, for example, domestic violence and child abuse.

the hearings address issues of judicial philosophy – barely half the number of comments involving civil rights issues. Our data thus demonstrate that, despite the hopes of many reformers,[8] the senators seem to have relatively little interest in limiting their discussion to abstract concepts of interpretation, preferring instead to focus their energies on more concrete inquires.

Table 4.1 thus illustrates that five issue areas have dominated the hearings: civil rights; hearing administration; nominee background; judicial philosophy; and law, crime, and family. As we show in Table 4.2, these issues have dominated not just the hearings overall, but the hearings of most individual nominees as well.

Table 4.2 reports the most frequently addressed issue area by nominee, excluding the nonsubstantive hearing administration category. The nominees are listed in the first column, and the second and third columns identify the issue most commonly canvassed by senators and nominees, respectively. Civil rights has been the most frequently discussed issue area at all but one of the hearings since 1971 and at seventeen of the thirty-two hearings in our data set.[9] Nominee background was the most discussed issue at eight of the hearings; law, crime, and family was the most discussed issue at three of the hearings; and judicial philosophy dominated two of them. Only two hearings, those of Byron White (1962) and Warren Burger (1969), were monopolized by issues other than these four. White's hearing focused on issues of standing and access to courts, and Burger's hearing for chief justice devoted a substantial amount of attention to issues implicating judicial administration.[10] As we demonstrate in the text that follows, the amount of hearing dialogue dedicated to an issue

---

[8] See, e.g., Ronald Dworkin, "Justice Sotomayor: The Unjust Hearings," *The New York Review of Books*, September 2, 2009; Robert F. Nagel, "Advice, Consent, and Influence," 84 *Northwestern University Law Review* 858 (1990); Denis Steven Rutkus, "CRS Report for Congress: Proper Scope of Questioning of Supreme Court Nominees: The Current Debate" (2009). Retrieved from: http://assets.opencrs.com/rpts/RL33059_20050901.pdf (Accessed October 4, 2012).

[9] The exception is Rehnquist's 1986 Chief Justice hearing. During that hearing, discussions of Rehnquist's background comprised 29% of comments, compared to 28% for civil rights. Much of the discussion of Justice Rehnquist's background, however, involved accusations that he had been involved in various efforts to harass voters in largely African American neighborhoods. These accusations had obvious civil rights implications, so the attention given to civil rights issues at his chief justice hearings is almost certainly understated in our data.

[10] Two hearings, those of Rehnquist in 1986 and White in 1962, exhibit discrepancies between the most frequently addressed issues for nominees and Senators. During the Rehnquist hearing, senators addressed the nominee's background in 24.1% of their questions (compared to 24.3% for civil rights), whereas Rehnquist spoke to his background in 36% of his statements. At the White hearing, senators engaged the nominee in discussions of his background in 28% of comments, whereas White discussed his background in 29% of his statements (compared to 43% for matters of standing and access to courts). Thus, although strictly speaking there are differences between the most frequently addressed issues at these hearings depending on

TABLE 4.2. *The most frequently addressed issues at the Senate Judiciary Committee confirmation hearings of Supreme Court nominees, 1939–2010*

Nominee name (Year)	Senators (%)	Nominees (%)
Frankfurter (1939)	Nominee Background (36.2)	Nominee Background (47.0)
Jackson (1941)	Law, Crime, and Family (78.1)	Law, Crime, and Family (97.0)
Harlan (1955)	Nominee Background (33.6)	Nominee Background (53.6)
Brennan (1957)	Civil Rights (50.2)	Civil Rights (58.6)
Whittaker (1957)	Nominee Background (62.2)	Nominee Background (78.9)
Stewart (1959)	Judicial Philosophy (29.6)	Judicial Philosophy (48.8)
White (1962)	Nominee Background (28.1)	Standing/Access to Courts (42.9)
Goldberg (1962)	Judicial Philosophy (29.8)	Judicial Philosophy (47.8)
Fortas (1965)	Nominee Background (31.5)	Nominee Background (42.4)
Marshall (1967)	Law, Crime, and Family (46.7)	Law, Crime, and Family (52.5)
Fortas (1968)	Law, Crime, and Family (21.4)	Law, Crime, and Family (23.9)
Thornberry (1968)	Civil Rights (40.4)	Civil Rights (58.0)
Burger (1969)	Judicial Administration (25.6)	Judicial Administration (41.7)
Haynsworth (1969)	Nominee Background (74.8)	Nominee Background (82.6)
Carswell (1970)	Nominee Background (32.8)	Nominee Background (40.9)
Blackmun (1970)	Nominee Background (27.9)	Nominee Background (43.3)
Rehnquist (1971)	Civil Rights (31.6)	Civil Rights (38.5)
Powell (1971)	Civil Rights (47.7)	Civil Rights (54.6)
Stevens (1975)	Civil Rights (22.0)	Civil Rights (23.9)
O'Connor (1981)	Civil Rights (23.7)	Civil Rights (28.2)
Rehnquist (1986)	Civil Rights (24.3)	Nominee Background (36.2)
Scalia (1986)	Civil Rights (26.2)	Civil Rights (32.9)
Bork (1987)	Civil Rights (36.9)	Civil Rights (45.2)
Kennedy (1987)	Civil Rights (24.7)	Civil Rights (28.2)
Souter (1990)	Civil Rights (30.0)	Civil Rights (36.9)
Thomas (1991)	Civil Rights (31.9)	Civil Rights (44.9)
Ginsburg (1993)	Civil Rights (28.1)	Civil Rights (40.0)
Breyer (1994)	Civil Rights (21.3)	Civil Rights (27.2)
Roberts (2005)	Civil Rights (37.7)	Civil Rights (44.0)
Alito (2006)	Civil Rights (21.2)	Civil Rights (25.6)
Sotomayor (2009)	Civil Rights (25.7)	Civil Rights (33.1)
Kagan (2010)	Civil Rights (21.5)	Civil Rights (24.7)

The numbers in parentheses indicate the percentage of comments represented by the most frequently addressed issue area at each hearing. Discussions of hearing administration are excluded from this table.

area very much reflects the salience of that issue area in the legal and political spheres at the time of the confirmation hearing.

whether the speaker is the senator or nominee, the substantive distinctions between the most frequently addressed topics are not especially meaningful.

A CLOSER LOOK AT CONFIRMATION HEARING DIALOGUE

Tables 4.1 and 4.2 demonstrate which issue areas were most frequently discussed at the hearings overall and at the hearing of each individual nominee. They do not, however, tell us how the discussion of these issues has changed over time. Identifying such temporal changes is key to illustrating the role the hearings play in debating and ratifying constitutional change. We therefore provide a more fine-grained analysis of those temporal changes within the five most frequently occurring issue areas at the hearings: civil rights; hearing administration; nominee background; judicial philosophy; and law, crime, and family. In doing so, we also break down the civil rights category and examine how attention to the various subissues within this issue area has changed over time.

Civil Rights

For much of the twentieth century, constitutional discourse in America *was* civil rights discourse. The opaque phrases of the First and Fourteenth Amendments in particular have generated some of our most noble constitutional moments, as well as many of our most bitter constitutional disputes. This century was marked by the rise of the civil rights movement, resulting in major congressional legislation addressing inequalities in the American political system, such as the Civil Rights Act of 1964 and the Voting Rights Act of 1965. Much of the Supreme Court's agenda in this era reflects this increased attention to civil rights.[11] It is not a surprise, then, that civil rights issues play a dominate role in a data set comprising almost exclusively twentieth-century hearings.

Figure 4.1 presents the percentage of comments regarding civil rights made by senators and nominees from 1939 to 2010. In this figure, and in those that follow, the nominees are arranged along the vertical *y*-axis, while the horizontal *x*-axis represents the percentage of comments involving civil rights. The percentages of comments made by nominees are indicated by the white bars, and comments from senators are denoted by the black bars.

As shown in Figure 4.1, civil rights has dominated the substantive issue areas covered at the hearings overall, and has done so with particular force since 1971.

---

[11] See, e.g., Robert G. McCloskey, *The American Supreme Court* (Chicago: University of Chicago Press, 2004); Pacelle, *The Transformation of the Supreme Court's Agenda*, supra, n. 4; Doris Marie Provine, *Case Selection in the United States Supreme Court* (Chicago: University of Chicago Press, 1980); Jeffrey A. Segal and Harold J. Spaeth, *The Supreme Court and the Attitudinal Model Revisited* (New York: Cambridge University Press, 2002) at 141.

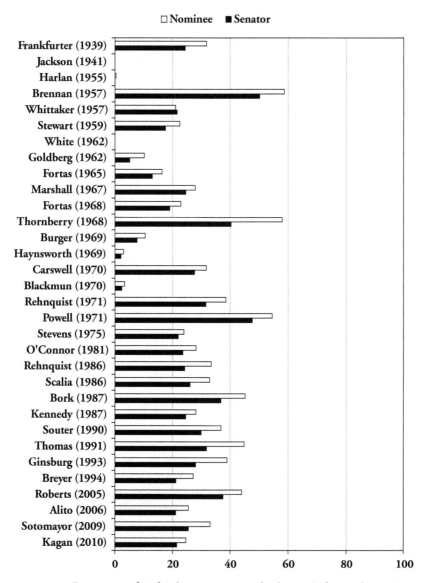

FIGURE 4.1. Percentage of civil rights comments at the Senate Judiciary Committee confirmation hearings of Supreme Court nominees, 1939–2010.

Although there was notable variation in the pre-1971 era, with the Jackson (1941) and White (1962) hearings containing no discussion of civil rights (and the Harlan hearing containing less than 1% of discussion on civil rights), it is apparent that civil rights has been an essential part of the confirmation hearings for some time. In fact, since 1971, interrogation by senators regarding a nominee's views of the pressing civil rights issues of the day has never constituted less than 20% of all questions asked at the hearings.

The dominance of civil rights comments is particularly remarkable given that the number of comments likely to have been motivated by civil rights concerns may be somewhat understated in the data. It is not unusual for senators to present substantive concerns about an issue area in comments that are, under our coding rules, identified as involving "judicial philosophy." The most obvious example of this is the 1959 hearing of Potter Stewart. Stewart was nominated just five years after the Court's landmark *Brown v. Board of Education*[12] decision (striking down the "separate but equal" doctrine) and his hearing was held at a time when *Brown* was still seen by many as an egregious overreaching by the Supreme Court. In this political environment, Stewart was bombarded with questions from southern Democrats about the dangers of judges replacing "the law" with their "personal notions" of good policy, the problem of judges trying to "amend" the Constitution, and the importance of *stare decisis*.

It seems unlikely that these comments, coming at the time and from the senators that they did, were unrelated to *Brown*. Indeed, the senators at the Stewart hearing often made the connection with *Brown* explicit. Consider, for example, the following question by Senator McClellan (D-AR), which was posed three times at the hearing:

> Do you agree with the premise used, the reasoning and logic applied, or the lack of application of either or both as the case may be, and the philosophy expressed by the Supreme Court in arriving at its decision in the case of *Brown vs. Board of Education* on May 7, 1954?[13]

Often, however, the senators did *not* link their inquiries about *Brown* so directly to their comments about judicial philosophy. Consider this question by Senator Johnston (D) of South Carolina: "Are you going to be what you call a 'creative judge' or are you going to to [sic] follow the law and the precedent?"[14] Under our coding rules, Senator McClellan's comment would be coded as involving civil rights, while Senator Johnston's would be coded as one of judicial philosophy. This is so despite the fact that Senator Johnston's statement is as likely to have been motivated by *Brown* (which he discussed shortly after the exchange in which the aforementioned comment appears) as

---

[12] Brown v. Board of Education, 347 U.S. 483 (1954).
[13] Stewart transcript, questioning by Senator McClellan (D-AR) at 34, 56, 62.
[14] Stewart transcript, questioning by Senator Johnston (D-SC) at 20–1.

was Senator McClellan's. We cannot presume to accurately perceive senatorial motivations, however, so comments such as Johnston's that are not articulated as civil rights issues are coded in our data as raising issues of judicial philosophy rather than civil rights.[15] Thus, the actual number of comments in fact motivated by concerns about civil rights may be higher than is reflected in our data.

Regardless, civil rights issues clearly have, even under our conservative coding regime, dominated the hearings. Civil rights, however, is a broad issue area. It includes race, gender, age, and disability discrimination; speech and religious freedoms; and the right to keep and bear arms. To understand more fully the role this issue area has played in the hearings, it is therefore worth examining the prevalence and distribution of the subissues within it. We present this information in Table 4.3. The civil rights issue areas appear in the first column; the percentage of statements made by senators and nominees corresponding to each issue area is reported in the second and third columns, respectively; and the fourth column provides the total percentage of comments involving each civil rights issue.

As Table 4.3 illustrates, statements involving discrimination constitute a plurality of comments within the civil rights issue area. Specifically, discussions of racial discrimination comprise 23% of civil rights comments; gender and sexual orientation discrimination constitute an additional 13%; and age and disability discrimination add 2%. Combined, dialogue involving discrimination thus constitutes 37% of the comments within the civil rights issue area. Freedom of speech and religion is the next most commonly discussed civil rights subissue, followed by non-abortion privacy (13%) and, at only 12% of the issue area, abortion rights. Dialogue implicating voting rights represents 9% of the civil rights category, while treatments of antigovernment activities constitute 4% this issue. Debates concerning the Second Amendment, first appearing at O'Connor's hearing in 1981 and constituting 11% of all dialogue at the Sotomayor hearing in 2009, make up only 3% of civil rights discourse overall. In the subsections that follow, we provide a detailed treatment of the

---

[15] Sonia Sotomayor's hearing provides additional examples of this. Many of the comments from her hearing coded as judicial philosophy involved whether she would allow her personal experiences to influence how she decided cases. Much of this commentary stemmed from concerns of racial bias allegedly revealed in a series of speeches Sotomayor gave before her nomination in which she said "I would hope that a wise Latina woman with the richness of her experiences would more often than not reach a better conclusion than a white male who hasn't lived that life." Sonia Sotomayor, "A Latina Judge's Voice." Retrieved from: http://www. law.berkeley.edu/4982.htm (Accessed May 6, 2011).

TABLE 4.3. *The civil rights issues addressed by senators and nominees who testified at the Senate Judiciary Committee confirmation hearings of Supreme Court nominees, 1939–2010*

Issue	Senators	Nominees	Total
Racial Discrimination	23.2 (1,071)	22.4 (969)	22.8 (2,040)
Freedom of Speech/Religion	17.3 (800)	17.9 (774)	17.6 (1,574)
Right to Privacy (non-abortion)	13.2 (610)	13.3 (576)	13.2 (1,186)
Gender/Sexual Orientation Discrimination	12.8 (590)	12.9 (559)	12.8 (1,149)
Abortion Rights	12.6 (582)	12.1 (524)	12.4 (1,106)
Voting Rights	8.5 (391)	8.6 (371)	8.5 (762)
Antigovernment Activities	3.8 (176)	3.5 (153)	3.7 (329)
Right to Keep and Bear Arms	3.2 (148)	3.3 (142)	3.2 (290)
Handicap/Disease Discrimination	1.3 (59)	1.1 (49)	1.2 (108)
Age Discrimination	0.5 (23)	0.5 (22)	0.5 (45)
Other Civil Rights Issues	10.9 (504)	11.4 (493)	11.1 (997)
Totals	107.3 (4,954)	107.0 (4,632)	107.0 (9,586)

The column entries represent the percentage of comments regarding each civil rights issue area. The percentages exceed 100% because a single comment by a senator or nominee can fall within multiple civil rights issue areas (e.g., abortion and freedom of speech). Accordingly, the number of comments exceeds the number of civil rights comments reported in Table 4.1. The numbers in parentheses indicate the total number of comments pertaining to each issue area falling within the civil rights category. Miscellaneous civil rights issue areas and civil rights issue areas representing less than 0.4% of the total column are combined into the "Other Civil Rights Issues" category.

five most frequently occurring subissues involving civil rights: discrimination relating to race, gender, and sexual orientation; freedoms of speech and religion; and the right to privacy, involving both abortion and non-abortion matters.

Racial, Gender, and Sexual Orientation Discrimination

The prevalence of racial discrimination comments is not surprising, given the importance of racial justice issues within constitutional law, as well as the fact that all but two of the hearings contained in the data set occurred after the Supreme Court's *Brown* decision, which helped elevate civil rights issues to the forefront of the Court's agenda.[16] Indeed, a recent article speculates that

[16] See, e.g., Michael J. Klarman, "How *Brown* Changed Race Relations: The Backlash Thesis," 81 *Journal of American History* 81 (1994); Michael W. McCann, "Reform Litigation on Trial," 17 *Law & Social Inquiry* 715 (1992); David S. Meyer and Steven A. Boutcher, "Signals and Spillover: *Brown v. Board of Education* and Other Social Movements," 5 *Perspectives on Politics* 81 (2007).

nominee testimony became the norm after 1955 precisely *because* of *Brown*.[17] Conflicts about racial issues, so prevalent in society throughout much of the time period covered in the data set, plainly were reflected in the confirmation hearings.

Interestingly, however, the dominance of race discrimination comments may be waning. While remaining the most frequently mentioned subissue within the civil rights issue area, the percentage of civil rights comments involving racial discrimination has actually declined since the mid-1980s, as reported in Figure 4.2. As this figure makes clear, discussions of racial discrimination dominated the civil rights category for several nominees – most notably Harlan (1955), Stewart (1959), Haynsworth (1969), and Carswell (1970) – but questions regarding racial discrimination have tapered off somewhat since the mid-1980s. For example, prior to 1987, discussions of racial discrimination constituted 30% of civil rights dialogue; beginning with the Bork hearing in 1987, this percentage dropped to 19%. As we demonstrate in Chapter 6, this decline reflects a constitutional consensus, clearly solidified by the mid-1980s, that the Constitution proscribes (and allows Congress to penalize) intentional discrimination against racial minorities.

As comments regarding racial discrimination declined, comments about gender and sexual orientation discrimination arrived to fill the gap. As illustrated in Table 4.3, discussions about gender and sexual orientation discrimination constitute 13% of the civil rights comments in the data set, making this the fourth most frequently commented on civil rights subissue. Figure 4.3 also shows that all of the activity in this area has occurred since 1970, with most of it coming after 1975.

The emergence of these issues in the 1970s is not surprising. The 1970s were pivotal for both the women's rights and the gay rights movements. The National Organization of Women marched on Washington; the Equal Rights Amendment was reintroduced in Congress; and Gloria Steinman founded *Ms. Magazine*.[18] Gay rights activists also gained momentum in the 1970s. The Stonewall Riot, widely considered the birth of the gay rights movement, occurred in New York City in 1969.[19] The country's first gay pride parades,

[17] Dion Farganis and Justin Wedeking, "'No Hints, No Forecasts, No Previews': An Empirical Analysis of Supreme Court Nominee Candor from Harlan to Kagan," 45 *Law & Society Review* 525 (2011) at 527.

[18] Barbara Burrell, *Women and Political Participation: A Reference Handbook* (Santa Barbara, CA: ABC-CLIO, 2004); Dorothy McBride-Stetson, *Women's Rights in the USA: Policy Debates and Gender Roles* (New York: Routledge, 2004).

[19] David Carter, *Stonewall: The Riots that Sparked the Gay Revolution* (New York: St. Martin's Press, 2004).

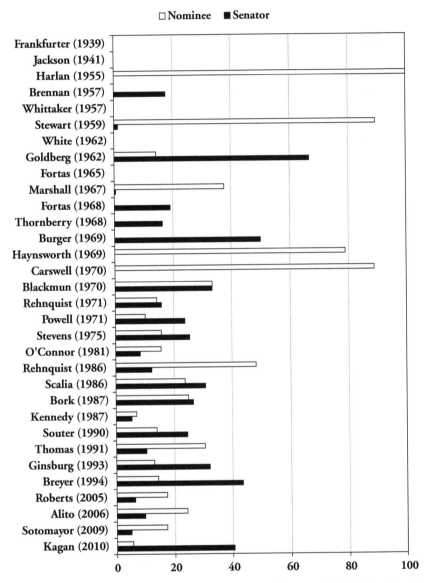

FIGURE 4.2. Percentage of civil rights comments involving racial discrimination at the Senate Judiciary Committee confirmation hearings of Supreme Court nominees, 1939–2010.

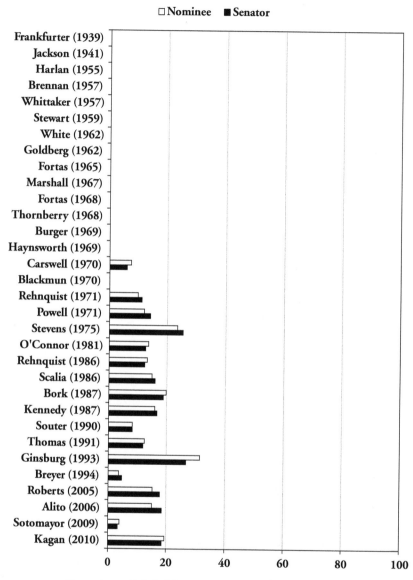

FIGURE 4.3. Percentage of civil rights comments involving gender and sexual orientation discrimination at the Senate Judiciary Committee Confirmation hearings of Supreme Court nominees, 1939–2010.

organized in remembrance of Stonewall, followed in 1970, and Ann Arbor, Michigan, passed the first gay-rights ordinance in 1972.[20] As with racial conflicts, it would be surprising if societal changes as revolutionary as these were not reflected in the confirmation hearings.

Gender and sexual orientation discrimination played a particularly prominent role at the Ginsburg hearing in 1993, making up 29% of all civil rights dialogue at that hearing. Ginsburg, an advocate for women's rights before her nomination and a cofounder of the Women's Rights Project at the American Civil Liberties Union (ACLU),[21] was queried on many of her early litigation activities battling gender discrimination. Senators asked Ginsburg about her role in landmark gender discrimination cases such as *Frontiero v. Richardson*[22] (striking down a law subjecting male and female military spouses to different qualifications regarding dependent benefits) and *Reed v. Reed*[23] (ruling unconstitutional a law that preferred men to women in estate administration).

Although much of this discussion focused on Ginsburg's opinion as to the appropriate standard of review in gender discrimination cases,[24] Senator DeConcini (D-AZ) questioned Ginsburg as to her choice of terminology in this issue area:

Senator DECONCINI: One of the stories that I would like to know is the reason why you refer to this area as "gender discrimination" instead of "sex discrimination." Is there a history to that?

Judge GINSBURG: Yes, there is. I hesitate every time I say "gender-based discrimination" because I have been strongly criticized by an academic colleague for whom I have the highest respect. He tells me, "That term belongs in the grammar books; the word for what you have in mind is 'sex' and why don't you use it?" And I will tell you why I don't use it.

In the 1970's, when I was at Columbia and writing briefs, articles, and speeches about distinctions based on sex, I had a bright secretary. She said one day, "I have been typing this word, sex, sex, sex, over and over. Let me tell you, the audience you are addressing, the men you are addressing" – and

[20] James W. Meeker, John Dombrink, and Gilbert Geis, "State Law and Local Ordinances in California Barring Discrimination on the Basis of Sexual Orientation," 10 *University of Dayton Law Review* 745 (1985).

[21] Amy Leigh Campbell, "Raising the Bar: Ruth Bader Ginsburg and the ACLU Women's Rights Project," 11 *Texas Journal of Women and the Law* 157 (2002).

[22] Frontiero v. Richardson, 411 U.S. 677 (1973).

[23] Reed v. Reed, 404 U.S. 71 (1971).

[24] Ginsburg transcript at 123, 136, 164–5, 243, 360. Traditionally, classifications based on race are subject to the strict scrutiny standard, whereas classifications based on gender are subject to the more lenient heightened (or intermediate) scrutiny standard.

they were all men in the appellate courts in those days – "the first association of that word is not what you are talking about. So I suggest that you use a grammar-book term. Use the word 'gender.' It will ward off distracting associations."[25]

Discrimination based on sexual orientation also made a goodly number of appearances at the Ginsburg hearing, as attention to this issue increased in the national dialogue.[26] Senator Thurmond (R-SC) pressed Ginsburg as to whether states may pass laws forbidding "homosexuals" from adopting children.[27] Senators Kennedy (D-MA) and Cohen (R-ME) questioned Ginsburg on her statement, made at a 1979 conference on women's rights, that "rank discrimination based on sexual orientation should be deplored."[28] Senator Hatch (R-UT) interrogated Ginsburg on the ACLU's position in support of equal rights for gay individuals, and praised her for voting to deny rehearing in *Dronenburg v. Zech*,[29] a District of Columbia Circuit Court of Appeals case in which the unanimous panel upheld the Navy's decision to dismiss Dronenburg for engaging in "homosexual conduct."[30] Further, Senator Brown (R-CO) asked whether sexual orientation should be treated as a suspect class under the Equal Protection Clause, or whether the acts of gay individuals should instead be considered a form of behavior unprotected by the Fourteenth Amendment.[31]

Freedoms of Speech and Religion

While a plurality of civil rights dialogue at the hearings involves issues of discrimination, there are other important topics included in this category. As noted in Table 4.3, speech and religious freedom is the second most frequently occurring subissue within the civil rights area. This subissue, which includes discussions of, among other things, flag burning, school prayer, obscenity, free exercise of religion, and campaign finance regulation, constitutes 18% of all civil rights dialogue.

---

[25] Ginsburg transcript, questioning by Senator DeConcini (D-AZ) at 166.

[26] See, e.g., Stephen H. Haeberle, "Gay and Lesbian Rights: Emerging Trends in Public Opinion and Voting Behavior," in *Gays and Lesbians in the Democratic Process*, ed. Ellen D. B. Riggle and Barry R. Tadlock (New York: Columbia University Press, 1999); Anthony J. Nownes, "The Population Ecology of Interest Group Formation: Mobilizing for Gay and Lesbian Rights in the United States, 1950–98," 34 *British Journal of Political Science* 49 (2004).

[27] Ginsburg transcript, questioning by Senator Thurmond (R-SC) at 146.

[28] Ginsburg transcript at 261, 322–4.

[29] Dronenburg v. Zech, 741 F.2d 1388 (D.C. Cir. 1984).

[30] Ginsburg transcript, questioning by Senator Hatch (R-UT) at 262, 365.

[31] Ginsburg transcript, questioning by Senator Brown (R-CO) at 341.

Unlike the dialogue concerning racial, gender, and sexual orientation dis-crimination, comments involving speech and religious freedom have been relatively evenly dispersed over time, particularly since the late 1960s, as shown in Figure 4.4. Although not every hearing involved substantial discussions of these issues, there was no time period in the last forty years in which this subissue did not play a relatively important role. Rather, its prevalence has remained quite stable over time, constituting about 10% to 30% of civil rights comments for most nominees.

Comments in this subissue were most prominent in the Goldberg, Burger, Breyer, and Kagan hearings. Most of the Goldberg hearing comments within this subissue occurred within an exchange between Goldberg and Senator Ervin (D-NC) in which Ervin asked Goldberg questions such as whether he agreed that "every American citizen has a right to think and to speak his own honest thoughts concerning all things under the sun including the decisions of Supreme Court majorities?"[32] Goldberg agreed, stating that "no institution in American life, including the Supreme Court of the United States, is immune from criticism by our citizens."[33]

The statements made at the Burger and Breyer hearings are more repre-sentative of the types of comments usually found in this category. Burger, confirmed in 1969, was asked very few questions overall (see Figure 2.2), but the ones he was asked within this area focused primarily on *Stein v. Oshinsky*,[34] a school prayer case in which the Court denied *certiorari*.[35] Despite prodding from the senators, Burger refused to speculate on why the Court declined to hear the case, saying that similar cases would no doubt find their way before the Court in the future. Breyer also was asked several questions about school prayer and the religion clauses, as well as numerous speech-related questions. Breyer was somewhat more forthcoming than Burger had been, expressing general agreement with the Court's Establishment Clause jurisprudence as set forth in *Lemon v. Kurtzman*[36] (ruling unconstitutional state aid to religious educational institutions), but refusing to give an opinion about Free Exercise cases such as *Sherbert v. Verner*[37] (reversing a state's decision to deny a Seventh-day Adventist unemployment compensation after she was fired for refusing to work on Saturdays) and *Employment Division v. Smith*[38] (upholding a state's

---

[32] Goldberg transcript, questioning by Senator Ervin (D-NC) at 23.
[33] Ibid. at 24.
[34] Stein v. Oshinsky, 382 U.S. 957 (1965).
[35] Burger transcript at 18–19.
[36] Lemon v. Kurtzman, 411 U.S. 192 (1973).
[37] Sherbert v. Verner, 374 U.S. 398 (1963).
[38] Employment Division v. Smith, 494 U.S. 872 (1990).

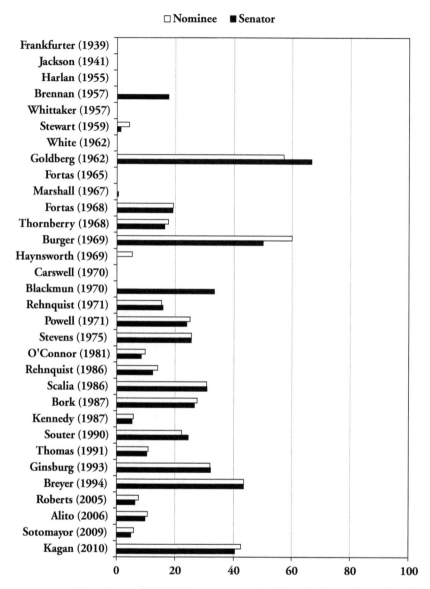

□ Nominee   ■ Senator

FIGURE 4.4. Percentage of civil rights comments involving freedom of speech and religion at the Senate Judiciary Committee Confirmation Hearings of Supreme Court Nominees, 1939–2010.

decision to deny unemployment benefits to an individual who used illegal drugs as part of a religious ceremony).[39]

Kagan, the most recent nominee for whom this subissue constituted an unusually high percentage of civil rights comments, was asked a variety of questions about the Court's then-recent decision in *Citizens United v. Federal Election Commission*,[40] which she argued as solicitor general. *Citizens United* struck down portions of the Bipartisan Campaign Reform Act prohibiting corporations from using general corporate revenue funds to finance certain types of electioneering activities in the time period running up to primary and general elections. The case is widely credited with opening up the door for the creation of "Super PACs."[41] Senator Hatch, who thought the case was correctly decided, spent a good deal of time pressing Kagan about the decision.[42] Prior to her nomination, Kagan stated that the case was wrongly decided. At her hearing, however, she took the opportunity to explain to Hatch that her positions as an advocate differ from those she would take as a judge. "I want to make a clear distinction between my views as an advocate and any views that I might have as a judge," she told the senators, "I do think *Citizens United* is settled law going forward. There's no question that it's precedent, that it's entitled to all the weight that precedent usually gets."[43]

Abortion and the Right to Privacy

Privacy issues also have had a role to play within the civil rights issue area. Our data divide privacy comments into two distinct categories: abortion-related privacy and privacy unrelated to abortion. Because of the nominees' (and perhaps the senators') reluctance to address abortion-related questions directly, abortion as an issue is frequently addressed at the hearings through proxy debates, usually involving contraception or *Griswold v. Connecticut*[44] (the 1965 decision that established the right of married couples to use contraception and recognized a constitutional right to privacy). To ensure that abortion-related comments were not thereby undercounted in the data, we coded comments involving contraception and *Griswold* as involving abortion rights. Non-abortion privacy, consequently, consists primarily of comments involving

[39] Breyer transcript at 223–224.
[40] Citizens United v. Federal Election Commission, 558 U.S. 50 (2010).
[41] See, e.g., Arthur S. Brisbane, "Big-Dollar Individual Campaign Giving and the Tie to Citizens United," *New York Times*, March 2, 2012; Richard L. Hasen, "The Numbers Don't Lie," *Slate*, March 9, 2012. Retrieved from:http://www.slate.com/articles/news_and_politics/politics/2012/03/the_supreme_court_s_citizens_united_decision_has_led_to_an_explosion_of_campaign_spending_.html.
[42] Kagan transcript, questioning by Senator Hatch (R-UT) at 21–7.
[43] Ibid. at 26.
[44] Griswold v. Connecticut, 381 U.S. 479 (1965).

personal or informational privacy, such as police wiretapping, employee drug testing, and the privacy of medical records.[45]

Discussions of privacy unrelated to abortion are more prevalent in the dataset than are abortion-related privacy issues, constituting the third most commonly raised subissue in the civil rights issue area (after racial discrimination and First Amendment issues). Abortion-related privacy, in contrast, places fifth within the civil rights issue area, coming in after gender and sexual orientation discrimination. Numerically, non-abortion privacy discussions constitute 13% of civil rights comments, while abortion rights comments comprise 12% of that issue area.

Figure 4.5 reports the percentage of civil rights comments involving privacy unrelated to abortion, and Figure 4.6 illustrates the percentage of civil rights comments touching on abortion rights. The distinction between the two types of privacy comments explains the prevalence of privacy as a subissue at Rehnquist's first confirmation hearing in 1971 – two years before *Roe v. Wade*[46] (providing constitutional protection to a woman's decision to have an abortion) was decided.

During that hearing, Rehnquist received a host of questions related to electronic wiretapping on the heels of the passage of the Omnibus Crime Control and Safe Streets Act of 1968.[47] This Act was a response to the Court's decisions in *Berger v. New York*,[48] which struck down a state law authorizing electronic eavesdropping, and *Katz v. United States*,[49] which required that police obtain a warrant before engaging in wiretapping.[50] Although Rehnquist declined to answer several direct questions as to his personal opinion regarding the constitutionality of the Act, he did affirm that it was within the power of Congress to pass such legislation: "I mean, Congress has it within its power any time it chooses to regulate the use of investigatory personnel on the part of the executive branch. It has the power as it did in the Omnibus Crime Act of 1968 of saying that Federal personnelsh [sic] all wiretap only under certain rather strictly defined standards."[51]

---

[45] As discussed in Chapter 6, discussions of *Griswold* are not always just proxies for abortion discussions. They are, however, distinct from the type of police procedure privacy concerns that dominated the discussion of privacy in the earlier hearings in our data set.

[46] Roe v. Wade, 410 U.S. 113 (1973).

[47] Rehnquist associate justice transcript at 63–9, 138–44, 184–7.

[48] Berger v. New York, 388 U.S. 41 (1967).

[49] Katz v. United States, 389 U.S. 347 (1967).

[50] Under the Act, Congress established a variety of procedures allowing law enforcement officials to utilize electronic surveillance. It also authorized police to engage in electronic wiretapping absent prior judicial consent when national security is at issue. See, e.g., Timothy Casey, "Electronic Surveillance and the Right to Be Secure," 41 *UC Davis Law Review* 977 (2008).

[51] Rehnquist associate justice transcript, questioning by Senator Bayh (D-IN) at 67.

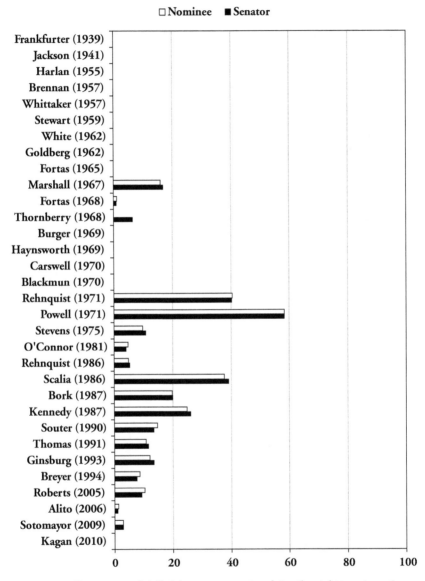

FIGURE 4.5. Percentage of civil rights comments involving the right to privacy (non-abortion) at the Senate Judiciary Committee confirmation hearings of Supreme Court nominees, 1939–2010.

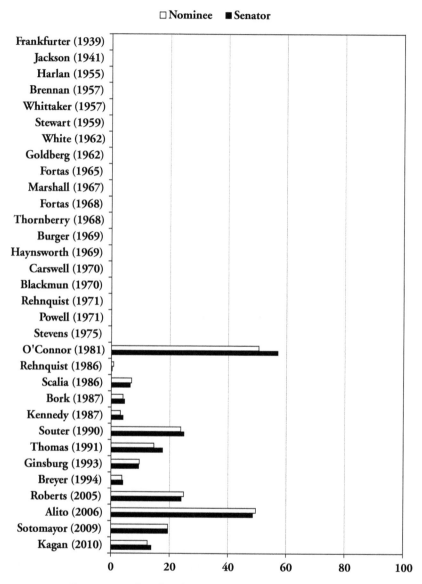

FIGURE 4.6. Percentage of civil rights comments involving abortion rights at the Senate Judiciary Committee confirmation hearings of Supreme Court nominees, 1939–2010.

Also of note is that comments involving abortion constitute a relatively small percentage of the civil rights comments at the Bork hearing, despite Senator Kennedy's (D-MA) famous statement, discussed further in Chapter 7, that "Robert Bork's America is a land in which women would be forced into back-alley abortions..."[52] Indeed, the distribution of civil rights comments at the Bork hearing was fairly evenly divided among the category's subissues. Abortion concerns, in other words, did not completely dominate that hearing. Issues of race discrimination, gender discrimination, speech and religious freedoms, and non-abortion privacy all played roughly equivalent roles.

That dialogue about abortion rights constitutes a relatively small percentage (12%) of the civil rights observations in the data set may be less surprising than it initially appears. Our data set goes back to 1939, and abortion became a constitutional issue only after 1973, the year *Roe* was decided. What is more surprising than the relative scarcity of abortion comments overall may be the fact that such comments have not played a larger role even in the post-*Roe* era. As shown in Figure 4.6, abortion rights comments – again, generously interpreted to include comments about contraception and *Griswold* – have constituted more than 20% of the civil rights observations in only four of the thirteen post-*Roe* hearings: those of O'Conner, Souter, Roberts, and Alito.[53] Moreover, even though *Roe* was decided in 1973, abortion did not become an issue in the hearings until the Reagan era: the first questions about it were raised at the 1981 O'Connor hearing. Overall, post-*Roe* dialogue concerning abortion rights constitutes only 16% of all civil rights comments and less than 5% of all post-*Roe* comments in the data set. Thus, although abortion may play a disproportionate role in the public's perceptions of the hearings (which we discuss in Chapter 8), abortion as a hearing issue took some time to gain traction and failed to dominate the hearings even after it did.

Hearing Administration

Having finished our in-depth examination of civil rights discourse, we now turn to the other categories that have regularly appeared at the individual

---

[52] James Reston, "Kennedy and Bork," *New York Times*, July 5, 1987.
[53] That all four of these nominees were appointed by Republican presidents is interesting, and may reflect a greater confidence on the part of pro-choice Democratic senators to push the issue when the nominee's position is either unclear or presumed to be opposed to abortion rights. We explore this further in Chapter 8.

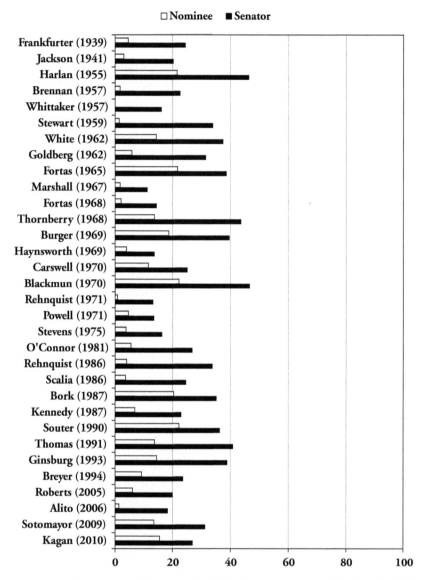

FIGURE 4.7. Percentage of hearing administration comments at the Senate Judiciary Committee confirmation hearings of Supreme Court nominees, 1939–2010.

hearings since 1939. We begin with hearing administration. Figure 4.7 shows the percentage of comments regarding hearing administration made by senators and nominees from 1939 to 2010. Hearing administration statements include discussions of scheduling, the order of questioning, and the social niceties that typically occur at the beginning and end of nominee questioning. The category also includes nonsubstantive clarifications, such as "could you repeat that?" The largest contributors to the hearing administration category are the Committee (or Subcommittee)[54] chairs, who make up 50% of all discussions of hearing administration, and more than 63% of all statements made by senators in this issue area.

As Figure 4.7 makes clear, the percentage of comments involving hearing administration has remained relatively constant over time, typically comprising about 30% of the comments made by senators and 10% of the comments made by nominees. Some hearings, however, have involved more chatter than others. For example, about 35% of the comments made by nominees and senators during the Harlan and Blackmun hearings involved administrative concerns. Similarly, about 30% of the comments proffered by nominees and senators at eight of the hearings involved hearing administration: Burger, Fortas (for associate justice), Ginsburg, Scalia, Souter, Thomas, Thornberry, and White. The hearings that concerned the smallest percentage of discussion regarding administrative concerns include those of Marshall, Powell, and Rehnquist (for associate justice): hearing administration constituted less than 10% of all dialogue for these hearings.

Sidebar: Of Vampires, Werewolves, and Chinese Restaurants

As we show throughout this book, the issues discussed at Supreme Court confirmation hearings closely reflect the salient legal and political issues of the day. They also very much reflect the mood and cultural phenomena of their moment. Reading, hearing transcripts spanning seven decades often brings this into sharp relief, in ways that can be both startling and amusing.

A comparison of the hearings of Felix Frankfurter (the first nominee in our dataset) and Elena Kagan (the last nominee in our data set) provides an excellent example of changes in the ways we talk about certain issues. Like Kagan, Felix Frankfurter was a member of the Harvard Law faculty and a well-respected lawyer. He also was a close friend and advisor of President Roosevelt. His nomination in 1939 nonetheless surprised people, because Frankfurter – again like Kagan – was Jewish. Anti-Semitism was common in America in the era between the two world wars, and many people assumed that the president could not politically afford to put another Jewish person on the high Court.[55]

---

[54] The hearings of Frankfurter (1939) and Jackson (1941) were conducted by the Subcommittee of the Committee on the Judiciary, chaired by Senators Neely (D-WV) and Hatch (D-NM), respectively.

[55] See John Anthony Maltese, *The Selling of Supreme Court Nominees* (Baltimore: Johns Hopkins University Press, 1995) at 104.

Anti-Semitism raged throughout Frankfurter's hearing. Witness after witness testified about Frankfurter's unfitness for the position, most of them barely attempting to mask the bigoted basis of their objections.[56] The issue came to a head in an exchange between the senators and one particular witness, Allen A. Zoll. Asked by Senator Neely (D-WV) why he opposed the Frankfurter nomination, Zoll replied as follows:

> There are two reasons why I opposed the appointment of Prof. Felix Frankfurter to the Supreme Court of the United States. One is because I believe his record proves him unfitted for the position, irrespective of his race, and the other is because of his race.[57]

Zoll went on to explain that he recognized that there are many "fine Jews," but that appointing Frankfurter to the bench would be bad policy because it would cause an "uprising" in the country.[58] Jews, he opined, had been "fostering movements that are subversive to the Government" and that to place on the highest Court "another of that race" would be a social and political mistake.[59]

Senator Borah (R-ID) interrupted Zoll to note that Zoll was raising the same issues that were "drenching Europe in blood" and that he did not want to hear "the race question" debated in "any public hearing in this country."[60] Zoll then asked whether Borah was forbidding him from making his statement. This led to a terse discussion between the senators, ending with the chair calling a vote as to whether Zoll should be allowed to continue. The ayes had it, and Zoll, continuing in more or less the same vein, finished his testimony.[61]

Compare that to the casual banter between Elena Kagan and the Judiciary Committee members seventy-one years later. Senator Graham (R-SC) was questioning Kagan on terrorism and the rights of detainees accused of engaging in terrorist acts. His questioning was setting the stage to ask Kagan about the attempted Christmas Day bombing, a failed effort to smuggle a bomb onto a Northwest Airlines flight on Christmas Day, 2009. The exchange continued as follows:

> **Senator GRAHAM:** Now, as we move forward and deal with law of war issues, Christmas day bomber, where were you at on Christmas Day?
>
> **Ms. KAGAN:** Senator Graham, that is an undecided legal issue, which – the – well, I suppose I should ask exactly what you mean by that. I'm assuming

---

[56] See Lori A. Ringhand, "Aliens on the Bench: Lessons in Identity, Race and Politics from the First 'Modern' Supreme Court Confirmation Hearing to Today," 2010 *Michigan State Law Review* 795 (2010).

[57] Frankfurter transcript at 74.

[58] Ibid. at 75, 76.

[59] Ibid. at 76.

[60] Ibid. at 75.

[61] Ibid. at 76.

that the question you mean is whether a person who is apprehended in the United States is . . .

Senator GRAHAM: No, I just asked you where you were at on Christmas.
(Laughter)

Ms. KAGAN: You know, like all Jews, I was probably at a Chinese restaurant.
(Laughter)

Senator GRAHAM: Great answer. Great answer.

Senator LEAHY: You know, I could almost – I could almost see that one coming, and I thought . . .

Senator GRAHAM: Me, too. So you were celebrating Hanukkah.

Senator LEAHY: Senator Schumer explained this to me earlier.

Senator GRAHAM: Yes, he did.

Senator SCHUMER: If I might, no other restaurants are open.
(Laughter)

Senator GRAHAM: Right. You were with your family on – on Christmas Day at a Chinese restaurant, OK.

Ms. KAGAN: Yes, sir.

Senator GRAHAM: That's great. That's what Hanukkah and Christmas is all about.[62]

Kagan's hearing took yet another foray into confirmation humor on her second day of testimony, this one showing the lighter side of the cultural contexts illustrated by the hearings. In an exchange that is certain to confound Supreme Court scholars fifty years from now, Senator Klobuchar (D-MN) queried Kagan, tongue firmly in cheek, as to whether she was a supporter of Edward or Jacob in the *Twilight* series:

Senator KLOBUCHAR: Solicitor General Kagan, you did – had an incredibly grueling day yesterday, and did incredibly well. But I guess it means you missed the midnight debut of the third "Twilight" movie last night.
(Laughter)
We did not miss it in our household, and it culminated in three 15-year-old girls sleeping over at 3 a.m. So I have this urge to ask you about the . . .

---

[62] Kagan transcript, questioning by Senator Graham (R-SC) at 66.

> **Ms. KAGAN:** I didn't see that.
>
> **Senator KLOBUCHAR:** I just had a feeling. I keep wanting to ask you about the famous case of Edward versus Jacob or the vampire versus the werewolf.
>
> **Ms. KAGAN:** I wish you wouldn't.
>
> **Senator KLOBUCHAR:** But I will refrain. I know you can't comment on future cases. So I'll leave that alone.[63]

Most of the comments in this category involve mundane scheduling or administrative matters. Some, however, take a more jovial turn. At the Alito hearing, for example, Senator Specter produced a chart listing thirty-eight cases decided since *Roe v. Wade* in which the Supreme Court had the opportunity to overrule *Roe*. In attempting to set up the chart, an aide placed the chart so close to Senator Hatch that he appeared in front of the television camera alongside the graphic. Recognizing this, Senator Leahy suggested "Just balance it on Orrin's head," upon which Senator Hatch remarked "Put that over by Leahy."[64] Such is the senatorial humor found in this issue area.

Nominee Background

Discussions of the nominees' backgrounds make up the third most frequently addressed category at the hearings, as shown in Table 4.1. This issue area also was the most frequently discussed substantive issue at eight of the fifteen hearings in our data set not dominated by civil rights discourse. Senators probe nominees on their backgrounds in 15% of their comments, whereas nominees devote slightly more of their statements – 18% – to discussions of their own backgrounds. Comments in this issue area typically pertain to the nominees' education, character, ethics, prior employment (including any previous judicial posts), health, and family.

Figure 4.8 presents the percentage of background discussion at each confirmation hearing. As this figure illustrates, there has been a substantial amount of variation over time with respect to dialogue involving the nominees' backgrounds. Perhaps unexpectedly, however, the nominees whose hearings include a large percentage of background questions are usually not those with inspiring personal stories who broke racial or gender barriers on their way

---

[63] Kagan transcript, questioning by Senator Klobuchar (D-MN) at 108–9.
[64] Alito transcript at 321.

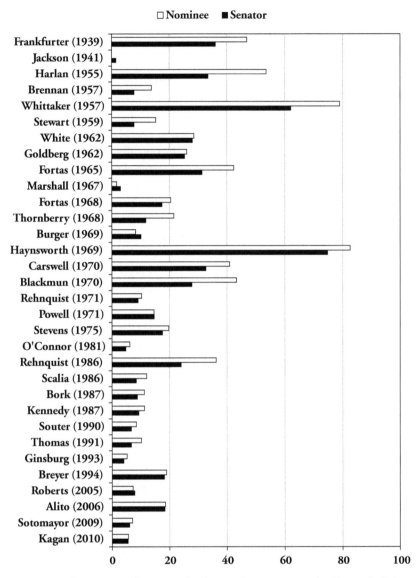

FIGURE 4.8. Percentage of nominee background comments at the Senate Judiciary Committee confirmation hearings of Supreme Court nominees, 1939–2010.

to the high Court, such as Thurgood Marshall, Sandra Day O'Connor, and Sonia Sotomayor. Rather, this issue has more often dominated the hearings of nominees whose prior conduct raises potential ethical issues the senators want to probe (or exploit).

For example, almost 80% of the Haynsworth hearing was dedicated to discussions of Judge Haynsworth's background. Much of this dialogue focused on his stock holdings in several businesses, including Vend-a-Matic, a vending machine business, and J. P. Stevens, a textile manufacture. Among other things, it was alleged that Haynsworth, as a Fourth Circuit Court of Appeals judge, should have recused himself in a series of cases in which these businesses had an interest.[65] These allegations stemmed in large part from the testimony of George Meany, who opposed the nomination on behalf of the AFL-CIO and pointed to seven antilabor decisions that Haynsworth rendered as a circuit court judge that were subsequently overturned by the Supreme Court.[66] The accusations, along with claims that Haynsworth was an opponent of civil rights, were enough to convince senators that Haynsworth was not fit to serve on the Court. He was rejected by the full Senate by a 55–45 vote.[67]

A substantial percentage (70%) of Whittaker's hearing likewise focused on the nominee's background. Unlike the ethical problems raised at the Haynsworth hearing, however, the discussion of Whittaker's background tread a more mundane path. Senator Eastland (D-MS), the Committee chair, began with a simple question: "Judge Whittaker, where were you born?"[68] Eastland would follow up with questions regarding Whittaker's education, trial court experience, marriage, and children. The senator even asked Whittaker his current address.[69] Things got more colloquial when Senator Watkins (R-UT) chimed in to ask the nominee how he transported himself to school:

> **Senator WATKINS:** . . . There was a matter you mentioned in connection with your schooling. It probably didn't mean very much, but I understood you to say that you rode a pony to school?
>
> **Judge WHITTAKER:** To high school.
>
> **Senator WATKINS:** For 6 miles back and 6 miles there?
>
> **Judge WHITTAKER:** Correct.
>
> **Senator WATKINS:** It may have a lot to do with the qualifications of a man who certainly had persistency. I would like to think so. I had the same experience . . .

---

[65] Haynsworth transcript at 270–311.

[66] Lisa Pruitt, "Haynsworth, Clement Furman, Jr.," in *Great American Judges: An Encyclopedia*, ed. John R. Vile (Santa Barbara, CA: ABC-CLIO, 2003).

[67] See also John P. Frank, *Clement Haynsworth, the Senate, and the Supreme Court* (Charlottesville: University Press of Virginia, 1991).

[68] Whittaker transcript, questioning by Senator Eastland (D-MS) at 32.

[69] Ibid.

Senator HENNINGS: You think he should have walked?

Judge WHITTAKER: I have a letter in my pocket on the subject, sir, the most beautiful Americana on this subject that I have seen among the thousands I have received. I would like for you to read it.

Senator WATKINS: I would like to read it. I had a similar experience. I rode for six miles to high school and back through mud and dirt.[70]

Senator Eastland, perhaps unsure just where this folksy discussion was headed, suggested at this point that the Committee move to executive session. The full Senate subsequently confirmed Whittaker by a voice vote.

More recent nominees have faced fewer questions regarding their backgrounds than did earlier nominees. The percentage of background questioning prior to 1971 was 31%, compared to only 11% since then. Indeed, the only hearing since 1971 that involved more than 20% of background questions was Rehnquist's 1986 hearing for chief justice. As in the Haynsworth hearing, most of the background questions Rehnquist faced had ethical underpinnings. Rehnquist was grilled about a memo, written when he was a law clerk, that endorsed *Plessy v. Ferguson* (the 1896 case that validated segregation and the separate but equal doctrine).[71] He also was interrogated over allegations that he engaged in voter intimidation in Phoenix, Arizona, in the early 1960s. These accusations had come up just after Rehnquist's hearing for associate justice concluded in 1971, but were not addressed by the Committee because Senator Eastland, the Committee Chair, refused to reopen the hearing to allow for questions on the topic.[72] Senator Kennedy took the opportunity presented by Rehnquist's chief justice hearing to query Rehnquist on these issues, as did Senators Laxalt (R-NV), Metzenbaum (D-OH), and Simpson (R-WY). Kennedy in particular pressed Rehnquist on claims made by eyewitnesses that Rehnquist "challenged black, elderly working class voters for literacy by having them read the Constitution out loud."[73] Rehnquist denied the charges, but offered no explanation as to why the eyewitnesses would fabricate such stories.[74]

Judicial Philosophy

Judicial philosophy is the fourth most frequently occurring issue at the hearings, following civil rights, hearing administration, and nominee background.

[70] Whittaker transcript, questioning by Senator Watkins (R-UT) at 34.
[71] Plessy v. Ferguson, 163 U.S. 537 (1896). Rehnquist chief justice transcript at 161–2.
[72] Rehnquist chief justice transcript at 144.
[73] Rehnquist chief justice transcript, questioning by Senator Kennedy (D-MA) at 145.
[74] Ibid. at 146–7.

Comments about judicial philosophy include discussions of constitutional interpretation, original intent, "living constitutionalism," *stare decisis,* and judicial activism. Statements in this issue area constitute 13% of all hearing discourse and played a leading role in hearings of Stewart and Goldberg.

The most interesting thing about the judicial philosophy category is the relatively small part it has played in the hearings overall. Figure 4.9 reports the percentage of comments involving judicial philosophy for each nominee in the data. With the exception of the Stewart and Goldberg hearings, the percentage of senatorial comments involving judicial philosophy at the hearings has not exceeded 20% and has consistently been in a range of approximately 10% to 20% of hearing comments. This is noteworthy, in that many commentators, senators, and legal scholars argue that this should be the primary if not exclusive area of senatorial questioning.[75] Clearly, neither the senators nor the nominees have conformed to such a practice: the substantive area of civil rights comprises more than twice as many comments in our data set than do comments about judicial philosophy. Nor is this a new development. The focus on concrete issues rather than abstract discussions of judicial philosophy has been remarkably consistent over time.

The following exchange between nominee Kagan and Senator Cornyn (R-TX) is typical of comments in this issue area. Cornyn has just asked Kagan if she believed that the Court's decision in *Brown* changed the meaning of the Constitution or restored the original purpose of the Fourteenth Amendment. They then continued as follows:

> **Senator CORNYN:** I appreciate your answer. What I'm trying to figure out is whether you and I agree or disagree about how the American people can change their Constitution. Do you think the court can change the Constitution? Or do you agree with me that Article V has the sole means by which the Constitution can be modified, that is, either through a constitutional amendment or a constitutional convention proposing constitutional amendments, which are later ratified by three-quarters of the states?

> **Ms. KAGAN:** I think the Constitution is a timeless document setting forth certain timeless principles. It's the genius of the Constitution that not everything was set forth in specific terms, but that instead certain provisions were phrased in very general terms that enabled people – that enabled the courts over time to apply the principle to new conditions and to new circumstances.

---

[75] See, e.g., Dworkin, "Justice Sotomayor," supra, n. 8; Nagel, "Advice, Consent, and Influence," supra, n. 8; Rutkus, "Proper Scope of Questioning of Supreme Court Nominees," supra, n. 8.

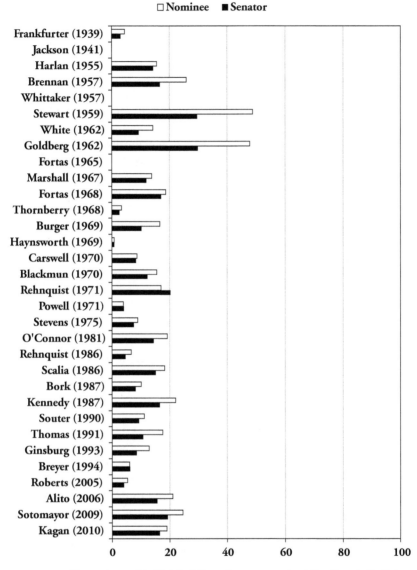

FIGURE 4.9. Percentage of judicial philosophy comments at the Senate Judiciary Committee confirmation hearings of Supreme Court nominees, 1939–2010.

And I think that that's the continuing obligation of the court to do that, to ensure that the Constitution does apply appropriately and that the time-less principles set forth in the Constitution do apply appropriately for our posterity.

Senator CORNYN: Do you believe in the idea of a living Constitution, that the Constitution itself has no fixed meaning?

Ms. KAGAN: You know, I – I think that – I – I don't particularly think that the term is apt, and I especially don't like what people associate with it. I think people associate with it a kind of loosey-goosey style of interpretation in which anything goes, in which there are no constraints, in which judges can import their own personal views and preferences. And I most certainly do not agree with that.

I think of the job of constitutional interpretation that the courts carry on as a highly constrained one, as constrained by text, by history, by precedent and the principles embedded in that – in that precedent.

So the courts are – are – are limited to specifically legal sources. It's a highly constrained role, a circumscribed role. So – so to the extent that that term is used in such a way as to suggest that that's not the case, I – I don't agree with that.

But I do think, as – as I just indicated, that the Constitution, and specifically – not the entire Constitution, but the general provisions of the Constitution, that the genius of the drafters was – was to draft those so that they could be applied to new conditions, to new circumstances, to changes in the world.[76]

As this excerpt illustrates, the judicial philosophy issue area includes observations in which the comment is specifically about constitutional interpretation and/or the nominee's preferred method thereof. When interpretive concerns are raised in the context of discussions about a particular substantive issue, in contrast, we coded the observation by that issue. So, for example, a comment such as that cited earlier from the Stewart hearing, in which Senator McClellan asked the nominee about judicial philosophy *within* a discussion of *Brown*, would be coded as a civil rights comment. As pointed out previously, however, remember that this coding rule in practice probably still over-counts judicial philosophy statements because comments touching on constitutional interpretation in which a substantive issue area is not raised are coded as statements about judicial philosophy, regardless of the senator's issue-driven motivation in asking the question. The data show, therefore, that it is simply indisputable that the hearings are and have since their inception been more focused on substantive, concrete issues of constitutional law rather than on generalized debates about theories of constitutional interpretation.

---

[76] Kagan transcript, questioning by Senator Cornyn (R-TX) at 77.

Law, Crime, and Family

Discussions of law, crime, and family are the last of the top five issue areas addressed at the hearings. As shown in Table 4.1, dialogue involving this issue area comprises 8% of the comments in the data set. This topic was the most frequently addressed issue area in three hearings, one more than judicial philosophy. As noted previously, although law, crime, and family is a seemingly broad category, this issue area is absolutely dominated by discussions of criminal justice, including comments about criminal procedure, capital punishment, and executive branch agencies dealing with law and crime.

Figure 4.10 indicates the percentage of comments dedicated to these issues by nominee. As this figure illustrates, the percentage of questions regarding law, crime, and family has been steadily decreasing over time. Prior to 1981, law, crime, and family constituted an average of 15% of hearing dialogue, whereas it has comprised only 5% since this date. The only hearing since 1981 in which law, crime, and family issues involved more than 10% of discussion was Breyer's hearing in 1994. During that hearing, Breyer was asked a host of questions regarding the death penalty, criminal sentencing, and search and seizure law.[77]

Robert Jackson, who was attorney general at the time of his nomination, faced the highest percentage of questions within this issue area and made the most comments about it: almost 85% of the Jackson hearing involved issues of law, crime, and family. Much of this discussion stemmed from Jackson's role, as attorney general, in a dispute between Senator Tydings (D-MD) and two newspaper reporters, Robert Allen and Drew Pearson. Tydings, a member of the Judiciary Committee, claimed that Jackson refused to prosecute the newspapermen for libel for writing that Tydings used Works Progress Administration resources to make improvements to his seaside estate. Using Tydings's displeasure with Jackson's decision as a starting point, this discussion evolved into a debate about the proper scope of prosecutorial discretion.[78]

Law, crime, and family was also a frequently occurring issue in hearings of Fortas (for both associate and chief justice), Marshall, and Rehnquist (for associate justice). Most of the questions raised in this issue area during the first three of these hearings – held in 1965, 1967, and 1968, respectively – were about the rights of criminal defendants versus the needs of law enforcement officials in protecting the people. These questions were motivated, in large

---

[77] See, e.g., Breyer Transcript at 192, 232–6 (death penalty), 182–3 (criminal sentencing), and 237–8 (search and seizure).
[78] Jackson transcript at 56–69.

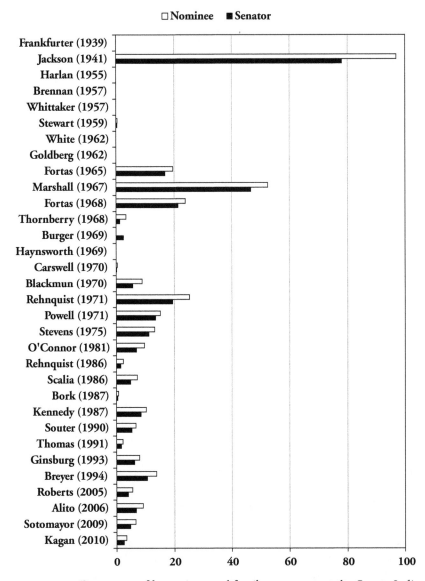

FIGURE 4.10. Percentage of law, crime, and family comments at the Senate Judiciary Committee confirmation hearings of Supreme Court nominees, 1939–2010.

part, by the growing crime rate in the 1960s and the protests related to the civil rights movement and the Vietnam War.[79] There can be little doubt that

---

[79] See, e.g., Dennis D. Loo and Ruth-Ellen M. Grimes, "Polls, Politics, and Crime: The 'Law and Order' Issue of the 1960s," 5 *Western Criminology Review* 50 (2004).

they also were driven by the Warren Court's string of decisions expanding the rights of the criminally accused. In Marshall's case, they almost certainly also were provoked by a thinly veiled racism that associated African Americans with crime.[80]

The following statement by Senator McClellan (D-AR) during the Fortas hearing illustrates the thought process of several of the senators engaged in questioning in this issue area:

> I may premise what I am about to say, the question I am about to ask you, with this statement. I do not believe that we can continue the course and path we are traveling now and preserve civilized society in this county. Lawlessness and chaos will take over. I think there is a very heavy responsibility on the courts, and I think that the pendulum has swung in court decisions in the other direction to where today it favors the criminal rather than protects society in some instances. I think that trend is noticeable. I think it is a trend that must be corrected.[81]

McClellan followed this statement by asking Fortas a series of questions regarding the rights of criminal suspects regarding police interrogations.

Hearing dialogue in this issue area at the Rehnquist associate justice hearing in 1971 was also motivated by social and political changes. Rehnquist was asked a series of questions regarding the Speedy Trial Act of 1971, the Bail Reform Act of 1966, the use of wiretaps by law enforcement officials, and the rights of criminal defendants more generally.[82] As these examples show, confirmation dialogue about law, crime, and family issues, like the other issue areas discussed earlier, is provoked by the senators' desire to engage in a national discussion about the constitutional consequences of issues of importance to the nation. As those issues change, so too does the amount of attention they are given at the hearings.

CONCLUSIONS

The Senate Judiciary Committee hearings of Supreme Court nominees represent the only institutionalized opportunity for nominees to engage in a face-to-face dialogue with members of the legislative branch. As part of the Senate's advice and consent role, these hearings provide information to senators and

---

[80] See, e.g., Stephen L. Carter, *The Confirmation Mess: Cleaning Up the Federal Appointments Process* (New York: Basic Books, 1994); Ringhand, "Aliens on the Bench," supra, n. 59.

[81] Fortas transcript, questioning by Senator McClellan (D-AR) at 41.

[82] Rehnquist associate justice transcript at 142–3, 187–95.

the American public regarding a host of issues implicating nominees' backgrounds, preferred means of judicial interpretation, and, most importantly, views on the most pressing issues of the day.

Despite the importance of Senate Judiciary Committee hearings, there has until now been little rigorous empirical scholarship on the topic. Building on the previous chapter, we have filled this gap by revealing in detail the issues discussed at the confirmation hearings. In doing so, we have shown that the past seventy years of Senate Judiciary Committee hearings have been marked by both continuity and change.

The continuity of the hearing process is shown by the consistent attention to substantive issues. Since the beginning of nominee testimony in 1939, senators have been remarkably consistent in their focus on concrete issues of constitutional law rather than abstract questions of judicial philosophy. Senators are and always have been more interested in constitutional outcomes than in the finer points of constitutional theory. Moreover, reading the constitutional interpretation questions in context makes it quite clear that much of the senators' attention to matters of judicial interpretation is itself likely to be driven by concerns about substantive outcomes, not generalized ideas about constitutionalism and the role of courts. We also see continuity in the types of issues discussed at the hearings. Several of the issues examined have exhibited remarkable levels of stability over the years. For example, since the early 1970s, civil rights have been a staple of hearing dialogue, while attention to matters of hearing administration has long been a necessary part of the hearings.

Some things have changed, however. Although civil rights issues have almost always played a leading role in the hearings, the type of civil rights comments engaged by the senators and the nominees has changed over time. Beginning in the mid-1980s, we witnessed a decrease in attention to discussions of racial discrimination. As discussions of racial discrimination tapered off, questions regarding gender and sexual orientation discrimination grew in number. Other issues have manifested themselves anew. Abortion, never a focal point of the hearings, has nonetheless taken a place on the hearing agenda, as, increasingly, have questions about gun rights and the Second Amendment – a topic we discuss in greater detail in Chapter 6.

Moreover, as we have demonstrated in the previous chapter, the transformation of confirmation dialogue is not random, but follows changes in public opinion and Supreme Court precedent. As different social and legal issues press their way into the public discourse, senators and nominees follow suit and use the confirmation hearings to explore the ways in which those new issues are absorbed into our system of constitutional values. Chapter 5 explores this idea more fully. In doing so, it takes the next step in building the central premise of this book: that the true value of the confirmation hearings is that they are a democratic forum for the discussion and ratification of constitutional change.

5

The Discussion of Precedent at the Hearings

The United States Supreme Court decisions do not just resolve the dispute between the immediate parties to the litigation. Instead, the Court's decisions affect – and are intended to affect – the broad American polity. Of course, the breadth of a decision's impact on American society varies. Some cases have a rather narrow impact, such as deciding whether New York or New Jersey owns most of Ellis Island.[1] Other cases result in significant change throughout the country, such as recognizing a constitutional right to privacy,[2] declaring racial segregation in public schools unconstitutional,[3] and requiring that law enforcement officials make criminal suspects aware of their rights before questioning can begin.[4]

The primary means by which the Court influences society is through its precedents. One of the core foundations of the American common law system is adherence to *stare decisis* ("let the decision stand"). According to this doctrine, judicial decisions create legal consequences that are to be respected in future disputes touching on similar factual circumstances. Thus, when the Court renders a decision, the rule of law announced in that decision becomes a precedent, directing the behavior of a variety of actors, including lower federal and state courts, executive branch agencies, legislative institutions, and future Supreme Courts.

Although a great deal of scholarship has been devoted to understanding the influence of precedent on the Supreme Court and in American society,[5] there

---

[1] New Jersey v. New York, 523 U.S. 767 (1998).
[2] Griswold v. Connecticut, 381 U.S. 479 (1965).
[3] Brown v. Board of Education, 347 U.S. 483 (1954).
[4] Miranda v. Arizona, 384 U.S. 436 (1966).
[5] See, e.g., Michael J. Gerhardt, *The Power of Precedent* (New York: Oxford University Press, 2008); Thomas G. Hansford and James F. Spriggs II, *The Politics of Precedent on the U.S. Supreme Court* (Princeton: Princeton University Press, 2006); Gerald N. Rosenberg, *The*

has been scant attention to comprehending the role of precedent as it relates to staffing the high bench.[6] This chapter, and those that follow, remedies this situation by investigating the role of precedent at the hearings. The discussion of precedent at the hearings is important to the argument we make in this book because nominees and senators often use the Court's precedents to talk about the constitutional choices made by the high Court. As we demonstrate, when senators and nominees debate the Court's choices, they often talk of "*Brown*" and "*Griswold*," not just "civil rights" and "privacy." In this way, the constitutional discourse that takes place at the hearings is to a large extent framed by the Court's precedents.

Understanding what precedents are discussed at the hearings, and how those precedents have changed over time, thus illustrates the ways in which the confirmation hearings operate as a forum to ratify constitutional change. As cases are accepted into or expelled from our constitutional consensus, nominees are expected to accept or reject them in order to win confirmation. These cases, in other words, function as confirmation conditions. When a case enjoys deep and sustained support over time, nominees are expected to affirm their agreement (or disagreement) with the case before being allowed to join the Court. Over time, this repeated affirmation or rejection of key cases works to publicly and formally validate the constitutional changes those cases represent.

We explore this issue in this chapter and Chapters 6 and 7. We begin here by analyzing the extent to which hearing dialogue revolves around the examination of the Court's precedents, the cases that most frequently make their way into hearing dialogue overall, and the cases that most commonly appear at each nominee's hearing. We continue in Chapter 6 by taking a closer look at how certain cases function as conditions of confirmation in areas such as racial and gender discrimination, the scope of congressional power, and the right to keep and bear arms. Finally, Chapter 7 provides additional examples of this process in action by contrasting the failed nomination of Robert Bork with the successful nomination of Anthony Kennedy and those of subsequent nominees.

AN OVERVIEW OF THE DISCUSSION OF PRECEDENT

In Chapter 3, we demonstrated that confirmation hearing dialogue is influenced by Supreme Court precedent: as the Court's attention to an issue

---

Hollow Hope: Can Courts Bring about Social Change? (Chicago: University of Chicago Press, 1991); Harold J. Spaeth and Jeffrey A. Segal, *Majority Rule or Minority Will: Adherence to Precedent on the U.S. Supreme Court* (New York: Cambridge University Press, 1999).

[6] For an exception to this, see Margaret Williams and Lawrence Baum, "Questioning Judges about Their Decisions: Supreme Court Nominees before the Senate Judiciary Committee," 90 *Judicature* 73 (2006).

area increases, so too does the discussion of that issue area at the hearings. Although this finding is essential to establishing the dialogical value of confirmation hearings, we treated the actual precedents debated at the hearings rather abstractly by focusing on the number of precedents handed down in an issue area. This chapter, in contrast, explores both how frequently Supreme Court precedents are addressed at the hearings and exactly which precedents are most commonly discussed.

Prior to presenting this information, a few words about the data employed in this chapter are in order (recall that a full description of the data appears in the Appendix). First, to determine the extent to which precedents are addressed at the hearings, we coded all situations in which a statement made by a nominee or senator relates to a named Supreme Court case as involving the discussion of a precedent, even if the nominee or senator does not identify the case in a given comment. For example, if a four-statement line of questioning begins with a senator inquiring about a specific case, and all four statements touch on the case, each of the four observations is coded to reflect the fact that these statements discussed a given precedent, regardless of whether one (or more) of the comments did not specifically name the case. Second, we have separately coded each named case in a given statement. Accordingly, a single statement by a nominee or senator can reference multiple cases.

To illustrate, consider the following conversation between Chairman Biden (D-DE) and Judge Souter:

> **The CHAIRMAN:** You very rightly and skillfully, Judge, always refer to the equal protection aspect of that case, which was not the basis upon which *Griswold* was decided. What would have happened had *Eisenstadt* come before the Court before *Griswold*, so that there was not an equal protection portion to it? Do you believe that there is a constitutional right to privacy in the liberty clause of the 14th amendment, not the equal protection clause of the 14th amendment for unmarried couples?

> **Judge SOUTER:** I don't know the extent an answer to that question can be given in the abstract without the kind of Harlan inquiry that I'm talking about. It was not made and I have not made it. The thing that I can say is that if that question had come up before *Griswold* as you posit, exactly the same kind of analysis that Harlan would have used and did use in his concurring opinion should be used to address the same issue of nonmarital privacy.

> **The CHAIRMAN:** That is worrisome, because I know of no tradition in American society where an inquiry into the history and traditions of the American people have guaranteed a right of privacy to unmarried couples relating to procreation or sexual activity. So it seems to me that you would have come down and concluded that married couples do not have a right to privacy, based on that set of inquiry.

Am I wrong about that?

Judge SOUTER: I think, yes, I think it is wrong simply to draw that conclusion because as you, yourself, have pointed out in the analyses that go on, there is a two-part inquiry. The first inquiry is No. 1: Is there a liberty interest to be asserted and how may it be valued? The other inquiry that goes on is, when, in fact, is the weight to be given to the State interest which may be brought up as a countervailing interest when the liberty interest is, in some way, restricted?

   One of the questions, of course, that would have to be asked if we were approaching *Eisenstadt* first and not *Griswold* first, is not merely the weight to be given to the privacy interest to be asserted, but the weight to be given to the State interest in asserting the right to preclude people under those circumstances from obtaining contraceptive information and devices. I do not think that is a simple question to answer.[7]

Given our coding rules, each of these statements is treated as referencing both *Griswold v. Connecticut* and *Eisenstadt v. Baird*,[8] despite the fact that only the first and fourth comments specifically name both precedents. This is because all four comments involve the back-and-forth between Biden and Souter regarding the relationship between these cases and the right to privacy in the Fourteenth Amendment.

   Finally, note that our focus in this chapter is on Supreme Court precedent. Although other courts' decisions occasionally make their way into confirmation hearings, typically relating to the nominees' prior judicial decisions (if any),[9] such discussions are nominee specific and therefore are short lasting. The decisions of lower courts do not lodge themselves in the public consciousness, and thus their affirmation or rejection do not become conditions of confirmation in the same way that Supreme Court decisions do.[10] Of the 8,538 statements exploring judicial decisions made at the confirmation hearings, 72% (6,138) involved Supreme Court precedents, compared to only 28% (2,400) of comments about the decisions of other courts.[11] Of those lower court

---

[7] Souter transcript, questioning by Senator Biden (D-DE) at 233–4.

[8] Eisenstadt v. Baird, 405 U.S. 438 (1972).

[9] Williams and Baum, "Questioning Judges about Their Decisions," supra, n. 6.

[10] See, e.g., Bryan Calvin, Paul M. Collins, Jr., and Matthew Eshbaugh-Soha, "On the Relationship between Public Opinion and Decision Making in the U.S. Courts of Appeals," 64 *Political Research Quarterly* 736 (2011) at 743.

[11] With one exception, all of the non-Supreme Court precedents discussed at the hearings involved the decisions of American lower federal or state courts. The aberration is Dudgeon v. United Kingdom, Series A, No. 45 (1981), in which the European Court of Human Rights declared that a law criminalizing male homosexual sodomy ran afoul of the European Convention on Human Rights. This case was mentioned at the Kennedy hearing in relation to the Supreme Court's decision in Bowers v. Hardwick, 478 U.S. 186 (1986), which upheld a

decisions, moreover, only three appeared at the confirmation hearing of more than a single nominee.[12] As we illustrate below, this positively pales in comparison to the host of Supreme Court decisions that were discussed at myriad confirmation hearings.

Figure 5.1 reports the extent to which Supreme Court precedents make their way into hearing dialogue. The nominees are arrayed along the vertical y-axis, and the horizontal x-axis reports the percentage of all statements at each hearing involving Supreme Court precedent. Nominee comments are indicated by the white bars, and senatorial comments are shown by the black bars.

This figure reveals three interesting patterns relating to the discussion of precedent at the confirmation hearings. First, it is evident that questioning nominees regarding the Court's decisions did not become a routine part of the process until the Marshall hearing in 1967. Prior to this, precedents were broached in fewer than 2% of all comments, and five hearings, those of Frankfurter, Jackson, Brennan, Whittaker, and White, featured no mentions of Supreme Court precedent. This is not to say that these hearings involved no discussion of constitutional issues; they plainly did. Rather, our data show that hearing dialogue was slow to take the form of discussions about particular cases. Beginning with Marshall, however, 14% of all comments at the hearings involved the Court's prior decisions. Moreover, dialogue relating to precedent played a particularly prominent role at the hearings of Marshall, Fortas (for chief justice), and Roberts. At each of these hearings, more than 25% of all statements involved the analysis of the Court's precedents, ranging from 26% for Marshall, to 30% for Roberts, to a high of 39% for Fortas. Thus, although the discussion of precedent took some time to gain traction, once it did, precedential inquiries became a mainstay of hearing colloquy.

Second, it is evident that precedential dialogue has remained quite stable since O'Connor's hearing in 1981. Prior to that hearing, there was wide variation in attention to precedent, even in the post-Marshall era. For example, inquiries into a nominee's views of precedent constituted fewer than 2% of the Carswell and Haynsworth hearings, compared to more than 25% of the Marshall and Fortas (for chief justice) hearings. Since 1981, however, attention to precedent

---

Georgia statute outlawing sodomy. Kennedy transcript, questioning by Senator Humphrey (R-NH) at 176.

[12] Masses Publishing v. Patten, 244 F. 535 (SDNY 1917) appeared at the hearings of Ginsburg and Roberts; Ollman v. Evans, 750 F.2d 970 (DC Cir. 1984) was featured at the hearings of Bork and Scalia; Richmond Medical Center for Women v. Gilmore, 144 F.3d 326 (4th Cir. 1998) was discussed at the hearings of Alito, Roberts, and Sotomayor.

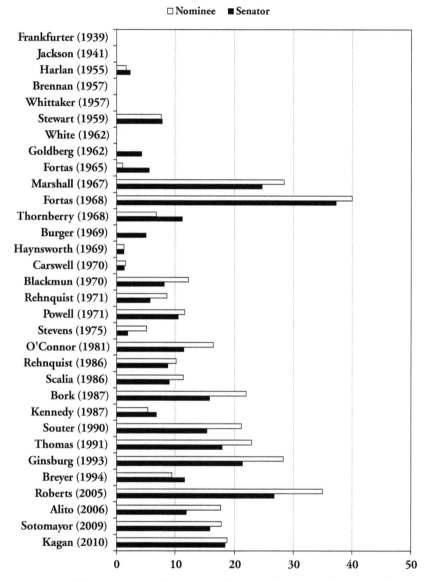

FIGURE 5.1. The percentage of comments discussing Supreme Court precedent at the Senate Judiciary Committee confirmation hearings of Supreme Court nominees, 1939–2010.

has stabilized, typically constituting about 16% of hearing dialogue.[13] Thus, in recent decades, we can expect about one-sixth of hearing discourse to be devoted to concrete examinations of Supreme Court precedents.

Third, Figure 5.1 indicates that nominees engage in the discussion of precedent more often than do senators. Although the overall average of precedential statements is quite close for the two types of participants, 11% for nominees, and 10% for senators ($P = 0.036$), only nine hearings featured senators referencing precedent more often than nominees. During the other 23 hearings, nominees discussed precedent in 18% of their comments, in contrast to 15% of statements for senators ($P < 0.001$). Though speculative, our impression is that this difference is attributable largely to the tendency of nominees to address specific cases in response to more general senatorial questions about a given issue. That is, senators query nominees with respect to a general concept and nominees reply by informing the senators how the Court has decided particular cases in the issue area. To illustrate, consider the following exchanges:

Senator TUNNEY: What do you consider to be the present state of the political question doctrine and do you see a trend?

Mr. STEVENS: We talked about that very briefly this morning and I pointed out what I am sure you are well aware of, Senator, that the term political question is used in two different senses: one, the jurisdictional sense and the other, the more or less popular sense. I think that really ever since *Baker v. Carr* the political question objection to Federal jurisdiction has been narrowed . . . [14]

***

Senator HUMPHREY: But I mean the question in more than the abstract sense. Is it your view that at times in our history, the Supreme Court has overreached, has exercised, rawly exercised political power?

Judge KENNEDY: There are a few cases where it is very safe to say that they did, the *Dred Scott* case being the paradigmatic example of judicial excess.[15]

***

Senator SCHUMER: . . . So I would like to find out a little bit more about modesty. So I would ask you – and these can be well settled, they could be 50 or 100 years ago, and please don't go on at length – can you give me a few

---

[13] From 1967 to 1975, statements involving precedent constituted an average of 11% of hearing dialogue, with a standard deviation of 12% and a range from 1.3% to 38.5%. From 1981 to 2010, comments relating to precedent comprised 16% of hearing colloquy, with a standard deviation of 7% and a range from 6.1% to 30.3%, clearly evincing the stabilization of the discussion of precedent beginning with the O'Connor hearing.

[14] Stevens transcript, questioning by Senator Tunney (D-CA) at 68.

[15] Kennedy transcript, questioning by Senator Humphrey (R-NH) at 175.

Supreme Court cases that are modest, or represent modesty, is a better way to put it, at least in your view, and a few Supreme Court cases that would represent immodesty?

Judge ROBERTS: Sure. I guess I would think the clearest juxtaposition would be the cases from the *Lochner* era. If you take *Lochner* on the one hand and, say, *West Coast Hotel*, which kind of overruled and buried the *Lochner* approach on the other, and the immodesty that I see in the *Lochner* opinion is in its re-weighing of the legislative determination. You read that opinion, it's about limits on how long bakers can work. And they're saying we don't think there's any problem with bakers working more than 13 hours.[16]

As these examples make clear, it is not uncommon for senators to question nominees on a somewhat broad issue, such as the political questions doctrine or judicial restraint, and have the nominees respond by bringing up specific Supreme Court precedents.

WHICH PRECEDENTS?

Having established the extent to which precedent is discussed at the confirmation hearings, we now turn to identifying exactly which precedents are most commonly featured at the hearings. Table 5.1 presents the Supreme Court precedents that generated fifty or more comments at the hearings, arranged by the total number of comments relating to each decision. The first column reports the name of the decision and the year it was decided. The second column indicates the total number of comments made by senators and nominees regarding the decision, as well as the percentage of comments represented by each decision as a function of all statements pertaining to the Court's precedents (in parentheses). Thus, this column provides information on the overall extent to which each precedent appeared at the hearings. Because older cases have more opportunity to be raised at multiple confirmation hearings, this column risks weighing older decisions more heavily than newer precedents. Given this, the third column reports the percentage of hearings, since the case was decided, that the precedent was discussed, in addition to the number of hearings, since the decision was rendered, that each case was mentioned (in parentheses). The purpose of this latter column is to ascertain how frequently each case appears at hearings subsequent to the decision being handed down.

For example, *Roe v. Wade*,[17] which established that the right to privacy protects a woman's decision to have an abortion, is the most frequently addressed

---

[16] Roberts transcript, questioning by Senator Schumer (D-NY) at 408.
[17] Roe v. Wade, 410 U.S. 113 (1973).

TABLE 5.1. *The most frequently addressed Supreme Court precedents at the Senate Judiciary Committee confirmation hearings of Supreme Court nominees, 1939–2010*

Decision	Number of comments	Percent of hearings since case was decided
Roe v. Wade (1973)	475 (7.7)	85.7 (12)
Brown v. Board of Education (1954)	322 (5.3)	73.3 (22)
Griswold v. Connecticut (1965)	259 (4.2)	58.3 (14)
Miranda v. Arizona (1966)	246 (4.0)	73.9 (17)
Planned Parenthood v. Casey (1992)	150 (2.5)	100.0 (6)
Katzenbach v. Morgan (1966)	125 (2.0)	17.4 (4)
Plessy v. Ferguson (1896)	121 (2.0)	50.0 (16)
Citizens United v. Federal Election Commission (2010)	117 (1.9)	100.0 (1)
District of Columbia v. Heller (2008)	99 (1.6)	100.0 (2)
Brandenburg v. Ohio (1969)	84 (1.4)	21.1 (4)
Marbury v. Madison (1803)	84 (1.4)	50.0 (16)
Stovall v. Denno (1967)	71 (1.2)	8.7 (2)
Lemon v. Kurtzman (1971)	67 (1.1)	50.0 (7)
Dred Scott v. Sandford (1856)	60 (1.0)	31.3 (10)
Escobedo v. Illinois (1964)	57 (0.9)	20.8 (5)
Morrison v. Olson (1988)	54 (0.9)	37.5 (3)
U.S. v. Lopez (1995)	52 (0.9)	100.0 (4)
Eisenstadt v. Baird (1972)	51 (0.8)	31.3 (5)
Youngstown Sheet and Tube Company v. Sawyer (1952)	50 (0.8)	20.0 (6)

This table lists the nineteen Supreme Court cases addressed fifty or more times at the confirmation hearings. The second column shows the total number of statements involving an individual decision. The numbers in parentheses in the second column indicate the percentage of comments pertaining to each decision as a function of all statements regarding Supreme Court decisions at the hearings. As a whole, senators and nominees made 6,138 statements that addressed 578 unique Supreme Court precedents. The third column shows the percentage of hearings, since the case was handed down, at which a decision was addressed. The numbers in parentheses in the third column report the number of hearings, since the case was decided, at which the case was discussed.

decision at the confirmation hearings, constituting 7.7% of all mentions of precedent (475 total comments). This decision appeared at 85.7% of the hearings since it was handed down (twelve of the fourteen hearings subsequent to the decision). The only hearings at which *Roe* was not discussed since its issuance in 1973 were those of Stevens and Rehnquist (for chief justice).

Several notable findings emerge from Table 5.1. First, with one exception, each of these cases falls into one of five issue areas: reproductive rights, racial discrimination, institutional powers, criminal rights, and the First

Amendment. The lone aberration is *District of Columbia v. Heller*,[18] in which the Court held that the Second Amendment right to keep and bear arms is an individual, rather than a collective, right. Though *Heller* was decided in 2008, it nonetheless is the ninth most frequently addressed precedent at the hearings, and it made appearances at each of the two hearings following its issuance (those of Sotomayor and Kagan). As a whole, treatments of *Heller* constituted 1.6% of all the precedents discussed at the hearings since their inception in 1939. Thus, although *Heller* is a relatively new precedent, it is evident that it is a particularly significant case that will no doubt continue to generate substantial attention at future hearings.[19]

Decisions related to reproductive rights constitute the most frequently addressed precedential issue area at the hearings, with four cases accounting for 15% of all named precedents. In addition to *Roe*, these cases include *Griswold v. Connecticut*, *Planned Parenthood v. Casey*,[20] and *Eisenstadt v. Baird*. *Griswold*, decided eight years before *Roe*, set the stage for reproductive freedom by, first, recognizing a constitutional right to privacy, and, second, determining that the right to privacy protects the ability of married couples to be counseled regarding the use of contraception. Given the importance of this case, it is not surprising that it is the third most frequently addressed precedent at the hearings, encompassing more than 4% of all mentions of precedent and appearing at almost 60% of hearings since it was decided.

Planned Parenthood v. Casey is the third most commonly addressed reproductive rights decision, making up 2.5% of all precedents and appearing at every hearing since it was handed down. This decision affirmed the central holding in *Roe* (that the right to privacy protects the abortion decision), but rejected the trimester framework established in *Roe*. In its place, the Court established the undue burden test, holding that state regulations regarding abortion are constitutional so long as they do not place a substantial obstacle in the path of a woman seeking the abortion of a nonviable fetus.

The fourth most frequently addressed reproductive rights precedent is *Eisenstadt v. Baird*. This decision constitutes 0.8% of all precedents named at the hearings and it made appearances at 31% of the hearings since it was decided. In *Eisenstadt*, the Court struck down a Massachusetts law that prohibited the distribution of contraceptive materials to unmarried couples on the grounds

---

[18] District of Columbia v. Heller, 171 L. Ed. 2d 637 (2008).

[19] See, e.g., Lindsay Goldberg, "Note: *District of Columbia v. Heller*: Failing to Establish a Standard for the Future," 68 *Maryland Law Review* 889 (2009); Eugene Volokh, "Implementing the Right to Keep and Bear Arms for Self-Defense: An Analytical Framework and a Research Agenda," 56 *UCLA Law Review* 1443 (2009).

[20] Planned Parenthood v. Casey, 505 U.S. 833 (1992).

that the law violated the Equal Protection Clause of the Fourteenth Amendment. To reach this conclusion, the Court determined that the state did not have a legitimate interest in enacting the legislation prohibiting access to contraceptive materials to nonmarried couples, but allowing their distribution to married couples (which the Court compelled in *Griswold*).

That four cases involving reproductive rights represent 15% of all precedents discussed at the hearings is particularly interesting given our findings in Chapter 4 regarding the extent to which abortion rights are addressed at the hearings. Recall that abortion rights were not raised at the hearings until 1981 – eight years after *Roe* was decided. Even since that date, comments regarding abortion have constituted less than 5% of all hearing dialogue. Nonetheless, precedents touching on abortion rights and reproductive rights do regularly make their way into hearing discourse. This seeming dichotomy is explained largely by the fact that when the senators and nominees debate reproductive rights, they almost always do so through discussion of widely known precedents. This is different than the way other popular constitutional issue areas are discussed. For example, references to the Court's precedents occur in 54% of comments related to abortion rights, compared to only 35% of statements involving racial discrimination and 29% of comments implicating gender and sexual orientation discrimination.

Thus, whereas senators and nominees routinely converse about other civil rights and liberties issues in broad terms, their attention to reproductive rights is much more case specific, often revolving around the Court's reproductive rights precedents, such as *Roe, Griswold, Casey*, and *Eisenstadt*. This may well explain why anecdotal accounts of the hearings suggest (incorrectly) that abortion rights constitute a focal point of hearing dialogue.[21] Abortion appears to play a larger role in the hearings than it actually does because it is discussed in widely recognized terms – typically involving seminal decisions, such as *Roe* and *Griswold* – rather than couched in abstract or more technical legal jargon that is less accessible (and thus less memorable) to casual observers.[22]

---

[21]   See, e.g., "Abortion Shouldn't Be Only Issue," *Wisconsin State Journal*, July 24, 2005; Hasani Gittens, "Thomas: Anita Who? Abortion was Key," *New York Post*, September 28, 2007; Jesse J. Holland, "Senators Say Alito Respects *Roe v. Wade*," *Houston Chronicle*, November 9, 2005; "Judge Alito and Abortion," *New York Times*, December 3, 2005; Neil A. Lewis, "The Supreme Court: Ginsburg Affirms Right of a Woman to Have an Abortion," *New York Times*, July 22, 1993; Margaret Talev and Michael Doyle Bee, "Senators Will Share in Roberts' Spotlight," *Sacramento Bee*, September 12, 2005.

[22]   We suspect that senators are motivated to discuss abortion rights in precedential terms because it allows them to engage in position-taking on cases that are familiar to the American public. This, in turn, can enhance their reelection prospectus, particularly given the highly public

Although precedents related to racial discrimination are not as common as reproductive rights cases, Table 5.1 indicates that they also often make their way into hearing colloquy. Three such cases account for 8% of all named precedents. This is not astonishing given that, for much of the twentieth century, many of our important constitutional debates centered on racial issues. *Brown v. Board of Education*, in which the Court declared that racially segregating public schools by law violated the Equal Protection Clause, is the most commonly scrutinized racial discrimination precedent and the second most frequently addressed decision overall. *Brown*, the evolution of which is discussed in detail in Chapter 6, comprised 5% of all mentions of precedent and appeared at 73% of hearings held since it was decided in 1954. *Plessy v. Ferguson*,[23] which was overruled by *Brown*, comes next, constituting 2% of precedents and making a showing at half of the hearings since their inception (*Plessy* is much older than the hearings; it was decided in 1896, four decades before modern hearings began). The infamous 1856 case of *Dred Scott v. Sandford*,[24] in which the Court determined that even freed slaves could not be citizens within the meaning of the Constitution, rounds out this category. *Dred Scott* was debated at 31% of all hearings, embodying 1% of all mentions of precedent.

The third most commonly addressed precedential issue area involves the institutional powers of the three branches of government. Because these cases often involve disputes about the scope of Congress's own powers, it makes sense that senators show a great deal of interest in this issue area. Five of the most frequently debated precedents fit into this category, constituting 6% of all precedents. Of these, *Katzenbach v. Morgan*,[25] a 1966 case in which the Court determined the scope of congressional power under the enforcement provision of the Fourteenth Amendment, received the most attention at the hearings. In it, the Court adjudicated whether Section 4e of the Voting Rights Act of 1965, which prohibits states from imposing literacy tests as a condition of voting, was a constitutional exercise of congressional power. New York State argued that Section 4e intruded upon state sovereignty, while the federal government claimed that it was a constitutionally acceptable way of enforcing the substantive components of the Fourteenth Amendment's Equal Protection Clause (the federal government won). *Katzenbach* makes up 2% of all of the

---

nature of the confirmation hearings. See, e.g., David R. Mayhew, *Congress: The Electoral Connection* (New Haven, CT: Yale University Press, 1974).

[23] Plessy v. Ferguson, 163 U.S. 537 (1896).
[24] Dred Scott v. Sandford, 60 U.S. 393 (1857).
[25] Katzenbach v. Morgan, 384 U.S. 641 (1966).

precedents discussed at the hearings and appeared at 17% of hearings since it was decided.

Two additional congressional powers cases show up regularly at the hearings, each constituting about 1% of all named precedents. *Morrison v. Olson*[26] upheld the ability of Congress to pass legislation establishing a special court and authorizing the Attorney General to appoint independent counsel to investigate allegations of criminal activity on the part of federal government officials. *Morrison* appeared at 50% of hearings since it was decided. In *U.S. v. Lopez*,[27] the Court struck down the Gun Free School Zones Act as beyond congressional authority on the grounds that the possession of a gun in a school zone is not economic activity and thereby was beyond the reach of the Commerce Clause. *Lopez* was the first case since 1937 in which the Court struck down a law as exceeding Congress's power to regulate interstate commerce. It is not surprising, therefore, that it has been discussed at every hearing since it was decided in 1995.

The two remaining institutional powers cases in Table 5.1 relate to the powers of the judicial and executive branches. *Marbury v. Madison*,[28] the seminal 1803 case asserting the Supreme Court's power to declare laws unconstitutional, makes up 1.4% of all named precedents and appeared at half of all confirmation hearings.[29] *Youngstown Sheet and Tube Company v. Sawyer*,[30] in which the Court limited the president's ability to seize and transfer the operation of steel mills to the secretary of commerce during the Korean War, was discussed at 20% of hearings since it was decided, comprising 0.8% of all precedents. Because *Youngstown* provided the framework through which the Court evaluates claims of presidential authority, it is not unexpected that it, like the other cases in this issue area, is of great concern to the senators and is debated regularly at the confirmation hearings.

Decisions involving the rights of the criminally accused constitute the next most common category of precedents discussed at the hearings. Three decisions in this area make up 6% of precedents debated at the hearings: *Miranda v. Arizona, Stovall v. Denno*,[31] and *Escobedo v. Illinois*.[32] *Miranda* required that law enforcement officials make criminal suspects aware of their

---

[26] Morrison v. Olson, 487 U.S. 654 (1988).

[27] U.S. v. Lopez, 514 U.S. 549 (1995).

[28] Marbury v. Madison, 5 U.S. 137 (1803).

[29] While endorsements of *Marbury* tend to be somewhat ritualistic, Antonin Scalia astonished the Committee at his hearing by refusing to comment on whether it had been properly decided Scalia transcript at 33–4.

[30] Youngstown Sheet and Tube Company v. Sawyer, 343 U.S. 579 (1952).

[31] Stovall v. Denno, 388 U.S. 293 (1967).

[32] Escobedo v. Illinois, 378 U.S. 478 (1964).

constitutional rights prior to questioning. It was a hotly debated decision when it was handed down in 1966, and has subsequently become one of the most widely known Supreme Court precedents, owing in no small part to police procedural television shows such as *Dragnet* and *Law & Order*.[33] It is no bombshell, therefore, to report that it is the fourth most commonly mentioned precedent at the hearings. *Miranda* accounts for 4% of all precedential statements and appeared at 74% of hearings since it was rendered.

Stovall v. Denno follows *Miranda* as the second most frequently canvassed criminal rights decision and the twelfth most commonly mentioned precedent overall. In *Stovall*, the Court determined that the pretrial identification of a criminal suspect, absent counsel, did not violate the defendant's due process rights based on the claim that the identification was unnecessarily suggestive that the suspect committed the crime. (The case also involved complicated questions of the retroactive effect of Supreme Court decisions.) Although *Stovall* accounts for 1.2% of all of the discussion of precedent at the hearings, it appeared only at two hearings, those of Thurgood Marshall and Abe Fortas (for chief justice). At the Marshall hearing, it constituted 15% of all Supreme Court cases mentioned, compared to only 2.5% for Fortas. The reason so much attention was devoted to this case at the Marshall hearing was almost certainly due to the fact that Marshall sat on the original three-judge Court of Appeals panel that handled the appeal.[34] Consequently, rather than representing a case that ingrained itself into the fabric of American constitutional discourse, *Stovall* is an excellent example of how senators occasionally interrogate nominees on their previous judicial opinions, frequently focusing on those decisions that were subsequently adjudicated by the Supreme Court.[35]

The third most referenced criminal rights case, accounting for almost 1% of all discussion of precedent, is *Escobedo v. Illinois*. This case was debated at 21% of the hearings since it was decided. In *Escobedo*, the Court held that criminal suspects have a Sixth Amendment right to an attorney during

---

[33] Todd S. Purdum, "*Miranda* as a Pop Cultural Icon," *New York Times*, July 2, 2000.

[34] The panel decision is U.S. ex rel. Stovall v. Denno, Docket Number 29208 (2nd Cir. 1965). The en banc decision is U.S. ex rel. Stovall v. Denno, 355 F.2d 731 (2nd Cir. 1966). Considering all cases discussed at the Marshall hearing collectively (Supreme Court and lower courts), the Supreme Court's decision in *Stovall* accounts for 11% of case-specific discussion, compared to 16% for the panel decision and 5% for the en banc decision.

[35] A more recent example of this involves Ricci v. DeStefano, 174 L. Ed. 2d 490 (2009), at the Sotomayor hearing. In *Ricci*, the Supreme Court reversed the three-judge panel that Sotomayor sat on, determining that a city's decision to set aside the results of a civil service examination because the results would have a disparate impact on minority firefighters ran afoul of Title VII of the Civil Rights Act of 1964. Discussion of the Supreme Court's decision in *Ricci* constituted 6% of all the decisions (Supreme Court and lower courts) debated at the Sotomayor hearing, and treatments of the Second Circuit's decision in *Ricci* comprised 16% of case-specific discussion.

police interrogations. Decided a year after *Gideon v. Wainwright*,[36] in which the Court established the right to counsel for indigent defendants, *Escobedo* extended this right to the point at which an individual becomes a suspect in a crime.

A set of three First Amendment cases round out the most frequently discussed Supreme Court precedents, collectively constituting more than 4% of all named precedents. Despite having been decided only in 2010, *Citizens United v. Federal Election Commission*[37] is the most commonly addressed First Amendment decision, accounting for 2% of all precedents mentioned at the hearings. In *Citizens United*, the Court struck down provisions of the Bipartisan Campaign Reform Act of 2002 that limited the ability of corporations to spend general corporate revenue on certain electioneering activities that specifically endorse or oppose a particular candidate for political office. The law also barred labor unions from spending unsegregated funds on this type of advocacy. The Court held that these restrictions violated the First Amendment. Interestingly, although *Citizens United* was decided in January of 2010, it actually made an appearance at the Sotomayor hearing six months earlier. Senator Russell Feingold (D-WI), one of the primary architects of the law, used the hearing to express to Sotomayor his concerns about the Court's intervention in this area.[38] Those concerns were even more pronounced after the case was actually decided: *Citizens United* was addressed in 115 comments at the Kagan hearing, making up 27% of all of the precedents discussed at that hearing. Like *Heller*, we predict that *Citizens United* will generate substantial attention at future confirmation hearings.

Brandenburg v. Ohio,[39] in which the Court concluded that the government may not criminalize inflammatory speech unless that speech is likely to incite immediate lawless action, appeared at 21% of hearings since it was decided, encompassing 1.4% of all precedential statements. The final First Amendment case (and first religion case) among the most frequently debated precedents is *Lemon v. Kurtzman*.[40] *Lemon* articulated the three-pronged "*Lemon* test" used to evaluate claimed violations of the Establishment Clause. Under this test, governmental engagement with religion will survive constitutional scrutiny if: (1) the statute has a secular purpose; (2) the statute's primary effect neither advances nor inhibits religion; and (3) the statute does not result in an

---

[36] Gideon v. Wainwright, 372 U.S. 335 (1963).
[37] Citizens United v. Federal Election Commission, 175 L.Ed.2d 753 (2010).
[38] Sotomayor transcript at 3.60–3.61.
[39] Brandenburg v. Ohio, 395 U.S. 444 (1969).
[40] Lemon v. Kurtzman, 403 U.S. 602 (1971).

excessive entanglement with religion.[41] *Lemon* comprises 1.1% of all precedents, appearing at 50% of the hearings since it was handed down.

Having explored the most commonly addressed precedents at the hearings overall, we now turn to the hearings of individual nominees. Table 5.2 presents the most frequently debated Supreme Court decision at each confirmation hearing. The first column indicates the nominee's name and hearing year; the second column reports the most commonly referenced precedent at each nominee's hearing; and the third column reveals the number of comments pertaining to that precedent at each hearing, along with the percentage of comments involving the case (in parentheses). Our purpose in presenting this information is to show how precedents are used over time. Accordingly, this analysis provides the opportunity to shed additional light on those precedents that are firmly entrenched into hearing colloquy in comparison to those that are more short lived.

Table 5.2 reveals several important findings with respect to the role of precedent at the confirmation hearings. First, although this table reports the most commonly referenced precedent at each hearing, it is clear that these high-profile cases do not absolutely dominate the discussion of precedent at each nominee's hearing. On average, each case represents 28% of all precedents debated at the hearings, ranging from a high of 67% (*Brown v. Board of Education* at the Carswell hearing) to a low of 7% (*DeGregory v. Attorney General of New Hampshire*[42] at the Fortas hearing for chief justice). Thus, although some of the Court's precedents gain enough traction to function as confirmation conditions – cases nominees are expected to accept or reject before being confirmed – many more are of only passing interest, failing over time to inspire the type of deep constitutional debate and commitment enjoyed by their more famous peers.

Second, the majority (61%) of the most commonly scrutinized cases at each hearing also appear in Table 5.1, which reports the most frequently addressed precedents overall. *Roe v. Wade* received the highest number of comments at seven hearings; *Brown v. Board of Education* at six hearings; *Griswold v. Connecticut* and *Miranda v. Arizona* at two hearings each; while *Citizens United v. Federal Election Commission*, *District of Columbia v. Heller*, and *Youngstown Sheet and Tube Company v. Sawyer* generated the most precedential inquires at one hearing each. This overlap between the two tables shows there is a reasonable amount of stability with respect to the precedents

---

[41] Lemon v. Kurtzman, 403 U.S. 602 (1971) at 612–613.
[42] DeGregory v. Attorney General of New Hampshire, 383 U.S. 825 (1966) (relating to the investigation of allegedly subversive activities).

TABLE 5.2. *The most frequently addressed Supreme Court precedents for each nominee at the Senate Judiciary Committee confirmation hearings of Supreme Court nominees, 1939–2010*

Nominee name (year)	Decision (year)	Number of comments
Frankfurter (1939)	No Supreme Court cases discussed	
Jackson (1941)	No Supreme Court cases discussed	
Harlan (1955)	*Youngstown Sheet and Tube Company v. Sawyer* (1952)	5 (38.5)
Brennan (1957)	No Supreme Court cases discussed	
Whittaker (1957)	No Supreme Court cases discussed	
Stewart (1959)	*Brown v. Board of Education* (1954)	16 (24.2)
White (1962)	No Supreme Court cases discussed	
Goldberg (1962)	*South Carolina v. U.S.* (1905)	2 (40.0)
Fortas (1965)	*Reynolds v. Sims* (1964)	6 (54.6)
Marshall (1967)	*Miranda v. Arizona* (1966)	131 (31.6)
Fortas (1968)	*DeGregory v. Attorney General of New Hampshire* (1966)	32 (7.2)
Thornberry (1968)	*Breedlove v. Suttles* (1937)	11 (40.7)
Burger (1969)	*Baker v. Carr* (1962)	1 (16.7)
	Brown v. Board of Education (1954)	1 (16.7)
	Kent v. U.S. (1966)	1 (16.7)
	Lucas v. Forty-Fourth General Assembly (1964)	1 (16.7)
	Miranda v. Arizona (1966)	1 (16.7)
	Reynolds v. Sims (1964)	1 (16.7)
Haynsworth (1969)	*Textile Workers Union v. Darlington Manufacturing* (1965)	9 (45.0)
Carswell (1970)	*Brown v. Board of Education* (1954)	6 (66.7)
Blackmun (1970)	*Minnesota Mining v. New Jersey Wood Finishing* (1965)	8 (36.4)
Rehnquist (1971)	*Konigsberg v. State Bar of California* (1961)	17 (19.8)
Powell (1971)	*Brown v. Board of Education* (1954)	14 (21.2)
Stevens (1975)	*Yamashita v. Styer* (1946)	5 (27.8)
O'Connor (1981)	*Roe v. Wade* (1973)	24 (16.0)
Rehnquist (1986)	*Brown v. Board of Education* (1954)	45 (21.7)
Scalia (1986)	*Roe v. Wade* (1973)	17 (20.7)
Bork (1987)	*Griswold v. Connecticut* (1965)	143 (18.4)
Kennedy (1987)	*Brown v. Board of Education* (1954)	10 (10.5)
	Griswold v. Connecticut (1965)	10 (10.5)
Souter (1990)	*Roe v. Wade* (1973)	82 (22.3)
Thomas (1991)	*Roe v. Wade* (1973)	78 (16.1)
Ginsburg (1993)	*Roe v. Wade* (1973)	36 (7.8)
Breyer (1994)	*Dolan v. City of Tigard* (1994)	15 (8.1)
Roberts (2005)	*Roe v. Wade* (1973)	104 (12.1)
Alito (2006)	*Roe v. Wade* (1973)	48 (11.1)
Sotomayor (2009)	*District of Columbia v. Heller* (2008)	57 (14.5)
Kagan (2010)	*Citizens United v. Federal Election Commission* (2010)	115 (26.7)

This table represents the most frequently addressed Supreme Court decisions at each nominee's confirmation hearing. The numbers in parentheses in the third column indicate the percentage of comments represented by the most frequently addressed Supreme Court precedent at each hearing as a function of all statements addressing Supreme Court decisions at each hearing.

senators and nominees do consider important enough to discuss repeatedly at the hearings. This supports our assertion, developed in Chapters 6 and 7, that confirmation hearings help to validate judicial choices over time.

Notably, though, almost 40% of the cases listed in Table 5.2 are *not* present among the most debated precedents overall, indicating that some precedents are more short lived than others. For example, *South Carolina v. U.S.*,[43] in which the Court upheld the ability of the Internal Revenue Service to tax state liquor agents, accounted for 40% of the discussion of precedent at the Goldberg hearing. This case it made its first appearance at the Stewart hearing in 1959; was broached at the hearings of Goldberg, Marshall, and Fortas (for chief justice); and then disappeared. Further evincing the short-lived nature of some precedents, seven decisions in Table 5.2 appeared at only a single hearing: *DeGregory v. Attorney General of New Hampshire* (Fortas for chief justice), *Kent v. United States*[44] (Burger), *Textile Workers Union v. Darlington Manufacturing*[45] (Haynsworth), *Minnesota Mining v. New Jersey Wood Finishing*[46] (Blackmun), *Konigsberg v. State Bar of California*[47] (Rehnquist for associate justice), *Yamashita v. Styer*[48] (Stevens), and *Dolan v. City of Tigard*[49] (Breyer).

On average, the twelve precedents listed in Table 5.2, but not Table 5.1, appear at two hearings each, whereas those listed in both Tables 5.1 and 5.2 are discussed at ten hearings each. (Two cases, *Heller* and *Citizens United*, were available for discussion only at two hearings.[50]) Only two cases reported in Table 5.2, but not Table 5.1, were advanced at five or more hearings: *Baker v. Carr*[51] and *Reynolds v. Sims*.[52] *Baker*, in which the Court determined that the redistricting of legislatures was no longer a political question, and thus open to judicial review, appeared at nine hearings – Fortas (for chief justice),

[43] South Carolina v. U.S., 199 U.S. 437 (1905).

[44] Kent v. U.S., 383 U.S. 541 (1966) (involving the due process rights of juvenile defendants).

[45] Textile Workers Union v. Darlington Manufacturing, 380 U.S. 263 (1965) (implicating the ability of employers to terminate their businesses after their employees unionize).

[46] Minnesota Mining v. New Jersey Wood Finishing, 381 U.S. 311 (1965) (dealing with the scope of federal antitrust laws).

[47] Konigsberg v. State Bar of California, 366 U.S. 36 (1961) (relating to whether the state can deny bar admission to an applicant for refusing to answer questions regarding his affiliation with the Communist Party).

[48] Yamashita v. Styer, 327 U.S. 1 (1946) (involving the jurisdiction of military commissions).

[49] Dolan v. City of Tigard, 512 U.S. 374 (1994) (dealing with the ability of cities to use zoning regulations to require land owners to make improvements to their property).

[50] Recall that, although Citizens United was decided in 2010, it nonetheless was discussed at the Sotomayor hearing in 2009.

[51] Baker v. Carr, 369 U.S. 186 (1962).

[52] Reynolds v. Sims, 377 U.S. 533 (1964).

Burger, Stevens, O'Connor, Bork, Kennedy, Souter, Thomas, and Ginsburg – a span of twenty-five years. *Reynolds*, which established the one-person, one-vote standard with respect to the reapportionment of legislative districts, was discussed at the hearings of Fortas (for associate justice), Marshall, Burger, Bork, and Souter, also covering a quarter century of confirmation hearings.

Thus, it is evident that, even though some cases may not find themselves among the most frequently addressed Supreme Court precedents overall, they are still capable of achieving confirmation longevity. As we illustrate in Chapter 6, another such case is *Lochner v. New York*.[53] In *Lochner*, the Court struck down a state law that established the maximum number of hours that bakers could work on the grounds that the law violated the liberty to contract found in the Fourteenth Amendment. Although this case addresses a seemingly mundane issue, it has nonetheless become one of the most significant, and assailed, Supreme Court decisions.[54] The case, famously, gave its name to an entire epoch in the Court's history – the *Lochner* era – used to denote the period from about 1890 to 1937 in which the Court regularly invalidated state and federal social welfare legislation.[55] Though it took *Lochner* until 1971 to be addressed by name at the hearings, the issues surrounding the *Lochner* era appeared much sooner and the case was subsequently debated by name at seven hearings – Rehnquist (for associate justice), Bork, Thomas, Ginsburg, Breyer, Roberts, and Alito – spanning more than three decades. Overall, *Lochner* is the thirty-first most frequently addressed Supreme Court precedent at the hearings.

CONCLUSIONS

Throughout this book, we argue that the confirmation hearings are a key mechanism through which the public helps shape the development of constitutional law over time. The hearings do this by acting as a forum in which the public, through its elected representatives on the Judiciary Committee, engages in a dialogue about constitutional meaning. At the hearings, senators and nominees debate the constitutional choices made by the high Court, and

---

[53] Lochner v. New York, 198 U.S. 45 (1905).
[54] See, e.g., Howard Gillman, *The Constitution Besieged: The Rise and Demise of Lochner Era Police Powers Jurisprudence* (Durham, NC: Duke University Press, 1993); William H. Rehnquist, "The Notion of a Living Constitution," 54 *Texas Law Review* 693 (1976); David A. Strauss, "Why Was *Lochner* Wrong?" 70 *University of Chicago Law Review* 373 (2003).
[55] See, e.g., Lewis F. Powell, Jr., "*Carolene Products* Revisited," 82 *Columbia Law Review* 1087 (1982); Stephen A. Siegel, "Understanding the *Lochner* Era: Lessons from the Controversy over Railroad and Utility Rate Regulation," 70 *Virginia Law Review* 187 (1984).

ultimately embrace some of those choices as conditions of confirmation – decisions or doctrines nominees are expected to accept or reject before being confirmed.

This chapter empirically explored the extent to which hearing dialogue focuses on the concrete discussion of Supreme Court precedents. Our data reveal that it took some time for the discussion of precedent to take hold at the hearings. Although many of the early hearings involved discussions of constitutional issues, they did not do so through the lens of the Court's decisions. Indeed, it was not until the hearing of Thurgood Marshall in 1967 that debates about the Court's precedents became a mainstay of hearing colloquy. Today, we can expect about one-sixth of hearing dialogue to devote itself to the specific discussion of the Supreme Court's decisions. Thus, although constitutional issues certainly were explored at earlier hearings, those issues rarely took the form of discussions about particular precedents.

This chapter also examined just which precedents are debated at the hearings. Several notable precedents have appeared at many or most of the confirmation hearings held since they were decided. Many of the cases that have ingrained themselves into hearing discourse are so familiar that even a casual observer of the Supreme Court will recognize them, such as *Brown v. Board of Education*, *Roe v. Wade*, and, most recently, *District of Columbia v. Heller*. Some of these high-profile cases remain controversial. Their role in the hearings, discussed in Chapter 8, is largely one of providing an accessible language (case names) through which we continue to debate contested constitutional issues. Senators use the hearings as a forum to argue why these currently controversial cases should or should not be deemed part of our constitutional consensus. While Chapter 8 addresses the issue of currently contested issues, Chapters 6 and 7 focus on the other high-profile cases – those on which a constitutional understanding has been embraced. It is these cases that are ratified over time as nominees are expected to accept or reject them as a condition of confirmation.

6

Confirmation Conditions

Chapter 5 provided an empirical foundation for understanding the use of precedent at Supreme Court confirmation hearings. This chapter and the one that follows build on our data by taking us to the heart of our story about the role of the confirmation process in ratifying constitutional change. In these chapters, we show how both nominees and senators employ Supreme Court precedents to construct a democratically accepted set of constitutional commitments capable of changing over time. Using our empirical data, we have identified a variety of such commitments, including *Brown v. Board of Education*,[1] *Griswold v. Connecticut*,[2] and (almost certainly) *District of Columbia v. Heller*.[3] As we illustrate in these chapters, nominees testifying before the Senate Judiciary Committee are expected to affirm their allegiance to, or rejection of, these decisions. This is so despite the fact that many of these cases embody what were once deeply contested constitutional meanings. The expectation that nominees will signal their acceptance (or rejection) of such cases at their hearings provides a democratically credentialed method through which these decisions are woven into our core constitutional understandings, despite the legal uncertainty they originally embodied.

As we demonstrate in the text that follows, cases and doctrines attain the status of confirmation conditions in a variety of ways. Hearing dialogue takes many forms, even about key cases, and it would be foolhardy to expect all such discourse to take a common form across multiple hearings. It is clear, however, that confirmation conditions share three common characteristics. First, they involve cases or doctrines that have a sufficiently high public profile such that they are discussed repeatedly over a series of confirmation hearings. Second,

---

[1] Brown v. Board of Education, 347 U.S. 483 (1954).
[2] Griswold v. Connecticut, 381 U.S. 479 (1965).
[3] District of Columbia v. Heller, 171 L. Ed. 2d 637 (2008).

they involve situations in which the routine tools of legal reasoning are capable of generating multiple legally plausible answers to the constitutional question presented. In other words, they represent situations in which the Court had to make a constitutional choice. Finally, they become conditions of confirmation only when the choice made by the Court has been accepted (or rejected) by a sufficiently broad and long-lasting segment of the American public, indicating that a social consensus exists with respect to the case or doctrine at the time of the hearing. This often is evidenced at the hearings by the fact that senators of both parties expect nominees to embrace (or reject) the case or doctrine as part of our constitutional canon.

Importantly, we are not arguing that the hearings create the consensus. To the contrary, the consensus develops independent of the hearings, through changes in public opinion and social norms.[4] Our point is that the hearings act as a democratically legitimate forum in which those changes are validated as constitutional choices. Thus, we offer a novel perspective on the importance of the confirmation hearings by illustrating how the hearings assimilate previously controversial cases or doctrines into an understanding of the Constitution that is endorsed in a formal and public setting.

In this chapter, we discuss four such cases or doctrines. The first two, *Brown v. Board of Education* and the cases surrounding the constitutionalization of gender equality,[5] are examples of norms today's nominees are expected to accept to win confirmation. Our third case, *Lochner v. New York*,[6] has for decades been a decision nominees were expected to reject at the hearings, although, as we show later, this norm may be changing. Finally, we discuss the development of what we believe is likely to become a new confirmation condition, triggered by the Court's recent decision in *District of Columbia v. Heller*. Although it is too soon for certainty, we predict that *Heller* will quickly

---

4 See, e.g., Larry D. Kramer, *The People Themselves: Popular Constitutionalism and Judicial Review* (New York: Oxford University Press, 2004); Mark Tushnet, *Taking the Constitution Away from the Courts* (Princeton: Princeton University Press, 2000). For a discussion of other ways in which public opinion and social norms influence judicial decisions, see Lee Epstein and Andrew D. Martin, "Does Public Opinion Influence the Supreme Court? Possibly Yes (But We're Not Sure Why)," 13 *University of Pennsylvania Journal of Constitutional Law* 263 (2010); Michael W. Giles, Bethany Blackstone, and Richard L. Vining, Jr., "The Supreme Court in American Democracy: Unraveling the Linkages between Public Opinion and Judicial Decision Making," 70 *Journal of Politics* 293 (2008).
5 As we discuss later, because it took the discussion of gender equality decades to appear at the hearings, no cases involving gender discrimination appear in Table 5.1. Nonetheless, gender equality provides an excellent example of changing norms regarding the development of a confirmation condition.
6 Lochner v. New York, 198 U.S. 45 (1905).

enter the corpus of cases nominees are expected to accept before taking their seats on the high Court (if it has not done so already).

Each of these cases or doctrines represents constitutional choices made by the Court that were neither self-evident nor inevitable. They have, nonetheless, become part of the Constitution that Americans today accept as their own and agree to be governed by. Each, moreover, obtained their status as a confirmation condition in quite different ways. *Brown's* long journey took it from being one of the most controversial decisions ever issued by the Supreme Court to being one of the most revered legal decisions in United States history. The issue of constitutional restrictions on gender discrimination, in contrast, was virtually invisible at the hearings for decades, but once raised was rather quickly and readily absorbed into our constitutional consensus. *Lochner* – and the practice of vigorous judicial oversight of economic regulation the case came to represent – spent years in the heart of the anti-canon, but now appears to be crawling its way back into the contested zone of our constitutional understandings. *Heller*, in contrast, shows the Court leading from behind: validating a constitutional right that the vast majority of American's already believed they enjoyed. The remainder of this chapter tells the story of how confirmation discourse about each of these cases or doctrines has evolved over time, while Chapter 7 illustrates that process at work in the context of more than two decades of the most recent hearings.

THE EVOLUTION OF *BROWN*

The paradigmatic example of a constitutional choice that today's nominees are expected to accept if they hope to be confirmed is *Brown v. Board of Education. Brown* has become so essential to our constitutional self-identity that it is easy to forget that when the case was first decided it was *legally*, not just socially, controversial. The "colorblind" reading of the Equal Protection Clause advocated by today's constitutional formalists was soundly rejected by the constitutional formalists of 1954. Professor Herbert Wechsler of Columbia Law School famously deemed it an insufficiently "neutral principle" on which to rest constitutional lawmaking.[7] In contrast, the "separate but equal" doctrine invalidated by *Brown* was, in 1954, seen as fully consistent with most accepted modes of constitutional interpretation: it was supported by precedent, compatible with the text of the Constitution, and was almost certainly consonant

---

[7]   Herbert Wechsler, "Toward Neutral Principles of Constitutional Law," 73 *Harvard Law Review* 1 (1959).

with the understandings held by most of the post–Civil War Americans who ratified the Fourteenth Amendment.[8]

The early disputes about *Brown* were on vivid display during the confirmation hearings of John Marshall Harlan II and Potter Stewart, who were among the first nominees to face the Senate Judiciary Committee after *Brown* was decided. Harlan's 1955 hearing – the first post-*Brown* hearing – was short, but the brand new case hung over the proceeding. The questions of Senator Eastland (D-MS), who had engaged in public battles with the Court since *Brown* was announced, nicely illustrate how anger about *Brown* was manifested at these early hearings. Eastland, seething with hostility toward the Court, repeatedly asked Harlan questions such as whether he agreed that "... the Supreme Court of the United States should change established interpretations of the Constitution to accord with the economic, political, or sociological views of those who from time to time constitute the membership of the Court."[9] He followed this by asking Harlan whether he believed that "the difficulty of amending the Constitution or the delay which is incident to the use of the amendment process prescribed in the Constitution ever justify the Supreme Court in changing established interpretations or provisions in the Constitution."[10] To make sure no one missed his point, Eastland closed by asking whether Harlan agreed that "the Constitution den[ies] legislative powers to the courts as well as it does to the Executive."[11] This rhetoric – accusing the justices of "amending" the Constitution, legislating from the bench, and failing to follow precedent – were at the time core and well understood components of the segregationist critique of *Brown*.[12]

---

[8] See, e.g., Raoul Berger, *Government by Judiciary: The Transformation of the Fourteenth Amendment* (Cambridge, MA: Harvard University Press, 1977); Alexander M. Bickel, "The Original Understanding and the Segregation Decision," 69 *Harvard Law Review* 1 (1955); Michael J. Klarman, "*Brown*, Originalism, and Constitutional Theory: A Response to Professor McConnell," 81 *Virginia Law Review* 1881 (1995); Mark V. Tushnet, "Following the Rules Laid Down: A Critique of Interpretivism and Neutral Principles," 96 *Harvard Law Review* 781 (1983). But see, e.g., Robert H. Bork, *The Tempting of America: The Political Seduction of the Law* (New York: The Free Press, 1989); Patrick J. Kelley, "An Alternative Originalist Opinion for *Brown v. Board of Education*," 20 *Southern Illinois University Law Journal* 75 (1996); Michael W. McConnell, "Originalism and the Desegregation Decisions," 81 *Virginia Law Review* 947 (1995).

[9] Harlan transcript, questioning by Senator Eastland (D-MS) at 140.

[10] Ibid. at 141.

[11] Ibid. at 141.

[12] See, e.g., Gerald D. Rosenberg, *The Hollow Hope: Can Courts Bring about Social Change?* (Chicago: University of Chicago Press, 1991); Clive Webb, "A Continuity of Conservatism: The Limitations of *Brown v. Board of Education*," 70 *Journal of Southern History* 327 (2004).

The questioning of Potter Stewart four years later was more direct. *Brown* had by this point become the flashpoint of Southern hostility to the Court, and Stewart was interrogated extensively by the senators about his opinion of the case. Senator McClellan (D-AR) informed Stewart that he "wholly disagree[d] with" the *Brown* decision and needed to know Stewart's opinion on it in order to do his duty with respect to Stewart's confirmation.[13] Senator Eastland was only slightly more subtle: "Before May 1954," he pointed out, "the Supreme Court in a number of cases held that the [separate but] equal doctrine met the test of the 14th Amendment. That was changed after that date, in *Brown vs. Board of Education*. Was that an amendment of the Constitution?"[14] Eastland went on a moment later, asking whether Stewart agreed that "the courts should be bound by precedent that is a century old."[15]

Stewart also was grilled about the methodology used by the Court in *Brown*. "Do you think," Eastland asked, "that the courts should cite as authority for decisions, textbooks, or documents written by individuals that have never been part of the record in the case. . . . Let us take the *Brown* case. There was a book written by a man named Murdock. I don't think Mr. Murdock could stand a security investigation. It was cited as an authority in that case. Do you think that is proper?"[16] Senator McClellan followed up in his round of questioning by asking Stewart if he agreed with "the view, the reasoning and the logic applied or the lack of application of either or both, as the case may be, and the philosophy expressed by the Supreme Court in arriving at its decision in the case of *Brown vs. Board of Education* on May 17, 1954?"[17] McClellan, plainly, did not.

Senator Ervin (D-NC) joined in the critique of *Brown*'s methodology. Arguing that *Brown* was based on factual assumptions "which are not really true,"[18] Ervin posed this question to Stewart:

> In my judgment those same words [factual assumptions which are not true] can be applied to the statement of the Court to the effect that history left this question inconclusive because the debates in the Congress which drafted the Amendment clearly showed that it was the purpose of Congress to embody in the equal protection of the laws clause of the Fourteenth Amendment the provisions of the Civil Rights Act of 1866. The debates in Congress showed that the Civil Rights Act of 1866 was amended by its own sponsors in order to make it clear that it was not intended to require mixed students.[19]

---

[13] Stewart transcript, questioning by Senator McClellan (D-AR) at 40.
[14] Stewart transcript, questioning by Senator Eastland (D-MS) at 15.
[15] Ibid.
[16] Ibid. at 17–18.
[17] Stewart transcript, questioning by Senator McClellan (D-AR) at 36.
[18] Stewart transcript, questioning by Senator Ervin (D-NC) at 125.
[19] Ibid.

Senator Ervin was equally explicit in his closing statement:

I think the *Brown v. Board of Education* was a most unfortunate decision from the standpoint of law, Constitutional law, in the United States. . . . [t]he Court said that it couldn't turn the clock back to 1868 when the Amendment was ratified or even to 1896 when *Plessy v. Ferguson* was decided, and yet since Constitutional provisions are to be interpreted to ascertain and give effect to the intention of the people who drew them and approved them, that is exactly what the Supreme Court should have done. They should have turned the clock back to 1868 when the Amendment was ratified. . . . [20]

As these statements make clear, *Brown* was, to the questioning senators, an unsupportable usurpation of state power by an out of control judiciary hell bent on imposing its personal preferences in lieu of constitutional law. Constitutional law, in turn, was seen as perfectly ascertainable through the standard interpretive tools of precedent, original intent, and text. And those tools clearly did not, in these senators' view, support *Brown*.

In the face of this assault, Stewart balked at giving an opinion of the case. Unlike today's nominees, who cannot say enough good things about *Brown*, Stewart worked hard to avoid a direct answer. His comments about the case, in fact, are much more reminiscent of the manner in which today's nominees respond to currently contested cases such as *Roe v. Wade*[21] than the way they respond to *Brown*. Stewart said that, of course, courts ought to give a very great deal of weight to precedent,[22] that the Court cannot amend the Constitution,[23] and that he did not necessarily agree with "all of the grammar, and all footnotes and everything" in *Brown*.[24] In the end, Stewart went only so far as to inform the senators that "I would not like you to vote for me for the top position that I am dedicated to because I am for overturning that decision, because I am not. I have no prejudgment against that decision."[25]

A nominee who waffled this much on *Brown* today would not be confirmed. But at the time of Stewart's hearing, the country was still debating *Brown* and the future of civil rights.[26] Opposition to *Brown* was not strong enough to make its *rejection* a condition of Stewart's confirmation, but nor was it essential for confirmation that a nominee unequivocally embrace the case. Instead, in 1959,

---

[20] Ibid. at 124.
[21] Roe v. Wade, 410 U.S. 113 (1973).
[22] Stewart transcript at 15–16.
[23] Ibid. at 15.
[24] Ibid. at 36–7.
[25] Ibid. at 63.
[26] See, e.g., Michael J. Klarman, *From Jim Crow to Civil Rights: The Supreme Court and the Struggle for Racial Equality* (New York: Oxford University Press, 2004); Rosenberg, *The Hollow Hope*, supra, n. 12.

Brown was a case on which no constitutional consensus had been reached and therefore no specific answer was required. In the end, only seventeen senators – all from former Confederate states – voted against Stewart's appointment.[27] Embracing *Brown* was not yet a condition of confirmation.

Nor would it be for some time. At the hearings of Johnson appointees Byron White, Arthur Goldberg, Abe Fortas (for associate justice), and Thurgood Marshall, *Brown* went largely underground. In fact, the case appeared by name at only two of these hearings, those of Fortas and Marshall.[28] But the rhetoric developed in the wake of *Brown* was on full display at each hearing. White, nominated in 1962, was asked very few questions (and, as discussed later, an unfortunate amount of his hearing dialogue was about his prowess on the football field). He was, however, pressed on his thoughts regarding "the Supreme Court attempting to legislate"[29] and the extent of congressional authority under the Exceptions Clause to pass bills restricting the Supreme Court's appellate jurisdiction,[30] a flurry of which had been introduced in Congress after *Brown*.[31]

The use of *Brown* at the Goldberg and Fortas (for associate justice) hearings was similarly opaque. Senator McClellan, who had made his dislike of *Brown* clear at the Stewart hearing, employed typical anti-*Brown* rhetoric to ask Goldberg whether he would "side with those who prefer so to interpret the Constitution as to permit them to actually write new law."[32] McClellan went on to ask whether Goldberg would lean "toward that reformist experimentation and innovation, that thirst to legislate the law and amend the Constitution from the High Bench rather than to referee the law as written by Congress, and the Constitution as written by the Founders."[33] Would Goldberg, McClellan

---

[27] Lee Epstein, Jeffrey A. Segal, Harold J. Spaeth, and Thomas G. Walker, *The Supreme Court Compendium: Data, Decisions, and Developments* (Washington, DC: CQ Press, 1994) at 289; Lori A. Ringhand, "'I'm Sorry, I Can't Answer That': Positive Legal Scholarship and the Supreme Court Confirmation Process," 10 *University of Pennsylvania Journal of Constitutional Law* 331 (2008) at note 91.

[28] Fortas transcript at 53; Marshall transcript at 168.

[29] White transcript at 23.

[30] Ibid. at 24–5.

[31] See, e.g., Theodore Eisenberg, "Congressional Authority to Restrict Lower Federal Court Jurisdiction," 83 *Yale Law Journal* 498 (1974); Wilfred Feinberg, "Constraining 'The Least Dangerous Branch:' The Tradition of Attacks on Judicial Power," 59 *New York University Law Review* 252 (1984); Walter F. Murphy, *Congress and the Court: A Case Study in the American Political Process* (Chicago: University of Chicago Press, 1962); C. Herman Pritchett, *Congress versus the Supreme Court, 1957–1960* (Minneapolis: University of Minnesota Press, 1961).

[32] Goldberg transcript, questioning by Senator McClellan (D-AR) at 7.

[33] Ibid. at 9.

continued, allow the senators to "indulge the hope that you will oppose making the Supreme Court a third legislative body?"[34]

Discussions of *Brown* continued in this manner at the Fortas associate justice hearing in 1965, at which the case was referenced directly only once, by Senator Ervin. Ervin was chiming in on a line of questioning from Senator Fong (R-HI) regarding whether the one-person, one-vote standard established in *Reynolds v. Sims*[35] could be interpreted to infer that the Fifth or Fourteenth Amendments supersedes the constitutional provisions guaranteeing each state two senators. Fong's concern appeared to be that if this were the case, smaller states such as Hawaii would lose representation in the Senate. Ervin briefed Fong and Fortas on his own position on the subject, expressing his displeasure with the Court's reasoning in *Bolling v. Sharp*,[36] the case in which the Court used the Fifth Amendment to declare unconstitutional racial segregation in public schools in the nation's capital (the Fourteenth Amendment, which *Brown* was based on, applies only to the states). Ervin opined that, if the Court could use the Fifth and Fourteenth Amendments interchangeably, it was only logical that the Senate would have to be reapportioned following *Reynolds*. In his response, Fortas did not directly address either *Brown* or *Bolling*, prompting Ervin to follow up with his by now familiar lecture about the Court's misuse of its judicial power. "I might add," he said, "more dangerous than that, though, is the fact that judges can take the due-process clause and make it mean almost anything they want it to mean. I think the Senators here learned that they do that on many occasions, and I hope you [Fortas] will not do so."[37]

This type of questioning – using the rhetoric deployed in response to *Brown* but not calling out nominees on the case itself – continued throughout the Thurgood Marshall and Warren Burger hearings. Thurgood Marshall led the NAACP Legal Defense Fund's litigation team during *Brown*. He was the first African American nominated to the Supreme Court, and his hearing was laced with thinly disguised racism.[38] Yet, the ground around *Brown* had shifted enough that his opponents dared not criticize the case directly, even with its primary architect sitting in front of them. In fact, the only specific mention of *Brown* at the hearing was made by Marshall, not the senators.[39]

---

[34] Ibid.

[35] Reynolds v. Sims, 377 U.S. 533 (1964).

[36] Bolling v. Sharpe, 347 U.S. 497 (1954).

[37] Fortas associate justice transcript, questioning by Senator Ervin (D-NC) at 55.

[38] See, e.g., Stephen L. Carter, *The Confirmation Mess: Cleaning Up the Federal Appointments Process* (New York: Basic Books, 1994).

[39] Marshall transcript at 168.

Instead, *Brown* once again was attacked by the senators through the rhetoric of judicial lawmaking (which by this point had been even further inflamed by the Warren Court's criminal procedure revolution).[40]

Senator Ervin again led the attack. Ervin introduced a resolution of state supreme court justices, circulated in 1958, stating that the Supreme Court was encroaching upon the areas reserved by the Constitution to the states.[41] Pegging his question to that resolution, Ervin asked whether Marshall agreed that the Supreme Court "has failed in recent years to confine itself to its allotted constitutional sphere, that of interpreting the Constitution rightly?"[42] Ervin then went on to talk about methods of constitutional interpretation. "Is not the role of the Supreme Court simply to ascertain and give effect to the intent of the framers of the Constitution and the people who ratified the Constitution. . . . it is the duty of the Supreme Court, is it not, to interpret the Constitution according to its true intent?"[43] The Constitution, Senator Eastland helpfully interjected, "cannot mean one thing today and another thing tomorrow, can it?"[44] Since "changes" to the Constitution are amendments to it, Ervin continued, and because the sole method of amending the Constitution is found in Article V of the Constitution, then no justice is "ever authorized by any provision of the Constitution to change its meaning while professing to interpret it, is he?"[45]

Questioning continued in this vein for some time. McClellan used his questions to ask Marshall how Supreme Court justices can be seen as complying with the law of the land when they are "free to reverse previous decisions that involve constitutional questions."[46] Such "changing of the law," he said, "is bringing chaos and confusion to our system of justice."[47] Senator Strom Thurmond (R-SC) grilled Marshall on the history of the Fourteenth Amendment.[48] Thurmond went on to ask Marshall how the original understanding of the Equal Protection Clause could be reconciled with Supreme Court cases "forbidding discrimination in State laws rendered since 1954?"[49] – an obvious reference to *Brown*.

---

[40] See, e.g., Jerold H. Israel, "Criminal Procedure, the Burger Court, and the Legacy of the Warren Court," 75 *Michigan Law Review* 1319 (1977).
[41] Marshall transcript, questioning by Senator Ervin (D-NC) at 27.
[42] Ibid.
[43] Ibid. at 49.
[44] Marshall transcript, questioning by Senator Eastland(D-MS) at 49.
[45] Marshall transcript, questioning by Senator Ervin (D-NC) at 50.
[46] Marshall transcript, questioning by Senator McClellan (D-AR) at 157.
[47] Ibid. at 156.
[48] Marshall transcript, questioning by Senator Thurmond (R-SC) at 175.
[49] Ibid. at 166.

Sidebar: Thurgood Marshall

President Lyndon B. Johnson nominated Thurgood Marshall to the Supreme Court in 1967, more than a decade after Marshall led the NAACP Legal Defense Fund (LDF) litigation team that successfully argued *Brown v. Board of Education*. By the time of Marshall's nomination, *Brown* had become a broadly accepted, albeit not yet canonized, part of our constitutional understandings. Consequently, even senators who opposed the decision rarely attacked the case by name. But residual hostility toward civil rights, racial equality, and Marshall himself certainly remained. Marshall's appointment five years earlier to the United States Court of Appeals for the Second Circuit had been held up for ten months by Olin D. Johnston (D-SC), the chair of the subcommittee considering the nomination. The subcommittee held six hearings on the nomination, and Johnston refused to move it on to the full Senate until he was faced with a bipartisan threat to force it out of the subcommittee for a vote.[50]

At Marshall's Supreme Court confirmation hearing, Senator Strom Thurmond, also from South Carolina, took up where Johnston left off. His questioning of Marshall was venomous. Thurmond began by stating that, given Marshall's work experience (presumably with the LDF), the Thirteenth and Fourteenth Amendments must be within his area of expertise. Thurmond then asked a series of detailed questions about the history of these amendments. As he goes on, the questions become more and more arcane. "What constitutional difficulties," he asked, "did Representative John Bingham of Ohio see, or do you see, in congressional enforcement of the privileges and immunities clause of article IV, section 2, through the necessary and proper clause of article I, section 8?"[51]

The colloquy continued:

Senator THURMOND: Now, on the 14th amendment, what committee reported out the 14th amendment and who were its members?

Judge MARSHALL: I don't know, sir.

Senator THURMOND: Why do you think the framers of the original version of the first section of the 14th amendment added the necessary and proper clause from article I, section 8, to the privileges and immunities clause of article IV, section 2?

Judge MARSHALL: I don't know, sir.

Senator THURMOND: What purpose did the framers have, in your estimation, in referring to the incident involving former Representative Samuel Hoar in Charleston, S.C., in December, 1844, as showing the need for the enactment of the original version of the 14th amendment's first section?

Judge MARSHALL: I don't know, sir.

[50] Warren Weaver, Jr., "Senate Hearings on Marshall End," *New York Times*, August 24, 1962.
[51] Marshall transcript, questioning by Senator Thurmond (R-SC) at 163.

Senator THURMOND: Why do you think the framer said that if the privileges and immunities clause of the 14th amendment had been in the original Constitution the war of 1860–65 could not have occurred?

Judge MARSHALL: I don't have the slightest idea.

Senator THURMOND: Why do you think the equal protection clause of the original draft of the first section of the 14th amendment required equal protection in the rights of life, liberty and property only?

Judge MARSHALL: I don't know.

Senator THURMOND: Did you understand that question?

Judge MARSHALL: Yes, sir.

Senator THURMOND: ... Now, what were the constitutional provisions of Indiana and Oregon which it was the purpose of the framer of the first section of the 14th amendment to override; and why did the framer say the Oregon constitution violated the U.S. Constitution as it then stood; and how would proposal and ratification of the first section of the 14th amendment, either in the original draft or the final draft, have overridden the Indiana and Oregon constitutions?"[52]

After continuing in this vein for some time, Thurmond argued that because Ohio (and several other states) had laws in place, at the time of passage of the Fourteenth Amendment, that prohibited African Americans from voting, "intermarrying with white persons," or attending desegregated schools, that therefore none of those rights could plausibly have been included in the protections provided by the Equal Protection Clause.[53]

Despite Thurmond's efforts to make the celebrated lawyer appear unqualified for the high Court, Marshall was confirmed by the full Senate by a vote of 69–11, with twenty senators not voting. All but one of the objecting senators, Robert Byrd (D-WV), hailed from the former Confederacy.[54]

Marshall's troubles with the Judiciary Committee did not end in 1967, however. Elena Kagan, nominated by President Barack Obama in 2010, clerked for Justice Marshall in his later years on the Court. Several senators used their opening comments at the Kagan hearing to take aim at Marshall's judicial legacy. Senator Kyl (R-AZ) critiqued Justice Marshall's jurisprudence, calling him the "epitome of a results-oriented judge" and questioned Kagan's admiration of his approach to decision making.[55] Senator Grassley (R-IA) repeated President Obama's statement that Kagan credited Marshall with teaching her that "behind the law there are stories,

---

[52] Ibid. at 164.
[53] Ibid. at 168.
[54] Fred P. Graham, "Senate Confirms Marshall as the First Negro Justice; 10 Southerners Oppose High Court Nominee in 69-to-11 Vote," *New York Times*, August 31, 1967.
[55] Kagan transcript, opening statement by Senator Kyl (R-AZ) at 19–20.

stories of people's lives as shaped by the law, stories of people's lives as might be changed by the law." This "empathy standard," Grassley said, "has been soundly rejected because it endorses the application of personal politics and preferences when judges decide cases."[56]

The constant critiques of Marshall in the opening statements of conservative senators led Senator Durbin (D-IL) to defend Marshall, declaring that America is a "better nation because of the tenacity, integrity, and values of Thurgood Marshall." "Some," Durbin continued, "may dismiss Justice Marshall's pioneering work on civil rights as an example of empathy; that somehow, as a black man who had been a victim of discrimination, his feelings became part of his passionate life's work; and I say, thank God."[57]

Opponents of *Brown*, however, were fighting a losing battle. By the late 1960s, *Brown* was widely accepted by the public and embraced by constitutional theorists.[58] Warren Burger's 1969 hearing featured just a few cryptic references to *Brown*. He was asked the standard set of post-*Brown* questions about whether the Supreme Court can "amend" the Constitution through interpretation, whether the Court has the power to "legislate," and whether the Court has an obligation to take "special care" to preserve the "rights and responsibilities" of state and local governments.[59] Senator Byrd (D-WV) also asked Burger if it was the "proper function" of federal judges to "incorporate their personal notions of what is socially, economically, or politically desirable" into judicial opinions.[60] But the direct attacks on *Brown* were gone. *Brown* was evolving from a hotly contested case that a nominee would be wise to avoid discussing to a consensus case that a nominee would be wise to embrace.

This transformation continued at the unsuccessful hearings of Clement Haynsworth in 1969 and Harrold Carswell in 1970. Although both of these nominees were defeated in the Senate in part due to their opposition to civil rights,[61] *Brown* failed to play a major role at either hearing. In fact, the senators referenced *Brown* only once at the Haynsworth hearing, though the reference,

---

[56] Kagan transcript, opening statement by Senator Grassley (R-IA) at 15.
[57] Kagan transcript, opening statement by Senator Durbin (D-IL) at 32.
[58] See, e.g., David G. Barnum, "The Supreme Court and Public Opinion: Judicial Decision Making in the Post- New Deal Period," 47 *Journal of Politics* 652 (1985); William E. Nelson, "*Brown v. Board of Education* and the Jurisprudence of Legal Realism," 48 *St. Louis University Law Journal* 795 (2004); Brad Snyder, "How the Conservatives Canonized *Brown v. Board of Education*," 52 *Rutgers Law Review* 383 (2000); Rosenberg, *The Hollow Hope*, supra, n. 12.
[59] Burger transcript at 5.
[60] Burger transcript, questioning by Senator Byrd (D-WV) at 15–16.
[61] See, e.g., John P. Frank, *Clement Haynsworth, the Senate, and the Supreme Court* (Charlottesville: University Press of Virginia, 1991); John Anthony Maltese, *The Selling of Supreme Court Nominees* (Baltimore: Johns Hopkins University Press, 1995); Richard E. Vatz and

and the nominee's response, were both supportive of the case. In the middle of a line of questioning regarding whether Haynsworth agreed with the decisions of Earl Warren,[62] Senator Hart (D-MI) engaged the nominee in the following brief exchange:

> **Senator HART:** I am speaking now of what he [Warren] did in terms of leading that Court in the direction that history will reflect was very timely, in the best long term interests of the country. He got into trouble because he said, among other things, that "separate but equal" wasn't equal and wasn't constitutional.
> Do you agree with him?

> **Judge HAYNSWORTH:** I certainly do.[63]

With that, the senator moved on, following up with a question regarding the right to counsel. Thus, it seems that Haynsworth felt compelled to support the reasoning of *Brown*, but not to elaborate on it or embrace it with vigor. This indicates that the case was gaining traction – Haynsworth's answer about the case was much more direct than Potter Stewart's had been – but had not yet entered our constitutional canon. This "in between" status of the case (moving out of the contested zone but not yet in the canon) is supported by the fact that Haynsworth would have been an ideal candidate to question aggressively for his opposition to *Brown* and the principles it stood for. As a Fourth Circuit Court of Appeals judge, Haynsworth had a less than stellar record of applying *Brown*.[64] Indeed, at his hearing, representatives from the Black American Law Students Association, the Congressional Black Caucus, the Leadership Conference on Civil Rights (made up of 125 civil rights organizations), and the NAACP all testified against the nominee, largely on the basis of his failure to properly enforce *Brown*. However, the senators did not press him on the case; it had not yet developed into a confirmation condition.

When Haynsworth's nomination was defeated in the Senate by a 55–45 vote, President Nixon nominated Harrold Carswell to fill the empty seat. *Brown* again played only a minor role in the process. At Carswell's hearing, Senator Scott (R-PA) posed the following question to Carswell: "The support of *Brown v. Board of Education* as a standing precedent of the Court does not give you any concern, does it?" Carswell's answer was succinct: "No, sir."[65] Neither the

---

Theodore Otto Windt, Jr., "The Defeats of Judges Haynsworth and Carswell: Rejection of Supreme Court Nominees," 60 *Quarterly Journal of Speech* 477 (1974).

[62] Haynsworth transcript, questioning by Senator Hart (D-MI) at 75.

[63] Ibid.

[64] See, e.g., Snyder, "How the Conservatives Canonized *Brown*," supra, n. 50 at 421–6.

[65] Carswell transcript, questioning by Senator Scott (R-PA) at 63.

senator nor the nominee elaborated or followed up on the question. *Brown* was also addressed by Senator Burdick (D-ND), who noted that "[i]n such areas covered by the *Brown* decision and some other areas, at the present time, at least, in your opinion, the law is pretty well set in that area." Carswell replied "I don't think there is any question about it."[66] Again, there was no follow-up and no elaboration.

As with Haynsworth, the discussion (or lack thereof) of *Brown* at the Carswell hearing is especially interesting given that Carswell, like Haynsworth, was far from a champion of civil rights, particularly those involving desegregation efforts.[67] For example, as a U.S. Attorney, he helped privatize a public golf course to evade complying with the Court's desegregation precedents.[68] During his tenure as a district court judge, he was frequently reversed by the Fifth Circuit in desegregation cases.[69] As Joseph Rauh, who testified on behalf of the 125-organization Leadership Conference on Civil Rights against Carswell, put it: "Judge Carswell is Judge Haynsworth with a cutting edge. He is Haynsworth with a bitterness and a meanness that Judge Haynsworth never had."[70] In spite of all this, however, the senators did not interrogate Carswell on *Brown* with any frequency or force. Although both Haynsworth and Carswell were defeated, in part due to their lackluster support for civil rights, *Brown* clearly had not yet fully entered our constitutional canon.

Brown's slow but steady shift from a contested case into one sitting in the center of our constitutional canon continued a year later at the 1971 associate justice hearing of William Rehnquist. Suspicious of Rehnquist's position on civil rights issues, Senator Edward Kennedy (D-MA) asked Rehnquist what the country should expect of him in this area, if he were confirmed. Rehnquist took the opportunity to say that *Brown* was the "established constitutional law of the land," and that he had no desire to revise it.[71] Arguments from precedent, which for more than a decade had been used against *Brown*, would now, it appeared, be given as a reason to support the case.

Senator Bayh (D-IN) explicitly noted this change, as did Rehnquist in his answer to Bayh's question:

---

[66] Carswell transcript, questioning by Senator Burdick (D-ND) at 65.

[67] See, e.g., Snyder, "How the Conservatives Canonized *Brown*," supra, n. 50 at 426–30.

[68] Jake C. Miller, "The NAACP and the Confirmation of Supreme Court Justices, 1930–1991," in *Contemporary Patterns of Politics, Praxis, and Culture*, ed. Georgia A. Persons (New Brunswick, NJ: Transaction Publishers, 2005).

[69] Snyder, "How the Conservatives Canonized *Brown*," supra, n. 50 at 428.

[70] Carswell transcript at 305.

[71] Rehnquist associate justice transcript, questioning by Senator Kennedy (D-MA) at 76.

Senator BAYH: Are you aware that probably few cases in history have provoked louder cries of anguish from some members of this committee than *Brown* versus *Board of Education*, and that there is probably not a better example that they would use to support the contention that you should not support "lawmaking" as a Supreme Court judge as symbolized in their minds in *Brown* versus *Board of Education*?

Mr. REHNQUIST: Of course, I do not support lawmaking as a Supreme Court judge; but as I stated yesterday, if nine Justices, presumably of the same varying temperaments that one customarily gets on the Supreme Court at the same time, all address themselves to the issue and all unanimously decide that the Constitution requires a particular result, that, to me, is very strong evidence that the Constitution does, in fact, require that result. But that is not lawmaking. It is interpretation of the Constitution just as was contemplated by John Marshall in *Marbury* versus *Madison*.[72]

This statement, as Senator Bayh recognized, was extraordinary. In seventeen years, *Brown* had gone from being the quintessential example of judicial overreaching and lawless decision making – the rallying cry of "strict constructionists" – to a valued precedent and act of constitutional interpretation worthy of John Marshall.

Brown's full canonization had not yet been revealed, however. That transformation took fifteen more years, not coming into fruition until the *next* time William Rehnquist sat before the Senate Judiciary Committee, as a nominee for the chief justice position. Rehnquist had been a law clerk for Supreme Court Justice Robert Jackson at the time *Brown* was decided. As Jackson's clerk, Rehnquist penned a memo supporting *Plessy* that urged Jackson to decline to overturn the "separate but equal" doctrine *Plessy* endorsed. The language of the memo is jarring. "[R]egardless of the Justice's individual views on the merits of segregation," it said, "it quite clearly is not one of those extreme cases which commands intervention from one of any conviction." "I realize," the memo went on, "that it is an unpopular and unhumantiarian position, for which I have been excoriated by 'liberal' colleagues, but I think *Plessy v. Ferguson* was right and should be re-affirmed."[73]

The memo was made public on December 5, 1971, a month after Rehnquist's associate justice hearing before the Judiciary Committee had ended, but before the full Senate began debating his nomination.[74] Thus, the memo

[72] Rehnquist associate justice transcript, questioning by Senator Bayh (D-IN) at 167.
[73] Rehnquist chief justice transcript at 325.
[74] The memo first appeared in an article in *Newsweek* that was released on December 5, a week before it was published in print: "Supreme Court: Memo from Rehnquist," *Newsweek*,

was not discussed during that hearing. His chief justice hearing, held in 1986, was different. Rehnquist was grilled relentlessly about the memo. By 1986, opposition to *Brown* was enough to disqualify a nominee and Rehnquist was repeatedly required to disavow the language contained in the memo. He told the Committee that the memo was written to reflect Justice Jackson's views, not his own (Justice Jackson voted with the unanimous Court in *Brown*), and that although he had, as Jackson's clerk, some hesitation about overturning *Plessy*, he attributed it to concerns about *stare decisis* and original intent, not to the merits of the argument presented in the case itself.[75] For our purposes, the point is not whether these assertions are accurate. Rather, the point is that by 1986, a Supreme Court nominee testifying before the Senate Judiciary Committee was compelled to make them. The Rehnquist chief justice hearing revealed that *Brown* had unquestionably entered our constitutional canon.

Subsequent nominations confirm this. Antonin Scalia, who answered very few specific questions at his hearing,[76] nonetheless felt it necessary to reject the "separate but equal" doctrine overturned by *Brown*.[77] The canonization of *Brown* was even more evident a year later, when Robert Bork, who aggressively defended an interpretive method that he readily acknowledged would rewind much of the work of the Warren Court, nonetheless felt compelled to explain in great detail how that interpretive approach could be made consistent with the outcome in *Brown*.[78] By the time Ruth Bader Ginsburg was confirmed in 1993, the initial rhetoric about *Brown* had been turned completely on its head. Far from decrying the case as judicial activism run amok, Senator Orin Hatch (R-UT), one of the more conservative members of the Senate Judiciary Committee, defended *Brown* as a case in which the Court properly applied a *conservative* interpretive method, describing it as one in which the Court was "actually interpreting the laws in accordance with the original meaning

---

December 13, 1971. See Brad Snyder, "What Would Justice Holmes Do (WWJHD)?: Rehnquist's *Plessy* Memo, Majoritarianism, and *Parents Involved*," 69 *Ohio State Law Journal* 873 (2008) at note 2. See also Mark Tushnet, *A Court Divided: The Rehnquist Court and the Future of Constitutional Law* (New York: W. W. Norton, 2005) at 20.

[75] Rehnquist chief justice transcript at 137–8: "Yes; that I thought *Plessey* [sic] had been wrongly decided at the time, that it was not a good interpretation of the equal protection clause to say that when you segregate people by race, there is no denial of equal protection. But *Plessey* [sic] had been on the books for 60 years; Congress had never acted, and the same Congress that had promulgated the 14th amendment had required segregation in the District schools."

[76] See, e.g., Ringhand, "'I'm Sorry, I Can't Answer That,'" supra, n. 27; Nina Totenberg, "The Confirmation Process and the Public: To Know or Not to Know," 101 *Harvard Law Review* 1213 (1988) at 1219.

[77] Scalia transcript at 86.

[78] Bork transcript at 132, 284–6.

which, of course, under the 14th Amendment meant equal protection, equal rights, equality."[79] *Brown* had come full circle.

Today, glowing endorsements of *Brown* are standard fare at confirmation hearings, regardless of the ideological inclinations of the nominee or questioning senator.[80] Methods of constitutional interpretation are judged by whether they can accommodate *Brown*, and proponents of competing interpretive methods fight to claim *Brown* as an example of their preferred methodology at work.[81] The country, in short, has embraced the constitutional proposition made by the Court in *Brown*. Adherence to that proposition, although previously contested, is now expected. Any nominee who spoke out against *Brown* today would not and should not be confirmed, and any senator who voted for such a nominee would do so at his or her immediate electoral peril. *Brown* is part of our current constitutional consensus.

Many things, of course, contributed to this canonization, most notably changes in public opinion and social mores. What the validation of *Brown* through the confirmation process adds is a mechanism through which the changes that *Brown* embodies were publically and formally debated and accepted as constitutional changes. Nor is *Brown* unique in this regard. Similar transformations have occurred in other areas, including the constitutionalization of restrictions on gender discrimination.

GENDER DISCRIMINATION

The Senate Judiciary Committee's treatment of gender issues did not undergo the dramatic, high-profile metamorphosis enjoyed by *Brown*. Gender, unlike race, snuck up on the senators. Once it took root, however, the constitutional norm of gender equality was embraced just as fully. The earliest hearings in our data set do not discuss gender issues at all; issues of gender discrimination were not broached until the Carswell hearing in 1970. Even though the early hearings did not deal with issues of gender discrimination directly, the language used by senators and nominees in these hearings is decidedly not the language of gender equity.

Byron White's hearing illustrates this. Prior to his nomination, White had a successful and impressive legal career. He graduated with honors from Yale Law School, worked in private practice, and served in the Kennedy

---

[79] Ginsburg transcript, questioning by Senator Hatch (R-UT) at 126.
[80] See, e.g., Roberts transcript at 178; Alito transcript at 452; Sotomayor transcript at 3.3; Kagan transcript at 96.
[81] See, e.g., Snyder, "How the Conservatives Canonized *Brown*," supra, n. 50.

Administration's Justice Department where he was, among other things, a vocal defender of the Freedom Rider's efforts to integrate transportation in the Jim Crow South. He also, and perhaps more famously, was a professional football player for the Pittsburgh Pirates (now Steelers) and the Detroit Lions.[82]

White's entire hearing testimony consists of only forty-six comments, taking up just four and a half pages in the bound version of the hearing transcripts compiled by Mersky and Jacobstein.[83] One and a half of those pages are dedicated to senatorial gushing about White's athletic and physical prowess. The senators talked about how wonderful it would be to have someone on the Court who understands professional football and baseball (why this would be so wonderful is not entirely clear, although apparently some of the senators were at the time working on some sports-related legislation). Senator Hart (D-MI) chimed in to say how "anybody charged with the responsibility, and everybody has at least an indirect responsibility in trying to raise children, male children, will find the job enormously helped by being able to point to an outstanding male such as Mr. White."[84] To this Senator Long (D-MO) helpfully replied that he was raising girls and that they too "can look with great admiration toward physical prowess."[85]

Senator Hruska (R-NE), practically alone among the chorus of admiring senators, did make some effort to focus his enthusiasm on White's impressive legal career. The comment he made in doing so, however, may be even more revealing of the gender norms of the era than were those of the other senators. "I do believe," Hruska said, "every lawyer in the land does rejoice when his ranks of the practicing attorney are called upon to fill the vacancy on the Supreme Court. It means one of their boys has 'made it.' "[86] As indeed it did.

Gender discussions at the hearings became more serious over time. Rehnquist received a few questions about gender equity at his associate justice hearing. The Equal Protection Clause, Rehnquist said, protects "women just as it protects other discrete minorities."[87] As he went on to point out, however, no case decided by the Court to that date actually found that a gender distinction violated the Constitution.[88] John Paul Stevens, nominated four

---

[82] Dennis J. Hutchinson, *The Man Who Once Was Whizzer White: A Portrait of Justice Byron R. White* (New York: The Free Press, 1998).

[83] Roy M. Mersky and J. Myron Jacobstein, eds., *The Supreme Court of the United States: Hearings and Reports on Successful and Unsuccessful Nominations of Supreme Court Justices by the Senate Judiciary Committee, 1916–1975* (Buffalo, NY: William S. Hein, 1977).

[84] White transcript, questioning by Senator Hart (D-MI) at 22.

[85] White transcript, questioning by Senator Long (D-MO) at 23.

[86] White transcript, questioning by Senator Hruska (R-NE) at 24.

[87] Rehnquist associate justice transcript at 163.

[88] Ibid.

years later, was asked a similar question, and gave a similar answer: women are "covered" by the Equal Protection Clause, but had not yet achieved full equality.[89]

The issue of gender equity was percolating into the hearings, however. The National Organization of Women (NOW) testified at the Stevens hearing, against his confirmation. NOW President Margaret Drachsler put the subject squarely on the table:

> ... NOW wishes to express the feelings of millions of women and men today, it is time to have a woman on the Supreme Court. After 200 years of living under laws written, interpreted, and enforced exclusively by men, we have a right to be judged by a court which is representative of all people, more than half of whom are women. The President owes us a duty to begin to eliminate the 200 years of discrimination against women. In our judicial system this could be partially accomplished by appointing a woman to the Supreme Court. He has failed us.[90]

President Reagan would succeed where President Ford failed. Reagan's nomination of Sandra Day O'Connor in 1981 finally brought the first woman to the high Court. The members of the Senate Judiciary Committee enthusiastically celebrated this milestone, and O'Connor (unlike Thurgood Marshall) was treated by the Committee with the respect such a trailblazer deserves.[91] Despite this celebration of her appointment, O'Connor was asked relatively few *substantive* questions about gender discrimination and the Constitution. Senator Denton (R-AL) broached the topic, asking about women in combat positions. "Would you," he asked O'Connor, "give your present personal position with respect to women serving in actual military combat or ships and planes which would likely become involved in combat?" "Mr. Chairman," O'Connor responded, "speaking as a personal matter only, I have never felt and do not now feel that it is appropriate for women to engage in combat if that term is restricted in its meaning to a battlefield situation, as opposed to pushing a button someplace in a missile silo."[92] The exchange then continued as follows:

---

[89] Stevens transcript at 15.

[90] Ibid. at 78–9.

[91] Senator Eastland, alone among the questioning Senators, repeatedly referred to O'Connor as "Mrs. O'Connor" rather than "Judge O'Connor," which was the address routinely used in other hearings in which a sitting judge was being questioned. Although we have no reason to think that Eastland did this to show intentional disrespect, we do note that it is unlikely that such a thing would happen today, or go unremarked if it did. O'Connor transcript at 105–6, 198, 200–2.

[92] O'Connor transcript, questioning by Senator Denton (R-AL) at 127.

Senator DENTON: In other words, you would not want them to be in a position to be shot?

Judge O'CONNOR: To be captured or shot? No, I would not. [Laughter]

Senator DENTON: Well, it may astound this audience, but at the Naval Academy not too many months ago there were young ladies standing up and demanding to be placed in just that position, and saying that that was their right to do so because they were accepted into the Naval Academy, so it really is not all this laughable, you know. I am glad to hear that is your opinion, Judge O'Connor.[93]

Senator Metzenbaum (D-OH) later asked O'Connor if it was "inappropriate judicial activism" for the Burger Court in *Reed v. Reed*[94] to say that discrimination on the basis of sex was unconstitutional. *Reed*, a case Metzenbaum clearly supported, had for the first time found that a gender distinction in a state law violated the Equal Protection Clause. O'Connor gave a limited reply, saying only that "it was in my view an appropriate consideration of the problem of gender-based discrimination."[95]

Hearing dialogue about gender evolved a bit further by 1986. Rehnquist and Scalia both faced hearings that year, Rehnquist for chief justice and Scalia for an associate justice position. Both nominees were pushed on the appropriate standard of review for gender discrimination claims, an issue that was obscured in *Reed*. Interestingly, both of these nominees drew a distinction in their answers with regard to gender between "invidious" (i.e., causing harm or malice) and "non-invidious" discrimination.

Defending an intermediate standard of review, Rehnquist noted that:

Women and men are virtually equal in our population. And much of the traditional discrimination against women by virtue of labor laws and so forth, while very unfair to them, nonetheless, does not have the – there are many situations in which distinctions between men and women are not genuinely invidious in the way that – it is not felt that it was the same thing to say, for example, that we do not hire blacks for heavy labor, which is a violently offensive thing, or to say we do not hire women for heavy labor. One may be as wrong as the other, but there is not the same invidious context.[96]

Scalia, asked the same question, gave an almost identical answer. Like Rehnquist, he began by acknowledging the Court's regime of tiered equal

---

[93] Ibid. at 128.
[94] Reed v. Reed, 404 U.S. 71 (1971).
[95] O'Connor transcript, questioning by Senator Metzenbaum (D-OH) at 160.
[96] Rehnquist chief justice transcript at 341.

protection review, noting that discrimination against what he identified as the "[s]o-called suspect categories" received heightened judicial scrutiny.[97] Scalia was not specifically asked additional questions about gender discrimination and the Equal Protection Clause, but he was asked about the propriety of a judge belonging to a men's-only club, as Scalia had prior to his nomination. Like Rehnquist, Scalia invoked the invidious/non-invidious distinction. Judges, Scalia said, should not be members of clubs that practice invidious discrimination, but the issue was whether the exclusion of women from his club was invidious. Drawing a distinction between race and gender, Scalia said he would not belong to a club that practiced racial discrimination, because such discrimination is clearly invidious: "I regard the two as quite different," he said, "and I would think that a club that discriminates on the basis of race or on the basis of religion, that would be invidious discrimination. I think the jury's out on whether it's invidious discrimination to have a men's club."[98]

Scalia was correct, of course: in 1986, the jury was very much still out on both the propriety and constitutionality of gender distinctions. By the time Ruth Bader Ginsburg appeared before the Committee in 1993, however, the issue had gained more constitutional traction, in large part because of the efforts of Ginsburg herself, along with growing support among the American public.[99] Ginsburg (who replaced Justice White) spent much of her legal career litigating – and winning – major gender discrimination cases such as *Reed v. Reed*, *Frontiero v. Richardson*,[100] and *Weinberger v. Wiesenfeld*.[101]

At her hearing, this history was roundly celebrated as the senators praised Ginsburg's accomplishments. Addressing the audience assembled in the hearing room, Ginsburg herself noted how far women had come in the past few decades. "It may be astonishing to some of the young people sitting behind you," she said, "that laws like [those challenged in *Reed v. Reed*] were on the books in the States of the United States in the early 1970s, but they were.

---

[97] Scalia transcript at 57.

[98] Ibid. at 100.

[99] See, e.g., Catherine I. Bolzendahl and Daniel J. Myers, "Feminist Attitudes and Support for Gender Equality: Opinion Change in Women and Men, 1974–1998," 83 *Social Forces* 759 (2004); Clem Brooks and Catherine Bolzendahl, "The Transformation of US Gender Role Attitudes: Cohort Replacement, Social-Structural Change, and Ideological Learning," 33 *Social Science Research* 106 (2004); Nancy Burns and Katherine Gallagher, "Public Opinion on Gender Issues: The Politics of Equity and Roles," 13 *Annual Review of Political Science* 425 (2010).

[100] Frontiero v. Richardson, 411 U.S. 677 (1973) (prohibiting the government from differently distributing military benefits on the basis of gender).

[101] Weinberger v. Wiesenfeld, 420 U.S. 636 (1975) (invalidating gender distinctions in the distribution of social security benefits).

And there were many of them."[102] Musing about how "shocked" some men were when she talked about laws restricting the role of women as discrimination, she described her role as "trying to educate the judges that there was something wrong with the notion 'sugar and spice and everything nice, that's what little girls are made of.'" That very notion, she said, "was limiting the opportunities, the aspirations of our daughters."[103]

Such a sentiment may not have been abhorrent to the men sitting on the Senate Judiciary Committee in earlier decades, but it also, self-evidently, had not struck them as worthy of discussion in a constitutional context. By 1993, it was. Senator DeConcini's (D-AZ) comments in this regard are typical. Questioning Ginsburg, he pointed out how the "heightened scrutiny test has made an enormous difference in combating laws that discriminate against women" and invited Ginsburg to opine on whether the standard of review should be even higher.[104] Subsequent nominees have embraced *Reed v. Reed* and the application of at least intermediate review to gender distinctions; several recent nominees, in fact, have gone further, stating or implying that strict scrutiny review may be more appropriate.[105] Gender equity, like racial equity, has been embraced as a core part of our constitutional understanding.

It is true – in gender as well as in race – that the cases and constitutional propositions addressed at the hearings are often accepted or rejected as much for the symbolic principles they have come to stand for as the legal weight they currently carry. This is particularly true the further in time a given hearing is from the date on which the case being discussed was decided.[106] This hardly renders the affirmation of these cases at the hearings meaningless, however. The repeated validation of *Brown*, for example, tells us that our constitutional consensus now requires that we accept people of color as full and equal citizens under law and that state-sanctioned, intentional, race-based subordination is

---

[102] Ginsburg transcript at 121.

[103] Ibid. at 122.

[104] Ginsburg transcript, questioning by Senator DeConcini (D-AZ) at 164. In addition, a variety of other Senators from both political parties asked Ginsburg similar questions with regard to gender discrimination. See, e.g., Ginsburg transcript, questioning by Senators Biden (D-DE) at 121; Kennedy (D-MA) at 136; Thurmond (R-SC) at 141; Specter (R-PA) at 189–93; Cohen (R-ME) at 223; Brown (R-CO) at 339.

[105] See, e.g., Kennedy transcript at 118; Souter transcript at 75–6; Thomas transcript at 204; Breyer transcript at 178–9; Roberts transcript at 191.

[106] Consider the recent fight in *Parents Involved* about the legacy of *Brown*. Each of the justices currently sitting on the Court would claim – did claim – fidelity with *Brown*. The justices nonetheless vehemently disagreed with each other about what that fidelity required in the case presented, as we discuss in Chapter 8. Parents Involved in Community Schools v. Seattle School District No. 1, 551 U.S. 701 (2007).

constitutionally prohibited. Our affirmation of heightened scrutiny for gender discrimination likewise tells us that women are now seen as entitled to constitutional protection against the grossest forms of state-sanctioned discrimination. Neither of these basic principles begins to answer *currently* contested race- and gender-related issues such as affirmative action, state-sanctioned integration efforts, and abortion. That fact does not, however, reduce the significance of the profound change represented by the adoption of the basic principles of racial and gender equity into the constitutional canon. It is important to remember that the principles these cases stand for, which today seem too abstract to be of much practical use, were *not* part of our constitutional consensus prior to and immediately after *Brown, Reed,* and *Frontiero.* Acceptance of them had real constitutional bite, and our distance from their original controversies should not mask that fact.

LOCHNER AND THE PATH NOT TAKEN

There are numerous cases and issues areas, like *Brown* and the gender discrimination cases, that have gained constitutional validation through repeated affirmation at the confirmation hearings, several of which we discuss in Chapter 7. Precedents also, however, can be used at the confirmation hearings to *reject* constitutional paths tentatively forged by the Supreme Court. These cases form the anti-canon: cases that a nominee is expected to renounce in order to be confirmed. In recent decades, such cases have included *Plessy v. Ferguson,*[107] *Dred Scott v. Sandford,*[108] and *Korematsu v. United States.*[109] Indeed, nominees appearing in the past three decades have routinely rejected these decisions by name.[110] These cases show how the confirmation process takes off the table what were once legally acceptable constitutional outcomes: in each of them, the Court used generally accepted tools of interpretation to reach what the justices saw at the time as acceptable – indeed constitutionally compelled – outcomes. Those outcomes, however, were rejected by the American people. Over time, they were rejected so soundly that nominees expecting to be

[107] Plessy v. Ferguson, 163 U.S. 537 (1896).
[108] Dred Scott v. Sandford, 60 U.S. 393 (1857).
[109] Korematsu v. United States, 323 U.S. 214 (1944).
[110] On *Plessy,* see Rehnquist chief justice transcript at 226; Bork transcript at 104; Kennedy transcript at 149; Souter transcript at 303; Thomas transcript at 469; Breyer transcript at 357; Roberts transcript at 241; Alito transcript at 379; Sotomayor transcript at 2.60; Kagan transcript at 153. On *Dred Scott,* see Bork transcript at 315; Kennedy transcript at 175; Thomas transcript at 464; Ginsburg transcript at 126, 188; Breyer transcript at 357; Roberts transcript at 241. On *Korematsu,* see Bork transcript at 314; Ginsburg transcript at 210; Breyer transcript at 226–227; Roberts transcript at 241; Alito transcript at 418; Sotomayor transcript at 2.60.

confirmed are obliged to voice their opposition to them. What where once legally defensible positions thus become constitutionally unacceptable. They become part of the anti-canon.[111]

But what constitutes the anti-canon (or the canon, for that matter) is always in flux.[112] The confirmation career of *Lochner v. New York* illustrates this. Open, transcribed confirmation hearings begin in 1939, just two years after the Supreme Court got out of the business of aggressively reviewing economic regulations enacted by state legislatures and Congress.[113] As we illustrated in Chapter 5, very few cases were broached during the first two decades of hearings in which the nominees testified. The senators discussed a wide array of constitutional issues at these early hearings, but they did not use cases as the vehicles for doing so.

Sidebar: Communism

Although most of this chapter focuses on high-profile cases nominees become expected to accept or reject as a condition of their confirmation, there also are important norms nominees are expected to conform to that are not tied as directly in the public mind to individual cases. Constitutional restrictions on gender discrimination are one example of this. Historically, however, the most striking of these is the use of the hearings to force nominees to denounce communism.

To today's ear, this may sound a bit quaint. But the fight against communism was very serious business for the first several decades of open hearing testimony. The first nominee in our data set, Felix Frankfurter, was excoriated on this front. The senators railed at Frankfurter for being a founding member of the American Civil Liberties Union, for being associated with a well-known British communist, and for having defended a group of striking miners in Arizona. To many of the senators (and to almost all of the testifying witnesses), these activities clearly meant that Frankfurter was likely to be harboring communist sympathies.[114] Question after question implicitly accused Frankfurter of just that. Finally, Senator Neely (D-WV), a Frankfurter ally who was chairing the Committee, initiated this exchange:

---

[111] See, e.g., J.M. Balkin and Sanford Levinson, "The Canons of Constitutional Law," 111 *Harvard Law Review* 963 (1998); Jamal Greene, "The Anticanon," 125 *Harvard Law Review* 379 (2011); Richard A. Primus, "Canon, Anti-Canon, and Judicial Dissent," 48 *Duke Law Journal* 243 (1998).

[112] Jack M. Balkin, "'Wrong the Day it was Decided:' *Lochner* and Constitutional Historicism," 85 *Boston University Law Review* 677 (2005).

[113] See, e.g., Robert G. McCloskey, "Economic Due Process and the Supreme Court: An Exhumation and Reburial," 1962 *Supreme Court Review* 34 (1962); Stuart S. Nagel, "Court-Curbing Periods in American History," 18 *Vanderbilt Law Review* 925 (1964).

[114] Lori A. Ringhand, "Aliens on the Bench: Lessons in Identity, Race and Politics from the First 'Modern' Supreme Court Confirmation Hearing to Today," 2010 *Michigan State Law Review* 795 (2010).

Senator NEELY: Some of those who have testified before the committee have, in a very hazy, indefinite way, attempted to create the impression that you are a Communist. Therefore, the Chair asks you the direct question: are you a Communist, or have you ever been one?

Dr. FRANKFURTER: I have never been and I am not now.[115]

Senator McCarran (D-NV) was not satisfied. "By that," he jumped in, "do you mean that you have never been enrolled as a member of the Communist Party?" "I mean," Frankfurter replied, "much more than that. I mean that I have never been enrolled, and have never been qualified to be enrolled, because that does not represent my view of life, nor my view of government."[116]

The specter of communism would appear over and over again at the hearings. John Marshall Harlan II was asked a series of questions about his involvement with the "Atlantic Union" movement, which worked after World War II to unite the world's democracies into a common federation. What would be the effect, Senator Jenner (R-IN) asked Harlan, of such an organization when "about a third of the members of the French Assembly are elected by the Communist vote?"[117] Harlan responded by citing his military service to the country and decrying the evils of communist nations.[118]

William Brennan, who testified in 1957 as a sitting justice after a recess appointment, was questioned extensively by the fading anti-communist crusader Senator Joseph McCarthy (R-WI). McCarthy, obviously piqued by comments Brennan had made earlier about the tactics being used by congressional investigatory committees such as McCarthy's Permanent Subcommittee on Investigations, grilled Brennan about his opinion of whether international communism was or was not a threat to the United States. At one point McCarthy asked Brennan whether he "adopted the gobbledegook" that communism is merely a political party, not a conspiracy (a legally meaningful distinction at the time).[119] Brennan, like Harlan and Frankfurter before him, responded by renouncing communism and affirming his loyalty to the American way.

The last hearing in which concerns about communism played a major role was that of Arthur Goldberg. Goldberg, nominated in 1962, was President Kennedy's secretary of labor, and was a noted union lawyer who, among other things, oversaw the merger of the American Federation of Labor and the Congress of Industrial Organizations. Senator Wiley (R-WI) began his questioning of Goldberg by observing that he received numerous letters "intimating" that Goldberg was a communist.[120] Goldberg responded by listing his anti-communist activities. As part of his work

[115] Frankfurter transcript, questioning by Senator Neely (D-WV) at 128.
[116] Frankfurter transcript, questioning by Senator McCarran (D-NV) at 128.
[117] Harlan transcript, questioning by Senator Jenner (R-IN) at 172.
[118] Ibid. at 172.
[119] Brennan transcript, questioning by Senator McCarthy (R-WI) at 18.
[120] Goldberg transcript, questioning by Senator Wiley (R-WI) at 43.

with the unions, Goldberg said, he supervised a purge of communist sympathizers. He offered a report of this work to the Committee, which was duly entered into the record.[121] He also gave this rousing speech:

> I regard and have regarded communism to be a dangerous international movement, incompatible with our democratic traditions. I have never deviated from that viewpoint from the earliest days of my life.... I regard the Communist movement to be a perversion of what people have a right to expect from government and from life. It is completely contrary to our way of life. We believe in freedom and democracy, and the right of people to speak their convictions, and their right to live in a society where they can criticize you or me, where they can take issue with a President of the United States, or a senator, or a congressman, or a private citizen.[122]

Senator Wiley was satisfied. "You have," he said later in the hearing, "made a presentation that ought to clearly convince anyone who is interested and not completely prejudiced that you have never been a Communist and you are not sympathetic toward their philosophy."[123]

That changed in the 1950s. Beginning with the Stewart hearing in 1959, all but one of the hearings (that of Byron White) involved the discussion of Supreme Court cases. *Lochner v. New York* was one of those cases, appearing by name at seven hearings, spanning the course of more than three decades.[124] *Lochner* involved a state law governing the working hours of bakers. The case survives in our legal lexicon, however, because it gave its name to the era – the *Lochner* era – in which the Court was seen as inappropriately using its power of judicial review to invalidate a host of state and federal laws involving various economic regulations.[125] Though the case may not be quite as publicly recognizable as *Brown* or as the idea that the Constitution prohibits gender discrimination, the doctrine established in *Lochner* – that the Court should stay out of the business of economic regulation – has deep roots in American politics. Indeed, debates about the scope of federal government involvement

---

[121] Ibid. at 56.
[122] Ibid. at 44.
[123] Ibid. at 63.
[124] As we demonstrate later, because nominees were quick to disavow *Lochner* at the hearings, it has not generated the same amount of discussion as cases that took longer to develop into confirmation conditions, such as *Brown*. This is evident in both Table 5.1 and in the discussion of economics in Chapter 3.
[125] See, e.g., Howard Gillman, *The Constitution Besieged: The Rise and Demise of Lochner Era Police Powers Jurisprudence* (Durham, NC: Duke University Press, 1993); William H. Rehnquist, "The Notion of a Living Constitution," 54 *Texas Law Review* 693 (1976); David A. Strauss, "Why Was *Lochner* Wrong?" 70 *University of Chicago Law Review* 373 (2003).

in economic regulation date to the founding era[126] and regularly appear in the platforms of American political parties.[127]

Potter Stewart, testifying in 1959, was not asked about *Lochner* by name, but the senators did quite explicitly discuss the extent to which the Court should review economic regulations passed by Congress. Senator Dirksen (R-IL) framed the issue as follows:

> **Senator DIRKSEN:** ... pending in another committee on which I serve is a bill which proposes to bring the service trades at the local level within the purview of the Fair Labor Standards Act, and I will tell you now I have got some difficulty in getting myself into a frame of mind that a clerk in a grocery store in my home town is in commerce because he reaches up and pulls a can of corn off the shelf that they brought from some wholesaler across the State line over in a neighboring State, and this is far from an academic matter when it comes to expanding, stretching the commercial clause of the Constitution, and sooner or later we are going to have to fight that one out.... [128]

The senators then engaged in a little friendly joking about the Court's retreat from the realm of economic regulation:

> **Senator KEATING:** Would the Senator yield?
>
> **Senator ERVIN:** Yes.
>
> **Senator KEATING:** If such legislation should be enacted and it was not within the purview of the Constitution, then the Supreme Court would so decide.
>
> **Senator DIRKSEN:** You say the Supreme Court would so decide? [Laughter]
>
> **Senator KEATING:** Well, it would be their duty to decide that issue. That perhaps would be a more accurate way to put it.[129]

Stewart, wisely, said nothing.

---

[126] Alexander Hamilton, "The Federalist No. 22," in *The Federalist Papers by Alexander Hamilton, James Madison, and John Jay,* ed. Garry Wills (New York: Bantam Books, 1982); Max Farrand, ed. *The Records of the Federal Convention of 1787* (New Haven: Yale University Press, 1937) at 625.

[127] See, e.g., Ian Budge, Hans-Dieter Klingemann, Andrea Volkens, Judith Bara, and Eric Tanenbaum, *Mapping Policy Preferences: Estimates for Parties, Electors, and Governments 1945–1998* (Oxford: Oxford University Press, 2001); Richard Franklin Bensel, *The Political Economy of American Industrialization, 1877–1900* (Cambridge: Cambridge University Press, 2000); Gerald Pomper, "'If Elected, I Promise': American Party Platforms," 11 *Midwest Journal of Political Science* 318 (1967).

[128] Stewart transcript, questioning by Senator Dirksen (R-IL) at 104–5.

[129] Stewart transcript, questioning by Senator Keating (R-NY) at 105.

Lochner made its inaugural hearing appearance by name relatively late in the day, showing up for the first time at the 1971 Rehnquist associate justice hearing. Rehnquist's treatment of *Lochner* is typical of how most nominees have approached the case: he renounced it. Asked by Senator Kennedy to distinguish the conservatism of Justice Felix Frankfurter from that of the justices who had stuck down economic regulations during the *Lochner* era, Rehnquist replied as follows:

> Well, I would say that the series of freedom of contract cases, *Lochner v. New York*, *Adkins v. Children's Hospital*, by the objective judgment of historians, represented an intrusion of personal political philosophy into constitutional doctrine which the framers had never intended, and that Frankfurter had criticized that from outside of the Court.[130]

A few exchanges later, Rehnquist elaborated, saying that the "sense of legal historians objectively evaluating it, has said that the so-called nine old men were wrong, at least a majority of them were wrong, in reading in freedom of contract."[131]

Nominees following Rehnquist repeatedly said the same thing: *Lochner* was wrong, and my interpretative method will not yield the same type of error. Bork, for example, used *Lochner* as an example of the dangers of the Court's use of the substantive due process doctrine.[132] Clarence Thomas declared at least twice at his hearing that the post-*Lochner* cases were correctly decided, and that it was the role of Congress, not the courts, to make complex decisions about health, safety, and work standards. The Court, Thomas went on, should not sit as a super-legislature to second guess Congress on such issues.[133] Senator Hatch, who like many senators uses *Lochner* as a vehicle to criticize *Roe v. Wade*'s reliance on substantive due process, immediately agreed, adding that "I too think that it would be wrong for judges to strike down economic regulation, just like you do."[134]

Later nominees were just as clear on this point. Ginsburg, also questioned by Senator Hatch, denounced *Lochner*, agreeing with the senator that the Court had exceeded its authority in the *Lochner* era cases.[135] Breyer,[136] Roberts,[137]

---

[130] Rehnquist associate justice transcript, questioning by Senator Kennedy (D-MA) at 159.
[131] Ibid. at 160.
[132] Bork transcript at 182, 717.
[133] Thomas transcript at 115–16, 173.
[134] Thomas transcript, questioning by Senator Hatch (R-UT) at 174.
[135] Ginsburg transcript, questioning by Senator Hatch (R-UT) at 270.
[136] Breyer transcript at 113.
[137] Roberts transcript at 144, 162, 270.

and Alito[138] each made similar comments. Whatever our Constitution stood for between 1971 and 2006, it decidedly did not embrace the type of judicial oversight of economic regulation embodied in *Lochner v. New York*.

Lochner's story, however, has taken an interesting turn. In the most recent confirmation hearing, that of Elena Kagan, the dialogue surrounding *Lochner* appears, ever so slightly, to have shifted. Reacting to the enactment of the federal Patient Protection and Affordable Care Act (the comprehensive health insurance legislation passed early in President Obama's first term), some senators on the Judiciary Committee began, ever so carefully, to broach the possibility that perhaps judicial oversight of economic regulation is not quite as off-limits as the typical *Lochner* dialogue suggests. In large part, this change has been motivated by the controversy surrounding the Act's minimum coverage provision that requires Americans to purchase health care insurance or pay a tax penalty for failing to do so. At the Kagan hearing (as in much of the public discourse about the Act[139]), this discussion intermingled the individual liberty concerns underlying the substantive due process doctrine with the reach of congressional power under the Commerce Clause.[140] Consider this exchange between Senator Cornyn (R-TX) and Kagan:

> **Senator CORNYN:** And would you agree with me that if the Supreme Court of the United States is not going to constraint the power grabs of the federal government and constrain Congress in terms of its reach down to people's everyday lives, that there remain only two constitutional options available: one is either to pass a constitutional amendment, for Congress to propose it, and then to have that ratified by three-quarters of the states, or for a constitutional convention to be convened for purposes of proposing

[138] Alito transcript, questioning by Senator Feinstein (D-CA) at 395–6 (discussing congressional power over economic regulation).

[139] See Bryan J. Leitch, "Where Law Meets Politics: Freedom of Contract, Federalism, and the Fight Over Health Care," 27 *Journal of Law and Politics* 177 (2011).

[140] Substantive due process is doctrinally linked to the Fifth and Fourteenth Amendments, both of which prohibit governmental actors from depriving persons of "liberty" without "due process of law." The Commerce Clause grants Congress the power to regulate interstate commerce. During the *Lochner* era, the Court used these two doctrines in tandem to reduce the power of states and the federal government to regulate economic relations: the "liberty" provisions were used to protect the right of individuals to enter into contracts as they saw fit, without regulatory restrictions on the content of those contracts, while the Commerce Clause was read narrowly to prevent Congress from imposing similar restrictions at the federal level. See, e.g., Allgeyer v. Louisiana, 165 U.S. 578 (1897) (using the due process clause to strike down a state law regulating insurance) and Hammer v. Dagenhart, 247 U.S. 251 (1918) (striking down a federal child labor law). As noted previously, public debate about the Patient Protection and Affordable Care Act was frequently framed in the realm of individual liberty, even though the legal debate took place in the language of the Commerce and Taxing and Spending Clauses.

constitutional limits on Congress, which would then have to be ratified by three-quarters of the states. Do you agree with me, that's the only recourse of the people to a limitless reach of the Federal Government, assuming the Supreme Court won't do it?

Ms. KAGAN: Well, I do think that there are limits on Congress' commerce power. They're the limits that were set forth in *Lopez* and *Morrison*, and they're basically limits saying that Congress can't regulate under the Commerce Clause where the activity in question is non-economic in nature. I think that that's the limit that the Court has set. But within that, you're quite right that Congress has broad authority under the Commerce Clause to act. To the extent that you or anybody else thinks that Congress ought not to have that authority under the Commerce Clause to act, an amendment to the Commerce Clause would be a perfectly appropriate way of changing the situation.[141]

Senator Coburn (R-OK) later picked up where Cornyn left off:

Senator COBURN: Let me go to one other thing. Senator Cornyn attempted to ask this, and I think it's a really important question. If I wanted to sponsor a bill and it said, Americans, you have to eat three vegetables and three fruits every day, and I got it through Congress and it's now the law of the land, you've got to do it, does that violate the Commerce Clause?

Ms. KAGAN: Sounds like a dumb law. [Laughter.]

Senator COBURN: Yes. I've got one that's real similar to it I think it equally dumb. I'm not going to mention which it is.

Ms. KAGAN: But I think the question of whether it's a dumb law is different from whether the question of whether it's constitutional, and – and – and I think that courts would be wrong to strike down laws that they think are – are senseless just because they're senseless.[142]

Coburn went on to say that "we find ourselves in trouble as a Nation because the judiciary and the executive branch has not slapped Congress down on the massive expansion of the Commerce Clause."[143]

Coburn's question, like most of the questions on this issue, invoked concerns about individual freedom and liberty. Thus, even though it was formally framed as one involving Congress's Commerce Clause power, not one involving substantive due process, Kagan replied by citing the anti-*Lochner*

---

[141] Kagan transcript, questioning by Senator Cornyn (R-TX) at 161–2.
[142] Kagan transcript, questioning by Senator Coburn (R-OK) at 180.
[143] Ibid. at 180–1.

rational: it is inappropriate for the judiciary to second guess legislative policy judgments in the economic realm. The national deficit (which Coburn invoked as an example of runaway congressional power), she said, "may be an enormous problem. It may be an enormous problem, but I don't think it's a problem for courts to solve. I think it's a problem for the political process to solve."[144] Coburn was having none of it. "You missed my whole point," he said, "[w]e're here because the courts didn't do their job in limiting our ability to go outside of original intent on what the Commerce Clause was supposed to be. Sure, you can't solve the problem now, but you help create it as a court because you allowed something other than what our original founders thought."[145]

In one sense, this line of questioning is not unusual. (John Roberts, as we discuss in Chapter 8, also waded into these waters at his hearing.) Concerns about the proper scope of congressional power have recurred throughout the hearings, and do not in and of themselves repudiate the perceived overreaching of the *Lochner* Court's substantive due process cases. On the second day of Kagan's testimony, however, Coburn went further. Referencing the above discussion, Coburn specifically invoked both liberty interests and 1937, the year the Court famously disavowed the *Lochner* doctrine and retreated from the realm of economic regulation:

> ... this very expansive view of it as held by the Supreme Court which is counter to what our founders wrote, there's nobody that – it started in 1937. It's counter to what our founders wrote, and as it has expanded, liberty has declined. We've seen that rapidly increase. And it's not just Republican or Democratic institutions – administrations that have overseen that, they've both been guilty.
>
> So I just wanted to – whether you'd ever contemplated that, because I think that can give you some insight into what America is concerned about.[146]

It seems America, at least in Senator Coburn's eyes, may be getting ready for *Lochner* to step out of the anti-canon and for the judicial protection of economic liberty to wiggle its way back into the contested zone of constitutional meaning – a development further highlighted by the public and legal debate about the constitutionality of the Patient Protection and Affordable Care Act.[147]

---

[144] Ibid. at 182.
[145] Ibid.
[146] Ibid. at 281.
[147] We discuss this in greater detail in Chapter 8.

THE RIGHT TO KEEP AND BEAR ARMS: A NEW CONSENSUS?

As our discussion of *Brown* illustrates, Supreme Court precedents can take decades to evolve from contested cases to cases nominees are expected to accept or reject as a condition of their confirmation. Other cases, however, travel this path more quickly. Though it is too early for certainty, it seems likely that the individual right to keep and bear arms, developed by the Court in the landmark decisions of *District of Columbia v. Heller* (finding an individual right to bear arms regardless of militia service) and *McDonald v. Chicago*[148] (incorporating this right against the states) presents just such a situation.

The Second Amendment was on full display at the confirmation hearings of Sonia Sotomayor and Elena Kagan, with both Democratic and Republican senators probing the nominees on the issue. An astonishing 11% of the Sotomayor hearing was devoted to the topic, and almost 4% of the Kagan hearing focused on Second Amendment issues. Senator Leahy (D-VT) was first to address gun rights at the Sotomayor hearing: "Is it safe to say that you accept the Supreme Court's decision [in *Heller*] as establishing that the Second Amendment right is an individual right? Is that correct?" Sotomayor responded, "Yes, sir."[149] Leahy pressed further, asking Sotomayor about the possibility of incorporating the newly adjudicated right against the states (*McDonald* would be decided a year later). Sotomayor did not push back; instead, she quickly indicated that she would have an "open mind" with respect to incorporation.[150] She went to affirm her gun-right's credentials. "Like you," she said, "I understand how important the right to bear arms is to many, many Americans. In fact, one of my godchildren is a member of the NRA, and I have friends who hunt. I understand the individual right fully that the Supreme Court recognized in *Heller*."[151]

Sotomayor continued to affirm her support for *Heller* in the face of somewhat more contentious questioning by Senator Hatch. Hatch, who appeared notably more skeptical than Leahy of Sotomayor's position, pushed the nominee on the brewing incorporation question. Although Sotomayor refused to say directly whether she would vote to incorporate the Second Amendment,[152] she did repeat that she would "bring an open mind to every case."[153]

---

[148] McDonald v. Chicago, 177 L. Ed. 2d 894 (2010).
[149] Sotomayor transcript, questioning by Senator Leahy (D-VT) at 2.7.
[150] Ibid. at 2.8.
[151] Ibid.
[152] Sotomayor transcript, questioning by Senator Hatch (R-UT) at 2.26.
[153] Ibid.

Moreover, Sotomayor, said (discussing *Heller*) "once there's Supreme Court precedent. . . then the Supreme Court has to look at that."[154]

Sotomayor further showed her appreciation of *Heller* in the face of questions from Senator Feingold (D-WI): "Senator, the Supreme Court did hold that there is in the Second Amendment an individual right to bear arms, and that is its holding and that is the court's decision. I fully accept that."[155] When asked by Senator Kyl (R-AZ) whether she would consider herself bound by *Heller*, Sotomayor responded "Absolutely."[156] Sotomayor gave similar answers in response to questions from Senators Klobuchar (D-MN),[157] Sessions (R-AL),[158] Graham (R-SC),[159] and Coburn.[160]

Like Sotomayor did before her, Kagan vocally endorsed *Heller* at her hearing. She also embraced *McDonald*, which had been decided the day before her testimony began. Again, Senator Leahy broached the issue first: "Is there any doubt," he asked, "after the court's decision in *Heller* and *McDonald* that the Second Amendment to the Constitution secures a fundamental right for an individual to own a firearm, use it for self-defense in their home?" Kagan's response was unequivocal: "There is no doubt, Senator Leahy. That is binding precedent entitled to all the respect of binding precedent in any case. So that is settled law."[161] She affirmed this position repeatedly in response to questions from Senators Feinstein (D-CA),[162] Feingold,[163] Grassley (R-IA),[164] Cornyn,[165] and Coburn.[166] In reply to Coburn's questioning, Kagan summarized her position as follows: "Senator Coburn, I very much appreciate how deeply important the right to bear arms is to millions and millions of Americans, and I accept *Heller*, which made clear that the Second Amendment conferred that right upon individuals and not simply collectively."[167]

As the use of the Second Amendment at the hearings in the post-*Heller* era demonstrates, the affirmation of an individual constitutional right to keep and bear arms is close to attaining the status of a confirmation condition

---

[154] Ibid. at 88.
[155] Sotomayor transcript, questioning by Senator Feingold (D-WI) at 2.57.
[156] Sotomayor transcript, questioning by Senator Kyle (R-AZ) at 2.61.
[157] Sotomayor transcript, questioning by Senator Klobuchar (D-MN) at 3.24.
[158] Sotomayor transcript, questioning by Senator Sessions (R-AL) at 3.50.
[159] Sotomayor transcript, questioning by Senator Graham (R-SC) at 4.11.
[160] Sotomayor transcript, questioning by Senator Coburn (R-OK) at 4.30.
[161] Kagan transcript, questioning by Senator Leahy (D-VT) at 65.
[162] Kagan transcript, questioning by Senator Feinstein (D-CA) at 95–6.
[163] Kagan transcript, questioning by Senator Feingold (D-WI) at 115–116.
[164] Kagan transcript, questioning by Senator Grassley (R-IA) at 122–3.
[165] Kagan transcript, questioning by Senator Cornyn (R-TX) at 163–4.
[166] Kagan transcript, questioning by Senator Coburn (R-OK) at 284.
[167] Ibid.

(if it has not already done so). The premise that the Second Amendment protects an individual's right to own a gun is supported by a reasonable interpretation of the Second Amendment, and is endorsed by senators from both political parties and an overwhelming majority of the American public. Like their view on *Brown*, it seems that Americans now expect nominees to accept that interpretation of the Amendment before being confirmed to the high Court.[168] Unlike *Brown*, however, it has not taken decades for public opinion about the propriety of this constitutional interpretation to gel. This is almost certainly because the Court in *Heller* was following, not forging, public opinion: a Gallup Poll conducted four months before the *Heller* decision revealed that 73% of Americans already believed the Second Amendment guarantees the right of individuals to own guns.[169] *Heller*, it turns out, simply gave the judicial stamp of approval to a right Americans already believed they enjoyed.

CONCLUSIONS

As we argue throughout this book, one of the central roles played by Supreme Court confirmation hearings is that they provide a democratically validated mechanism through which the Supreme Court's choices can be accepted or rejected by the public. The Court's constitutional decisions are accepted when nominees and senators affirm and reaffirm previously contested cases, thereby absorbing them into our constitutional understanding. To secure confirmation, nominees are expected to embrace these decisions. Constitutional decisions representing unpopular interpretations, in contrast, are thrust out of the realm of acceptable constitutional alternatives when nominees and senators repeatedly disclaim them. To win confirmation, nominees are expected to rebuff these decisions. This constant process of accepting and rejecting cases provides a type of formal democratic validation to constitutional change over time.

In this chapter, we demonstrated this process in action by investigating the confirmation history of four cases or issues: *Brown v. Board of Education*,

---

[168] That said, we have little doubt that more complicated questions involving the Second Amendment, particularly regarding the extent to which governments may place restrictions on the right to keep and bear arms, will generate substantial discussion at the hearings of future nominees. Thus, although the proposition that the Second Amendment protects an individual right to own a gun is likely a settled constitutional issue, questions as to the extent to which governments may restrict such a right are contestable.

[169] Jeffrey M. Jones, "Americans in Agreement With Supreme Court on Gun Rights." Retrieved from: http://www.gallup.com/poll/108394/americans-agreement-supreme-court-gun-rights .aspx (Accessed November 3, 2010).

gender equality, *Lochner v. New York,* and *District of Columbia v. Heller.* When it was decided in 1954, *Brown* was a hotly contested decision, and controversy surrounding the case continued at the first post-*Brown* hearings. Slowly, however, *Brown* was transformed from a contested case into a confirmation condition. By 1986, public opinion was firmly in favor of *Brown,* and nominees were all but required to praise the decision before they could hope to win confirmation.

Unlike *Brown,* issues of gender discrimination were completely absent from the hearings until 1970. The issue made sporadic appearances in the 1970s and 1980s, illustrating its growing importance in our constitutional discourse. It also, as we discuss in Chapter 7, played an important role in the failed nomination of Robert Bork in 1987. By the Ginsburg hearing in 1993, the issue had come fully into its own, and nominees since then have regularly embraced the idea that the Constitution requires that gender distinctions made by state actors be reviewed by the Court under at least an intermediate standard of review.

Lochner, in contrast, is a case that nominees for decades have been expected to reject to win confirmation. In hearing after hearing, nominees and senators regularly used *Lochner* as an example of judicial overreaching into the area of economic regulation. Thus, *Lochner* sat firmly in the anti-canon as a case nominees have been expected to renounce as falling outside of our constitutional consensus. Yet, the tide may be turning with respect to *Lochner*: during the Kagan hearing, several senators, reacting to the passage of the Patient Protection and Affordable Health Care Act in 2010, suggested that the Court has retreated too far from the oversight of economic regulation. Consequently, rejecting *Lochner* and the doctrine of aggressive judicial oversight it has come to stand for may not be something that is routinely expected of future nominees.

Finally, the rapid embrace of *Heller* at the hearings illustrates how a case can rapidly work its way into our constitutional canon. The Court's holding that the Second Amendment protects an individual right to gun ownership was endorsed by the vast majority of the American public when it was constitutionalized, and the decision was quickly embraced by nominees, as well as senators of both political parties. Though it is too soon to reach a firm conclusion, it seems likely that avowing the individual right interpretation of the Second Amendment may be the latest judicial choice nominees are expected to endorse in order to win confirmation.

As these examples make clear, there are varying paths by which cases and issues develop into conditions of confirmation. Some take decades to evolve, such as the issues of racial segregation and gender quality. Some develop almost immediately, such as the individual right to keep and bear arms. Some call for affirmation (*Brown*), while others call for rejection (*Lochner*). And even those tests that appear to necessitate a firm answer, such as *Lochner*, may, as public opinion on an issue shifts, lose that status and become once again contested constitutional propositions. Chapter 7 further explores the development of confirmation conditions by examining the failed nomination of Robert Bork in 1987 and the successful appointments that followed.

7

The 104th Justice

It has been twenty-five years since President Ronald Reagan nominated Judge Robert Bork to become the 104th Justice of the U.S. Supreme Court. The passage of time has done little to lessen our fascination with Bork's story; even now, decades later, every Supreme Court nomination renews a discussion of Robert Bork. The Bork nomination, people say, changed everything.[1] Variations on the theme exist, but the general gist of the story is the same: Robert Bork was the last nominee to actually answer questions put to him by the senators. Because he did so, he was rejected. Consequently, nominees since Bork have avoided saying much of anything at all.

---

[1] See, e.g., Ethan Bronner, *Battle for Justice: How the Bork Nomination Shook America* (New York: Sterling, 1989); Stephen L. Carter, *The Confirmation Mess: Cleaning Up the Federal Appointments Process* (New York: Basic Books, 1994); Richard Davis, *Electing Justice: Fixing the Supreme Court Nomination Process* (New York: Oxford University Press, 2005); Lee Epstein, René Lindstädt, Jeffrey A. Segal, and Chad Westerland, "The Changing Dynamics of Senate Voting on Supreme Court Nominees," 68 *Journal of Politics* 296 (2006); Morton J. Horwitz, "The Meaning of the Bork Nomination in American Constitutional History," 50 *University of Pittsburgh Law Review* 655 (1989); Ayo Ogundele and Linda Camp Keith, "Reexamining the Impact of the Bork Nomination to the Supreme Court," 52 *Political Research Quarterly* 403 (1999); Norman Vieira and Leonard Gross, *Supreme Court Appointments: Judge Bork and the Politicization of Senate Confirmations* (Carbondale: Southern Illinois University Press, 1998); Stephen J. Wermiel, "Confirming the Constitution: The Role of the Senate Judiciary Committee," 56 *Law and Contemporary Problems* 121 (1993). For alternative views of the impact of the Bork nomination, see, e.g., Frank Guliuzza, III, Daniel J. Reagan, and David M. Barrett, "Character, Competency, and Constitutionalism: Did the Bork Nomination Represent and Fundamental Shift in Confirmation Criteria?," 75 *Marquette Law Review* 409 (1992); Frank Guliuzza, III, Daniel J. Reagan, and David M. Barrett, "The Senate Judiciary Committee and Supreme Court Nominees: Measuring the Dynamics of Confirmation Criteria," 56 *Journal of Politics* 773 (1994); John Anthony Maltese, *The Selling of Supreme Court Nominees* (Baltimore: Johns Hopkins University Press, 1995); Henry Paul Monaghan, "The Confirmation Process: Law or Politics?" 101 *Harvard Law Review* 1202 (1988); Robert F. Nagel, "Advice, Consent, and Influence," 84 *Northwestern University Law Review* 858 (1990).

This chapter looks at the Bork story in a new light. As we show, Bork's nomination did not fail because he answered too many questions; it failed because he gave the wrong answers. Nominees confirmed since Bork have indeed learned a lesson from Bork's experience, but that lesson is quite different than that ritualistically repeated by the punditry.[2] The lesson learned is not to avoid discussing the issues that stymied Bork, but to recognize that those issues now have constitutionally correct answers – answers nominees are expected to endorse as a condition of their confirmation. As we show, every nominee, whether appointed and confirmed by Democratic or Republican presidents and Senates, who was nominated in the two decades subsequent to Bork has in fact done this. Nominees following Bork did not run from the questions that got Bork in trouble; like Bork, they answered the questions. Unlike Bork, they gave the answers Americans have agreed to be governed by.

The Bork hearing, consequently, was transformative, but not in the ways people talking about it usually mean. What was transformed was not the process itself, but our understanding of which issues continue to be constitutionally debatable and which have been settled (for the time being, at least).[3] Constitutional choices that were seen as contested prior to the Bork hearing were revealed by that and subsequent hearings to instead be part of our constitutional consensus. Although alternative outcomes in those cases continued to be legally defensible, they were no longer constitutionally defensible: Americans saw and debated their constitutional alternatives, and made their constitutional choices.

A BRIEF OVERVIEW OF THE BORK NOMINATION

The summer of 1987 was not going well for Ronald Reagan. The Iran-Contra hearings were playing on television for months, slowly revealing an unsavory story of illegal arms sales to Iran, cash-for-hostages negotiations with terrorists, and the funneling of money to Nicaraguan rebels in contravention of U.S. law. Confidence in Reagan was much lower than it was before the scandal broke: 69% of Americans polled by Gallup believed that the president was more

---

[2] See, e.g., Nancy Benac, "Tough Confirmation Hearings Relatively New," *Telegraph Herald*, August 29, 2005; Linda Greenhouse, "Judge Ginsburg: A Nominee With a Short 'Paper Trail,'" *New York Times*, November 1, 1987; Henry J. Reske, "Did Bork Say Too Much?," *ABA Journal*, December 1, 1987; Guy Taylor, "Politics and Justice for All," *Washington Times*, July 24, 2005.

[3] See also Bruce A. Ackerman, "Transformative Appointments," 101 *Harvard Law Review* 1164 (1988).

involved in the scandal than he admitted,[4] and 61% of Americans believed that history would judge his presidency as only average or below.[5]

There was a bright spot in Reagan's summer, however. Justice Lewis Powell announced in June that he would step down from his seat on the Supreme Court. Powell was the critical "swing justice" on an ideologically divided Court.[6] He played a key role in deciding contentious cases such as *Regents of the University of California v. Bakke*[7] (forging a compromise on affirmative action) and *Gregg v. Georgia*[8] (doing the same for the death penalty). His retirement would give Reagan the chance to finally, fundamentally, reshape the high Court.

Reagan was not new to the Supreme Court appointments game. As a candidate, he campaigned vigorously against the Court and promised that he, if elected president, would use his appointments to change its direction. He used his first appointment to fulfill a campaign pledge to put a woman – Sandra Day O'Connor – on the high Court.[9] His next two appointments, the elevation of William Rehnquist to chief justice and the appointment of Antonin Scalia to fill Rehnquist's associate justice seat, were both seen as furthering his promise to use his presidency to change the direction of the Court.

Although the O'Connor, Rehnquist, and Scalia appointments were important steps in that effort, none of these appointments had the potential impact that replacing Powell would. O'Connor, who was seen at the time of her appointment as a reliably conservative jurist, replaced Potter Stewart, who was himself relatively conservative. Scalia replaced Rehnquist, while Rehnquist in turn replaced Chief Justice Warren Burger. Each of Reagan's prior appointments therefore more or less replaced conservatives with conservatives.[10]

---

[4] George Gallup, Jr., *The Gallup Poll: Public Opinion 1987* (Wilmington, DE: Scholarly Resources, 1988) at 148.

[5] Ibid. at 172.

[6] See, e.g., Lee Epstein and Tonja Jacobi, "Super Medians," 61 *Stanford Law Review* 37 (2008); Margaret Meriwether Cordray and Richard Cordray, "The Supreme Court's Plenary Docket," 58 *Washington and Lee Law Review* 737 (2001) at 784; Andrew D. Martin, Kevin M. Quinn, and Lee Epstein, "The Median Justice on the U.S. Supreme Court," 83 *North Carolina Law Review* 1275 (2005); Richard L. Revesz, "Congressional Influence on Judicial Behavior?" 76 *New York University Law Review* 1100 (2001) at 1141. But see Janet L. Blasecki, "Justice Lewis F. Powell: Swing Voter or Staunch Conservative?" 52 *Journal of Politics* 530 (1990).

[7] Regents of the University of California v. Bakke, 438 U.S. 265 (1978).

[8] Gregg v. Georgia, 428 U.S. 153 (1976).

[9] See, e.g., Henry J. Abraham, *Justices, Presidents, and Senators: A History of U.S. Supreme Court Appointments from Washington to Bush II* (Lanham, MD: Rowman & Littlefield, 2008) at 268.

[10] See, e.g., Andrew D. Martin and Kevin M. Quinn, "Dynamic Ideal Point Estimation via Markov Chain Monte Carlo for the U.S. Supreme Court, 1953–1999," 10 *Political Analysis*

The Powell seat was different. Replacing the moderate, centrist Powell with a jurist in the model of Scalia or Rehnquist would change the ideological balance of the Court and had the potential to truly unwind the work of the Warren Court in a way the Burger Court never had – exactly what Reagan promised to do during his campaign.[11]

Robert Bork seemed just the man for the job. He had impeccable conservative credentials. He was solicitor general under Presidents Nixon and Ford, and stepped in as acting attorney general for Nixon when Nixon's attorney general and deputy attorney general both resigned rather than follow Nixon's order to fire Watergate special prosecutor, Archibald Cox. Bork's six years of service on the U.S. Court of Appeals for the District of Columbia Circuit, moreover, showed him to be a reliably conservative jurist, while his writings and speeches demonstrated him to be a vocal and sharp critic of many of the Court's left-leaning decisions.[12] To Reagan's more socially conservative followers, stymied for years in their efforts to accomplish social change through the Democratically controlled Congress, Bork represented nothing less than their last chance to end the Reagan era with a bang.

But it would not be easy. Everyone knew the Powell seat was important. Supreme Court nominees must, of course, be confirmed by the Senate, and the Senate was firmly in Democratic hands. The chair of the Senate Judiciary Committee, then-Senator Joseph Biden (D-DE), was running for the Democratic nomination for president, which would further elevate partisan tensions. The Reagan White House understood that naming a nominee who would fulfill the constitutional dreams of Reagan's core supporters thus risked alienating the centrist and Southern Democrats the administration would need to get the nominee confirmed. Consequently, a debate raged within the administration about whether Bork should give full voice to the conservative constitutional vision that so excited his supporters, or back away from it to appeal to the moderates whose votes the administration needed if Bork was to be confirmed.[13]

---

134 (2002); Jeffrey A. Segal and Albert D. Cover, "Ideological Values and the Votes of U.S. Supreme Court Justices," 83 *American Political Science Review* 557 (1989).

[11] See, e.g., David M. O'Brien, *Storm Center: The Supreme Court in American Politics* (New York: W. W. Norton, 2005) at 69; Christopher E. Smith and Thomas R. Hensley, "Unfulfilled Aspirations: The Court-Packing Efforts of Presidents Reagan and Bush," 57 *Albany Law Review* 1111 (1994).

[12] Kenneth B. Noble, "New Views Emerge of Bork's Role in Watergate Dismissals," *New York Times*, July 26, 1987; Peter Phillips, "A Study of Robert Bork," 19 *Arizona State Law Journal* 425 (1987).

[13] Abraham, *Justices, Presidents, and Senators*, supra, n. 9 at 282–3; Bronner, *Battle for Justice*, supra, n .1

The administration chose the latter path, and decided to position Bork as a constitutional moderate in the model of Justice Powell. Given Bork's writings, this strategy seemed unlikely to succeed. The strategy also infuriated many of the president's conservative supporters. Far from wanting to hide the more controversial of Bork's constitutional opinions, they wanted to celebrate them. They were fighting for nothing less than the repudiation of Earl Warren's legacy, and they wanted the world to know it.[14]

Americans understood what was at stake. By the end of the hearing, more than 83% of Americans held an opinion about whether Bork should be confirmed.[15] A majority of them, including at least a plurality of individuals in each racial, educational, age, income, and geographical group distinguished by Gallup, believed he should not be confirmed.[16] Invited by the Bork hearing to accept or reject specific constitutional choices made by Warren Court, Americans embraced them. Robert Bork, it turned out, was voicing a constitutional vision that large swaths of America no longer shared. Far from rolling back the constitutional changes of the preceding decades, Bork's confirmation hearing served primarily to reveal a new constitutional consensus, one so broadly accepted that no nominee in the two decades following Bork would refute it.

THE REJECTED CONSTITUTION

What was Bork's constitutional vision? The late Senator Ted Kennedy (D-MA) famously proclaimed from the floor of the U.S. Senate on the day the nomination was announced that Robert Bork's America was one in which "women would be forced into back-alley abortions, blacks would sit at segregated lunch counters, rogue police could break down citizens' doors in midnight raids, schoolchildren could not be taught about evolution, writers and artists would be censored at the whim of government, and the doors of the federal courts would be shut on the fingers of millions of citizens for whom the judiciary is often the only protector of the individual rights that are the heart of our democracy."[17]

This statement was widely criticized, and we do not defend it here. The best way to characterize it may be that it was a hyperbolic articulation of some of the permissible but not inevitable consequences of Robert Bork's

---

[14] Bronner, *Battle for Justice*, supra, n. 1.
[15] Gallup, *The Gallup Poll*, supra, n. 4 at 241.
[16] Ibid. at 241.
[17] James Reston, "Kennedy and Bork," *New York Times*, July 5, 1987.

constitutional vision, and an exaggeration of others. Although there is little reason to think that Bork was personally racist or sexist, his own writings and his confirmation testimony do nonetheless show a constitutional vision in which many of the issues raised by Senator Kennedy are seen not as implicating core constitutional values, but rather as subjects appropriately dealt with in most cases through the give and take of ordinary politics.

Contemporaneous news reports consistently identified the same issues as the ones that stymied Bork: a disavowal of any sort of constitutionally protected privacy right; a view of the Equal Protection Clause that did not give heightened scrutiny to state actions discriminating on the basis of gender; a skepticism of constitutional or congressional authority over voting rights issues; a restricted view of the speech rights contained in the First Amendment; and a rejection of almost all judicial protection of rights not specifically enumerated in the text of the Constitution.[18]

Bork's own words at his hearing illustrate his positions on these issues quite clearly.[19] Although he did distance himself from some of his most inflammatory opinions, and flatly repudiated a few others, he more often used his testimony to affirm and elaborate on his earlier positions. The hearing transcripts thus give us an accurate picture, in Bork's own words, of his positions on these key issues.

---

[18] See, e.g., Phil Gailey, "Bork Bends, Leans But Doesn't Break," *St. Petersburg Times*, September 17, 1987; Linda Greenhouse, "Stakes of the Bork Fight: With Senate Hearings Starting Tomorrow, Both Sides Have Much to Gain or to Lose," *New York Times*, September 14, 1987; Al Kamen and Edward Walsh, "Bork Lays Out Philosophy: 'Neither Liberal Nor Conservative,' Court Nominee Testifies," *Washington Post*, September 16, 1987; Michael Kramer, "The Brief on Judge Bork," *US News & World Report*, September 14, 1987; Larry Margasak, "Justice Says Bork Nomination 'All Right,' Scholar Says Bork Won't Change," *Associated Press*, September 22, 1987; Aric Press and Ann McDaniel, "Where Bork Stands," *Newsweek*, September 14, 1987; Stuart Taylor, Jr., "Judge Bork: Restraint v. Activism," *New York Times*, September 13, 1987; Stuart Taylor, Jr., "The Bork Hearings: Bork Backs Away From His Stances on Rights Issues," *New York Times*, September 17, 1987; Stuart Taylor, Jr., "How Bork Recast Ideas in His Senate Testimony," *New York Times*, September 21, 1987; Kirk Victor, "Drawing Lightening," *The National Journal*, September 12, 1987. See also Richard Davis, *Electing Justice: Fixing the Supreme Court Nomination Process* (New York: Oxford University Press, 2005).

[19] Michael Gerhardt, reviewing Bork's book, *The Tempting of America: The Political Seduction of the Law* (New York: The Free Press, 1989), noted that *Tempting* aptly demonstrates that the constitutional views attributed to Bork during his hearing did in fact accurately reflect Bork's underlying constitutional vision. In the book, Gerhardt says, Bork "denounces . . . the Court's decisions to uphold virtually all New Deal legislation . . . criticizes the Court's construction of the equal protection clause . . . rejects the Court's application of the Bill of Rights to the states . . . [and rejects the] reading of the fourteenth amendment due process clause to protect any aspect of individual privacy." See Michael Gerhardt, "Interpreting Bork: *The Tempting of America: The Political Seduction of the Law*," 75 *Cornell Law Review* 1358 (1990) at 1360–1.

These positions, it is worth noting, were entirely *legally* defensible, meaning that they are among the outcomes that could be reasonably reached using traditional tools of constitutional construction. Moreover, as Bork's supporters repeatedly pointed out, his positions had frequently been embraced by esteemed justices of earlier eras, including some still sitting on the Court he hoped to join. In an important way, both of these things illustrate our core point. Bork was not rejected because he was legally inept; he was rejected because, in a system in which justices must frequently choose *among* legally acceptable outcomes, he repeatedly made the wrong choices. Bork's constitutional choices, articulated by him in his own words at his confirmation hearing, were simply not within the constitutional consensus that the American people in 1987 agreed to be governed by. The Reagan administration, committed to its rhetorical war against the Warren Court, failed to realize that key battles in that war – those about basic privacy rights, gender discrimination, some types of racial discrimination, certain voting rights, and issues involving the scope of the First Amendment – were already lost.

The Right to Privacy

Confirmation discussions about the "right to privacy" sometimes are mere proxies for debates about abortion and *Roe v. Wade*.[20] That was not true at Bork's hearing. Bork's writings and speeches made it perfectly clear what he thought of *Roe*, so the senators hardly needed proxy conversations to tease out his opinion. Moreover, and more interestingly for our purposes, Bork's position on the constitutional protection of privacy (or, more accurately, the lack thereof) became the most potent symbol of a constitutional vision that turned out to be out of step with America's.

The constitutional right to privacy was developed in a series of Supreme Court cases. The most well-known of these cases is *Griswold v. Connecticut*.[21] *Griswold* involved a challenge to a Connecticut law that prohibited the use or sale of contraceptives. The law was challenged by a married couple and their doctor. The Court, building on a series of cases protecting "fundamental" but not specifically enumerated rights (such as the right to teach children a foreign language[22] or to send them to a private school[23]) struck down the law

---

[20]   Roe v. Wade, 410 U.S. 113 (1973).
[21]   Griswold v. Connecticut, 381 U.S. 479 (1965).
[22]   Meyer v. Nebraska, 262 U.S. 390 (1923).
[23]   Pierce v. Society of Sisters, 268 U.S. 510 (1925).

for violating the right to privacy implicit in the Constitution's First, Third, Fourth, Fifth, and Ninth Amendments.

Bork's pre-hearing criticisms of *Griswold* were sharp. In earlier writings, he called the decision "unprincipled."[24] As recently as 1985, two years before the hearing, he told the *Conservative Digest* that he did not think there was a "supportable method of constitutional reasoning" underlying *Griswold*.[25] In 1982, he listed the case, along with *Lochner v. New York*[26] and *Roe v. Wade*, as among the most "dramatic examples" in our history of a noninterpretivist method of constitutional interpretation (in the lexicon of the era, Bork earlier identified himself as an interpretivist). "In not one of those cases," he wrote, "could the result have been reached by interpretation of the Constitution."[27] In a speech given at Catholic University, Bork reiterated this idea, saying that, "[t]he result in *Griswold* could not have been reached by proper interpretation of the Constitution."[28]

Bork did not deviate from this position at his hearing. Asked by Senator Biden to explain why *Griswold* was so unprincipled, Bork affirmed his earlier views, saying that the Court "has not demonstrated that the Constitution speaks in this area."[29] Biden went on to draw Bork's attention to an argument Bork made in a 1971 *Indiana Law Review* article. The article compared the constitutional claim of marital privacy to a hypothetical claim brought by an electric company attempting to void a pollution ordinance as unconstitutional.[30] In the article, Bork wrote:

> Neither case is covered specifically or by obvious implication in the Constitution. Unless we can distinguish forms of gratification, the only course for a principled Court is to let the majority have its way. It is clear that the Court cannot make the necessary distinction. There is no principled way to decide that one man's gratifications are more deserving of respect than another's, or that one form of gratification is more worthy than another. Why is sexual gratification more worthy than moral gratification? Why is sexual gratification more noble than economic gratification?[31]

---

[24] Bork transcript at 128.
[25] Ibid. at 553.
[26] Lochner v. New York, 198 U.S. 45 (1905).
[27] Bork transcript at 373.
[28] Ibid. at 121.
[29] Ibid. at 128.
[30] Ibid. at 114.
[31] Robert H. Bork, "Neutral Principles and Some First Amendment Problems," 47 *Indiana Law Journal* 1 (1971) at 1.

Asked about this comparison at the hearing, Biden and Bork engaged in the following exchange:

> **The CHAIRMAN:** Then I think I do understand it, that is, that the economic gratification of a utility company is as worthy of as much protection as the sexual gratification of a married couple, because neither is mentioned in the Constitution.
>
> **Judge BORK:** All that means is that the judge may not choose.
>
> **The CHAIRMAN:** Who does?
>
> **Judge BORK:** The legislature.
>
> **The CHAIRMAN:** Well, that is my point, so it is not a constitutional right. I am not trying to be picky here. Clearly, I do not want to get into a debate with a professor, but it seems to me that what you are saying is what I said and that is, that the Constitution – if it were a constitutional right, if the Constitution said anywhere in it, in your view, that a married couple's right to engage in the decision of having a child or not having a child was a constitutionally-protected right of privacy, then you would rule that that right exists. You would not leave it to a legislative body no matter what they did.
>
> **Judge BORK:** That is right.
>
> **The Chairman:** But you argue, as I understand it, that no such right exists.
>
> **Judge BORK:** No, Senator, that is what I tried to clarify. I argued that the way in which this unstructured, undefined right of privacy that Justice Douglas elaborated, that the way he did it did not prove its existence.
>
> **The CHAIRMAN:** You have been a professor now for years and years, everybody has pointed out and I have observed, you are one of the most well-read and scholarly people to come before this committee. In all your short life, have you come up with any other way to protect a married couple, under the Constitution, against an action by a government telling them what they can or cannot do about birth control in their bedroom? Is there any constitutional right, anywhere in the Constitution?
>
> **Judge BORK:** I have never engaged in that exercise.[32]

Although Bork's testimony thus never completely rejected the idea that *some* constitutional foundation for *some* type of privacy right might exist in the Constitution – something he seemed to reject in his earlier writings and

---

[32] Bork transcript, questioning by Senator Biden (D-DE) at 115–116.

speeches – Bork made clear at the hearing that he had as yet to find any such right.

Bork compounded his problems in this area by appearing to accept some nontextual rights, rights that appear to float as unmoored from the text of the Constitution as does the privacy right asserted in *Griswold*. Bork acknowledged a constitutional right to travel,[33] as well as a constitutional right to educate children outside of the public school system.[34] He also seemed to accept a constitutional right to teach children a foreign language,[35] although he had rejected this in his written work.[36] In these cases, in short, Bork appeared to approve of extending constitutional protection to rights that were not specifically textually enumerated. At no point, however, did he explain why these rights were entitled to more judicial protection than the right of married couples to use birth control in the privacy of their own homes – a right, which he repeatedly pointed out, that also does not enjoy specific textual support.

By appearing to accept some unspecified rights but rejecting others, Bork seemed to discredit his jurisprudential argument that a judge could find truly neutral constitutional principles only by hewing close to text and a narrow version of intended applications originalism.[37] His mantra of deference to the framers and legislatures thus began to look more like the doctrine of a man willing to protect as fundamental nonspecified rights he personally deemed important, while rejecting those whose importance he did not understand or value. This apparent blindness to the constitutional concerns of others would animate one of the most notorious aspects of the Bork hearing: his discussion of female sterilization and the *American Cyanamid* case.[38]

Gender Discrimination

Going into the hearing, the Reagan administration knew that gender issues were going to be problematic for Bork. The American Association of University

---

[33] Bork transcript at 185, 335.

[34] Ibid. at 190, approving of *Pierce v. Society of Sisters*, which held that parents have a substantive due process right to send their children to schools other than those sanctioned by the state. See also Bork transcript at 351–2, positing a possible First Amendment basis for *Pierce*.

[35] Ibid., approving of *Meyer v. Nebraska*, which struck down a state law prohibiting the teaching of foreign languages as a violation of the Due Process Clause of the Fourteenth Amendment. See also Bork transcript at 352, supporting a possible First Amendment basis for *Meyer*.

[36] Bork, "Neutral Principles," supra, n. 31 at 11.

[37] In brief, this method of judicial interpretation asserts that judges must closely follow the specific intentions of the framers or ratifiers of the Constitution to resolve constitutional disputes. See, e.g., Robert H. Bork, "The Constitution, Original Intent, and Economic Rights," 23 *San Diego Law Review* 823 (1986); Bork, *The Tempting of America*, supra, n. 19.

[38] Oil, Chemical, and Atomic Workers v. American Cyanamid, 741 F.2d 444 (D.C. Cir. 1984).

Women, League of Women Voters, National Organization of Women, National Women's Bar Association, National Women's Law Center, and the Women's Legal Defense Fund all opposed the nomination.[39] Early in his testimony, Bork was asked about a case of particular interest to these groups, *Oil, Chemical, and Atomic Workers v. American Cyanamid. American Cyanamid* involved a statutory challenge brought under the Occupational Safety and Health Act (OSHA). Bork sat on the panel that decided the case three years earlier on the U.S. Court of Appeals for the District of Columbia Circuit.[40]

American Cyanamid's manufacturing process exposed workers to lead. The problem with this was that lead had been determined to cause harm to developing fetuses. The company responded to this dilemma by informing its female employees, regardless of their marital status or plans to have children, that they must either be sterilized or be fired. The company's action was challenged under a provision of OSHA that required employers to provide a workplace "free from recognized hazards that are likely to cause death or serious physical harm."[41] The employees' union argued on behalf of the female employees that the forced sterilization policy violated this statute because it subjected female workers to a workplace hazard, that is, sterilization.

Bork's court unanimously rejected this claim, holding that the workplace hazards Congress intended to regulate under the statute were hazards within the physical workplace, not hazards caused by company policies such as the sterilization policy. The opinion, which Bork wrote, noted that the agency charged with enforcing the statute reached the same conclusion. Because that conclusion was not unreasonable, basic administrative law principles entitled the agency's decision to judicial deference. Bork also suggested in the opinion that the case may have come out differently if the plaintiffs were able to show that there was a way the company could have reduced the lead exposure to levels that did not threaten fetal safety.

The case itself, therefore, involved the interpretation of a statute, rather than a constitutional provision, and deference to a reasonable interpretation of a statute by the administrative agency charged with enforcing it. None of this is extraordinary, from a legal perspective. In describing the case at his hearing, however, Bork made the following comment:

> The company chose the latter alternative and the women involved were thus faced with a distressing choice. Some chose sterilization. Some did not. The fact is, if they had not been offered that choice, these women would have

39 Bork transcript at 1233; Joseph Michael Green, *Your Past and the Press: Controversial Presidential Appointments* (Lanham, MD: University Press of America, 2004) at 109.

40 Bork transcript at 467.

41 *American Cyanamid*, supra, n. 38 at 447.

been put in lower paying jobs or would have been discharged. They offered a choice to the women. Some of them, I guess, did not want to have children.[42]

He later added this:

I suppose the [five] women who chose to stay on that job with higher pay and choose sterilization – I suppose that they were glad to have the choice – they apparently were – that the company gave them.[43]

The idea that women told to choose between their job and their fertility would be *glad* to be given the choice, or that women would choose their job only because they did not *want* to have children shows, at best, a shocking insensitivity to the devastating dilemma posed by being asked to choose between your job and your fertility. This apparent callousness led to concerns about whether Bork actually understood the challenges, some of which would present themselves as constitutional choices, faced by women in the workplace. As Senator Metzenbaum (D-OH), questioning Bork at the hearing, explained:

Congress said, no hazards in the workplace, but you wrote an opinion which said it was okay for a company to achieve safety at the expense of women by preventing its female employees from ever having children. I have to say to you that that is a distortion of the statute beyond recognition. I think it is unfair. I think it is inhumane and maybe it somehow explains the concerns that women of this country have and have evidenced about your appointment.[44]

Betty Riggs, one of the women sterilized under the American Cyanamid policy, put it more succinctly in a letter read to the Committee the next day:

I cannot believe that Judge Bork thinks we were glad to have the choice of getting sterilized or getting fired. Only a judge who knows nothing about women who need to work could say that. I was only 26 years old, but I had to work, so I had no choice. . . . This was the most awful thing that happened to me. I still believe it's against the law, whatever Bork says.[45]

After being confronted with Rigg's letter, Bork acknowledged that the case presented the women involved with a "terrible choice" and a "wrenching decision."[46] He then reiterated the panel's holding that the company's decision to require the woman to make the choice simply did not violate the hazardous conditions provision of the statute. The damage, however, was already done.

---

[42] Bork transcript at 467–8.
[43] Ibid. at 470.
[44] Ibid. at 468.
[45] Ibid. at 678.
[46] Ibid. at 679.

Bork's awkward discussion of *American Cyanamid* presented a lasting image of Bork as insensitive to the workplace difficulties faced by women. It was Bork's position on the Equal Protection Clause, however, that caused him constitutional difficulties in this area. His comments about *American Cyanamid* may have framed the constitutional discussion, but it is that discussion itself that best illuminates Bork's position on gender discrimination.

The Fourteenth Amendment's Equal Protection Clause holds that "no state . . . shall deny to any person within its jurisdiction . . . the Equal Protection of the law."[47] Modern equal protection doctrine rests on a system of tiered judicial review. Laws that distinguish between people on the basis of "suspect" classifications, or that deprive some citizens but not others of fundamental rights, are subjected to heightened judicial scrutiny. Heightened review takes different forms, but the gist of it is that the government must in such situations show an important (sometimes compelling) need for the classification it has drawn, and must write its law in a way that is substantially or narrowly tailored to meet that need. Classifications not deemed suspect, or not involving fundamental rights, are subjected to less rigorous review. In those cases, the state need only show that drawing the classification it did was a rational way to pursue a legitimate state interest.

By the time of Bork's confirmation hearing, the Supreme Court had begun subjecting gender classifications in laws to a form of heightened scrutiny, using what came to be known as intermediate review. In his 1971 *Indiana Law Review* article, Bork objected to this. The Equal Protection Clause, he wrote, has "two legitimate meanings. It can require formal procedural equality, and, because of its historic origins, it does require that the government not discriminate along racial lines. But much more than that cannot properly be read into the clause."[48]

He went on to add this:

> There is no principled way in which anyone can define the spheres in which liberty is required and the spheres in which equality is required. These are matters of morality, of judgment, of prudence. They belong therefore in the political community. In the fullest sense, they are political questions.[49]

His speeches were even more explicit. In an interview published just two months before the hearing, Bork said "I do think the Equal Protection Clause probably should have been kept to things like race and ethnicity."[50] Criticizing

---

[47] U.S. Constitution, Amendment XIV.
[48] Bork, "Neutral Principles," supra, n. 31 at 11.
[49] Ibid. at 12.
[50] Bork transcript at 373.

the Court's approach in a 1982 speech to the Federalist Society, Bork stated:

> This is a process that is going on. It happens with the extension of the Equal Protection Clause to groups that were never previously protected. When they begin to protect groups that were historically not intended to be protected by that clause, what they are doing is picking out groups which current morality of a particular social class regards as groups that should not have any disabilities laid upon them.[51]

Asked at his hearing to elaborate on these comments, Bork said that what he objected to was the tiered system of review generally rather than the extension of the Equal Protection Clause to gender discrimination specifically.[52] His position, he said now, was that all classifications – whether involving race, gender, ethnicity, or economics – should be subject to a "reasonableness" standard. As he described it at his hearing:

> What the Court was doing with the equal protection clause for many years, and to which I objected more generally in this article, is that they would decide whether a whole group was in or out and then they would decide what level of scrutiny they would give to the statute to see whether it was constitutional or not. . . . It would be much better if instead of taking groups as such and saying this group is in, that group is out, if they merely used a reasonable basis test and asked whether the law had a reasonable basis.[53]

A proper equal protection analysis, Bork argued, would thus ask the same question regardless of the type of classification drawn: is the classification reasonable or not? If so, the law would be constitutional; if not, it would be struck down. Racial classifications, he went on, would almost always be unconstitutional because it would be virtually impossible for the state to show that any distinction based on race was reasonable.[54]

It was less clear, however, when and how a court would determine when gender discrimination was or was not reasonable. When asked to explain how his reasonableness test would work in such cases, Bork said this:

Senator DECONCINI: . . . What about the sex discrimination cases?

---

[51] Ibid. at 372.
[52] Ibid. at 133. This statement is in some tension with a comment Bork made later at the hearing. Asked about the need to respect precedents in constitutional adjudication, Bork added "the extension of the equal protection clause" to a list of issue areas that could no longer be reversed. Bork transcript at 465.
[53] Ibid. at 119.
[54] See, e.g., Bork transcript at 253, 256.

Judge BORK: Well, sometimes it will be reasonable and sometimes it will not because I do not... We know that it is irrational to make a distinction between persons on racial grounds, utterly irrational. We also know that for some purposes it is rational, reasonable to make a distinction between the genders, between the sexes.[55]

Senator Kennedy wondered whether this was any different than the rational basis test used to evaluate gender discrimination claims in the past – a test, as Kennedy pointed out in the following exchange, which had not provided much protection against gender discrimination:

Senator KENNEDY: Well, the point as I see it, Judge Bork, is that talking about the rational basis test, it was the test the Supreme Court used for a 100 years to deny equality for women. Some years ago, the Court altered that to a rigorous standard for sex discrimination. As I understand the rational basis test, it is the same test which is used in terms of economic regulations and pollution ordinances. You have restated earlier in your response to Chairman Biden that this is still your test whereas the Court itself has moved to a much more rigorous standard to sex discrimination.

Judge BORK: I do not think in the case of gender, Senator, that my test – or what you call my test, which is a test the Court has been applying in one way or another for 90 years – would come out that much different than an intermediate scrutiny standard.

Senator KENNEDY: Well, it was the test that was used when women were discriminated against back in 1896.... What I hear you saying here now is that the test that was used about 90 years ago and which was the basis for discrimination against women is the standard that you would use.

Judge BORK: I do not know that it was the basis for discrimination against women. I think that society saw all kinds of distinctions, legal distinctions between men and women as entirely reasonable and rational. This society no longer sees them that way, and that is fine.[56]

Bork did give one hint of how his test might work in practice, using a case challenging an Oklahoma[57] law establishing different drinking ages for men

---

55 Bork transcript, questioning by Senator DeConcini (D-AZ) at 255.
56 Ibid. at 161.
57 Although he does not name the case, it appears Bork was talking about *Craig v. Boren*, 429 U.S. 190 (1976). *Craig* involved an Oklahoma law, but was misidentified by Bork as addressing an Idaho statute.

and women. In describing the case, Bork said:

> That was a case about – I forget it; it was Idaho, I think – but it had a law
> that in order to drink 3.2 beer, a man had to be 21 but a woman could be 18
> years of age. And I said I thought that was to trivialize the Constitution in a
> way. They produced six opinions in that case about whether you could have
> a different drinking age for men and women for 3.2 beer. You would have
> thought it was the steel seizure case the way they went at it. And I thought,
> as a matter of fact, the differential drinking age probably is justified, because
> they have statistics on it.[58]

Senator Biden next questioned how Bork's reasonableness test could be
reconciled with the nominee's insistence in other areas that judges use neutral
principles in deciding cases. After all, reasonableness, as Biden pointed out, "is
very subjective."[59] Bork agreed, in part, stating that "unless you are going to [go]
compelling all the way, or unless you are going to let it stand all the way, there
is an element of subjectivity that cannot be avoided."[60] Bork went on to add
that his understanding of the tiered system of review used by the Court was that
the Court has "supposed that interest group politics was at work" in questions
of economic rights and that the justices therefore "didn't examine [those laws]
too closely."[61] This observation is certainly relevant to explaining why the
Supreme Court adopted a tiered approach to equal protection analysis, but
seems to shed little light on how a judge would, applying neutral principles,
determine whether a particular gender distinction drawn in a law is or is not
a reasonable one.

The degree to which gender discrimination would be judicially scrutinized
under Bork's reasonableness test became even more unclear when Bork was
asked to connect his test to comments he made about the proposed Equal
Rights Amendment (ERA). The operative language of the ERA was very similar
to that of the Equal Protection Clause, stating that "Equality of rights under
the law shall not be denied or abridged by the United States or by any State
on account of sex."[62] In a 1974 speech, Bork objected to the ERA, arguing it
would "ratify and forward a dangerous constitutional revolution" by handing
to the courts "without legislative guidance of any sort, the task of making the
infinite number of political decisions required in deciding when men and

---

[58] Bork transcript at 392.
[59] Ibid. at 699.
[60] Ibid. at 700.
[61] Ibid. at 706.
[62] Ruth Bader Ginsburg, "Sexual Equality under the Fourteenth and Equal Rights Amendments," 1979 *Washington University Law Quarterly* 161 (1979).

women must be treated alike, when they need not be, and, perhaps, when they may not be."[63]

At his hearing, Bork repeated this criticism, saying that his objection to the ERA was that it would "put all the relationships between the sexes in the hands of judges where it should be in the hands of legislatures, except when it violates the Constitution."[64] Senator DeConicini asked Bork if this same criticism could be made of judicial protection against gender discrimination under the Equal Protection Clause, even (or especially) using Bork's reasonableness test.[65] Bork replied by saying this:

> My objection to the Equal Rights Amendment was that legislatures would have nothing to say about these complex cultural matters, and had no chance to express a judgment. People would go straight to court and challenge any distinction, and the court would have to write the complete body of what is allowable, discrimination or whatever it is. A reasonable basis test allows a little more play in the joints, I think, for the court to listen to the legislatures and look at the society and bring evidence in and so forth. If you want to say that the Equal Rights Amendment really would enact the same thing as the reasonable basis test, then my objection to the Equal Rights Amendment drops out.[66]

The question, Bork continued, is "[h]ave you got a good reason for the distinction? Is there some good reason for the distinction being made?"[67] There are, he said, a "million kinds of judgments to be made about that in many different contexts."[68] Bork repeatedly insisted that most gender discrimination cases adjudicated under his test would be decided the same way as existing case law, even without the protection of heightened scrutiny review.[69] But it was unclear just why this would be so. Given Bork's earlier skepticism of courts' ability to make the types of "complex cultural judgments" necessary under the ERA, his trivialization of the imposition of different drinking ages in the Oklahoma case, his earlier objections to the Court's jurisprudence in this area, and his insistence on "reasonableness" as the appropriate standard of review, the Senators were not reassured that a Justice Bork interpreting the

---

[63] See Bork transcript at 173.
[64] Ibid. at 162.
[65] Ibid. at 255.
[66] Ibid. at 255–6.
[67] Ibid. at 257.
[68] Ibid.
[69] Ibid. at 734.

Equal Protection Clause would scrutinize gender-based discriminations in a way they – or their constituents – considered sufficiently protective.[70]

Racial Discrimination and Voting Rights

Bork also faced difficulties with a cluster of race and voting rights issues. Years earlier, as a law professor at Yale, Bork had been an outspoken critic of the Civil Rights Act of 1964. The Act, he said, intruded too far into what he saw as the right of property owners to exclude those with whom they did not want to do business. In an article he wrote for the *New Republic*, Bork said that the public accommodations provisions of the Act, which prohibited owners of places such as restaurants and hotels from discriminating on the basis of race, were based on a "principle of unsurpassed ugliness."[71] The law, he wrote:

> [W]ould inform a substantial body of the citizenry that in order to continue to carry on the trades in which they are established they must deal with and serve persons with whom they do not wish to associate.[72]

This position was not unusual in 1963. Questions about the wisdom and constitutionality of the Civil Rights Act were widely debated at the time.[73] Moreover, Bork, well before the hearing, publicly changed his position on the Act, writing off his earlier objections as part of a "free market libertarianism" that he said he had since outgrown.[74] Bork did, however, continue to question the constitutional underpinning of several important race or racially salient Supreme Court cases. Most notable among these were *Bolling v. Sharpe*,[75] *Shelley v. Kraemer*,[76] and several voting rights cases.

Bolling v. Sharpe involved a challenge to racial segregation in District of Columbia public schools. Earlier in the hearing, Bork agreed that *Brown v. Board of Education*,[77] which declared such segregation unconstitutional when sanctioned by states, was properly decided. *Bolling*, however, was a more difficult case. *Brown* was decided under the Equal Protection Clause, a clause that by its own terms restricts only state, not federal, action. Consequently, there was no textual way to use the Equal Protection Clause to limit the

---

[70] Ibid. at 733.
[71] Robert Bork, "Civil Rights – A Challenge," *The New Republic*, August 31, 1963, at 21.
[72] Ibid.
[73] See, e.g., Hugh Davis Graham, *The Civil Rights Era: Origins and Development of National Policy, 1960–1972* (New York: Oxford University Press, 1990).
[74] Bork transcript at 152–3. See also Bork transcript at 251–2.
[75] Bolling v. Sharpe, 347 U.S. 497 (1954).
[76] Shelley v. Kraemer, 334 U.S. 1 (1948).
[77] Brown v. Board of Education, 347 U.S. 483 (1954).

actions of public school districts in the District of Columbia, which is, of course, a federal entity.

The *Bolling* Court sidestepped this problem by using the Fifth Amendment. As part of the original Bill of Rights, the Fifth Amendment, unlike the Fourteenth, applies to the federal government. It does not, however, include an Equal Protection Clause, meaning that the Court could not follow the same reasoning it used in *Brown* to find that racial segregation violated the equal protection of the laws. What it did have was a Due Process Clause, prohibiting the federal government from depriving any person of "life, liberty or property" without due process of law. Following the "fundamental rights" reasoning used in the line of cases developed under the Fourteenth Amendment's Due Process Clause, the *Bolling* Court held that race-based discrimination violated the liberty provision of the Due Process Clause of the Fifth Amendment. Chief Justice Warren, speaking for a unanimous Court, wrote:

> Although the Court has not assumed to define "liberty" with any great precision, that term is not confined to mere freedom from bodily restraint. Liberty under law extends to the full range of conduct which the individual is free to pursue, and it cannot be restricted except for a proper governmental objective. Segregation in public education is not reasonably related to any proper governmental objective, and thus it imposes on Negro children of the District of Columbia a burden that constitutes an arbitrary deprivation of their liberty in violation of the Due Process Clause.[78]

This reasoning, as both Bork and the senators understood, is the same reasoning used by the Court in its Fourteenth Amendment substantive due process cases – the reasoning Bork rejected so vehemently in his discussions of *Griswold*. To be consistent, therefore, Bork needed to reject the reasoning used in *Bolling*. Much to the senators' astonishment, he did.

Senator Specter (R-PA) questioned Bork closely on this point:

Senator SPECTER: ... [I]f you can apply the due process clause as they did in *Bolling v. Sharpe*, why not in *Griswold v. Connecticut*?

Judge BORK: Well, if they apply the due process clause that way, Senator, I quite agree with you. Why not in *Griswold v. Connecticut*, and why not in all kinds of cases? You are off and running with substantive due process which I have long thought is a pernicious constitutional idea.

Senator SPECTER: I think it is as you articulate it, but if you start to deal with the needs of the nation and you accept in *Bolling v. Sharpe* to strike down

---

[78] *Bolling*, supra, n. 75 at 499.

segregation in the District of Columbia, and you accept it in the commerce clause, what happens to your principle?

Judge BORK: Senator, I did not accept it in *Bolling v. Sharpe*. And when I say I accepted it in the commerce clause, I accept it because what has happened is irreversible."[79]

Senator Specter questioned him further:

Senator SPECTER: Final question: Do you accept *Bolling v. Sharpe* or not?

Judge BORK: I have not thought of a rationale for it because I think you are quite right, Senator [that *Bolling* raises the same substantive due process issues as *Griswold*].

Senator SPECTER: You say you have or have not?

Judge BORK: Have not. I think you are quite right, Senator, because if you say it is due process and we will do whatever is fair or good under due process, the court's powers are unlimited. That is the problem I have with that substantive due process.[80]

Bork was clear – and senators fully understood – that he had no intention of overturning *Bolling* and allowing Congress to legally segregate public schools in the nation's capital. *Bolling*, he said, is precedent, and he saw "absolutely no reason" to overrule it.[81] To say that the reasoning of any case is not adequate, he said, is "not to say you want to overrule it, and it is certainly not to say you want to bring back the underlying statute."[82]

The difficulty with this was that Bork's approach left *Bolling*, an important and symbolic decision in the fight against racial discrimination, with the status of a constitutional mistake; something to be tolerated rather than celebrated. Senator Specter, for one, was looking for something more:

Well, I know that you will not reverse *Bolling v. Sharpe* in any event, but it is a very uneasy conclusion, Judge Bork, when you talk about the needs of the Nation.... [Y]ou get into Holmes, who was very much against substantive due process but talked about striking laws on which reasonable men could

---

[79] Bork transcript, questioning by Senator Specter (R-PA) at 287.
[80] Bork transcript, questioning by Senator Specter (R-PA) at 287. Briefly stated, the doctrine of substantive due process asserts that the Due Process Clause protects substantive rights, such as the right to privacy. See, e.g., Erwin Chemerinsky, "Substantive Due Process," 15 *Touro Law Review* 1502 (1999).
[81] Bork transcript at 405.
[82] Ibid.

not differ. . . . and where the courts have been and what the tradition of this country is, and I think that what so many of us are looking for here is some reassurance that you would follow in that tradition. That is what I am looking for.[83]

Bork also ran into problems with three other racially salient cases, *Shelley v. Kraemer* (1948), *Katzenbach v. Morgan*,[84] and *Harper v. Virginia Board of Elections*.[85] *Shelley* read the Equal Protection Clause, which as noted earlier applies by its terms only to state action, to prohibit racially restrictive housing covenants entered into by private parties. The *Shelley* Court reasoned that the state action requirement was met when courts were asked to enforce the covenants. *Shelley*, Bork said, was wrongly decided, although not worth overturning because the Court did not follow it in subsequent cases.[86]

Katzenbach and *Harper*, unlike *Bolling* and *Shelley*, did not directly involve race. *Katzenbach* involved a challenge to a provision of the Voting Rights Act that prohibited states from requiring literacy tests as a condition of voting. Although literacy tests had long been used to suppress African American votes in the South, *Katzenbach* was not an equal protection case. Rather, the case involved the extent to which Congress can prohibit such tests even when they were used in a nondiscriminatory manner. Congress grounded its power to prohibit the use of such tests in Section 5 of the Fourteenth Amendment. Section 5 gives Congress the power to enforce the substantive provisions of the Amendment, which includes the Equal Protection Clause. In *Katzenbach*, the Court held that this power was sufficiently broad to allow Congress to legislate in ways it deemed necessary to prevent or remedy constitutional violations, even when such legislation reached behaviors that were not themselves judicially recognized transgressions of the Constitution.

Bork disagreed. Testifying before the Senate Judiciary Committee six years earlier at his hearing for a seat on the Court of Appeals for the District of Columbia Circuit, he said that *Katzenbach* "represent[ed] a very bad and, indeed, pernicious constitutional law."[87] Asked about the case at his Supreme Court hearing, he affirmed his disagreement with the case. *Katzenbach*, he said, allowed Congress to define the Equal Protection Clause and to "change

---

[83] Ibid. at 287–8.
[84] Katzenbach v. Morgan, 384 U.S. 641 (1966).
[85] Harper v. Virginia Board of Elections, 383 U.S. 663 (1966).
[86] Bork transcript at 114: "[*Shelley*] has never been applied again. It has had no generative force. It has not proved to be a precedent. As such, it is not a case to be reconsidered. It did what it did; it adopted a principle which the court has never adopted again. And while I criticized the case at the time, it is not a case worth reconsidering."
[87] Ibid. at 371.

the Constitution by statute."[88] His views on the case, he said, "have not changed."[89]

Bork also disagreed with the Court's decision in *Harper v. Virginia Board of Elections. Harper*, like *Katzenbach*, involved the nondiscriminatory use of a mechanism with a long history of being employed to suppress African American voting. In *Harper*, the challenged mechanism was a state poll tax. The Court held that such taxes were unconstitutional even when used in ways that are not racially discriminatory. "Voter qualifications," the Court said, "have no relation to wealth."[90] State poll taxes, consequently, were unconstitutional.

Bork again disagreed. In his 1973 confirmation hearing for solicitor general, he said that the poll tax at issue in *Harper* was "very small" and that he doubted it had "much impact on the welfare of the nation one way or the other."[91] He affirmed this reasoning at this hearing. The tax struck down in *Harper*, he said, was not applied in a discriminatory fashion, but rather "was just a $1.50 poll tax."[92] Moreover, he went on, the poll tax "was familiar in American history and nobody ever thought it was unconstitutional unless it was racially discriminatory."[93] The case, Bork added, was therefore "hard to square with out [sic] constitutional history" and was wrongly decided.[94]

Bork confronted similar difficulties with another voting rights case, *Reynolds v. Sims*.[95] Although *Reynolds* does not have obvious racial connotations, it is nonetheless one of our most famous Supreme Court cases. It involved a challenge to state legislative districts in Alabama. The districts were not apportioned by population, meaning that residents of smaller (usually rural) population districts were given much more influence over who was elected to the legislature than were voters in larger (usually urban) population districts. The challengers argued that the unequal apportionment scheme violated the Equal Protection Clause. The Court agreed. In doing so, it held that the Equal Protection Clause required state legislative districts to be apportioned under what came to be known as the one-person, one-vote rule.

Yet again, Bork disagreed with the Court. In his earlier writings, Bork said that there was "no reputable theory of constitutional adjudication" that could

---

[88] Ibid. at 253.
[89] Ibid.
[90] *Harper*, supra, n. 85 at 666.
[91] Bork transcript at 155.
[92] Ibid.
[93] Ibid.
[94] Ibid.
[95] Reynolds v. Sims, 377 U.S. 533 (1964).

support the result in *Reynolds*.[96] The one-person, one-vote rule of *Reynolds*, he testified before Congress in 1973, was "too much of a straightjacket" and lacked a "theoretical basis."[97] A state, Bork said, must be "free to apportion as it sees fit, so long as the apportionment plan has rationality and so long as a majority has a way to change [it]."[98] In imposing the one-person, one-vote rule, he said in an interview, the Court "stepped beyond its allowable boundaries."[99]

Bork confirmed at his hearing that this continued to be his opinion regarding *Reynolds*. Senator Kennedy and Bork then engaged in the following exchange:

Senator KENNEDY: [T]he people of this country, Judge Bork, accept the fundamental principle of one man, one vote even though they are not burdened with a law school education.

Judge BORK: Well, Senator, if the people of this country accept one man, one vote, that is fine. They can enact it anytime they want to. I have no desire to go running around trying to overturn that decision. But as an original matter, it does not come out of anything in the Constitution.[100]

As in *Bolling, Shelley, Katzenbach*, and *Harper*, Bork's position on *Reynolds* was not legally unsupportable. All of these decisions were controversial when they were decided, and they continue to provoke rich debate in constitutional law courses across the country. *Shelley* and *Katzenbach* may fairly be described as representing the outer edges of judicial interpretations of the Fourteenth Amendment. *Harper* was criticized for imposing, as an equal protection requirement, a rule Congress declined to put into the Twenty Fourth Amendment (which prohibited the use of poll taxes in federal elections, but did not govern state elections). *Reynolds* was vigorously questioned by legislators across the country.[101]

It is not surprising, therefore, that Bork could articulate solid legal criticisms of these cases, or that he was able to point to other distinguished judges who shared his concerns. What is surprising is how oblivious, or uninterested, he seemed to the constitutional weight those decisions had come to carry. *Bolling* and *Shelley* ended a scourge of officially sanctioned racial discrimination opposed by most Americans.[102] The type of voting restrictions prohibited by

---

[96] See Bork transcript at 156.
[97] Ibid. at 157.
[98] Ibid.
[99] Ibid.
[100] Ibid.
[101] See, e.g., Alexander Keyssar, *The Right to Vote: The Contested History of Democracy in the United States* (New York: Basic Books, 2000).
[102] See, e.g., William G. Mayer, *The Changing American Mind: How and Why American Public Opinion Changed Between 1960 and 1988* (Ann Arbor: University of Michigan Press, 1993);

Congress in *Katzenbach* and *Harper* were long used to repress black voting in the South and were still associated with such practices in the minds of many Americans.[103] And despite its unpopularity with legislatures, the one-person, one-vote rule of *Reynolds* was almost immediately accepted by the American public as a constitutionally protected guarantee of political equality.[104]

In other words, these cases came to represent ideals of racial and political equality that Americans, in the years leading up to the Bork hearing, embraced as their own. To note as Bork did that these particular cases were not all litigated as race cases, or that the reasoning in them was (and is) legally contestable, is to fundamentally miss the point. After all, Supreme Court cases, almost by definition, generate legally contestable outcomes: that is how they get to the Supreme Court. The salient fact about cases like these is decidedly not that they are impenetrable to legal criticism, but rather that legal criticism of them is no longer relevant. Outcomes that were legally available when the cases were decided have become constitutionally unacceptable over time. In 1987, *Bolling, Shelley, Katzenbach, Harper*, and *Reynolds* were such cases. Americans embraced the constitutional meanings these cases represented, and simply did not want those victories overturned or written off as constitutional mistakes.

Freedom of Speech

Bork's writings about the scope of the First Amendment's freedom of speech protections also bedeviled him at his hearing. In his 1971 *Indiana Law Review* article, Bork opined:

> Constitutional protection should be accorded only to speech that is explicitly political. There is no basis for judicial intervention to protect any other form of expression be it scientific, literary, or that variety of expression we call obscene or pornographic. Moreover, within that category of speech we

Howard Schuman, Charlotte Steeh, Lawrence Bobo, and Maria Krysan, *Racial Attitudes in America: Trends and Interpretations* (Cambridge, MA: Harvard University Press, 1997).

[103] See, e.g., Keyssar, *The Right to Vote*, supra, n. 101; Donald R. Matthews and James W. Prothro, "Political Factors and Negro Voter Registration in the South," 57 *American Political Science Review* 355 (1963).

[104] For example, a Gallup Poll conducted one month after *Reynolds* was handed down in 1964 revealed that 47% of Americans supported reapportionment based on equality, 30% disapproved, and 23% expressed no opinion. Five years later, 52% supported apportioning state legislative districts equally, whereas 23% preferred "earlier plans" that were not based on population criteria, and 23% offered no opinion. Related, 76% of Americans polled in 1963 supported allowing the federal government to send voting registrars to areas suspected of voter disenfranchisement, 16% opposed, and 8% expressed no opinion. George H. Gallup, *The Gallup Poll: Public Opinion 1935–1971*, Vol. 3 (New York: Random House, 1972) at 1837, 1897–8, 2205-6.

ordinarily call political, there should be no constitutional obstruction to laws making criminal any speech that advocates forcible overthrow of the Government or the violation of the law.[105]

Explicitly political speech, he went on, did *not* include scientific, educational, commercial, or literary expression. "A novel," Bork wrote, "may have impact upon attitudes that affects politics, but it would not for that reason receive judicial protection."[106]

At his Supreme Court hearing, Bork was asked if he still believed that only explicitly political speech warranted First Amendment protection, and, if not, what his current position about the scope of First Amendment protections was. Bork was clear on the first point: he repudiated his earlier views. He was less clear, however, on the second, leaving senators a bit puzzled as to just what his current position was.

Senator Leahy (D-VT) began his questioning on this issue by asking Bork if the aforementioned statements represented his current position. They did not, Bork replied.[107] The assertion that free speech protections extend only to explicitly political speech, Bork now said, was based on his search for a bright line test that could clearly distinguish protected from unprotected speech.[108] Such a line, he came to realize, could not exist because a great deal of speech that was not explicitly political would nonetheless be "central to a democratic government and deserve protection."[109]

Asked to more clearly explain his current position, Bork said he was "about to where the Supreme Court currently is."[110] He then added this:

I do not think a bright line test is available in this area. It is a spectrum. Furthermore, as another professor pointed out to me, the realm of politics extends much more through life than it used to, particularly in part because of the spread of government throughout life. So that the area of what is political or what affects politics has expanded enormously, and fiction affects it and so forth and so on.[111]

---

[105] Bork, "Neutral Principles," supra, n. 31 at 20.
[106] Ibid. at 28.
[107] Bork transcript at 270–1.
[108] Ibid. at 270.
[109] Ibid. at 274–5, citing a letter to the editor written by Bork and read into the transcript by Senator Leahy. After citing the letter, Leahy asked Bork if it is a "pretty accurate statement of [his] views." Bork responded "Well, it is. It does not take in all the forms of speech that would be protected, but it clearly states that it is not just political speech and I think I go on to say that I do not think this rationale requires protection of pornography." Bork transcript at 275.
[110] Ibid. at 269.
[111] Ibid. at 270.

When pushed on whether this rational meant that artistic or other speech that did *not* affect politics was protected by the First Amendment, Bork's reply was ambiguous:

> [T]he political core will, in some sense, confine the first amendment's protections, but it will not be confined to politics . . . Political speech is the paradigm case. Other kinds of speech inform our society and make it freer and make it better able to be efficient and govern itself, and they are all protected. But when you get to something, for example, to take the outer case, when you get to pornography, it is a little hard to see what that has to do with any connection with the way this society lives and governs itself.[112]

Whether expression that had nothing to do with the way "society lives and governs itself," would be protected by Bork's approach, not to mention how a court would determine what speech met this criteria in the first instance, remained unclear.

By the end of the hearing, however, Bork's larger constitutional vision, as stated in his own words, was clear. He did not see a constitutionally defensible way of reaching the result in *Griswold* and he did not agree that gender discrimination should be subjected to heightened scrutiny under the Equal Protection Clause. He thought, and continued to think, that *Bolling, Shelley, Harper, Katzenbach,* and *Reynolds* were wrongly decided, although he would not necessarily overturn them at this point. And, finally, he was suspicious of judicial protection of rights not specifically enumerated in the text of the Constitution, at least to the extent that such protection extended beyond that recognized by the Court in its very early substantive due process cases.

That was Bork's constitutional vision, expressed in his own words. It was not, it turned out, the constitutional vision of the American people. Bork's nomination was defeated by a vote of 58–42. As importantly, it also was not the constitutional vision of the person who would ultimately succeed in becoming our 104th justice: Anthony Kennedy.

THE KENNEDY HEARING

Anthony Kennedy's hearing before the Senate Judiciary Committee took place just three months after Robert Bork's ended. To read the transcripts of these hearings back-to-back, however, is like time traveling from one era into another. "It is central to our American tradition," Kennedy said in his opening remarks, that "there is a zone of liberty, a zone of protection, a line

[112] Ibid. at 276.

that is drawn where the individual can tell the Government: Beyond this line you may not go."[113] "Most Americans," he said, "believe that liberty includes protection of a value that we call privacy."[114] That value, he further specified under questioning, is not just an aspirational one, but is one protected by the Constitution. It is, he said, part of the liberty protected by the Due Process Clause, which, he went on, is itself "quite expansive, quite sufficient, to protect the values of privacy that Americans legitimately think are part of their constitutional heritage."[115]

When asked specifically about *Griswold*, Kennedy distinguished himself from Bork. Although initially declining to comment on the case, he went on to state that "If you were going to propose a statute or a hypothetical that infringed upon the core values of privacy that the Constitution protects, you would be hard put to find a stronger case than *Griswold*."[116] Asked flatly if marital privacy was protected by the Constitution, he said, simply, "yes."[117] Kennedy then went even further. Marital privacy, he said, was unlikely to be the only privacy right protected by the Due Process Clause:

> I think there is a substantive component to the due process clause.... And with reference to the right of privacy, we are very much in a stage of evolution and debate. I think that the public and the legislature have every right to contribute to that debate. The Constitution is made for that kind of debate.... And it may well be that we are still in a very rudimentary state of the law so far as the right of privacy is concerned.[118]

Asked how justices were to determine what unremunerated rights are protected by the Due Process Clause under the rubric of liberty, Kennedy's answer was again quite encompassing. The Court, he said, must look to "essentials of the right to human dignity, the injury to the person, the harm to the person, the anguish to the person, the inability of the person to manifest his or her own personality, the inability of a person to obtain his or her own self-fulfillment, the inability of a person to reach his or her own potential."[119]

Kennedy was similarly expansive about the other areas that caused problems for Bork. The First Amendment, he proclaimed, applies not just to speech that relates to self-governance, but to "all ways in which we express ourselves as

---

[113] Kennedy transcript at 86.
[114] Ibid. at 88.
[115] Ibid. at 164.
[116] Ibid. at 164.
[117] Ibid. at 165.
[118] Ibid. at 165–6.
[119] Ibid. at 180.

persons," including dance, art, and music.[120] These features, Kennedy said, are "to many people as important or more important than political discussions or searching for philosophical truth."[121] The First Amendment, he affirmed, covers all of these forms of speech.[122]

Nor was there any doubt in Kennedy's mind that gender discrimination was properly subjected to some form of heightened review under the Equal Protection Clause. The only open question, he declared, was whether the intermediate scrutiny standard adopted by the Court would adequately protect women: "The law there really seems to me in a state of evolution at this point," he said. "It is going to take more cases for us to ascertain whether or not the heightened scrutiny standard is sufficient to protect the rights of women, or whether or not the strict standard should be adopted."[123] He also indicated agreement with congressional power to enact civil rights legislation prohibiting gender discrimination, declaring himself to be "absolutely committed to enforcing congressional policy to eliminate barriers that discriminate against women, particularly in employment or in the market place or in any other area where it is presented to me. We do not have a free society when those barriers exist."[124]

Kennedy further distinguished himself from Bork in his treatment of civil rights issues and voting rights. Civil rights statutes, Kennedy said, must not be "interpreted grudgingly."[125] Rather than seeing statutory restrictions on private racial discrimination as embodying a principle of "unsurpassed ugliness,"[126] Kennedy proclaimed that "we simply do not have any real freedom if we have discrimination based on race, sex, religion or national origin."[127] Rather than embracing a skepticism of congressional power to regulate in this area, Kennedy expressed the "greatest respect" for the lead Congress has taken in combating discrimination.[128] On voting rights, Kennedy said that restrictions on such rights trigger "rigorous" scrutiny under the Equal Protection Clause.[129] Although not specifically asked about *Reynolds v. Sims*, in earlier speeches, reaffirmed at the hearing, Kennedy spoke highly of *Baker v. Carr*[130] (the

---

[120] Ibid. at 111.
[121] Ibid.
[122] Ibid.
[123] Ibid. at 118.
[124] Ibid. at 161.
[125] Ibid. at 103.
[126] Bork, "Civil Rights – A Challenge," supra, n. 71 at 21.
[127] Kennedy transcript at 101.
[128] Ibid. at 102.
[129] Ibid. at 122 (affirming an earlier writing to this effect).
[130] Baker v. Carr, 369 U.S. 186 (1962).

case that precipitated *Reynolds v. Sims*), classifying it with *Brown v. Board of Education* and *Gideon v. Wainwright*[131] as among the accomplishments of the federal judiciary.[132] He also, as the senators knew, had authored an opinion on the Ninth Circuit Court of Appeals that expanded the one-person, one-vote rule beyond that required by the Supreme Court.[133]

Kennedy likewise rejected Bork's restrictive approach to judicial protection of rights or liberties not specifically enumerated in the Constitution.[134] In determining which such rights to protect, Kennedy did say that a judge must always tie his or her interpretations to the "intentions" of the framers. His understanding of their relevant intentions, however, was cast at an astronomically high level of abstraction, including within it "the ideas, the values, the principles" set forth by the framers.[135] It was those higher ideals that must animate judicial understandings of constitutional meanings. "We are in a much better position" to interpret the Constitution today, Kennedy said, because time has distanced us from the "particular political concerns" of the framers, thereby giving their intentions a "purity and a certain generality now that they did not previously."[136] It would "serve no purpose," he said, "to have a Constitution which simply enacted the status quo."[137] This was particularly true in regard to judicial understandings of the equal protection and due process guarantees found in the Fourteenth Amendment. The Fourteenth Amendment, he declared, was not "designed to freeze into society all of the inequities that then existed."[138]

As Kennedy made clear at his hearing, he fully understood what Robert Bork had not: that enforcing "the Constitution" requires a judge to understand and anticipate "what the society expects of the law."[139] Frequently, there will be no such understanding for a justice to reference. The Court will often be called upon to decide cases involving issues the public has not fully debated or thought about. Or sometimes an issue will have been fully vetted, but no deep or lasting societal consensus has been reached. In those cases, justices must exercise the discretion the tools of legal reasoning leave them with and make the best decisions they can. Other times, however, there *will* be a settled societal expectation about what the Constitution requires. In such

---

[131] Gideon v. Wainwright, 372 U.S. 335 (1963).
[132] Kennedy transcript at 100.
[133] James v. Ball, 613 F.2d. 180 (9th Cir. 1980).
[134] Kennedy transcript at 167.
[135] Ibid. at 141.
[136] Ibid. at 184.
[137] Ibid. at 152.
[138] Ibid. at 151.
[139] Ibid. at 171.

cases, outcomes that were once among those that were legally acceptable are taken off the constitutional table and the constitutional meaning chosen by the people must be embraced, not as something a wiser jurist must grudgingly accept as an irrevocable constitutional error, but as a knowingly chosen and fully validated part of our Constitution. Anthony Kennedy understood this; Robert Bork did not.

THE AFFIRMATION OF THE NEW CONSENSUS

The Bork and Kennedy hearings illustrate how the confirmation process helps to reveal and democratically validate shifts in constitutional meaning. But ratifying a true change in our constitutional consensus requires more. It requires repeated affirmation by numerous nominees, of all political persuasions, over an extended period of time. The six nominees confirmed in the two decades following Kennedy's hearing give us precisely that. Every one of these nominees, from relatively liberal nominees such as Ruth Bader Ginsburg and Stephen Breyer to staunch conservatives such as Clarence Thomas, has embraced the constitutional consensus rejected by Bork and embraced by Kennedy. They have affirmed *Griswold*, *Bolling*, and *Harper*. They have, at their hearings and under oath, stated that gender discrimination warrants heightened scrutiny under the Equal Protection Clause, that the Constitution protects a fundamental and judicially protectable right to privacy, that nontextual liberty interests are protected under the substantive due process doctrine, and that the First Amendment extends beyond self-government–related expression. It is these nominees, appointed by both Democratic and Republican presidents, and confirmed by both Democratic and Republican senators, who solidified the constitutional consensus revealed by the Bork and Kennedy hearings.

David Souter was the first nominee to face the Senate Judiciary Committee after Kennedy was confirmed. Nominated just three years after Bork, Souter was appointed by Republican president George H. W. Bush and confirmed by a Democratically controlled Senate. As in the Bork and Kennedy hearings, the senators opened with *Griswold*. Souter made short work of it: "I believe that the due process clause of the Fourteenth Amendment does recognize and does protect an unenumerated right of privacy," he told the Committee.[140] Contraception, he added, is at the heart of the marital privacy protected by that clause,[141] although the scope of privacy extends contraception rights to nonmarried couples as well.[142]

---

[140] Souter transcript at 54.
[141] Ibid. at 59, 232, 268–9.
[142] Ibid. at 233.

Unenumerated rights, Souter went on, also are protected either by the Ninth Amendment or by the Due Process Clause.[143] These rights, moreover, go beyond the "immediately intended applications" of the founders: justices must take changing attitudes into account when deciding what rights to include within this protection.[144] Confining such liberty rights to those ascertainable through a narrow, "specific intentionalism" is not, Souter told the Judiciary Committee, a valid interpretive approach.[145]

Souter was no less emphatic on civil and voting rights. Bork, Souter said directly, was wrong in worrying that the Civil Rights Act intruded inappropriately on liberty interests. Souter, instead, agreed with Senator Simon's (D-IL) statement that "[W]hen you expand the liberty of any of us, you expand the liberty for all of us."[146] Congress, Souter went on, has "sweeping"[147] powers under the Fourteenth Amendment, including the power to prohibit literacy tests as a condition of voting.[148] He also declared that *Katzenbach* was correctly decided and that the Civil Rights Act of 1964 was clearly constitutional.[149] Arguments to the contrary, Souter went on, have no validity.[150] He was equally clear on *Reynolds v. Sims* and *Bolling v. Sharpe*. *Reynolds* (creating the one-person, one-vote rule) was properly decided, as was *Bolling* (prohibiting racial discrimination by the federal government).[151]

First Amendment and gender discrimination issues also posed no difficulties for Souter. Freedom of speech, he agreed, covers all kinds of expression, regardless of its connection to self-governance.[152] As to gender, the only open constitutional question Souter saw in that area is whether gender-based distinctions should be subjected to heightened or strict scrutiny.[153] There is no "reasonable debate," Souter declared, that rational basis was appropriate.[154]

That Souter rejected Bork's constitution so emphatically may not surprise Court watchers; Souter, after all, ended up on the more liberal wing of the Court on which he sat.[155] Perhaps, one can argue, the constitutional consensus

---

[143] Ibid. at 55.
[144] Ibid. at 235, 267.
[145] Ibid. at 330, 128–9, 161.
[146] Ibid. at 295.
[147] Ibid. at 142, 184.
[148] Ibid. at 216.
[149] Ibid. at 236.
[150] Ibid.
[151] Ibid. at 304–5.
[152] Ibid. at 204, 301.
[153] Ibid. at 75–6, 106, 127, 198.
[154] Ibid.
[155] See, e.g., Thomas M. Keck, "David H. Souter: Liberal Constitutionalism and the Brennan Seat," in *Rehnquist Justice: Understanding the Court Dynamic*, ed. Earl M. Maltz (Lawrence: University Press of Kansas, 2003).

we claim was revealed by the Bork and Kennedy hearings was not a consensus at all, but just the articulation by more liberal nominees of a more liberal constitutional vision. Clarence Thomas's hearing refutes that.

Like Kennedy and Souter, Thomas affirmed at his hearing that the Due Process Clause includes a substantive component, and that privacy is part of the liberty protected by that clause.[156] The privacy protected, he said, includes a marital right to privacy that can be infringed on only by a compelling governmental interest.[157] Asked directly if the right to marital and family privacy was a fundamental liberty protected by the Constitution, Thomas, like Kennedy, said "yes."[158] Like Souter, he also went further, stating that he had "no quarrel" with the Court's extension of contraceptive privacy rights to nonmarried couples.[159]

Echoing Kennedy and Souter, Thomas also said – repeatedly – that constitutionally protected liberty includes more than just the specific protections envisioned by the framers. The framers, he said, used the broad concept of "liberty" precisely because it "evolves" over time.[160] "The world," Thomas said, "didn't stop with the framers. The concept of liberty was not self-defining at that point."[161] Consequently, the quest to determine the scope of constitutional liberty must begin with the framers, but does not end there.[162] "I am skeptical," Thomas said, "when one looks at tradition and history, to narrow the focus to the most specific tradition. I think that the effort should be to determine the appropriate tradition or the tradition that is most relevant to our inquiry, and to not take a cramped approach or narrow approach that could actually limit fundamental rights."[163]

Thomas also concurred with Kennedy's, not Bork's, understanding of other key issues and cases. The First Amendment, Thomas readily affirmed, protects more than politically enriching speech.[164] He also accepted the Court's tiered system of evaluating equal protection claims, and agreed that gender discrimination warrants at least intermediate scrutiny.[165] He explicitly distanced himself from Bork in regard to both *Bolling* and *Katzenbach*, saying in his discussion of *Katzenbach* that it "makes eminent sense to me to find unlawful

---

[156] Thomas transcript at 275.
[157] Ibid. at 127, 255.
[158] Ibid. at 277.
[159] Ibid. at 278–9.
[160] Ibid. at 274.
[161] Ibid. at 270.
[162] Ibid. at 269.
[163] Ibid. at 484.
[164] Ibid. at 466.
[165] Ibid. at 204.

literacy tests that are used to deprive people of the right to vote."[166] He similarly distinguished himself from Bork's initial skepticism of the constitutionality of the Civil Rights Act of 1964, saying without qualification that Congress acted well within its Fourteenth Amendment powers in passing the law.[167]

Ruth Bader Ginsburg and Stephen Breyer, nominated by Democratic president Bill Clinton in 1993 and 1994, respectively, continued in this vein. Both recognized a constitutional right to privacy,[168] accepted a substantive component within the Due Process Clause,[169] and rejected a "narrow" or "rigid" specific intentions approach to determining the content of that substantive protection.[170] Each accepted that gender discrimination is appropriately reviewed with at least an intermediate level of scrutiny,[171] and that the First Amendment extends beyond self-governance–related speech.[172]

Of more interest are the responses John Roberts and Samuel Alito gave to these questions. Unlike Kennedy, Souter, Breyer, and Ginsburg, Roberts and Alito were separated from the Bork hearing by more than two decades. Also unlike those nominees, Roberts and Alito were appointed by a Republican president *and* faced a Republican-controlled Senate – a situation that seemingly would have presented a perfect opportunity to reassert the constitutional vision presented by Bork. Neither of them did. Like their predecessors, Roberts and Alito each explicitly rejected Bork's constitution and embraced Kennedy's.

Alito was the most precise about this, whereas Roberts was the most expansive. Alito repeatedly distinguished himself, by name, from Bork. He specifically rejected Bork's understanding of *Griswold*, *Baker*, and *Reynolds*.[173] He affirmed the correctness of both *Griswold* and *Eisenstadt v. Baird*[174] (extending contraceptive privacy rights to non-married couples).[175] Like Kennedy and Souter, he also rejected Bork's version of a specific intentions-based originalist approach to constitutional interpretation.[176] Roberts likewise went through this post-Bork litany, passing with flying colors. He affirmed that privacy is part of the liberty interest protected by the substantive component of the Due

---

[166] Ibid. at 415.
[167] Ibid. at 414.
[168] Ginsburg transcript at 185; Breyer transcript at 270.
[169] Ginsburg transcript at 271; Breyer transcript at 222–3.
[170] Ginsburg transcript at 223, 270–1; Breyer transcript at 113, 126, 170, 208–9.
[171] Ginsburg transcript at 121, 164; Breyer transcript at 179.
[172] Ginsburg transcript at 314; Breyer transcript at 160, 246.
[173] Alito transcript at 380, 383–4.
[174] Eisenstadt v. Baird, 405 U.S. 438 (1972).
[175] Alito transcript at 318, 400, 453.
[176] Ibid. at 320, 465.

Process Clause,[177] a liberty interest he described as a "living thing,"[178] not bound by the specific intended applications foreseen by the framers.[179] He accepted *Bolling*[180] and *Griswold*[181] and affirmed that the Equal Protection Clause necessitates that gender discrimination be subjected to nothing less than heightened scrutiny.[182] Like Thomas and Alito, he added that he had no quarrel[183] with *Eisenstadt* and declared he was "not aware" of any serious issues regarding the constitutionality of the Civil Rights Act of 1964.[184]

By 2006, when President Barak Obama named his first Supreme Court nominee, the issues that so inflamed the Bork hearing were so obviously part of the constitutional consensus that most of them were mentioned only in passing.[185] The war against the Warren Court was over. It was, in fact, over in 1987. Robert Bork just failed to realize it.

CONCLUSIONS

The Bork hearing, as one scholar put it a few years after it ended, was one of the most "serious and fundamental consideration[s] of constitutional direction . . . we have ever had in America."[186] It showed that many of the constitutional battles of the seventies and eighties were now settled. Rhetoric about "the Warren Court" may still inflame, but many (perhaps most) of the specific cases decided by that Court no longer do. They have, simply put, been absorbed into our constitutional fiber. Americans considered their constitutional options and made their constitutional choices. Kennedy, Souter, Thomas, Ginsburg, Breyer, Roberts, and Alito have vastly different approaches to the Constitution. But yet each of these seven nominees, named by four different presidents, facing Senates controlled by both political parties, testifying over the course of two decades, embraced the post-Bork constitutional consensus on the issues

---

[177] Roberts transcript at 146–7, 186, 259, 325–6.

[178] Ibid. at 148.

[179] Ibid. at 159.

[180] Ibid. at 186.

[181] Ibid. at 207.

[182] Ibid. at 182, 192–3.

[183] Ibid. at 351.

[184] Ibid. at 169.

[185] Pressing issues at the Sotomayor and Kagan hearings included the meaning of the Second Amendment, affirmative action, executive power, campaign finance regulation, and the scope of the public purpose provision of the Takings Clause of the Fifth Amendment. See, e.g., Sotomayor transcript at 2.4–2.6, 2.14–2.15, 2.21, 2.26–2.28, 2.53–2.55, 3.60–3.61; Kagan transcript at 65–6, 88–92, 98–100, 115–118, 142–5, 170–2.

[186] Morton J. Horwitz, "The Meaning of the Bork Nomination in American Constitutional History," 50 *University of Pittsburgh Law Review* 655 (1989) at 655.

that caused Bork so much difficulty. Repeatedly, publicly, and under oath, they again and again gave the answers that Americans have come to accept as part of our constitutional meaning.

At least until the constitutional consensus shifts again – as we are sure it will – our Constitution now protects a fundamental right to privacy, subjects gender discrimination to heightened scrutiny review, guarantees political equality through a one-person, one-vote rule, extends First Amendment protections beyond speech that enriches political discourse, allows Congress and the courts to protect voting rights and prevent even private racial discrimination, and rejects a view of liberty restricted to those liberties explicitly listed in the Constitution or recognized by very early judicial decisions. Our Constitution protects these things not because no other answers to these constitutional questions are legally available, but because these are the answers the American people have chosen.

8

Currently Contested Constitutional Questions

The previous chapters showed how the Court's constitutional choices are ratified over time by their repeated affirmation or rejection at the confirmation hearings. We believe that this is the key role played by the confirmation process: prior to confirmation, nominees, in public and under oath, are expected to affirm their agreement with the current constitutional consensus. When a series of nominees affirm or reject previously contested cases before taking their seats on the high Court, those cases are ushered into (or out of) our constitutional canon. Changes in our constitutional understandings thereby receive a democratically validated stamp of approval.

But what about constitutional issues on which there is no contemporary consensus? Currently contested issues, by definition, are those in which no constitutional agreement exists.[1] Confirming nominees without demanding answers to questions about such issues reflects the fact that neither side in the debate has yet won sufficient support for its position to require affirmation of it as a condition of confirmation. In such cases, we allow presidents to appoint, and Senate majorities to confirm, candidates they *hope* will nudge the Court in their preferred direction, but we do not impose true confirmation conditions.

---

[1] These issues are often the focal point of critiques of the confirmation process. See, e.g., Michael Comiskey, "Can the Senate Examine the Constitutional Philosophies of Supreme Court Nominees?" 26 PS: *Political Science and Politics* 495 (1993); William G. Ross, "The Questioning of Supreme Court Nominees at Senate Confirmation Hearings: Proposals for Accommodating the Needs of the Senate and Ameliorating the Fears of the Nominees," 62 *Tulane Law Review* 109 (1987); Denis Steven Rutkus, "CRS Report for Congress, Questioning Supreme Court Nominees about Their Views on Legal or Constitutional Issues: A Recurring Issue" (2005). Retrieved from: http://www.fas.org/sgp/crs/misc/R41300.pdf (Accessed December 13, 2011); Denis Steven Rutkus, "CRS Report for Congress, Proper Scope of Questioning of Supreme Court Nominees: The Current Debate" (2005). Retrieved from: http://assets.opencrs.com/rpts/RL33059_20050901.pdf (Accessed December 13, 2011).

This does not mean that confirmation discourse about these issues plays no useful role, however. At the hearings, senators repeatedly frame their questions about currently contested constitutional issues in ways that flatter their preferred position.[2] They then press nominees to agree with that position, or to acknowledge that their position either is "settled law," or, depending on the legal status quo, that cases supporting the other side are *not* settled law.[3] In doing so, the senators both signal their constitutional priorities to future justices and present their best case for what should and should not be considered part of our constitutional consensus.

The discussion of "super precedent" at John Roberts' confirmation hearing illustrates this point. Throughout the hearing, Democratic senators pushed Roberts to agree that *Roe v. Wade*[4] was a "super precedent" and was thus either immune from being overturned or, at a minimum, should be subject to a much higher standard than other cases before it properly could be invalidated. Senator Arlen Specter (R-PA) in particular explored the "super precedents" idea with Roberts. After noting that the Supreme Court has declined to overturn *Roe* despite having the opportunity to do so thirty-eight times (by his count), Specter asked Roberts if he agreed that *Roe* might be a "super precedent."[5] The exchange then went on as follows:

Chairman SPECTER: Judge Roberts, in your confirmation hearing for circuit court, your testimony read to this effect, and it has been widely quoted: "*Roe* is the settled law of the land." Do you mean settled for you, settled only for your capacity as a circuit judge, or settled beyond that?

Judge ROBERTS: Well, beyond that, it's settled as a precedent of the Court, entitled to respect under principles of *stare decisis*. And those principles, applied in the *Casey* case, explain when cases should be revisited and when they should not. And it is settled as a precedent of the Court, yes.[6]

---

[2] See, e.g., Anna Batta, Paul M. Collins, Jr., Tom Miles, and Lori A. Ringhand, "Let's Talk: Judicial Decisions at Supreme Court Confirmation Hearings," 96 *Judicature* 7 (2012); George Watson and John Stookey, "Supreme Court Confirmation Hearings: A View from the Senate," 71 *Judicature* 186 (1988).

[3] Nominees at times disagree about what is "settled law." See Lori A. Ringhand, "'I'm Sorry: I Can't Answer That': Positive Scholarship and the Supreme Court Confirmation Process," 10 *University of Pennsylvania Journal of Constitutional Law* 331 (2008). The term, therefore, is not perfectly synonymous with the confirmation conditions that we describe throughout this book: only those issues or cases that are repeatedly affirmed (or rejected) at multiple hearings over time function as true conditions of confirmation. The discussion of what is and is not "settled" is therefore best thought of as an effort to move more cases and issues into the category of confirmation conditions, rather than precisely reflecting what those conditions are.

[4] Roe v. Wade, 410 U.S. 113 (1973).

[5] Roberts transcript, questioning by Senator Specter (R-PA) at 145.

[6] Ibid.

To employ the nomenclature we have developed in this book, Senator Specter was making the case that the Court's repeated affirmation of *Roe* and the decades of reliance on the precedent by the public (which Specter discussed earlier in the exchange) mean that *Roe* should be considered part of our constitutional consensus. Roberts, presumably well aware that *Roe* continues to generate significant constitutional controversy, replied with a noncommittal statement about the general applicability of the principles of *stare decisis*.

Senator Orrin Hatch (R-UT) used his next round of questioning to challenge Specter's narrative about *Roe*, and to frame the issue in a manner more sympathetic to his preferred position. Hatch described *Roe* as a dubious precedent whose validity remains an open question. He supported this view by noting that *Roe* had already been modified by the Court, and thus should not be treated as uniquely settled (or "super") in any way:

> **Senator HATCH:** ... Now, my friend, the Chairman, held up a chart with the number of cases that he said relied on *Roe* v. *Wade*. In fact, if I heard him correctly he called *Roe* a super-duper precedent. Now, I am not sure that a super-duper precedent exists, between you and me, but some have said that *Planned Parenthood* v. *Casey*, a very important case, reaffirmed *Roe*. But let me just ask you, am I correct that *Casey* reaffirmed the central holding in *Roe*, but substantially changed its framework?[7]

Roberts again agreed: yes, he said, *Casey* modified *Roe*.[8] Senator Hatch, having drawn this admission from Roberts, went on to note that, in his view, this meant that the *Roe* framework had proven to be "unworkable."[9] Roberts again responded with a noncommittal statement about *stare decisis*:

> **Judge ROBERTS:** Well, the question of the workability of the framework is I think one of the main considerations that you look to under principles of *stare decisis*, along with the settled expectations, whether a precedent has been eroded. That was one of the factors that the Court looked at in *Casey* in determining I think to alter the framework of *Roe*, the trimester framework and the strict scrutiny approach, at least in the terms that were applied by the joint opinion.[10]

The relevance of this exchange is that both Senators Specter and Hatch presented competing arguments about whether and why *Roe* should be considered part of our constitutional consensus. Specter asserted that it should

---

[7] Roberts transcript, questioning by Senator Hatch (R-UT) at 159.
[8] Ibid.
[9] Ibid. at 160.
[10] Ibid.

because it had been affirmed (by his count) thirty-eight times, whereas Hatch argued that it should not because it had proven "unworkable" and had already been modified by the Court. Neither of the senators, however, was able to draw from Roberts a firm statement about how *he* viewed the status of the case. In fact, in his exchange with Specter, Roberts explicitly refused to provide his opinion on the case directly, noting his belief that he "should stay away from discussions of particular issues that are likely to come before the Court again."[11] Roberts was allowed to appear open to both arguments, without committing to either. Thus, although each side used the hearing to present arguments for and against the canonization of *Roe*, neither side in fact had the political support necessary to make the affirmation or rejection of the case a true condition of Roberts' confirmation.[12]

This chapter explores the discussion of currently contested cases and issues, like *Roe*, at the hearings by illuminating what topics senators and nominees treat as open versus settled constitutional questions. To do this, we investigate the issues and cases that cause nominees to invoke the privilege of declining to discuss on the grounds they may encounter these topics if they are confirmed to the Court. Our definition of "privilege" is quite narrow: we code only those statements in which nominees are pushed hard enough that they are no longer being merely evasive, but instead must resort to a direct refusal to reply. This measure has the obvious advantage of presenting a clear line in an area rife with ambiguity, but we use it primarily because it focuses our inquiry on only those issues that nominees deem too contested to comment on, even when pushed by senators for their position. As a result, our definition limits our query to those issues on which senators are confronted with the choice of either forcing the point by withholding their vote, or confirming nominees despite their express refusal to accept or reject the senator's preferred position.

We begin by identifying the issue areas and cases in which nominees most frequently invoke the privilege to not answer questions. We then examine whether and how the issues triggering such responses have changed over the course of more than seventy years of hearings. Changes to the issues and cases in which nominees invoke privilege evidences alterations to what is

---

[11]   Roberts transcript, questioning by Senator Specter (R-PA) at 142.

[12]   Gerhardt has framed the issue of super precedents in a similar way, defining a super precedent in part as one enjoying "the culmination of sustained support from political leaders and the federal judiciary generally, including the Court, over time." Gerhardt also notes, as we do, that the confirmation process is a mechanism through which the Senate "use its confirmation authority to weaken Supreme Court decisions with which it disagrees and strengthen those with which a critical mass of senators agree." Michael J. Gerhardt, "Super Precedent," 90 *Minnesota Law Review* 1204 (2006) at 1221, 1226.

and is not considered part of our constitutional consensus. Exploring such changes thus illuminates our point about the role the hearings play in validating constitutional change over time: as issues are absorbed or expelled from our constitutional canon, the nominees' willingness to comment on them changes.

Next, we address the related question of whether nominee candor has changed over time. If nominees are increasingly unwilling to make constitutional commitments, the ability of the hearings to play the role we assign to them here would be reduced. Simply put, the hearings cannot act as a forum for the democratic ratification of constitutional change if nominees are increasingly unwilling to commit to such changes at their hearings.

We conclude by examining the extent to which nominees, once confirmed, vote in ways contrary to the constitutional commitments they affirmed at their hearings. Although we believe that the key role of the hearings is ratifying the existing constitutional consensus, which does not itself require that nominees conform to that consensus once on the Court, a system in which justices repeatedly and casually reject the constitutional agreements they endorsed at their hearings would nonetheless be troubling. Consequently, we investigate "mismatches" between what nominees say at their hearings about those issues and cases we have identified as confirmation conditions and how they vote in relation to those same cases and issues once on the Court.

INVESTIGATING PRIVILEGED RESPONSES

In order to analyze systematically the extent to which nominees refuse to answer questions posed by senators, we have coded nominee responses that invoke what we refer to as the "privilege" against answering certain types of questions.[13] As numerous scholars have observed, there is a long-standing practice at the confirmation hearings of nominees refusing to directly answer questions that they believe raise issues likely to come before them if they are seated on the high Court.[14] To capture this type of statement, a response is coded as invoking privilege if the nominee explains his or her refusal to answer a question by asserting that doing so would create the reality or appearance

---

[13] As with Chapters 4 and 5, the unit of analysis is the change of speaker.

[14] See, e.g., Dion Farganis and Justin Wedeking, "'No Hints, No Forecasts, No Previews': An Empirical Analysis of Supreme Court Nominee Candor From Harlan to Kagan," 45 *Law & Society Review* 525 (2011); Albert P. Melone, "The Senate's Confirmation Role in Supreme Court Nominations and the Politics of Ideology Versus Impartiality," 75 *Judicature* 68 (1991); Rutkus, "Proper Scope of Questioning of Supreme Court Nominees, supra, n. 1; Margaret Williams and Lawrence Baum, "Questioning Judges about Their Decisions: Supreme Court Nominees Before the Senate Judiciary Committee," 90 *Judicature* 73 (2006).

TABLE 8.1. *The issue areas in which nominees most frequently invoke privilege, 1939–2010*

Issue	Percent of privileged responses
Civil Rights	51.1 (304)
Law, Crime, and Family	20.5 (122)
Judicial Philosophy	11.1 (66)
Government Operations	6.1 (36)
Miscellaneous Substantive Topics	2.0 (12)
Public Lands and Public Water	2.0 (12)
Other Issues	7.2 (43)
Totals	100.0 (595)

The column entries represent the percentage of comments in each issue area in which nominees invoked privilege in their responses to senatorial questions. The numbers in parentheses indicate the total number of comments pertaining to each issue area. Issue areas representing less than 2% of the column totals are combined into the "Other Issues" category.

of bias; would interfere with judicial independence; or would be inappropriate for some other, similar reason. For example, John Roberts' responses to Senator Graham's (R-SC) questioning are demonstrative of a nominee claiming privilege:

> **Senator GRAHAM:** I think it is not right for elected officials to be unable to talk about or protect the unborn. What do you think about that?
>
> **Judge ROBERTS:** Well, again, Senator, these are issues that are likely to come before the Court, and I cannot comment on those particulars because —
>
> **Senator GRAHAM:** Why are judges more capable of protecting or talking about the unborn than elected officials?
>
> **Judge ROBERTS:** Well, again, those are issues that come before the Court on a regular basis in particular cases, and whether on my current court or the future court, I need to be able to approach those cases with an open mind and not on the basis of statements I make during a confirmation hearing.[15]

We begin our investigation into nominee candor by exploring the issue areas in which nominees most frequently invoke privilege, based on the issue and subissue categories discussed in Chapter 4. This information appears in Table 8.1. The first column lists the issue area, while the percentage of privileged responses corresponding to each issue area appears in the second column. The numbers in parentheses indicate the total number of privileged

[15] Roberts transcript, questioning by Senator Graham (R-SC) at 253.

TABLE 8.2. *The civil rights issue areas in which nominees most frequently invoke privilege, 1939–2010*

Issue	Percent of privileged responses
Abortion Rights	24.0 (73)
Voting Rights	15.5 (47)
Freedom of Speech/Religion	14.8 (45)
Right to Privacy (non-abortion)	14.1 (43)
Racial Discrimination	10.2 (31)
Antigovernment Activities	9.9 (30)
Gender/Sexual Orientation Discrimination	8.9 (27)
Other Civil Rights Issues	8.2 (25)
Totals	105.6 (321)

The column entries represent the percentage of comments in each civil rights issue area in which nominees invoked privilege in their responses to senatorial questions. The percentages exceed 100% because a single comment by a nominee can fall within multiple civil rights issue areas (e.g., abortion and freedom of speech). Accordingly, the number of comments exceeds the number of civil rights comments reported in Table 8.1. The numbers in parentheses indicate the total number of comments pertaining to each issue area falling within the civil rights category. Miscellaneous civil rights issues and civil rights issue areas representing less than 2% of the column totals are combined into the "Other Civil Rights Issues" category.

responses nominees gave in each issue area. Of the 13,452 remarks made by nominees from 1939 to 2010, claims of privilege constitute 595 statements, accounting for 4.4% of all nominee comments.

As this table illustrates, civil rights issues generate by far the most claims of privilege, making up more than half of all privileged responses (51%). This is expected. Although some of the most important constitutional settlements of recent decades have arisen in the civil rights area, such as those involving First Amendment protections, basic privacy rights, and racial and gender equality, it also is true that this issue area includes most of the currently *contested* constitutional issues. As we discuss in the text that follows, such issues include abortion, affirmative action, religious freedoms, and gay rights. Table 8.1 further shows that 21% of the comments in which nominees invoke privilege involve the law, crime, and family issue area; 11% implicate judicial philosophy; 6% involve government operations; and the miscellaneous substantive topics (such as matters of judicial administration and standing) and public lands and water issue areas each account for just 2% of privileged responses.

Because of the breadth and importance civil rights issues play in invoking claims of privilege, a more detailed breakdown of the subissues triggering this response in the civil rights category is warranted. Table 8.2 provides this information, reporting the civil rights issue areas in which nominees most frequently invoked privilege. Questions involving abortion rights generate the most privilege claims from nominees, accounting for almost of quarter of such claims in the civil rights area (24%). As a whole, abortion issues account for more than 12% of claims of privilege across *all* issue areas and more than 22% of *all* claims in the post-*Roe* era. A typical response to abortion-related questions is demonstrated in the following exchange between Senator Biden and nominee Souter:

> **Senator BIDEN:** Now, you have just told us that the right to use birth control, to decide whether or not to become pregnant is one of those fundamental rights – the value placed on it is fundamental. Now, let us say that a woman and/or her mate uses such a birth control device and it fails. Does she still have a constitutional right to choose not to become pregnant?

> **Judge SOUTER:** Senator, that is the point at which I will have to exercise the prerogative which you were good to speak of explicitly. I think for me to start answering that question, in effect, is for me to start discussing the concept of *Roe v. Wade*. I would be glad – I do not think I have to do so for you – but I would be glad to explain in some detail my reasons for believing that I cannot do so, but of course, they focus on the fact that ultimately the question which you are posing is a question which is implicated by any possibility of the examination of *Roe v. Wade*. That, as we all know, is not only a possibility, but a likelihood that the Court may be asked to do it.[16]

Below, we take a closer look at abortion-related privilege claims in our examination of the specific cases that result in nominees invoking privilege; for now, we note simply that it is the most common civil rights issue about which claims of privilege arise.

The next most common types of civil rights issues resulting in claims of privilege are voting rights, freedom of speech and religion, and non-abortion privacy, each of which account for about 15% of claims of privilege. Matters of racial discrimination, antigovernment activities, and gender and sexual orientation discrimination each comprise about 10% of privilege claims. We discuss each of these areas in turn.

The vast majority of privileged responses in the voting rights area came from the hearings of Abe Fortas (for both associate and chief justice) and Homer Thornberry.[17] Fortas was nominated as an associate justice in 1965, just a

---

[16] Souter transcript, questioning by Senator Biden (D-DE) at 59.
[17] While both of Rehnquist's hearings involved numerous questions about his involvement in what his opponents referred to as "voter suppression" efforts in Arizona, Rehnquist did not respond to these questions with claims of privilege. Rather, he denied the assertions or said

year after the Supreme Court declared in *Reynolds v. Sims*[18] that legislative districts must be equally apportioned on the basis of population. The senators at the Fortas hearing showed keen interest in this development. Senator Fong (R-HI) was particularly concerned about the case, and asked Fortas a series of questions about whether the logic of *Reynolds* could be extended to require the population-based apportionment of the Senate as well as the House of Representatives. As the representative of a small population state, Fong pushed Fortas to renounce any such extension of *Reynolds*. Fortas repeatedly refused to answer the senator's questions, noting that he was not at liberty to state his opinion because he had not studied the subject.[19]

Fortas' chief justice hearing was marked by voting rights issues of a different nature. This hearing occurred in 1968 – just two years after the Supreme Court decided *Katzenbach v. Morgan*.[20] *Katzenbach* upheld the Voting Rights Act of 1965, most notably its prohibition on the imposition of literacy tests as a condition of voting, as a valid exercise of congressional power. Southern senators viewed *Katzenbach* as an egregious extension of congressional power to interfere in what they saw as the internal concerns of the states. Fortas, who was on the Court when *Katzenbach* was decided, repeatedly declined to answer questions about the case.[21] He likewise claimed privilege in response to a series of questions from Senator Thurmond about other voting-related issues, such as those arising in *Baker v. Carr*[22] (legislative redistricting), *Reynolds* (apportionment), and *Harper v. Virginia Board of Elections*[23] (poll taxes).[24]

Homer Thornberry also claimed privilege on a host of voting rights–related issues. Thornberry was nominated to fill what was expected to be the vacancy created by Fortas' elevation to chief justice. When the Fortas promotion failed, Thornberry's nomination necessarily was withdrawn. Given that the two hearings occurred within days of one another, it is not surprising that they involved a similar set of issues. Like Fortas at his chief justice hearing, Thornberry was repeatedly asked about the constitutionality of the Voting Rights Act and federal prohibitions on literacy tests and poll taxes as a prerequisite to voting.[25]

he did not remember the details of the facts underlying the allegations. See, e.g., Rehnquist associate justice transcript at 71–2; Rehnquist chief justice transcript at 169–72.

[18] Reynolds v. Sims, 377 U.S. 533 (1964).
[19] Fortas associate justice transcript, questioning by Senator Fong (R-HI) at 51–3.
[20] Katzenbach v. Morgan, 384 U.S. 641 (1966).
[21] Fortas chief justice transcript at 180–1.
[22] Baker v. Carr, 369 U.S. 186 (1962).
[23] Harper v. Virginia Board of Elections, 383 U.S. 663 (1966).
[24] Fortas chief justice transcript, questioning by Senator Thurmond (R-SC) at 189–90.
[25] See, e.g., Thornberry transcript at 256–60, 262–3, 266–9, 271–3.

Senator Ervin (D-NC) posed just such a question, asking Thornberry whether he believed that state-imposed poll taxes violated the Constitution.[26] Thornberry refused to answer, generating this interesting exchange with the Committee Chair, Senator Eastland (D-MS):

> **Senator EASTLAND:** Let me ask a question. Judge, how long were you a district judge?
>
> **Judge THORNBERRY:** A year and a half.
>
> **Senator EASTLAND:** I want to ask you a question in all seriousness. Did you permit any witness on the stand to refuse to answer questions as you have refused to answer them in these hearings?
>
> **Judge THORNBERRY:** I don't recall – that the occasion ever arose, Senator. But I expect you are right.
>
> **Senator EASTLAND:** You know I am right.[27]

Nominees in the 1960s were not the only ones to assert privilege on voting rights issues. John Roberts, appearing before the Committee in 2005, also responded to a notable number of voting rights questions with claims of privilege. These questions were, once again, focused primarily on the Voting Rights Act:[28]

> **Senator KENNEDY:** So, I'll assume that you don't feel that there are any doubts on the constitutionality of the 1964 Act. Do you have any doubts as to the constitutionality of the 1965 Voting Rights Act?
>
> **Judge ROBERTS:** That's an issue, of course, as you know, it's up for renewal and that is a question that could come before the Court. The question of Congress's power, again, without expressing my views on it, I do know that it's going to be –[29]

After voting rights, the next most common civil rights issue areas in which privilege was invoked involved the freedoms of speech and religion. A plurality of such claims occurred at Fortas' chief justice hearing, although Ginsburg, Breyer, and Rehnquist (for associate justice) also provided a significant number of such responses. The following comment by Breyer is typical of this type of exchange:

---

[26] Thornberry transcript, questioning by Senator Ervin (D-TX) at 273.

[27] Thornberry transcript, questioning by Senator Eastland (D-MS) at 274.

[28] Roberts also claimed privilege when asked about Bush v. Gore, 531 U.S. 98 (2000). Roberts transcript at 338.

[29] Roberts transcript, questioning by Senator Kennedy (D-MA) at 169.

Judge BREYER: On the one hand, I know I had a case in which I wrote that the school system, when they have a place open for public meetings, has to let churches meet there, too, religious groups, too. Certainly, there is support for religion in the Constitution. When you come to the establishment clause, it is well established that that clause does not prohibit tax exemption. To the contrary, there is tax exemption.

Senator SPECTER: But the tax exemption is very narrowly tailored and cannot cross the line where there is any support for a political candidate – any support.

Judge BREYER: And when you get into areas beyond that, when you get into areas of definition when the support is greater, what I have said before – and it is hard to go beyond this – is there are difficult problems of line-drawing. The principle is fairly clear in the establishment area at the extremes. Some is absolutely permitted – the fire department, the tax exemptions of certain kinds, busing of certain kinds. Some is quite clearly prohibited. And then what you find are a difficult set of cases in this middle area, and what is going too far. It is hard for me to be more specific than that, because those are the cases that do come up, that are difficult, that I would have to think about in light of the particular context. That is in the legal area; outside the legal area, I am not expert.

Senator SPECTER: Well, you have not given me too much on how you would approach the legal issues, really, Judge Breyer; and you have not given me anything on your sense of values aside from the legal issues. We probe to get your thinking.

Judge BREYER: Yes.[30]

Questions involving the right to privacy outside of the abortion context con-stitute the fourth most frequently addressed civil rights issue area in which privilege is invoked. The plurality of such claims of privacy occurred at Rehn-quist's associate justice hearing in 1971. These questions involved Rehnquist's support for the Omnibus Crime Act of 1968, which authorized federal agents to install wiretapping devices, absent judicial approval, in cases of national secu-rity. As an Assistant U.S. Attorney General, Rehnquist spoke out in favor of the legislation.[31] When asked whether he continued to support such policies, Rehnquist repeatedly refused to answer, noting that "I think it inappropriate in a case in which I have appeared as an advocate to now give personal views."[32]

---

[30] Breyer transcript, questioning by Senator Specter (R-PA) at 377.
[31] See, e.g., Rehnquist associate justice transcript at 64–6.
[32] Ibid. at 64.

Issues of racial discrimination account for 10% of privilege claims in the civil rights issue area. Although many of these claims of privilege occurred during the early hearings in the data, when civil rights issues were largely unsettled, several more recent nominees also have refrained from answering questions on these matters. For example, Clarence Thomas claimed privilege in response to questions involving affirmative action programs and the Civil Rights Act of 1964.[33] Likewise, Ruth Bader Ginsburg refused to give her opinion on *Shaw v. Reno*,[34] a case involving the "racial gerrymandering" of congressional districts.[35]

Antigovernment activities, the sixth most frequent civil rights issue area in which claims of privilege were made, arose in only two hearings, those of Fortas (for chief justice) and Brennan. In both of these relatively early hearings, the questions resulting in privileged responses involved the nominees' opinions about communism or the Court's decisions involving communism. As noted in the Sidebar in Chapter 6, Brennan was asked a number of questions about his opinions on international communism by Senator Joseph McCarthy (R-WI). Brennan invoked privilege in many of his responses.[36] Fortas behaved similarly at his hearing in response to questioning by Senator Strom Thurmond.

One such exchange between Thurmond and Fortas is particularly interesting. Thurmond pushed Fortas about a then-recent decision by the Supreme Court, *U.S. v. Robel*.[37] *Robel* struck down a state-imposed loyalty oath administered as a condition of employment in public schools. After Senator Thurmond set out these basic facts, the exchange continued as follows:

Senator THURMOND: Mr. Justice Fortas, do you think the parent of a child who has a Communist for a teacher has cause for concern?

Justice FORTAS: Oh, I don't know how I can answer that, Senator. Of course, parents are concerned about the quality of the people who teach them. If there were somebody teaching the child subversive doctrine, or subversive attitudes toward the United States, a parent has every reason for indignation, not merely concern.

Senator THURMOND: Mr. Justice Fortas, what alternatives does a parent of the State have other than screening by oath or affirmation to prevent subversives from corrupting the minds of our children?

---

[33] Thomas transcript at 253, As noted in Chapter 7, Thomas later in his testimony affirmed that Congress was acting within its power when passing the Civil Rights Act. Thomas Transcript at 414.

[34] Shaw v. Reno, 509 U.S. 630 (1993).

[35] Ginsburg transcript at 252.

[36] Brennan transcript, questioning by Senator McCarthy (R-WI) at 17–20.

[37] U.S. v. Robel, 389 U.S. 258 (1967).

Justice FORTAS: Senator, I cannot answer that question . . . It is a very delicate area of the Constitution, as everybody knows. The problem is for legislation to be drafted which draws a careful and precise constitutional line. It is not a question of objectives. It is a question of the precise means. Beyond that I cannot with propriety go.[38]

Gender and sexual orientation discrimination is the next most frequent civil rights area in which nominees claim privilege. These topics constitute 9% of privileged responses within the civil rights issue area. Issues of gender discrimination first appeared at the Carswell hearing in 1970. During that hearing, Carswell invoked privilege in response to a question regarding Carswell's vote, as a Fifth Circuit Court of Appeals judge, to deny en banc rehearing to a case in which an employer refused to hire mothers with preschool children.[39] A year later, Rehnquist refused to answer questions on the Equal Rights Amendment.[40] More recent nominees have claimed privilege in response to questions involving gender and sexual orientation discrimination that generate substantial controversy in contemporary American politics, such as whether gender should be treated as a fully suspect classification (Ginsburg),[41] if the Constitution prohibits discrimination against gays and lesbians (Roberts),[42] whether there is a constitutional right for same-sex couples to marry (Sotomayor and Kagan),[43] and whether the Defense of Marriage Act violates the Full Faith and Credit Clause of the Constitution (Kagan).[44]

After civil rights, the law, crime, and family issue area is the second most frequent topic in which nominees invoke the privilege of not responding. As noted earlier, this issue area is composed almost entirely of criminal procedure questions. Thurgood Marshall's hearing in particular was dominated by questions in this area, many of which he refused to answer. Marshall served as President Johnson's solicitor general prior to his nomination and sat on a presidential commission investigating crime and law enforcement problems. These facts may account for the prevalence of this type of question at his hearing. Marshall's hearing also offered an opportunity for senators opposed to civil rights and *Brown* (which Marshall argued on behalf of the NAACP Legal Defense Fund) to stoke the anti-Court sentiment that was building among

---

[38] Fortas chief justice transcript, questioning by Senator Thurmond (R-SC) at 205–6.
[39] Carswell transcript at 40.
[40] Rehnquist associate justice transcript at 163–4.
[41] Ginsburg transcript at 165, 243–4.
[42] Roberts transcript at 360.
[43] Sotomayor transcript at 4.20; Kagan transcript at 149.
[44] Kagan transcript at 180.

those who did not (necessarily) object to *Brown*, but who did oppose the Warren Court's pro-defendant criminal procedure decisions.[45] As Marshall was the first African American appointed to the high Court, there was also an effort by some senators to associate him with what they were eager to portray as an out of control crime wave perpetrated by black Americans.[46]

The following exchange between Senator McClellan (D-AR) and Marshall illustrates the tone of comments in this issue area:

> **Senator McCLELLAN:** . . . You talk about democracy and liberty and all these things; I think they are in jeopardy today in this country. Look at the riots everywhere. A sentiment has been built up over the country to the point where some people feel that, if you don't like the law, violate it. And the Supreme Court takes the position that at its whim it can reverse decisions on constitutional issues, on constitutional questions, constitutional laws that have been the law of the land for a century. And they can change the law. They don't feel very strongly bound to enforce it, to observe it and to follow it. No wonder the fellow out in the street, thinks that, if the Supreme Court has no regard for precedent in law, and can change it when it wants to, why can't I do as I please? We have an intolerable situation in this country, and I would like to find some way to check it. I would like to start at the top, for I think that is where you need to start. You may lecture me if you want to. I have told you what I think.

> **Judge MARSHALL:** Far be it from me to attempt to lecture you, sir. I appreciate what you said, and appreciate your problem. And at the same time I am equally certain that you would not want me to prejudge a case that is certain to come up to the Court.[47]

The next most common area in which nominees claim the privilege of not responding (after civil rights and law, crime, and family) is judicial philosophy. Although there is a general consensus that it is appropriate for senators to question nominees regarding matters of judicial philosophy,[48] occasionally

---

[45] Jeff Woods, *Black Struggle, Red Scare: Segregation and Anti-Communism in the South, 1948–1968* (Baton Rouge: Louisiana State University Press, 2004).

[46] Juan Williams, *Thurgood Marshall: American Revolutionary* (New York: Random House, 1998).

[47] Marshall transcript, questioning by Senator McClellan (D-AR) at 190.

[48] See, e.g., Charles L. Black, Jr., "A Note on Senatorial Consideration of Supreme Court Nominees," 79 *Yale Law Journal* 657 (1970); Jason J. Czarnezki, William K. Ford, and Lori A. Ringhand, "An Empirical Analysis of the Confirmation Hearings of the Justices of the Rehnquist Natural Court," 24 *Constitutional Commentary* 127 (2007); Donald E. Lively, "The Supreme Court Appointment Process: In Search of Constitutional Roles and Responsibilities," 59 *Southern California Law Review* 551 (1986); William G. Ross, "The Functions, Roles, and Duties of the Senate in the Supreme Court Appointment Process," 28 *William & Mary*

nominees will refuse to answer such inquiries by invoking privilege. For example, William Brennan claimed privilege in response to a question involving whether "the Constitution and amendments thereto have a fixed and definite meaning when they are adopted."[49] Likewise, Robert Bork refused to elaborate on the "constitutional principles" that should be "reconsidered" by the Court.[50] More recent nominees have invoked privilege in response to senators' questions involving, for example, whether courts should be compelled to recognize societal changes with regard to constitutional interpretation (Ginsburg),[51] and whether it is appropriate for judges to consider foreign law in interpreting the U.S. Constitution (Roberts).[52]

The remainder of the claims of privilege in our data set comprise a hodgepodge of substantive issue areas. These include questions about government operations, judicial administration (coded under miscellaneous substantive topics), and issues involving public lands and water. In the government operations issue area, John Roberts refused to opine as to whether Congress has the power to stop a president from engaging in an unauthorized war.[53] With regard to judicial administration, Sandra Day O'Connor invoked privilege in response to a question involving setting term limits for federal judges.[54] An example in the public land and water issue area – a very rare topic of discussion – appeared at the hearing of Ruth Bader Ginsburg. The nominee asserted privilege in a series of questions involving the relationship between the federal government and Native American Indian tribes.[55]

Having established the issue areas in which nominees most frequently invoke privilege, we now turn to the analysis of each individual nominee's hearing. The purpose here is to shed light on the development of general trends over time in the nominees' claims of privilege. Table 8.3 presents the issue and subissue areas in which each nominee most commonly invoked privilege.

As discussed previously, claims of privilege in response to questions about voting rights were widespread in the years immediately following passage of the Voting Rights Act of 1965 and subsequent Supreme Court case upholding key

Law Review 633 (1986); Rutkus, "Proper Scope of Questioning of Supreme Court Nominees, *supra*, n. 1.

[49] Brennan transcript at 36.
[50] Bork transcript at 710.
[51] Ginsburg transcript at 222.
[52] Roberts transcript at 200.
[53] Ibid. at 150.
[54] O'Connor transcript at 100.
[55] Ginsburg transcript at 236–8.

TABLE 8.3. *The issue areas and subissue areas in which nominees most frequently invoke privilege, 1939–2010*

Nominee name (year)	Issue area	Subissue area
Frankfurter (1939)	Government Operations (1)	Federal Government Branch Relations (1)
Jackson (1941)	No claims of privilege	
Harlan (1955)	Judicial Philosophy (8)	Separation of Powers (7)
Brennan (1957)	Civil Rights (13)	Antigovernment Activities (13)
Whittaker (1957)	No claims of privilege	
Stewart (1959)	Civil Rights (4)	Racial Discrimination (4)
White (1962)	No claims of privilege	
Goldberg (1962)	Government Operations (1)	Federal Government Branch Relations (1)
Fortas (1965)	Civil Rights (3)	Voting Rights (3)
Marshall (1967)	Law, Crime, and Family (39)	*Miranda* Rights (22)
Fortas (1968)	Civil Rights (53)	Voting Rights (22)
Thornberry (1968)	Civil Rights (8)	Voting Rights (6)
Burger (1969)	Civil Rights (2)	Voting Rights (1)/Freedom of Speech/Religion (1)
Haynsworth (1969)	Judicial Philosophy (3)	General Judicial Philosophy (3)
Carswell (1970)	Civil Rights (3)	Racial Discrimination (2)
Blackmun (1970)	Civil Rights (2)	Other Civil Rights Issues (2)
Rehnquist (1971)	Civil Rights (28)	Right to Privacy (non-abortion) (11)
Powell (1971)	Civil Rights (5)	Right to Privacy (non-abortion) (3)
Stevens (1975)	Law, Crime, and Family (4)	Death Penalty (4)
O'Connor (1981)	Civil Rights (7)	Abortion Rights (5)
Rehnquist (1986)	Judicial Philosophy (11)	Separation of Powers (10)
Scalia (1986)	Civil Rights (16)	Racial Discrimination (9)
Bork (1987)	Civil Rights (6)	Abortion Rights (2)
Kennedy (1987)	Law, Crime, and Family (3)	Death Penalty (3)
Souter (1990)	Civil Rights (22)	Abortion Rights (19)
Thomas (1991)	Civil Rights (20)	Abortion Rights (14)
Ginsburg (1993)	Civil Rights (26)	Freedom of Speech/Religion (8)
Breyer (1994)	Civil Rights (13)	Freedom of Speech/Religion (5)
Roberts (2005)	Civil Rights (26)	Abortion Rights (15)
Alito (2006)	Judicial Philosophy (12)	Text as Interpretive Tool (6)
Sotomayor (2009)	Civil Rights (8)	Right to Keep and Bear Arms (4)
Kagan (2010)	Civil Rights (4)	Gender/Sexual Orientation Discrimination (2)
	Law, Crime, and Family (4)	Legal Issues (2)

The numbers in parentheses indicate the number of comments represented by the issue area and subissue area at each hearing in which each nominee invoked privilege in his or her responses to senatorial questions.

parts of the Act (such as *Katzenbach v. Morgan*). Attesting to this, Fortas (for both associate and chief justice), Thornberry, and Burger all asserted privilege in their responses to questions involving voting rights more than they did in any other issue area. Potter Stewart, whose hearing was the first held after *Brown* was issued, claimed privilege most often in response to questions about racial discrimination, as did later nominees Carswell and Scalia. Beginning in 1981, and continuing through Roberts' hearing in 2005, privilege was most commonly invoked in questions relating to abortion rights. Most recently, the scope of Second Amendment rights and gender and sexual orientation discrimination were, in turn, the topics in which Sotomayor and Kagan most frequently asserted privilege. This finding is consistent with our assertion that nominees' claims of privilege change as different issues move in and out of our constitutional consensus.

The most striking thing shown in Table 8.3, however, may be the distribution of claims of privilege in the abortion area. Nominees named by Republican presidents have asserted privilege in response to inquiries involving abortion rights much more frequently than have nominees appointed by Democratic presidents. Of the ten Republican nominees testifying before the Judiciary Committee since *Roe v. Wade* was decided in 1973, five of them – O'Connor, Bork, Souter, Thomas, and Roberts – have claimed privilege in abortion discussions more so than in any other issue area. The same is not true of nominees named by Democratic presidents in this time period. Each of these nominees – Ginsburg, Breyer, Kagan, and Sotomayor – invoked privilege more often in areas unrelated to abortion rights. Overall, 20.2% of all privilege claims made by Republican nominees implicate abortion rights, compared to only 1.6% for Democratic nominees, a statistically significant difference ($P < 0.001$).

This is an intriguing finding, and there are many possible explanations for it. Nominees appointed by Democratic presidents may have more well-known views on abortion than their Republican counterparts. This was certainly the case with Ginsburg, whose work on women's rights issues was familiar to senators and who was relatively forthright at her hearing about her support for abortion rights.[56] It also may be because three of the nominees appointed by Republican presidents – Bork, Kennedy, and Alito – were vying to replace justices (Powell and O'Connor) who were seen as the median justice or "swing vote" on their respective Courts.[57] Nominations for pivotal seats perceived as

[56] Ibid. at 207.
[57] See, e.g., Lee Epstein and Tonja Jacobi, "Super Medians," 61 *Stanford Law Review* 37 (2008); Andrew D. Martin, Kevin M. Quinn, and Lee Epstein, "The Median Justice on the U.S. Supreme Court," 83 *North Carolina Law Review* 1275 (2005).

likely to change the ideological direction of the Court have tended to be far more contested than those in which the nominee is seen as replacing a less critical justice or a justice holding an ideological perspective similar to that of the nominee.[58] It also could be that Democratic and Republican senators have different political incentives to grill nominees on abortion. To again put it in the nomenclature of this book, Democratic senators may feel that their view of abortion is closer to being a viable confirmation condition than do their Republican counterparts. Regardless of the reason, however, it is clear that abortion-related issues play a much larger role in motivating privilege claims for Republican appointees than Democratic appointees.

Also of interest in Table 8.3 are the four nominations in which questions about judicial philosophy most commonly resulted in privilege claims. This is unusual because, as noted previously, questions about judicial philosophy are widely seen as an appropriate and necessary part of the nominee vetting process. Nonetheless, Harlan, Haynsworth, Rehnquist (for chief justice), and Alito refused to answer more questions in this issue area than in any other.[59]

These claims of privilege, however, are not necessarily quite what they first appear. An exchange from Rehnquist's nomination to chief justice provides an illustration of the type of situation in which he and other nominees claimed privilege in this issue area. Senator Specter was questioning Rehnquist about *Ex Parte McCardle*,[60] a Civil War–era case in which the Court addressed the ability of Congress to limit the Supreme Court's appellate jurisdiction.[61] The question was primarily about Rehnquist's opinion about the power of the Court to exercise judicial review and the ways in which it should exercise that power. It therefore was captured in the judicial philosophy issue area. It is clear, however, that Rehnquist's claim of privilege was grounded in his assertion that questions about the scope of the Exceptions Clause, which allows Congress to strip the Court's appellate jurisdiction in some situations, would likely come before the Court again. Our review of the exchanges in which nominees claimed privilege in this issue area confirms that this type of question – a question that closely skirts the line between issues of constitutional interpretation and substantive questions of law – account for many of the

---

[58] P.S. Ruckman, Jr., "The Supreme Court, Critical Nominations, and the Senate Confirmation Process," 55 *Journal of Politics* 739 (1993).

[59] These exchanges raise the question of whether the affirmation or rejection of particular methods of constitutional interpretation can act as confirmation conditions. We think this is an interesting possibility, but exploring it is beyond the scope of this project.

[60] Ex Parte McCardle, 74 U.S. 506 (1869).

[61] Rehnquist Chief Justice transcript, questioning by Senator Specter (R-PA) at 188.

TABLE 8.4. *The Supreme Court cases in which nominees most frequently invoke privilege,* 1939–2010

Decision (year)	Number of privileged responses	Nominee who most frequently invoked privilege
Roe v. Wade (1973)	37 (13.6)	Souter (1990)
Miranda v. Arizona (1966)	27 (9.9)	Marshall (1967)
Planned Parenthood v. Casey (1992)	14 (5.1)	Roberts (2005)/Alito (2006)
Brown v. Louisiana (1966)	10 (3.7)	Fortas (1967)
Beacon Theatres v. Westover (1959)	7 (2.6)	Marshall (1967)
Cardona v. Power (1966)	7 (2.6)	Fortas (1967)
Katzenbach v. Morgan (1966)	7 (2.6)	Fortas (1967)
Fortson v. Morris (1966)	7 (2.6)	Fortas (1967)
DeGregory v. Attorney General of New Hampshire (1966)	6 (2.2)	Fortas (1967)
Griswold v. Connecticut (1965)	6 (2.2)	Souter (1990)
Harper v. Virginia State Board of Elections (1966)	6 (2.2)	Fortas (1967)
Marbury v. Madison (1803)	6 (2.2)	Scalia (1986)
Total	272 (100.0)	Fortas (1967)

This table lists the Supreme Court cases in which nominees most commonly invoked privilege in their responses to senatorial questions. The second column is the total number of privileged responses involving an individual decision. The numbers in parentheses in the second column indicate the percentage of comments pertaining to each decision as a function of all statements invoking privilege regarding Supreme Court decisions. The third column identifies the nominee who most frequently invoked privilege in statements involving each Supreme Court decision

nominees' claims of privilege in this issue area and are thus less surprising than they first appear.

A CASE-BASED ANALYSIS OF PRIVILEGE CLAIMS

To this point, we have investigated nominees' responses by focusing on the issue and subissue areas in which the nominees, both as a group and individually, most commonly invoked privilege, and how those issues have changed over time. But much of the debate about nominees' reticence to answer questions focuses on cases, not issue areas.[62] We therefore now examine claims of privilege in exchanges in which specific cases are the focus of nominees asserting privilege. This information is reported in Table 8.4.[63] The first column

---

[62] See, e.g., Rutkus, "Questioning Supreme Court Nominees about Their Views on Legal or Constitutional Issues," supra, n. 1.

[63] This information is based on the data collection effort discussed in Chapter 5.

provides the name of the case implicated in the invocation of privilege and the year it was decided. The second column indicates the number and percentage of privileged responses, while the third column reports the nominee who most frequently asserted privilege with respect to each case.[64]

As shown in Table 8.4, cases involving reproductive rights, and abortion rights in particular, abound, collectively accounting for more than 20% of privileged responses relating to Supreme Court precedents. *Roe v. Wade*, the seminal case providing constitutional protection to a woman's right to choose an abortion, is the single case nominees most commonly refuse to discuss on privilege grounds. *Planned Parenthood v. Casey*[65] and *Griswold v. Connecticut*[66] bring an additional 20 abortion-related privilege claims, indicating that such claims account for 57 of the 272 case-related assertions of privilege made at the hearings. This is almost double the number of such claims made by the abortion cases' closest competitor, *Miranda v. Arizona*,[67] which accounts for a relatively paltry twenty-seven claims.

Of the thirty-seven instances in which privilege was claimed in a discussion of *Roe*, more than 60% occurred at the hearings of Souter (thirteen) and Thomas (ten). In addition, Roberts explicitly asserted privilege five times in relation to *Roe*, while O'Connor made three such claims. *Casey*, a 1992 case upholding the core right to abortion, brings an additional fourteen claims of privilege to abortion-related discussions. Alito and Roberts invoked privilege five times each in discussions of *Casey*, while Ginsburg did so three times and Breyer did so once. Including *Griswold* – a case that sometimes, but not always, is used as a proxy for *Roe* – adds six abortion-related privilege claims, three by Souter and one each by Alito, Kennedy, and Roberts.[68]

The supremacy of abortion-related cases in claims of privilege is striking. *Roe*, *Casey*, and *Griswold* account for more than one-fifth of claims of privilege involving named cases. This is particularly notable given that, of the seventy-plus years of hearings in the data, more than half took place before *Roe* was decided. This is even more extraordinary because, unlike *Roe*, most of the named cases generating claims of privilege show up only a few times in our

---

[64] Some comments invoking privilege include more than one named case. Accordingly, the total number of named cases generating privileged responses is larger than the number of individual responses in which privilege is claimed. There are also occasionally instances in which a case is named in a comment, but the nominee's invocation of privilege is not made in relation to the case itself. We have excluded such cases from Table 8.4.

[65] Planned Parenthood v. Casey, 505 U.S. 833 (1992).

[66] Griswold v. Connecticut, 381 U.S. 479 (1965).

[67] Miranda v. Arizona, 384 U.S. 436 (1966).

[68] As noted in Chapter 7, many of these justices nonetheless did affirm the existence of the basic privacy right at issue in *Griswold*.

dataset before disappearing into historical oblivion. Just twelve cases generated more than five claims of privilege; the remaining seventy-five named cases provoking privileged responses each did so five or fewer times. Among just this pool of more frequently discussed cases (appearing in Table 8.4), the share of claims of privilege involving abortion-related cases leaps to more than 40%, making abortion's dominance among well-known, historically significant cases even more dramatic. The issue of unanswered questions is, it appears, largely an issue about *Roe v. Wade* and abortion, and this is especially true in the contemporary era.

Questions about other cases, nonetheless, do, of course, result in nominees claiming privilege. After *Roe*, *Miranda v. Arizona* generated the most privilege claims. *Miranda* provoked twenty-seven explicit refusals to answer on privilege grounds, twenty-four of which occurred at Thurgood Marshall's hearing. The remaining three instances of nominees claiming privilege in relation to *Miranda* were evenly divided between Fortas's chief justice hearing and the hearings of Scalia and Thornberry.

The next most common case nominees refuse to discuss is *Brown v. Louisiana*,[69] a 1966 decision involving the First Amendment rights of civil rights protestors. By a 5–4 vote, the Court in *Brown* held that protestors engaged in a sit-in in a segregated public library were exercising a protected First Amendment right to peacefully protest. Not surprisingly, this decision was not popular with Senator Thurmond, who repeatedly interrogated Justice Fortas about it at the nominee's chief justice hearing.[70] All of the invocations of privilege in relation to this case come from that hearing.

A cluster of cases, shown in Table 8.4, each generated either seven or six claims of privilege. Privilege claims relating to five of the cases in this group, *Cardona v. Power*,[71] *DeGregory v. New Hampshire*,[72] *Fortson v. Morris*,[73] *Harper v. Virginia*, and *Katzenbach v. Morgan* were made exclusively by Justice Fortas at his chief justice hearing, whereas only Thurgood Marshall claimed privilege with respect to *Beacon Theatres v. Westover*.[74] Among the remaining

---

[69] Brown v. Louisiana, 383 U.S. 131 (1966).

[70] Fortas Chief Justice Hearing at 184–7.

[71] Cardona v. Power, 384 U.S. 672 (1966) (involving the imposition of literacy requirements as a condition of voting).

[72] DeGregory v. New Hampshire 368 U.S. 19 (1961) (upholding a First Amendment challenge to a New Hampshire law giving the state attorney general wide latitude to investigate alleged subversive activities).

[73] Fortson v. Morris, 385 U.S. 231 (1966) (upholding a provision of the Georgia Constitution that authorized the General Assembly to elect the governor provided that no candidate received a majority of votes in the general election).

[74] Beacon Theatres v. Westover, 359 U.S. 500 (1959) (involving the circumstances under which a jury trial may be withheld by a trial court judge).

cases in this cluster, the most interesting surely is *Marbury v. Madison*.[75] Marbury, which stands for the proposition that the U.S. Supreme Court has the power to strike down laws on the grounds that they violate the Constitution, resulted in six privilege claims.

Given that the Court's power of judicial review is exceptionally well established, the prevalence of *Marbury* in generating claims of privilege is a bit surprising. Our data show, however, that all but one of these claims arose at Scalia's hearing. Scalia asserted privilege five times in response to questions about *Marbury*. Scalia's claims to privilege in this area were framed by him as a principled refusal to affirm or reject any cases (although he did do so in a few instances).[76] Rehnquist's chief justice hearing generated the only other claim of privilege raised in relation to *Marbury*. Rehnquist's assertion of privilege in this area, unlike Scalia's, involved a broader discussion (referenced previously) of congressional power to strip the Supreme Court's appellate jurisdiction.[77]

All other named cases in our data set generated claims of privilege five or fewer times. Among this array of cases, one is particularly notable: Roberts claimed privilege twice in relation to questions about *Wickard v. Filburn*.[78] *Wickard* is a key case in the constitutional settlement resulting from President Roosevelt's fights with the Court over the constitutionality of New Deal legislation.[79] Along with a series of other cases decided in the post-*Lochner* era, *Wickard* established the foundation for the modern understanding that Congress has broad power under the Commerce Clause, unrestricted by any substantive due process rights, to regulate economic activity. As mentioned in Chapter 6 – and evidenced by the constitutional battle over the Patient Protection and Affordable Care Act[80] – this almost certainly is one of the areas in which a new constitutional clash is brewing.

---

[75] Marbury v. Madison, 5 U.S. 137 (1803).

[76] See, e.g., Scalia transcript at 33: "Well, *Marbury* is of course one of the great pillars of American law. It is the beginning of the Supreme Court as the interpreter of the Constitution. I hesitate to answer, and indeed think I should not answer the precise question you ask – do I agree that *Marbury v. Madison* means that in no instance can either of the other branches call into question the action of the Supreme Court. As I say, *Marbury v. Madison* is one of the pillars of the Constitution. To the extent that you think a nominee would be so foolish, or so extreme as to kick over one of the pillars of the Constitution, I suppose you should not confirm him. But I do not think I should answer questions regarding any specific Supreme Court opinion, even one as fundamental as *Marbury v. Madison*."

[77] Rehnquist Chief Justice transcript at 188.

[78] Wickard v. Filburn, 317 U.S. 111 (1942). See Roberts transcript at 261, 265.

[79] See, e.g., Barry Cushman, *Rethinking the New Deal Court: The Structure of a Constitutional Revolution* (New York: Oxford University Press, 1998); Laura Kalman, "The Constitution, the Supreme Court, and the New Deal," 110 *American Historical Review* 1052 (2005).

[80] National Federation of Independent Business v. Sebelius, 132 S. Ct. 2566 (2012).

Seen in this light, Roberts' discussion of *Wickard* at his 2005 hearing is of great interest. Senator Schumer (D-NY) asked Roberts about a series of cases, such as *Brown v. Board of Education*, that Schumer saw as settled law. Schumer then inquired as to whether Roberts believed that the Court's post–New Deal Commerce Clause cases are likewise well settled. The subsequent exchange is lengthy, but worth reading in full:

> **Judge ROBERTS:** Well, that's obviously the Court's holding in *Wickard v. Filburn*, and reaffirmed recently to a large extent in the *Raich* case. But I would say that because it has come up again so recently in the *Raich* case that it's an area where I think it's inappropriate for me to comment on my personal view about whether it's correct or not. That's unlike an issue under *Marbury v. Madison* or *Brown v. Board of Education*, which I don't think is likely to come up again before the Court. This was just before the Court last year, and so I should, I think, avoid commenting on whether I think it's correct or not.
>
> **Senator SCHUMER:** This is not a recent case. This is *Wickard v. Filburn*. It is from 1942, I guess it was. It is a basic bedrock of our constitutional law, law after law, the civil rights laws of 1982 and 1965 and 1964 that you talked about previously, are based on the Commerce Clause, not necessarily on *Wickard*.
>
> **Judge ROBERTS:** No, not on *Wickard*.

A few moments later, the exchange continued:

> **Senator SCHUMER:** . . . I didn't ask you if you fully support *Wickard*. I asked you if you support the proposition that under the Commerce Clause, you don't need the actual article crossing the State line, and you are not willing to say that is settled law, that that is a part of our established way of law?
>
> **Judge ROBERTS:** Well, Senator, all you have to do is look at the arguments, the briefs in the *Raich* case where that was the issue that was argued, whether or not *Wickard v. Filburn* was still good law, whether or not *Wickard v. Filburn* should be applied in that situation. Nobody in recent years has been arguing whether *Marbury v. Madison* is good law. Nobody has been arguing whether *Brown v. Board of Education* was good law. They have been arguing whether *Wickard v. Filburn* is good law. Now, it was reaffirmed in the *Raich* case and that is a precedent of the Court, just like *Wickard*, that I would apply like any other precedent. I have no agenda to overturn it. I have no agenda to revisit it. It's a precedent of the Court. But I do think it's a bit much to say it's on the same plane as a precedent as *Marbury v. Madison* and *Brown v. Board of Education* –

Senator SCHUMER: Or *Griswold?*

Judge ROBERTS: Or *Griswold.*[81]

It appears that *Griswold,* once so controversial that Robert Bork's refusal to affirm the basic right to privacy it embodies helped deprive him of a seat on the high Court, was seen by Roberts in 2005 as *less* in play than the New Deal settlement. That, we posit, is a very interesting development – one that burst into public view with a vengeance in the Court's decision upholding the constitutionality of the Patient Protection and Affordable Care Act.[82] What is more, that decision, and the debate surrounding it, revealed a Court – and a nation – bitterly divided about the extent of congressional power to regulate the economy in a way not seen since 1937.

CHANGES IN NOMINEE CANDOR

Our examination thus far has explored the cases and issues in which the nominees have been most reluctant to answer questions through the invocation of privilege. But one of the most common concerns expressed about the confirmation process today is that the nominees have become more reticent *overall* than were their predecessors.[83] This concern is frequently tied to the failed Bork hearings, in that commentators assert that nominees since Bork have been less willing to give candid replies to the senator's questions.[84] If correct, this could undermine the role of the confirmation hearings in ratifying constitutional change: the hearings cannot act as a forum in which previously controversial constitutional choices are validated if nominees increasingly refuse to express opinions about those (or any) cases and issues.

In the first large-scale empirical studies to address nominee candor at the hearings, Farganis and Wedeking found no "strong pattern of decline" in such candor in recent years.[85] Although they did evince a very gradual decline in

---

[81] Roberts transcript, questioning by Senator Schumer (D-NY) at 261–3.

[82] *National Federation of Independent Business,* supra, n. 79.

[83] See, e.g., Richard Brust, "No More Kabuki Confirmations," 95 *ABA Journal* 39 (2009); Stephen L. Carter, *The Confirmation Mess: Cleaning Up the Federal Appointments Process* (New York: Basic Books, 1994); Elena Kagan, "Review: Confirmation Messes, Old and New," 62 *University of Chicago Law Review* 919 (1995); Jonathan Turley, "Retire the Ginsburg Rule," USA Today, July 16, 2009; David A. Yalof, "Confirmation Obfuscation: Supreme Court Confirmation Politics in a Conservative Era," 44 *Studies in Law, Politics, and Society* 141 (2008).

[84] Farganis and Wedeking, "'No Hints, No Forecasts, No Previews,'" supra, n. 14 (canvassing work making this argument).

[85] Justin Wedeking and Dion Farganis, "The Candor Factor: Does Nominee Evasiveness Affect Judiciary Committee Support for Supreme Court Nominees?" 39 *Hofstra Law Review* 329

forthrightness over time, that decline originated very early in the process and was driven by an unusally high level of candor among some of the very first nominees to testify before the Judiciary Committee. The "decline," in other words, was neither dramatic nor tied to the failed 1987 Bork nomination.

The work of Farganis and Wedeking has been instrumental in bringing some much-needed empirical scrutiny to the ongoing debate about candor at the confirmation hearings. We further contribute to our understanding of this issue by investigating temporal trends regarding claims of privilege. Our analysis differs from that of Farganis and Wedeking in two important ways. First, whereas those authors employed the exchange as the unit of analysis (treating a question and its corresponding answer as an exchange), we use the change of speaker as the unit of analysis, meaning that a new observation begins whenever the speaker changes. Second, our focus is on privilege claims (defined previously), whereas Farganis and Wedeking explored additional types of responses, such as when a nominee provides a factual answer to a question calling for a nominee's views on an issue. Given these differences in research design, similarities between our findings and those of Farganis and Wedeking should be viewed as especially robust evidence of nominees' willingness to answer questions at the hearings.

Figure 8.1 reports the percentage of privileged responses made by nominees from 1939 to 2010. The vertical y-axis reports the percentage of comments in which each nominee invoked privilege, while the horizontal x-axis lists each nominee. The black bars indicate the percentage of all statements made by each nominee in which privilege was invoked, and the dashed line represents the fitted linear trend of privilege claims. Like Wedeking and Farganis, we find no strong increase in privilege claims over time. In fact, there is no temporal pattern in the data with respect to the extent to which nominees' invoke privilege, as indicated by the fact the trend line is effectively flat.[86]

Thus, there is no evidence that more recent nominees (those testifying in the post-Bork era) invoke privilege more often than earlier candidates for the

---

(2010) at 343. See also Farganis and Wedeking, "'No Hints, No Forecasts, No Previews,'" supra, n. 14.

[86] This is corroborated by a regression model in which the percentage of privileged answers is the dependent variable and the year of the hearing is the independent variable. The year of hearing variable fails to achieve statistical significance anywhere near conventional levels ($P = 0.85$). When a post-Bork dummy variable is included in the model, we obtain substantively identical results, as neither the year of hearing variable ($P = 0.47$) nor the post-Bork dummy variable ($P = 0.30$) attains statistical significance. In addition, we also ran models using a counter variable, scored such that Frankfurter = 1, Jackson = 2, Harlan = 3, etc., as well as a model that introduced a squared term to account for possible curvilinear effects. As before, we find no evidence of a decline in nominee candor over time.

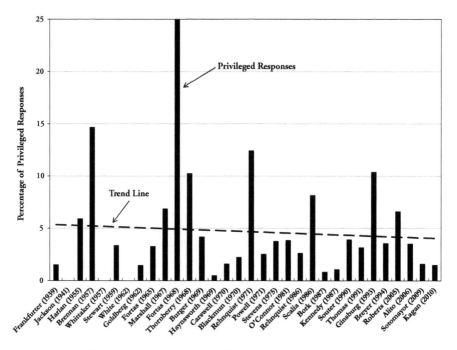

FIGURE 8.1. The percentage of privileged responses provided by each nominee, 1939–2010.

Court. The average percentage of privileged responses provided by nominees in the post-Bork era is lower than that of earlier hearings, although this difference is not statistically significant: 3.9% since Bork and 5.0% before Bork ($P = 0.61$). Moreover, nominees providing the highest percentage of privileged responses – the nominees, in other words, who refused to answer a greater portion of questions than their peers – are Fortas in 1968 (24.9%), Brennan in 1957 (14.7%), and Rehnquist in 1972 (12.4%), followed by Ginsburg in 1993 (10.4%), Thornberry in 1968 (10.2%), and Scalia in 1986 (8.1%). Of these, only Ginsburg testified in the post-Bork era.

Among the nominees who provided the lowest percentage of privileged responses, we see less of a temporal trend, although three early nominees – Jackson (1941), Whittaker (1957), and White (1962) – made no claims of privilege at their hearings. Among those nominees who did invoke privilege at least once, Haynsworth gave the lowest percentage of such responses (0.5%), followed by Bork in 1987 (0.8%), Kennedy in 1987 (1.1%), Goldberg in 1962 (1.4%), and Kagan in 2010 (1.5%). Thus, although the nominees providing the highest percentage of privileged responses tended (contrary to common assumptions) to come from the pre-Bork era, those giving the lowest percentage of privileged answers are more dispersed throughout time.

Our findings with respect to nominee candor are consistent with the "pattern of ebbs and flows" reported by Farganis and Wedeking.[87] Rather than being a recent phenomenon, nominees' practice of avoiding answering questions on privilege grounds has long been a part of the hearings. Together with their work, this research should put to rest the confirmation myth that nominees have become less responsive in the post-Bork era.

MISMATCHES

Throughout this book, we argue that the repeated affirmation of the existing constitutional agreement by nominees testifying at the confirmation hearings provides a formal mechanism through which constitutional choices made by the Court are ratified over time in a democratically credentialed way. In doing so, the Court's previously controversial constitutional choices are recognized as part of our constitutional consensus – the constitutional understandings under which we agree to live. But what happens when nominees deviate from that consensus once on the bench?

Such deviations are, in an important sense, somewhat irrelevant to our view of the confirmation hearings. A justice who fails to conform to the constitutional consensus he or she expressed agreement with as a nominee may be open to criticism for the deviation, but the deviation itself does not change the fact that acceptance of the constitutional consensus was expected as a condition of confirmation. It is the imposition of the condition, not compliance with that condition once confirmed, that demonstrates the public's endorsement of the reigning constitutional consensus. Nonetheless, a system in which justices routinely vote in ways contrary to the essential constitutional understandings they endorsed at their hearings would be troubling. Accordingly, this section explores certain "mismatches" between the positions nominees take at their hearings and the votes they cast once on the Court.

We expect such mismatches to be rare for at least two reasons. First, the key role of the confirmation hearings, in our view, is to act as forums in which

---

[87] Farganis and Wedeking do provide evidence of a slight decline in nominee candor in response to the senators' questions on civil rights issues following the Kennedy (not Bork) hearing. However, it is not evident that this decrease in forthrightness is attributable to nominees being more evasive over time in this issue area. It is plausible that the decrease in nominee forthrightness in questions involving civil rights is a function of nominee candor returning to historic levels following Bork and Kennedy's willingness to provide an especially large percentage of direct answers to senatorial questioning in this issue area. Farganis and Wedeking, "'No Hints, No Forecasts, No Previews,'" supra, n. 14 at 542, 547.

previously contested constitutional agreements are ratified. This ratification does not depend on judicial compliance with statements, ambivalent or otherwise, that nominees make about *currently* contested issues. The "mismatches" we are looking for, consequently, involve only those cases or issues that enjoy sufficiently wide and broad support that the acceptance or rejection of them can be imposed as true conditions of confirmation. Because the nominees are part of "We the People," they are subject to the same trends and influences involving such issues as are their fellow citizens. That they would genuinely share the core constitutional commitments of their era, and vote accordingly once confirmed, is therefore not surprising.[88] Second, a nominee who rejects the broadly accepted constitutional understanding of his or her era is likely to be seen as outside of the constitutional "mainstream" and thus unlikely to be either nominated or confirmed to the Supreme Court in the first place.[89] Presidents are, after all, political actors and are not likely to nominate a candidate whose constitutional views do not conform to the reigning constitutional consensus. Robert Bork may be the quintessential example of a nominee who failed to convince the senators that he accepted the constitutional consensus of his era, but he was (and remains) somewhat of an anomaly.[90]

Further complicating the picture is the fact that, as demonstrated earlier, what is and is not part of the constitutional consensus changes over time. Confirmation hearings often act as one of the first bellwethers, outside of think tanks and academia, that a new constitutional consensus is forming (or has formed). Consider nominee Roberts' comments about *Wickard*, discussed in the preceding text. His refusal to give a firm opinion on *Wickard* signaled that whatever constitutional consensus existed about Congress's broad

---

[88] See, e.g., Lee Epstein and Andrew D. Martin, "Does Public Opinion Influence the Supreme Court? Possibly Yes (But We're Not Sure Why)," 13 *University of Pennsylvania Journal of Constitutional Law* 263 (2011).

[89] Discussion of nominees as within or outside the constitutional "mainstream," like discussions of "settled law," are related to but not synonymous with the theory we are advancing here. The constitutional commitments that deem a nominee within the "mainstream" may overlap significantly with the cases and issues we describe as being within the constitutional consensus of an era, but the language of "mainstream" versus "extreme" constitutional beliefs fails to capture the idea of constitutional change, relating instead to notions of constitutional correctness and incorrectness. For a general discussion of how the concept of the "mainstream" is used in judicial nominations, see Michael J. Gerhardt, "Merit vs. Ideology," 26 *Cardozo Law Review* 353 (2005).

[90] See Mark Silverstein, *Judicious Choices: The New Politics of Supreme Court Confirmations* (New York: W. W. Norton, 2008) at 120–1. For a discussion of the inadvisability of using judicial appointments to impose constitutional change without building broad and deep political support for that change, see Bruce A. Ackerman, "Transformative Appointments," 101 *Harvard Law Review* 1164 (1988).

regulatory power under the Commerce Clause had or was in the process of breaking down – a breakdown made exquisitely clear in the subsequent litigation over the Patient Protection and Affordable Care Act. Given the ambiguity of his confirmation statements, Roberts' subsequent choices in that case – to limit Congress's Commerce Clause authority while nonetheless upholding the legislation under Congress's taxing power – are not surprising, nor are they troubling for our theory.[91] Roberts signaled in 2005 his understanding that the post–New Deal consensus might be faltering, and he was confirmed anyway. That he subsequently affirmed in part and limited in part the earlier consensus is perhaps exactly what should be expected.

Finally, some of the votes pointed to as judicial deviations from statements made by nominees at their hearings actually involve, upon closer inspection, disputes about how general statements made by nominees should be applied to specific cases, or how to expand or apply a canonical case, not whether to repudiate it.[92] The justices' continuing disagreements in cases involving racial integration, despite the canonical status of *Brown v. Board of Education*, is the most obvious example of this. Consider *Parents Involved v. Seattle School District*.[93] Parents Involved in Community Schools, a nonprofit interest group, challenged school assignment programs adopted by school boards in Seattle and Louisville. The programs, designed to promote racial integration in the public schools, each used race (in varying and limited ways) when assigning students to particular schools. The challengers compared the programs' use of race to the system of racial school segregation struck down in *Brown*.

---

[91] See *National Federation of Independent Business*, supra, n. 79.

[92] See, e.g., Alliance for Justice, "What a Difference a Justice Makes: A Review of the 2006–2007 Supreme Court Term: The Impact of Justices Roberts and Alito on the Bench." Retrieved from: http://www.afj.org/end-of-term-review.pdf (Accessed September 25, 2012) (reviewing apparent contradictions in statements nominees made at their confirmation hearings as compared to their voting behavior on the Court); Kasie Hunt, "Patrick Leahy: Decision Most 'Partisan' Since Bush v. Gore," *Politico*, January 28, 2010. Retrieved from: http://www.politico.com/news/stories/0110/32155.html (Accessed September 28, 2012) (citing a floor speech by Senator Leahy regarding the Court's invalidation of a federal statute, in which Leahy stated, "In his confirmation hearing, Justice Alito – I might say under oath – testified that the role of the Supreme Court is a limited role. . . . It has to be equally vigilant of not overstepping the bounds and invading the authority of Congress. That was then, when he was seeking confirmation. This is now."); William McGurn, "Chief Justice Roberts Taxes Credibility," *Wall Street Journal*, July 2, 2012. Retrieved from: http://online.wsj.com/article/SB10001424052702304708604577502933866909916.html (Accessed September 28, 2012) (questioning, in light of his vote in the Affordable Care Act case, the sincerity of Roberts' confirmation statements comparing justices to umpires).

[93] Parents Involved in Community Schools v. Seattle School District No. 1, 551 U.S. 701 (2007).

Of the nine justices who sat on the *Parents Involved* Court, all but Justice
Scalia had explicitly and affirmatively endorsed *Brown* at their confirmation
hearings, and Scalia did so indirectly by condemning *Plessy v. Ferguson*[94]
(which *Brown* overturned).[95] If the opinions of these justices in *Parents Involved*
in fact disavowed *Brown*, then the case would illustrate a clear mismatch
between their confirmation statements and their subsequent votes. Despite
heated rhetoric to the contrary,[96] however, none of the opinions in *Parents
Involved* betrayed the core constitutional consensus, represented by *Brown*,
that state-imposed racial segregation for the purpose of subordination is constitutionally unacceptable. Rather, all of the opinions worked within *Brown*,
claiming it as authority for their preferred outcome. The justices in *Parents
Involved*, in other words, were fighting about the legacy of *Brown*, not about
its rescission.[97]

There are instances, however, of a genuine mismatch between what a nominee says at the confirmation hearings and the votes the nominee casts as a
justice. To find examples of such situations, we examined the voting records of
the currently sitting justices in cases citing each of the confirmation conditions
discussed in Chapter 6: *Brown v. Board of Education*, *Griswold v. Connecticut*,
Craig v. Boren[98] (which we employ as a proxy for the issue of gender discrimination), and *District of Columbia v. Heller*.[99] In none of the cases citing these
precedents did a justice directly advocate for invalidating the canonical constitutional case. A few instances, however, did come close. Of these, three are of
particular interest: Justice Sotomayor's decision to join a dissenting opinion in
McDonald v. Chicago,[100] the precedent that incorporated the individual right
to keep and bear arms identified in *Heller* against the states; Justice Scalia's

---

[94] Plessy v. Ferguson, 163 U.S. 537 (1896).

[95] Scalia transcript at 86.

[96] For example, in a concurring opinion, Justice Thomas likened the argument of the dissenting
justices in the case to those made by segregationist school boards in *Brown*. *Parents Involved*,
supra, n. 92 at 773–4.

[97] A review of Potter Stewart's hearing transcript, in which the legitimacy of *Brown* itself was truly
questioned, makes this difference strikingly clear.

[98] Craig v. Boren, 429 U.S. 190 (1976). This was the first time the Court applied the heightened
scrutiny standard to evaluate claims of gender discrimination.

[99] We identified cases citing the key precedent (*Brown*, *Griswold*, *Craig*, or *Heller*) by searching
for the name of the precedent in the Westlaw Supreme Court database and setting the date
range to correspond to each justice's tenure on the Court. As discussed previously, because we
believe that these mismatches are not directly relevant to our view of the hearings, our purpose
here is to provide a limited investigation into this phenomenon for illustrative purposes.
For a discussion of the difficulties associated with comparing confirmation statements with
subsequent voting behavior, see Czarnezki, Ford, and Ringhand, "An Empirical Analysis of
the Confirmation Hearings of the Justices of the Rehnquist Natural Court," supra, n. 48.

[100] McDonald v. Chicago, 130 S. Ct. 3020 (2010).

comments in *United States v. Virginia*[101] regarding the appropriate level of scrutiny in gender discrimination cases; and Justice Thomas' disavowal of a general right to privacy in *Lawrence v. Texas*.[102]

In *McDonald*, Sotomayor joined a dissenting opinion written by Justice Stevens that heavily criticized *Heller*, arguing that the Court in *Heller* "badly misconstrued" the Second Amendment.[103] She signed this opinion despite stating at her hearing – under friendly questioning from Senator Leahy, a Democrat – that she accepted the Court's decision in *Heller* establishing that the Second Amendment protects an individual right to keep and bear arms.[104] Likewise, Scalia, dissenting in *U.S. v. Virginia*, deviated from the constitutional norm we have identified regarding gender discrimination, rejecting the idea that heightened scrutiny should be used to evaluate laws that discriminate on the basis of gender, at least to the extent that the law being challenged is grounded in our "constant and unbroken national traditions."[105] Finally,

---

[101] United States v. Virginia, 518 U.S. 515 (1996).

[102] Lawrence v. Texas, 539 U.S. 558 (2003). Other examples of behavior that is close to representing true mismatches involve Justice Scalia and *Griswold v. Connecticut* and *Wickard v. Filburn*. Scalia has been critical of some of the reasoning in *Griswold*, as well as the way other courts have interpreted *Griswold*. See, e.g., Lawrence v. Texas, 539 U.S. 558 (2003) at 595 and National Aeronautics and Space Administration v. Nelson, 131 S. Ct. 746 (2011) at 766. He nonetheless has construed his opinions as not inconsistent with the core outcome of that case. See, e.g., Michael H. v. Gerald D., 491 U.S 110 (1989) at 127. Scalia has also made extrajudicial comments regarding his willingness to revisit *Wickard*. Although the endorsement of *Wickard* is not one of the specific confirmation conditions discussed in Chapter 6, it is worth noting that the four-justice dissenting opinion in *National Federation of Independent Business v. Sebelius* was quite careful, despite Justice Scalia's off the bench comments, to argue within *Wickard*, not to advocate overturning it. Compare Antonin Scalia and Bryan A. Garner, *Reading Law: The Interpretation of Legal Texts* (St. Paul, MN: Thomson/West, 2012) at 405–6 (identifying *Wickard* as a "willful judicial distortion" of the Constitution that "expanded the Commerce Clause beyond all reason") to *National Federation of Independent Business*, supra, n. 79 at 2588 (explaining with apparent acceptance the use of the commerce power in *Wickard* and distinguishing *Wickard* from the case at bar).

[103] *McDonald*, supra, n. 99 at 3107.

[104] Sotomayor transcript, questioning by Senator Leahy (D-VT) at 2.7.

[105] More specifically, Scalia argued, "I have no problem with a system of abstract tests such as rational basis, intermediate, and strict scrutiny (though I think we can do better than applying strict scrutiny and intermediate scrutiny whenever we feel like it). Such formulas are essential to evaluating whether the new restrictions that a changing society constantly imposes upon private conduct comport with that 'equal protection' our society has always accorded in the past. But in my view the function of this Court is to *preserve* our society's values regarding (among other things) equal protection, not to *revise* them; to prevent backsliding from the degree of restriction the Constitution imposed upon democratic government, not to prescribe, on our own authority, progressively higher degrees. For that reason it is my view that, whatever abstract tests we may choose to devise, they cannot supersede – and indeed ought to be crafted *so as to reflect* – those constant and unbroken national traditions that embody the people's understanding of ambiguous constitutional texts. More specifically, it is my view that 'when a

Thomas, dissenting for himself in *Lawrence v. Texas*, embraced one of the dissenting opinions in *Griswold* that denied a constitutionally protected right to privacy – a right he affirmed at his confirmation hearing.[106]

Each of these examples, however, comes with caveats and qualifications. Although Sotomayor affirmed her acceptance of *Heller* at her hearing, she went on to maintain that the incorporation question – the question actually at issue in *McDonald* – was an open one that would certainly be coming before the Court. She therefore refused to comment on it in detail.[107] Moreover, as discussed in Chapter 6, although the individual right to keep and bear arms embraced in *Heller* appears well on its way to becoming a condition of confirmation (if it has not already achieved this status), there continues to be substantial public debate and litigation regarding the extent to which governments can regulate gun ownership. If *Heller* is used to strike down gun regulations broadly seen as fair and reasonable, the case itself may become more controversial among the public at large, rendering Sotomayor's rejection of it less a mismatch regarding a core constitutional commitment and more a step in the process of determining whether *Heller* does in fact embody such a commitment.

The Scalia example also is not what it may first appear. Scalia, nominated and confirmed a year before the 1987 Bork hearing, was asked about the appropriate standard of review in sex discrimination cases, but refused to comment on it.[108] He also expressed uncertainty about whether sex-based discrimination was "invidious" in the same way that racial discrimination is.[109] Thus, although the Bork hearing, along with the subsequent hearings of the remainder of the now sitting justices, established acceptance of heightened scrutiny in sex discrimination cases as a condition of confirmation, Scalia was confirmed before the constitutional consensus on this point was fully revealed through those hearings. Given this, his opinion in *Virginia*, as well as his extrajudicial statements on the subject,[110] perhaps reveals more about the difficulties that arise when a justice's tenure on the bench is too distant in

---

practice not expressly prohibited by the text of the Bill of Rights bears the endorsement of a long tradition of open, widespread, and unchallenged use that dates back to the beginning of the Republic, we have no proper basis for striking it down.'" (internal citation omitted). *United States v. Virginia*, supra, n. 100 at 568.

[106] Thomas transcript at 255.

[107] Sotomayor transcript at 2.7–2.8, 2.26–2.28.

[108] Scalia transcript at 56–7.

[109] Ibid. at 100.

[110] Stephanie Condon, "Scalia: Constitution Doesn't Protect Women and Gays from Discrimination," *CBS News*, January 4, 2011. Retrieved from: http://www.cbsnews.com/8301-503544_162-20027240-503544.html (Accessed September 16, 2012).

time from the era in which he or she was confirmed than it does about the ability of the hearings to ratify constitutional change. Although the former is a genuine problem, it is one that is beyond the scope of this work to solve.[111]

Justice Thomas' dissenting opinion in *Lawrence* is the most demonstrative of our three examples of a real mismatch between nominee testimony and subsequent behavior on the Court. Asked at his hearing whether the Constitution protected a right of privacy, Thomas said yes: there was a right to privacy in the Constitution, and the marital right to privacy (at issue in *Griswold*) was the "core" of that right.[112] Asked later to elaborate, he aligned himself with the approach taken by Justice Harlan in *Poe v. Ullman*,[113] a position Thomas said was "reaffirmed" in *Griswold*.[114] When specifically pressed whether he was basing his conception of privacy on Harlan's opinion in *Poe v. Ullman*, which embraced a constitutional right to privacy via the liberty provision of the Due Process Clause,[115] Thomas replied "exactly."[116] He went on to further affirm that he had "no quarrel" with the Court's decision in *Eisenstadt v. Baird*,[117] which extended the right to use contraception to single people, thus moving the range of constitutionally protected privacy beyond the marital realm and into a more generalizable form.[118]

Given the relative proximity of Thomas' nomination to the failed appointment of Robert Bork, Thomas' answers to these questions were important, and were vigorously pursued by the senators. Thomas' separate opinion in

---

[111] For a discussion of this issue, see Steven G. Calabresi and James Lindgren, "Term Limits for the Supreme Court: Life Tenure Reconsidered," 29 *Harvard Journal of Law and Public Policy* 769 (2006); David R. Stras and Ryan W. Scott, "An Empirical Analysis of Life Tenure: A Response to Professors Calabresi & Lindgren," 30 *Harvard Journal of Law and Public Policy* 791 (2007).

[112] Thomas transcript at 255.

[113] Poe v. Ullman, 367 U.S. 497 (1961).

[114] Thomas transcript at 225, 275.

[115] *Poe*, like *Griswold*, was a challenge to the Connecticut law prohibiting the use of contraception by married couples. Issued four years before *Griswold*, the Court in *Poe* dismissed the claim on standing grounds. Justice Harlan dissented, arguing both that the Court should hear the case on the merits and that the law was unconstitutional.

[116] Thomas transcript at 276.

[117] Eisenstadt v. Baird, 405 U.S. 438 (1972).

[118] Thomas transcript at 278. Recognizing that *Eisenstadt* could be justified on either equal protection or privacy grounds, Senator Biden (D-DE) framed his follow-up question as follows: "I am asking you whether the principle that I read to you, which had, in fact, been pointed to and relied upon in other cases, is a constitutional principle with which you agree; which is that single people have the same right of privacy – not equal protection, privacy – as married people on the issue of procreation." Thomas replied by saying "I think that the Court has so found, and I agree with that." Thomas transcript, questioning by Senator Biden (D-DE) at 279.

Lawrence, however, appears to step back from the positions he took on this issue at his hearing. Rather than once again affirming Harlan's opinion in *Poe*, Thomas instead took the opportunity in *Lawrence* to embrace one of the dissenting opinions from *Griswold*. Citing Stewart's dissent in that case, Thomas in *Lawrence* wrote as follows: "just like Justice Stewart, I 'can find [neither in the Bill of Rights nor any other part of the Constitution a] general right of privacy.'"[119]

As in the Sotomayor and Scalia examples, however, even this apparently blatant mismatch is somewhat less obvious a mismatch than it first appears. Justice Harlan's opinion in *Poe*, embraced by Thomas at his hearing, recognized a constitutional right to privacy, but also explicitly denied that it would necessarily extend to state prohibitions on "homosexual" conduct – which of course was the issue presented in *Lawrence*.[120] Thomas' statement in *Lawrence* that he could find no "general" right of privacy is not, consequently, precisely the same thing as a disavowal of the specific applications of the right to privacy he endorsed at his hearing relating to Harlan's opinion in *Poe*. This may make Thomas' *Lawrence* opinion more akin to the fights about *Brown* played out in *Parents Involved*: a dispute about how to extend a key precedent, rather than whether or not to reject the precedent itself. Nonetheless, Thomas' choice in *Lawrence* to frame his objection against the privacy right in general, rather than its specific application in that case, and, more strikingly, to source his disagreement in an opinion dissenting from a case he affirmed at his hearing, makes this perhaps the most troubling of the mismatches explored here.

CONCLUSIONS

Ultimately, we believe that the nominees' failure to answer questions about currently contested constitutional issues is less important than their repeated validation or rejection of the constitutional choices that the American people have embraced or rebuffed as part of our constitutional consensus. After all, nominees cannot be expected to affirm a consensus that does not exist. As we have shown in this and the previous two chapters, this theory is consistent with nominee behavior at the hearings. Nominees do in fact provide answers to specific questions about legal issues and cases that have entered into our constitutional canon, although they occasionally invoke privilege on issues in which there is no constitutional agreement. The purpose of this chapter was to

---

[119] *Lawrence*, supra, n. 101 at 605–06 (the bracketed text is as it appears in the Thomas opinion).
[120] *Poe*, supra, n. 112 at 552.

explore more thoroughly the role of currently contested constitutional issues at the hearings.

We found that the specific issue areas and cases in which nominees refuse to answer questions have changed over time. This supports our view of the confirmation hearings working to validate a gradually, but regularly shifting constitutional consensus: as cases and issues move out of the contested zone of constitutional meaning into our constitutional consensus, it is no longer acceptable for nominees to refuse to provide their opinions on such cases or issues.

This chapter has also demonstrated that questions about *Roe v. Wade* and abortion account for a substantial number of privilege claims, and that this is especially true for nominees appointed by Republican presidents in the post-*Roe* era. To a large extent, our data show that concerns about the nominees' lack of candor should really be reframed as concerns about the nominees' refusal to discuss abortion-related cases and issues. We are less concerned about this refusal than other commentators tend to be: the constitutional status of abortion rights remains, for better or worse, an issue in which the American people disagree.[121] In such cases, the confirmation process cannot work to democratically validate constitutional change because deep disagreement about the appropriate constitutional choice continues. The Court, like the rest of us, must simply keep muddling through, working within the range of acceptable legal arguments until a larger constitutional consensus emerges.

We also have shown that nominee candor has not declined over time. Although nominees do, as expected, refuse to answer questions about currently contested issues, there is no temporal trend to this practice. Two of the earliest nominees in our data set, Felix Frankfurter and John Harlan, each invoked the obviously misnamed "Ginsburg" rule[122] and refused to answer questions about issues they believed were likely to come before the Court. Another relatively early nominee, Abe Fortas, refused to answer an astonishing 25% of all questions put to him during his hearing for chief justice. William

---

[121] See, e.g., Lydia Saad, "More Americans 'Pro-Life' Than 'Pro-Choice' for First Time." Retrieved from: http://www.gallup.com/poll/118399/more-americans-pro-life-than-pro-choice-first-time.aspx (Accessed April 25, 2012). See also R. Michael Alvarez and John Brehm, "American Ambivalence Towards Abortion Policy: Development of a Heteroskedastic Probit Model of Competing Values,' 39 *American Journal of Political Science* 1055 (1995); Danette Brickman and David A. M. Peterson, "Public Opinion Reaction to Repeated Events: Citizen Response to Multiple Supreme Court Abortion Decisions," 28 *Political Behavior* 87 (2006); Charles H. Franklin and Liane C. Kosaki, "Republican Schoolmaster: The U.S. Supreme Court, Public Opinion, and Abortion," 83 *American Political Science Review* 751 (1989).

[122] See, e.g., "The Ginsburg Rule," *Washington Times*, August 3, 2005; Turley, "Retire the 'Ginsburg Rule,'" supra, n. 82.

Brennan refused to answer questions about communism; Potter Stewart refused to answer questions about *Brown*; and Thurgood Marshall refused to answer questions about *Miranda*. Clearly, nominees have, since the beginning of the hearings, declined to answer questions about controversial issues. Though this has not changed, what has changed are the cases and issues deemed too controversial to comment on. Although nominees refusing to provide their opinions about communism or *Brown* today would have a very difficult time winning confirmation, this was not true during the hearings of Brennan and Stewart, as those issues were far more contentious than they are in the contemporary era.

Finally, this chapter investigated whether "mismatches" between what nominees say at their hearings and how they vote once confirmed to the high Court pose a serious difficulty for our view of the confirmation hearings as forums in which to ratify constitutional change. As we note, such mismatches appear to be rare, and would not in any event change the fact that the affirmation of the contemporary consensus is expected as a condition of confirmation. Such mismatches, consequently, may raise problems of judicial accountability or length of tenure, but they present little difficulty for the thesis presented here. Fundamentally, it is the affirmation of the consensus over time, not a given justice's subsequent adherence to it, that allows the confirmation hearings to function as a public forum for the ratification of widely embraced changes to our core constitutional commitments.

9

Our Constitution

Brown v. Board of Education[1] is rightly one of the most celebrated decisions ever issued by the U.S. Supreme Court. The decision sits proudly and properly at the very core of our constitutional understandings. No nominee today who refused to accept *Brown* as part of our constitutional canon would, could, or should be confirmed. But this was not always the case. When it was first decided, *Brown* was legally, not just socially, controversial. Herbert Wechsler was not alone when, delivering the Holmes Lecture at Harvard Law School in 1959, he found himself unable to articulate a sufficiently neutral principle on which to justify the *Brown* decision.[2] Although sympathetic to the outcome, Wechsler simply could not see his way through the legal thicket to the Court's result.

Like all of us, Wechsler was constrained by the era in which he lived, but he was far from a bigot or a segregationist. Rather, the difficulty for Wechsler was that the case *Brown* overturned – *Plessy v. Ferguson*[3] – seemed to many lawyers of his era to be perfectly consistent with well-accepted tools of legal reasoning. *Plessy* had been the law of the land for almost sixty years, was the dominant precedent in the area of racial segregation, and was almost certainly true to the specific expectations of the enactors of the Fourteenth Amendment. Moreover, although difficult to see today, *Plessy* also was, in its time, a reasonable interpretation of the text of the Equal Protection Clause: to separate things is not always or obviously to render them unequal.[4]

---

[1] Brown v. Board of Education, 347 U.S. 483 (1954).
[2] Herbert Wechsler, "Toward Neutral Principles of Constitutional Law," 73 *Harvard Law Review* 1 (1959).
[3] Plessy v. Ferguson, 163 U.S. 537 (1896).
[4] See, e.g., Raoul Berger, *Government by Judiciary: The Transformation of the Fourteenth Amendment* (Cambridge, MA: Harvard University Press, 1977); Alexander M. Bickel, "The

Brown also, of course, is perfectly consistent with well-accepted tools of legal reasoning. Separate *can* be unequal, particularly when separation sends, as it did in *Brown*, a message of subordination and inferiority. And while *Plessy* was the most relevant precedent before *Brown* was decided, the Court by 1954 had been for several years chiseling away at the legal foundations of America's racial apartheid regime, striking down segregation in a variety of settings.[5] Moreover, numerous originalist scholars, determined to make *Brown* consistent with their preferred method of constitutional interpretation, have made gallant efforts to show that segregated schools were in fact contrary to the specific intentions of at least some of the advocates of the Fourteenth Amendment.[6] Others have argued (with perhaps more success) that at the very least, the original principle behind the Fourteenth Amendment was to prohibit racial distinctions that inhibited equal citizenship – a principle that, by 1954, seemed incompatible with segregated schools.[7]

Both *Plessy* and *Brown*, then, could be supported by arguments from text, history, precedent, and principle. *Plessy* was the most on-point precedent governing the question presented in *Brown*. *Plessy's* side of the legal scale was also ballasted by a plausible textual interpretation of the Fourteenth Amendment and the weight of specific original intent. *Brown* had recent and evolving precedents; a plausible textual interpretation of the Fourteenth Amendment; and the weight of a generalized, originally intended principle on its side.

This type of interpretive tension is hardly unusual in Supreme Court cases. Similar stories have been told about the many of the most famously "wrong" cases in Supreme Court history. The legal reasoning underlying the substantive due process cases of the *Lochner* era has been reconstructed by a host of

---

Original Understanding and the Segregation Decision," 69 *Harvard Law Review* 1 (1955); Michael J. Klarman, "*Brown*, Originalism, and Constitutional Theory: A Response to Professor McConnell," 81 *Virginia Law Review* 1881 (1995); Mark V. Tushnet, "Following the Rules Laid Down: A Critique of Interpretivism and Neutral Principles," 96 *Harvard Law Review* 781 (1983).

[5] See, e.g., McLaurin v. Oklahoma State Regents, 339 U.S. 637 (1950); Sweatt v. Painter, 339 U.S. 629 (1950).

[6] See, e.g., Robert H. Bork, *The Tempting of America: The Political Seduction of the Law* (New York: The Free Press, 1989); Patrick J. Kelley, "An Alternative Originalist Opinion for *Brown v. Board of Education*," 20 *Southern Illinois University Law Journal* 75 (1996); Michael W. McConnell, "Originalism and the Desegregation Decisions," 81 *Virginia Law Review* 947 (1995). But see Klarman, "*Brown*, Originalism, and Constitutional Theory," supra, n. 4.

[7] Michael J. Perry, "The Legitimacy of Particular Conceptions of Constitutional Interpretation," 77 *Virginia Law Review* 669 (1991).

scholars,[8] as has the legal logic of *Dred Scott v. Sandford*.[9] Defensible strands of legal argument have even been presented in defense of *Korematsu v. United States*[10] (the World War II era case upholding the internment of Japanese Americans).

When confronted with this type of legal ambiguity, we resolve it in different ways, and do so differently in different cases. Sometimes we prioritize specific intended applications over plain text. For example, the text of the First Amendment states, "Congress shall make no law...abridging the freedom of speech."[11] Yet it is clear that the founding generation intended perjury to remain punishable in federal courts. So, we ignore the plain text in favor of a specific intended application. Sometimes we prioritize general principles over text: the term "speech" does not self-evidently include movies, silent protests, or campaign contributions, but the Court nonetheless has used the principles embodied in the First Amendment to protect all of these things. Sometimes we follow precedent – *Planned Parenthood v. Casey*[12] refused to overturn *Roe v. Wade*,[13] and *Dickerson v. United States*[14] refused to overturn *Miranda v. Arizona*.[15] But sometimes we don't – *McDonald v. Chicago*[16] overturned *Presser v. Illinois*[17] and, of course, *Brown* overturned *Plessy*.

So, which case was legally correct, *Plessy* or *Brown*?

To even ask the question is to commit constitutional heresy in today's America. Simply put, *Brown* cannot be wrong. And, to be perfectly clear, it isn't. *Brown* is properly considered one of our core constitutional commitments. But this is not – indeed, cannot be – because the decision is obviously correct as a matter of pure legal reasoning. The *Brown* case presented the Court with two legally viable options. It could adhere to precedent, thereby following a reasonable interpretation of the text and remaining true to the most likely

---

[8] See, e.g., Barry Cushman, "Some Varieties and Vicissitudes of Lochnerism," 85 *Boston University Law Review* 881 (2005); Howard Gillman, "De-Lochnerizing *Lochner*," 85 *Boston University Law Review* 859 (2005); Logan E. Sawyer III, "Creating *Hammer v. Dagenhart*," 21 *William & Mary Bill of Rights Journal* 67 (2012).

[9] Dred Scott v. Sandford, 60 U.S. 393 (1857). Mark A. Graber, *Dred Scott and the Problem of Constitutional Evil* (New York: Cambridge University Press, 2006).

[10] Korematsu v. United States, 323 U.S. 214 (1944). Jamal Greene, "The Anticanon," 125 *Harvard Law Review* 379 (2011).

[11] U.S. Constitution, Amendment I.

[12] Planned Parenthood of Southeastern Pennsylvania v. Casey, 505 U.S. 833 (1992).

[13] Roe v. Wade, 410 U.S. 113 (1973).

[14] Dickerson v. United States, 530 U.S. 428 (2000).

[15] Miranda v. Arizona, 384 U.S. 436 (1966).

[16] McDonald v. Chicago, 177 L. Ed. 2d 894 (2010).

[17] Presser v. Illinois, 116 U.S. 252 (1886).

specific expectations of the ratifiers of the Fourteenth Amendment, or it could build on its more recent precedents, thereby embracing a different textual interpretation bolstered by a more general principle of equal justice.

Faced with this type of legal underdeterminacy, the Court did what it has always done in such situations: it made a choice. The Court, however, could not unilaterally install that choice into our constitutional canon. Only we – the true keepers of the Constitution – could do that. And we did so in an abundance of ways. Rosa Parks refused to give up her seat on a segregated bus. Civil rights advocates marched together across the Edmund Pettis Bridge on Bloody Sunday. Linda Brown's little sister attended a racially integrated elementary school. It was those actions, and their widespread endorsement by subsequent generations of Americans, that made *Brown* an unassailable part of our constitutional commitment. And it is that commitment that is democratically ratified through the Supreme Court confirmation process. The confirmation hearings provide a forum at which senators and nominees engage in a discussion about constitutional issues of importance to the public. In doing so, senators quarrel about what should and should not be considered part of our constitutional consensus. Over time, as the consensus on a given issue becomes sufficiently broad and deep, nominees are expected to endorse that consensus as a condition of confirmation. In this way, Supreme Court confirmation hearings are a democratic forum for the discussion and ratification of constitutional change.

We have done more than just assert these claims, however: we have backed them up with both quantitative and qualitative evidence. Chapter 3 used our original data on confirmation hearings to investigate the influence of public opinion on hearing dialogue. We demonstrated that, contrary to common assumptions, the hearings in fact do much more than focus on the idiosyncratic traits or personal histories of the individual nominees. Rather, they provide a forum through which public sentiments about important issues are conveyed to future members of the Court. The senators' questions closely reflect those contemporary legal and political debates in which the Court plays an active role. Although a highlight film of any given confirmation hearing may feature nominee-specific things such as discussions of Sonia Sotomayor's "wise Latina" comment or William Rehnquist's *Plessy* memo, Chapter 3 confirms that individualized issues such as these do not dominate the hearings. In fact, we believe these types of idiosyncratic facts are memorable precisely because, and only to the extent that, they capture issues already salient to the public, not because the hearings themselves are inexorably shaped by the personal characteristics of individual nominees.

Chapter 3 also demonstrates that the constitutional conversation held at the confirmation hearings works in both directions. The Court is not a passive player in the process. Rather, it actively shapes confirmation dialogue through the content of its cases. Discussion of Supreme Court precedents at the hearings allows the public, acting through its elected representatives, to probe the Court's cases and pass judgment on its work, but it also gives the Court a mechanism to shape public opinion about constitutional law. The Court, of course, does not speak directly at the hearings, but the process helps the Court communicate to the public by giving legal experts – the nominees – a chance to explain the Court's decisions to the senators and to the public at large. Our data confirm this conversational aspect of the hearings by showing that, when the Court hands down decisions in a particular issue area, the senators respond by querying subsequent nominees about those decisions. The hearings thereby provide a mechanism through which public values are conveyed to the Court, and the Court's decisions are in return engaged by the public.

Chapter 4 develops this point further by investigating which issues are addressed at the hearings, and how the discussion of these issues has and has not changed over more than seven decades of nominee testimony. This chapter reveals that hearing dialogue within major issue areas, such as civil rights, has shifted over the years. For example, as public debates about racial discrimination, gender discrimination, and gay rights evolve, so too does confirmation discourse about these issues. As different types of issues move in and out of public consciousness, confirmation dialogue follows.

Chapter 4 also illustrates an additional, important, point: confirmation hearings have always been driven by concerns about substantive issues. Even in the earliest hearings in our data set, before the discussion of specific cases became common, the senators asked many more questions about concrete issues than they did about nominees' abstract judicial philosophies or preferred methods of constitutional interpretation. Despite the lip service frequently paid to the idea that senators should limit their questions to those more abstract matters, the senators, undoubtedly reflecting the priorities of the people they represent, have long understood their jobs to be to ascertain the nominees' positions on more substantive points of constitutional meaning, not on abstract theories of constitutional interpretation. This is consistent with other work in this area that tracks the predictive value of different types of confirmation testimony, finding that comments about substantive issues are more predictive of a nominee's voting behavior than are statements about political philosophy or interpretive methods.[18]

---

[18] Jason J. Czarnezki, William K. Ford, and Lori A. Ringhand, "An Empirical Analysis of the Confirmation Hearings of the Justices of the Rehnquist Natural Court," 24 *Constitutional Commentary* 127 (2007).

Taking its cue from the senators' focus on concrete issues and cases, Chapter 5 looks at the specific precedents addressed at the hearings. The discussion of specific cases, as we show, has constituted about a sixth of all confirmation dialogue since Thurgood Marshall's hearing in 1967. Not surprisingly, we found that the Court's landmark decisions – *Roe v. Wade*, *Brown v. Board of Education*, *Griswold v. Connecticut*,[19] and *Miranda v. Arizona* – are the most frequently discussed cases. We also demonstrate, however, that *Roe v. Wade* has played less of a role in the hearings than one might expect. Although *Roe* is the most frequently discussed case at the hearings, it constitutes fewer than 8% of all comments involving Supreme Court precedent, and only 2% of all hearing dialogue conducted since the case was decided. *Roe*, therefore, obviously is an important part of our hearing discourse, but it is not dominant: discussions of precedent at the hearings are in fact quite heterogeneous.

Our illustration of the dialogical nature of the hearings in Chapters 3 through 5 lays the framework for the second, more normative, point of this work: to cast light on the role the hearings play in democratically ratifying the constitutional choices made by the Supreme Court. Chapters 6 and 7 illustrate how this process works in practice. Chapter 6 identifies four cases or constitutional principles that nominees are expected to accept or reject before being confirmed. As we show in Chapter 6, the path forged by each of these conditions of confirmation has been quite different. Although agreement with *Brown* is today's quintessential confirmation condition, the case was vigorously contested when first issued and aggressively assailed at the earliest hearings at which it was mentioned. It then went underground for some time, becoming the unnamed anchor of proxy fights about interpretive methods and the proper role of courts in our governing system. Eventually, however, *Brown* began inching its way into the constitutional canon. This movement was evident at William Rehnquist's associate justice hearing in 1971, and acceptance of *Brown* was fully revealed as a condition of confirmation in Rehnquist's 1986 chief justice hearing, when Rehnquist felt compelled to denounce his infamous memo endorsing *Plessy v. Ferguson* and avow his belief in the fundamental correctness of *Brown*. Since then, nominees and senators of both political parties have routinely celebrated *Brown* as exemplifying constitutional lawmaking at its best.

The validation of other constitutional changes has followed different paths. Gender discrimination issues took a long time finding their way into hearing discourse, but agreement that the Constitution requires at least heightened judicial scrutiny of laws making distinctions on the basis of gender was

---

[19] Griswold v. Connecticut, 381 U.S. 479 (1965).

embraced as a condition of confirmation soon after it was introduced to the hearings. The probable canonization of *District of Columbia v. Heller*[20] seems to be happening even more quickly. *Lochner v. New York* followed yet a different path. For decades, nominees were expected to reject *Lochner* and embrace the post-1937 consensus about the limited role courts should assume in overseeing the economic policy choices of legislatures. To the extent that *Lochner* is used at the hearings to represent that broader consensus (rather than the narrower point about using substantive due process as the vehicle to strike down such legislation), John Roberts' confirmation comments about *Wickard v. Fillburn*,[21] as well as the controversial decision issued by the Court in the Patient Protection and Affordable Care Act cases,[22] may evidence a fracturing of our constitutional agreement in this area. Finally, we concluded Chapter 6 by making an important point about each of the cases or issues we have identified as confirmation conditions: even though the legal principles these cases have come to stand for do not and cannot dictate outcomes in *today's* constitutional controversies, these cases had real constitutional bite when they were decided. Their absorption into the canon thus evidences a true change in our constitutional commitments, despite nominees' occasional refusal to discuss their application to today's constitutional disagreements.

Chapter 7, with its examination of the failed nomination of Robert Bork and the successful nominations of Anthony Kennedy and those that followed, evinces the sometimes dramatic consequence of a nominee's failure to acknowledge that a new constitutional consensus has emerged. Bork, as we demonstrated, either ignored or misunderstood the shifts in the constitutional consensus that had occurred since the heyday of the Warren Court. His refusal to affirm the most salient of the constitutional choices made by that Court cost him his confirmation. Importantly, however, Chapter 7 does not stop there. Instead, it goes on, through the examination of subsequent nominees, to show that the constitutional preferences revealed by the Bork hearings had in fact been absorbed into our constitutional consensus. Multiple nominees, appointed and confirmed by presidents and senators of both political parties over more than two decades, rejected key parts of Robert Bork's constitutional vision and embraced that of Anthony Kennedy. This powerfully illustrates that the role we are claiming for the confirmation process is not one of holding nominees hostage to short-term political preferences, but

---

[20] District of Columbia v. Heller, 171 L. Ed. 2d 637 (2008).
[21] Wickard v. Filburn, 317 U.S. 111 (1942).
[22] National Federation of Independent Business v. Sebelius, 132 S. Ct. 2566 (2012).

of ensuring that the ongoing project of constitutional law making, aided by newly arrived justices, continues to reflect those constitutional commitments that are both deeply held and broadly accepted. Together, Chapters 6 and 7 demonstrate that the confirmation process both can and has played an important role in providing democratically validated legitimacy to new constitutional constructions.

The nominees' reluctance to give firm answers to questions about today's currently contested constitutional questions is, under this view of the confirmation process, rather beside the point. After all, nominees cannot be expected to confirm a consensus that does not exist. Nonetheless, Chapter 8 provides some important insights into the role of contested issues at the hearings. For example, we illustrated that nominees' reluctance to answer such questions has not in fact – despite abundant speculation to the contrary – increased meaningfully over the years. This finding confirms the only other quantitative research on this point[23] and will, we hope, put this particular criticism of the confirmation hearings to rest. Although we do feel that nominees could and perhaps should answer more questions than they do, forcing nominees to take positions on currently contested issues as a condition of confirmation is not essential to our approach. The Court needs to be accountable to the public over time, but it need not and should not be accountable in the same way, or in the same time frame, as elected officials.

Nor do we believe that the criticism that the process has become too "political" is particularly meaningful. It is not at all clear as a matter of history that this has in fact happened. As Figure 2.4 illustrates, the margin of positive senatorial roll call votes received by nominees has actually gone up over time, not down. Moreover, presidents from George Washington forward have had their choices for the high Court disputed or rejected by the Senate, often for plainly political reasons. The Senate refused to approve Washington's elevation of Justice John Rutledge to chief justice because of Rutledge's vocal objection to the then-recently negotiated and politically controversial Jay Treaty.[24]

---

[23] Dion Farganis and Justin Wedeking, "'No Hints, No Forecasts, No Previews': An Empirical Analysis of Supreme Court Nominee Candor from Harlan to Kagan," 45 *Law & Society Review* 525 (2011); Justin Wedeking and Dion Farganis, "The Candor Factor: Does Nominee Evasiveness Affect Judiciary Committee Support for Supreme Court Nominees?" 39 *Hofstra Law Review* 329 (2010).

[24] Henry J. Abraham, *Justices and Presidents: A Political History of Appointments to the Supreme Court* (New York: Oxford University Press, 1992). President Washington apparently did not dispute the propriety of the Senate's actions. See George L. Watson and John Alan Stookey, *Shaping America: The Politics of Supreme Court Appointments* (New York: Harper Collins, 1995) at 13 (citing President Washington as saying, "As the President has a right to nominate without assigning his reasons, so has the Senate a right to dissent without giving theirs.").

President James A. Garfield's nomination of Stanley Mathews barely passed the Senate after being subjected to vocal senatorial concerns about Mathew's connections to finance and railroad interests. President Herbert Hoover's effort to promote Justice Charles Evan Hughes' to the chief justice position was vigorously fought in the Senate because of senatorial concerns about Hughes' economic views. John J. Parker, another Hoover nominee, was voted down for similar reasons, and also because of concerns raised by the NAACP about his record on civil rights issues. Although two of Richard Nixon's nominees, Clement Haynsworth and Harrold Carswell, were both rejected by the Senate, so too were *five* of James Tyler's nominees.[25] Clearly, Supreme Court appointments have always been controversial, and opposition to them has frequently been overtly political.

Although not all of these disputes were public in the way that today's confirmation battles are, all of them did give the Senate an opportunity to direct the development of constitutional law through the confirmation process. The relatively recent increase in direct political engagement with the process by members of the public, elected officials, and an array of interests groups, reflects, we suspect, an expanding understanding of what it means for governmental decision makers to be democratically accountable, not a change in the fundamental understanding that choices about who sits on the high Court should be subject to such accountability. What used to go on behind closed Senate doors now occurs in public, under the scrutiny of television lights, bloggers, and reporters. But the basic idea behind the process – that constitutional changes that come to enjoy broad and deep public support are over time validated through their repeated endorsement by Supreme Court nominees at their confirmation hearings – is the same. As Larry Kramer has argued, Americans have long used both political and legal means to shape and change the meaning of vague constitutional language.[26] What we have shown in this book is that the confirmation process provides a public and formal mechanism through which the public can channel their efforts to accomplish exactly that.

Accepting our view of the role that the confirmation process actually plays in our governing system also has implications for efforts to change (or "reform") the process. Many reform proposals are premised on assumptions we have empirically rejected – namely, that nominees have become less responsive

---

[25] Abraham, *Justices and Presidents*, supra, n. 24 at 137 (Mathews), 201 (Hughes), 202 (Parker), 15–16 (Haynsworth and Carswell), and 106 (Tyler).

[26] Larry D. Kramer, *The People Themselves: Popular Constitutionalism and Judicial Review* (New York: Oxford University Press, 2004).

over time, or, more broadly, that the process is not contributing anything positive to our public discourse or governance. Proposals sprouting from such premises include suggestions that senators limit their questioning solely to issues of character and competence (not issues or cases);[27] that the Senate's "advice and consent" role be conducted behind closed doors in "private little debates between the president and the Senate;"[28] and even that the public hearing portion of the process be eliminated entirely.[29]

The desirability of such proposals (setting aside the perhaps insurmountable problem of their infeasibility) depends on one of two beliefs. People making these proposals either believe that Supreme Court decision making is in fact like calling balls and strikes, and that therefore the ability to cleverly deploy the tools of legal reasoning is the only qualification a justice needs; or they believe that the discretion necessarily exercised by Supreme Court justices needs to be hidden from public view and protected from public influence.

We reject both of these premises. More than two hundred years of constitutional lawmaking in action, as well as decades of scholarly searching for a more perfect method of interpretation, give lie to the assertion that Supreme Court justices can, do, or ever have been able to apply traditional tools of legal reasoning to find single, legally correct answers to complex constitutional questions. Our tools of legal reasoning can constrain judicial discretion, but they cannot eliminate it. As discussed in Chapter 1, in a world in which judicial choices are sharply isolated from public opinion, this type of constitutional underdeterminacy can be seen as a disturbing thing. After all, if the best legal reasoning available to us is not capable of providing determinate answers to hard constitutional questions, how can we reconcile judicial review with our ideals of self-governance? In such a world, it is much more reassuring to believe that justices are in fact umpires who just call them as they see them, using their top-notch case-crunching skills to extract a single, legally correct answer from the constitutional cacophony created by less skilled litigants and lower courts.

But the Constitution does not work that way. Constitutional questions find their way to the Supreme Court precisely when traditional tools of legal reasoning fail to provide exclusively correct constitutional answers. Whether

---

[27] See, e.g., Stephen Carter, "The Confirmation Mess," 101 *Harvard Law Review* 1185 (1988) at 1186–8, 1198–1201; Donald R. Songer, "The Relevance of Policy Values for the Confirmation of Supreme Court Nominees," 13 *Law & Society Review* 927 (1979) at 928.

[28] Carter, *The Confirmation Mess*, supra, n. 27 at 6.

[29] Stephen Choi and Mitu Gulati, "A Tournament of Judges?" 92 *California Law Review* 299 (2004); Glenn Harlan Reynolds, "Taking Advice Seriously: An Immodest Proposal for Reforming the Confirmation Process," 65 *Southern California Law Review* 1572 (1992).

we want to acknowledge it or not, our system in such cases gives the Court the power to choose from among the legally viable alternatives. At some point, though, those judicial choices are constrained by the constitutional commitments of the people. Answers that were legally acceptable become constitutionally unacceptable. This happens, as we show in this book, when previously contested constitutional choices made by the Court enter public discourse, are discussed and debated, and are accepted or rejected by the American people. When this happens, Supreme Court nominees are likewise expected to accept or reject those changes before taking their seat on the high Court. It is through this process that constitutional change is, over time, democratically ratified by the actions of our elected officials. It is not mandated from on high by nine unaccountable and unelected Supreme Court seers. It is a change that we, acting through those elected officials, have accepted as part of the Constitution under which we agree to be governed.

This vision of constitutional change need not deny constitutional under-determinacy; it can embrace it as a strength of our constitutional system. Examining seventy years of confirmation hearings reveals quite clearly that the public is fully capable of making choices about constitutional values and meanings, and of effectively conveying those choices to Supreme Court nominees. Indeed, we doubt very much that our Constitution could continue to awe and inspire us if this were not the case. We are even more certain that it would not be allowed to continue to govern us. Our hope is that revealing this democracy-enhancing aspect of the confirmation process will help facilitate a more mature constitutional conversation, one that moves past the unhelpful and false rhetoric of umpires versus activists.

In the end, each generation of Americans makes the Constitution its own. This happens through social movements and constitutional discourse. It happens through good faith debate and bare-knuckled politics. It happens through acts of violence and acts of bravery. Sometimes it happens quickly; at other times, it takes decades. Sometimes the Court leads the way, and sometimes it follows. But it never goes it alone. To adapt a phrase made famous by the great Chief Justice John Marshall, we must never forget that it is *our* Constitution they are expounding.

Appendix: Data and Data Reliability

The quantitative data on hearing dialogue used throughout this volume were coded from Supreme Court confirmation hearing transcripts. With two exceptions, these data are based on the official transcripts of the Senate Judiciary Committee. The transcripts of the early hearings, Frankfurter (1939) to Blackmun (1970), are found in Mersky and Jacobstein.[1] The transcripts of Powell (1971) through Alito (2006) are available on the Senate Judiciary Committee's webpage.[2] The Bork (1987) transcript is found on the Library of Congress's webpage.[3] Because official Senate Judiciary Committee transcripts of the Sotomayor and Kagan hearings were not available when those hearings were coded, we relied on transcripts from *The New York Times* (Sotomayor)[4] and *The Washington Post* (Kagan).[5] The citations to the hearing transcripts appearing

[1] Roy M. Mersky and J. Myron Jacobstein, eds., *The Supreme Court of the United States: Hearings and Reports on Successful and Unsuccessful Nominations of Supreme Court Justices by the Senate Judiciary Committee, 1916–1975* (Buffalo, NY: William S. Hein, 1977).

[2] United States Senate, "Nomination Hearings for Supreme Court Justices." Retrieved from: http://www.senate.gov/pagelayout/reference/one_item_and_teasers/Supreme_Court_Nomination_Hearings.htm (Accessed January 30, 2012).

[3] Library of Congress, "Supreme Court Nominations – Not Confirmed or Withdrawn." Retrieved from: http://www.loc.gov/law/find/court-withdrawn.php (Accessed January 30, 2012).

[4] *New York Times*, "Sotomayor Confirmation Hearings, Day 2." Retrieved from: http://www.nytimes.com/2009/07/14/us/politics/14confirm-text.html?_r=1&pagewanted=all (Accessed January 30, 2012); *New York Times*, "Sotomayor Confirmation Hearings, Day 3." Retrieved from http://www.nytimes.com/2009/07/15/us/politics/15confirm-text.html?pagewanted=all (Accessed January 30, 2012); *New York Times*, "Sotomayor Confirmation Hearings, Day 4." Retrieved from: http://www.nytimes.com/2009/07/16/us/politics/16confirm-text.html?pagewanted=all (Accessed January 30, 2012).

[5] *Washington Post*, "Transcript: The Elena Kagan Hearings – Day 2." Retrieved from: http://www.washingtonpost.com/wp-srv/politics/documents/KAGANHEARINGSDAY2.pdf (Accessed January 30, 2012); *Washington Post*, "Transcript: The Elena Kagan Hearings – Day 3." Retrieved from: http://www.washingtonpost.com/wp-srv/politics/documents/KAGANHEARINGSDAY3.pdf (Accessed January 30, 2012).

throughout this book correspond to the page numbers from these sources (as reported in *The U.S. Supreme Court Confirmation Hearings Database*).

The unit of analysis in the data is the change of speaker, meaning that a new observation begins whenever the speaker changes (e.g., from senator to nominee). To illustrate, the following discussion between Senator Metzenbaum (D-OH) and nominee Sandra Day O'Connor represents two observations, one for Metzenbaum and one for O'Connor:

> **Senator METZENBAUM:** Do you think there was inappropriate judicial activism in 1971 for the Burger Court to rule for the first time in *Reed v. Reed* that sex discrimination was unconstitutional?

> **Judge O'CONNOR:** Senator Metzenbaum, it was in my view an appropriate consideration of the problem of gender-based discrimination.[6]

Because our focus is on the heart and soul of the hearings – the questioning of nominees – we excluded opening statements made by senators and nominees from the data collection effort. In addition, we excluded comments made during the three days of testimony at the hearing of Clarence Thomas that involved allegations of sexual harassment brought by Anita Hill. The Thomas hearings, which had ended, were reopened for the sole purpose of taking additional testimony related to those allegations.[7] Consequently, the reopened hearing testimony did not involve unrestricted questioning. Including it would have thus biased our understanding of the hearings because almost all of the dialogue during this restricted portion of the Thomas hearing would be coded under our rules as involving the nominee's background (which includes ethical concerns based on a nominee's past behavior).[8]

Each comment is coded by both its primary issue and any relevant subissues. Senatorial comments and nominee comments are coded separately and therefore need not (although usually do) involve the same issue and subissue(s). A single unit of analysis can have only one issue, but may have up to six subissues. So, for example, a senatorial comment inquiring about the nominee's opinion on *Miranda* warnings and involuntary confession would

---

[6] O'Connor transcript, questioning by Senator Metzenbaum (D-OH) at 160.

[7] Thomas transcript, October 11, 1991, opening statement of Chairman Biden (D-DE) at 1–2.

[8] For discussion of this portion of the Thomas hearing, see, e.g., William L. Benoit and Dawn M. Hill, "A Critical Analysis of Judge Clarence Thomas' Statement Before the Senate Judiciary Committee," 49 *Communication Studies* 179 (1998); Jill Smolowe, "Sex, Lies and Politics: He Said, She Said," *Time*, October 21, 1991; Dan Thomas, Craig McCoy, and Allan McBride, "Deconstructing the Political Spectacle: Sex, Race, and Subjectivity in Public Response to the Clarence Thomas/Anita Hill 'Sexual Harassment' Hearings," 37 *American Journal of Political Science* 699 (1993).

have one issue ("law, crime, and family") and two subissue codes ("*Miranda* rights" and "involuntary confession"). Subissue codes are unique to their issue in that the same subissue does not appear in multiple issue codes.

The issue and subissue codes used in the data set are based on the Policy Agendas Project,[9] with some confirmation-specific codes added. The issue codes include topics such as "civil rights," "law, crime, and family," "judicial philosophy," and "hearing administration." Subissues include such topics as "age discrimination" and "religion: free exercise" (in the civil rights issue area); "*Miranda* rights" and "death penalty/capital punishment" (in the law, crime, and family issue area); "precedent" and "original intent" (in the judicial philosophy issue area); and "hearing administration and chatter," and "nominee background" (in the hearing administration issue area). Table A.1 provides a complete list of the issues and subissues appearing in the database.

Each comment also is coded for identification variables, such as the year of the hearing, the chair of the Judiciary Committee, the name of the questioning senator, the questioning senator's political party, the party holding majority control in the Senate at the time of the hearing, and the party of the nominating president. Political party variables are coded as of the date of the hearing. So, for example, a senator such as Arlen Specter, who served on the Judiciary Committee as both a Republican and a Democrat, will appear in the data as both a Republican and a Democrat, with his party affiliation depending on the date of the relevant hearing.

In addition, we coded each statement to identify whether it referenced a judicial decision. If it did, we collected information on the full name of each decision, the case's citation, the court that decided each case, and the date each decision was handed down, using information found in Westlaw, an online legal database. Although most statements reference a single court case, on occasion, a lone comment may identify several judicial decisions. In such instances, each case is coded separately.

We coded all situations in which a statement made by a nominee or Senator relates to a named judicial decision as involving the discussion of a case, even if the nominee or senator does not specifically identify the case in a given comment. Thus, if a senator asks a nominee about a specific case, and the nominee's response addresses the judicial decision without specifically naming the case, both observations are coded to reflect the fact that these statements discussed a given judicial decision. Consequently, the observations in the database corresponding to the aforementioned conversation between

---

9 Frank R. Baumgartner and Bryan Jones, *Policy Agendas Project.* Retrieved from: http://www. policyagendas.org/ (Accessed January 30, 2012).

TABLE A.1. *Issues, subissues, and itemized subissues appearing in the data*

Issue	Subissues and itemized subissues
Macroeconomics	Taxation, Tax Policy, and Tax Reform; Price Control and Stabilization; Other and General Macroeconomic Issues
Civil Rights	Ethnic Minority and Racial Group Discrimination; Gender and Sexual Orientation Discrimination; Age Discrimination; Handicap or Disease Discrimination; Voting Rights and Issues; Freedom of Speech and Religion; Right to Privacy and Access to Government Information; Abortion; Antigovernment Activities; Second Amendment; Speech: Political Speech and Campaign Finance; Speech: Commercial; Speech: Obscenity and Pornography; Speech: Other; Religion: Free Exercise; Religion: Establishment; Other Civil Rights Issues
Health	Comprehensive Health Care Reform; Regulation of Drug Industry, Medical Devices, and Clinical Labs; Provider and Insurer Payment and Regulation; Prevention, Communicable Diseases, and Health Promotion; Long-term Care, Home Health, Terminally Ill, and Rehabilitation Services; Research and Development; Other Health Issues
Labor, Employment, and Immigration	Worker Safety and Protection, Occupational and Safety Health Administration (OSHA); Employee Benefits; Employee Relations and Labor Unions; Fair Labor Standards; Parental Leave and Child Care; Immigration and Refugee Issues; Other Labor and Employment Issues
Education	Higher Education; Elementary and Secondary Education; Education of Underprivileged Students; Special Education; Educational Excellence; Other Education Issues
Environment	Drinking Water Safety; Waste Disposal; Hazardous Waste and Toxic Chemical Regulation, Treatment, and Disposal; Air Pollution, Global Warming, and Noise Pollution; Species and Forest Protection; Pollution and Conservation in Coastal and Other Navigable Waterways; Other Environment Issues
Energy	Nuclear Energy and Nuclear Regulatory Commission Issues; Natural Gas and Oil; Coal

Issue	Subissues and itemized subissues
Law, Crime, and Family Issues	Executive Branch Agencies Dealing With Law and Crime; White Collar Crime and Organized Crime; Illegal Drug Production, Trafficking, and Control; Prisons; Juvenile Crime and the Juvenile Justice System; Child Abuse and Child Pornography; Family Issues; Police, Fire, and Weapons Control; Riots and Crime Prevention; Death Penalty/Capital Punishment; *Miranda* Rights; Double Jeopardy; Search and Seizure; Right to Counsel; Self-Incrimination, Involuntary Confession, Refusal to Testify; Confrontation Clause, Right to Confront Witnesses Against You; Habeas Corpus Reform; Other Criminal Justice Issues
Social Welfare	Poverty and Assistance for Low-Income Families; Assistance to the Disabled and Handicapped; Other Social Welfare Issues
Community Development and Housing Issues	Low and Middle Income Housing Programs and Needs; Other Community Development and Housing Issues
Banking, Finance, and Domestic Commerce	U.S. Banking System and Financial Institution Regulation; Securities and Commodities Regulation; Corporate Mergers, Antitrust Regulation, and Corporate Management Issues; Small Business Issues and Small Business Administration; Copyrights and Patents; Consumer Safety and Consumer Fraud; Sports and Gambling Regulation; Other Banking, Finance, and Domestic Commerce Issues
Defense	Military Intelligence, CIA, Espionage; Manpower, Military Personnel and Dependents (Army, Navy, Air Force, Marines), Military Courts; Civil Defense and Homeland Security; Direct War Related Issues; Relief of Claims Against U.S. Military; Other Defense Issues
Space, Science, Technology, and Communications	Broadcast Industry Regulation (TV, Cable, Radio); Computer Industry, Computer Security, and General Issues Related to the Internet
International Affairs and Foreign Aid	Human Rights; International Organizations Other Than Finance: United Nations (UN), UNESCO, International Red Cross; Terrorism, Hijacking; Other International Affairs and Aid Issues

(*continued*)

TABLE A.1 *(continued)*

Issue	Subissues and itemized subissues
Government Operations	Intergovernmental Relations; Government Efficiency and Bureaucratic Oversight; Nominations and Appointments; Presidential Impeachment and Scandal; Federal Government Branch Relations and Administrative Issues, Congressional Operations; Regulation of Political Campaigns, Political Advertising, PAC Regulation, Voter Registration, Government Ethics; Relief of Claims Against the U.S. Government; Constitutional Roles of the President and Congress in Declaring and Waging War, Limits on Presidential War Powers; Other Government Operations Issues
Public Lands and Water Management	Native American Affairs; Natural Resources, Public Lands, and Forest Management; Water Resource Development and Research; U.S. Dependencies and Territorial Issues
State and Local Government	State and Local Government Administration
Federalism	Scope of Federal Preemption of State Law; Scope of Congressional Power Under the Thirteenth, Fourteenth, or Fifteenth Amendments; Commerce Clause; Tenth Amendment; Other Federalism Issues
Miscellaneous Substantive Topics	Judicial Administration; Statutory Interpretation; Best/Favorite Justices; Best/Favorite Cases or Opinions; Worst Cases or Opinions; Standing/Access to Courts; Non-Standing Justiciability Issues, Political Questions Doctrine, Mootness and Ripeness, Advisory Opinions
Judicial Philosophy	Judicial Restraint, Activism, Humility, Deference, Hubris; Original Intent, Original Meaning, Founders, Framers' Purposes; Living Constitutionalism, Constitution as Evolving or Incorporating Current Norms; Text as Interpretive Tool; Precedent, Stare Decisis; Separation of Powers; General Judicial Philosophy Issues
Hearing Administration	Hearing Administration and Chatter; Character and Background, Ethics of Nominee; Discussion of Media Coverage or Spin About the Hearings or the Nominee; Discussions of Pre-Hearing Conversations or Coaching or Contact between the Nominee and Executive Officials or Others

Senator Metzenbaum and Judge O'Connor are both coded as referencing the Supreme Court's decision in *Reed v. Reed*,[10] even though O'Connor did not explicitly name the case in her response to Metzenbaum's question. We did not, however, code comments as involving a judicial decision when the statements concerned the discussion of an issue strongly associated with a particular decision, if the decision itself was not named by the senator or nominee. For example, an exchange about abortion would not be coded as involving *Roe v. Wade*[11] unless either the senator or the nominee identified the case itself during the exchange.

THE CODING OF VARIABLES IN *THE U.S. SUPREME COURT CONFIRMATION HEARINGS DATABASE*

In this section, we provide an abbreviated discussion of the coding of the variables used in this book. The database, along with a full codebook that provides a more detailed description of the variables, can be accessed on Paul Collins' website (http://www.psci.unt.edu/~pmcollins/).

NID is a unique identification number given to each nominee.

YEAR represents the year of the confirmation hearing.

CITE indicates the page number of the transcript corresponding to the observation.

PRESPRTY represents the political party of the president who appointed the nominee.

SENCONTRL indicates which political party controlled the Senate at the time of the confirmation hearing.

SENID is a unique identification number given to the questioning senator.

SENPAR represents the political party of the questioning senator.

CHAIR indicates the identification number of the chair of the Senate Judiciary Committee during each nominee's hearing.

SPEAK indicates whether the statement was made by the nominee or senator.

ISSUE represents the main issue discussed in each statement.

SUBIS denotes the subissue discussed in each statement.

ITEMSB1 ... iTEMSB5 indicate the itemized subissues discussed in each statement.

---

[10] Reed v. Reed, 404 U.S. 71 (1971).
[11] Roe v. Wade, 410 U.S. 113 (1973).

RSPTYPE1 is the nominee's response type to a senator's question, which has three values. 1 = nominee gave a firm, current position on a clearly identified, legal issue; 2 = nominee refused to provide a clear answer citing privilege (e.g., the appearance of bias); 3 = the nominee neither gave a firm response to the senator's question nor refused to answer the question by citing privilege.

CASE indicates whether the statement involved the discussion of a named judicial decision.

CNAME1 ... CNAME8 represent the full name of the judicial decision named in a statement.

CCITE1 ... CCITE8 indicate the case citation of the judicial decision named in a statement.

CDATE1 ... CDATE8 represent the date the judicial decision named in a statement was decided.

CCOURT1 ... CCOURT8 identify the name of the court that rendered the judicial decision named in a statement.

DATA RELIABILITY

To conduct reliability analyses of the variables in the database, we extracted a random sample of 96 pages of transcript (out of 4,021 pages). Because the average number of observations per page is 6.1 (standard deviation = 4.7), we sought to obtain a sample of approximately 2.5% of the data. Our random sample constitutes 740 observations, making up 2.4% of the data. This sample size gives us precision of ± 3.6% with 95% confidence. An independent coder collected the data for the reliability sample.

The number of observations in the main data file for the 96 pages of transcript is 744. The number of observations in the reliability sample for the 96 pages of transcript is 745. There are four observations in the main data set that do not appear in the reliability sample and five observations in the reliability sample that do not appear in the main database. Thus, nine observations do not match in the reliability sample and the main data file. Consequently, the agreement rate with regard to the number of observations is 98.8%. As we are unable to compare observations that are present in one data set and absent from the other, we excluded the nine nonmatching observations from the reliability analyses.

Because the variables corresponding to the identity of the judicial decisions discussed at the confirmation hearings are not ordered, it was necessary to sort them to conduct the reliability analyses. For example, a given observation might discuss two cases (e.g., *Brown v. Board of Education*[12] and *Plessy v. Ferguson*[13]). Coder 1 may have ordered these cases such that CNAME1 = *Brown* and CNAME2 = *Plessy*, whereas Coder 2 may have sorted these cases such that CNAME1 = *Plessy* and CNAME2 = *Brown*. In such an instance, both coders agree that the observation contained discussions of *Brown* and *Plessy*, although they ordered the cases differently. To ensure the reliability analyses reflect the fact that the coders were in perfect agreement with respect to the cases discussed in this example, the variables corresponding to the discussion of cases were ordered to match for the purpose of the reliability analyses. For this same reason, the SUBIS and ITEMSB1 through ITEMSB5 variables were sorted in the data used in the reliability analyses.

We report information pertaining to the reliability of each variable in Table A.2.[14] This table reports the agreement rate for both samples, the expected agreement (that which would be expected by chance), along with a kappa statistic for each variable. The kappa statistic ranges from zero to one, with a value of one indicating perfect agreement among coders and values less than one representing the proportion of agreement between two coders corrected for chance.[15] The average agreement rate for all of the variables is 96.2%, indicating that the data are highly reliable. Considering the variables individually, it is evident that the agreement rate between coders is very high, ranging from a low of 85.7% to a high of 100% for several variables.

Although there are no firm guidelines with regard to exactly how strong kappa should be to determine a variable's reliability, Landis and Koch[16] suggest

---

[12] Brown v. Board of Education, 347 U.S. 483 (1954).

[13] Plessy v. Ferguson, 163 U.S. 537 (1896).

[14] As Table A.2 illustrates, there are insufficient observations to conduct reliability tests on several of the variables in the database. These variables identify the third, fourth, and fifth subissues addressed in a statement, as well as the name, citation, date, and court that rendered the fifth, sixth, seventh, and eighth judicial decisions addressed in a statement. Because most statements involve a single subissue and, of those statements referencing judicial decisions, a single court case, these variables contain missing values for the vast majority of observations. For example, there are no statements in the sample of cases used in the reliability analyses that mention more than four judicial decisions. As such, we are unable to conduct reliability analyses on these variables.

In addition, four variables – CCOURT3, CNAME4, CCITE4, CDATE4, and CCOURT4 – do not exhibit sufficient variation to conduct reliability tests. This means that there are not enough categories in these variables for reliability analyses. For example, CCOURT3 contains eight observations, all coded as "Supreme Court of the United States."

[15] Jacob Cohen, "A Coefficient of Agreement for Nominal Scales," 20 *Educational and Psychological Measurement* 37 (1960).

[16] Richard J. Landis and Gary G. Koch, "The Measurement of Observer Agreement for Categorical Data," 33 *Biometrics* 159 (1977).

TABLE A.2. *Intercoder reliability tests*

Variable	Agreement rate (%)	Expected agreement	Kappa	Standard error	Probability
NID	100.0	5.91	1.000	0.009	<0.001
YEAR	100.0	7.38	1.000	0.010	<0.001
CITE	100.0	1.69	1.000	0.005	<0.001
PRESPRTY	100.0	57.06	1.000	0.037	<0.001
SENCONTRL	100.0	63.05	1.000	0.037	<0.001
SENID	98.24	5.98	0.981	0.009	<0.001
SENPAR	97.84	56.94	0.950	0.037	<0.001
CHAIR	100.0	22.38	1.000	0.018	<0.001
SPEAK	97.43	51.12	0.948	0.037	<0.001
ISSUE	93.65	19.72	0.921	0.017	<0.001
SUBIS	87.38	7.84	0.863	0.001	<0.001
ITEMSB1	100.0	13.02	1.000	0.035	<0.001
ITEMSB2	100.0	35.73	1.000	0.138	<0.001
ITEMSB3	Insufficient observations for calculation				
ITEMSB4	Insufficient observations for calculation				
ITEMSB5	Insufficient observations for calculation				
RSPTYPE1	94.63	70.62	0.817	0.049	<0.001
CASE	95.14	64.45	0.863	0.037	<0.001
CNAME1	96.08	5.06	0.959	0.018	<0.001
CCITE1	96.08	5.06	0.959	0.018	<0.001
CDATE1	96.08	5.06	0.959	0.018	<0.001
CCOURT1	100.0	46.69	1.000	0.048	<0.001
CNAME2	96.15	4.59	0.960	0.043	<0.001
CCITE2	96.15	4.59	0.960	0.043	<0.001
CDATE2	100.0	4.73	1.000	0.044	<0.001
CCOURT2	100.0	78.99	1.000	0.157	<0.001
CNAME3	85.71	12.24	0.837	0.138	<0.001
CCITE3	85.71	12.24	0.837	0.138	<0.001
CDATE3	85.71	12.24	0.837	0.138	<0.001
CCOURT3	Insufficient variation for calculation				
CNAME4	Insufficient variation for calculation				
CCITE4	Insufficient variation for calculation				
CDATE4	Insufficient variation for calculation				
CCOURT4	Insufficient variation for calculation				
CNAME5	Insufficient observations for calculation				
CCITE5	Insufficient observations for calculation				
CDATE5	Insufficient observations for calculation				
CCOURT5	Insufficient observations for calculation				
CNAME6	Insufficient observations for calculation				
CCITE6	Insufficient observations for calculation				
CDATE6	Insufficient observations for calculation				
CCOURT6	Insufficient observations for calculation				

Variable	Agreement rate (%)	Expected agreement	Kappa	Standard error	Probability
CNAME7		Insufficient observations for calculation			
CCITE7		Insufficient observations for calculation			
CDATE7		Insufficient observations for calculation			
CCOURT7		Insufficient observations for calculation			
CNAME8		Insufficient observations for calculation			
CCITE8		Insufficient observations for calculation			
CDATE8		Insufficient observations for calculation			
CCOURT8		Insufficient observations for calculation			

that kappa values between 0.00 and 0.20 are poor; values between 0.21 and 0.40 are fair; values between 0.41 and 0.60 are moderate; values between 0.61 and 0.80 are substantial; and values above 0.81 are almost perfect. Using this as a guide, it is evident that the data are extremely reliable. The average kappa score over all variables is 0.95, which is almost perfect. What is more, each of the variables achieves almost perfect reliability (i.e., kappa > 0.81).

Index

Lightning Source UK Ltd.
Milton Keynes UK
UKHW020701090123
415042UK00012B/1810